D0065480

The Writings of Thomas Hooker

The Writings of
THOMAS HOOKER

Spiritual Adventure in Two Worlds

SARGENT BUSH, JR.

THE UNIVERSITY OF WISCONSIN PRESS

Published 1980

The University of Wisconsin Press
114 North Murray Street
Madison, Wisconsin 53715

The University of Wisconsin Press, Ltd.
1 Gower Street
London WC1E 6HA, England

First printing

Printed in the United States of America

For LC CIP information see the colophon

ISBN 0-299-08070-6

Publication of this book was made possible in part
by a grant from the National Endowment for the Humanities

for Cynthia

Contents

Acknowledgments

During the extended period of my work on this book I have incurred many debts which I am pleased to acknowledge. I am especially grateful for grants for released time from my normal teaching duties from the National Endowment for the Humanities, whose Summer Stipend enabled me to begin by reading extensively at Harvard's Houghton Library, and from the late Cooperative Program in the Humanities, the American Council of Learned Societies, and the University of Wisconsin Graduate School. My debt also extends to several individuals whose interest and assistance have been invaluable, among whom I would especially single out John C. Gerber, C. F. Burgess, Frederick P. W. McDowell, and G. Thomas Tanselle. My colleague Merton M. Sealts has been a generous critic and counsellor throughout. Everett Emerson, Karl Keller, William T. Lenehan, E. N. Feltskog, and William M. Gibson have also read the manuscript at various stages of its evolution, and their constructive criticisms have helped to improve the work substantially. Hubert Pellman and Thompson R. Harlow gave early assistance on bibliographical matters. Two other scholar-teachers deserve mention: the late John T. Frederick first introduced me to the writings of Thomas Hooker and taught me how to appreciate the Puritans as writers and as real people, and Severn Duvall, head of the English Department at Washington and Lee University, encouraged me to pursue the outside fellowship support which gave me the substantial beginning that such a project requires. Many librarians have been of great service, particularly those at the Houghton Library, Duke University's Perkins and Divinity School Libraries, and the Cambridge University Library's Rare Books Room, at each of which I worked for extended periods. Closer to home, I am especially grateful to those at Wisconsin who saw to the acquisition of a virtually complete collection of microfilm of the Hooker canon. The editors of the *William and Mary Quarterly* and *Resources for American Literary Study* have given permission to reprint here in substantially altered form portions of articles which have appeared in their journals. And the Massachusetts State Archives has permitted me to quote from Hooker manuscript letters in its possession. I have benefitted greatly from the work of innumerable scholars whose work has preceded my own, including especially such recent Hooker experts as George H. Williams, Norman Pettit, Winfried Herget, Frank Shuffleton, and Keith Sprunger. Mere footnotes sometimes seem an inadequate acknowledgment but they serve here nonetheless as the chief means of indicating the considerable body of scholarship by these and others which has made my work not only possible but also exciting.

Finally, I want to thank my sons, Charlie and Jamie, for their normal blithe disregard of their father's labors on this book as well as for their occasional exciting interest and understanding. Deserving thanks above all is my wife Cynthia, who gracefully conveys her appreciation for the value of scholarship while also being my constant reminder that there are, after all, more important things in the world.

Madison, Wisconsin
January, 1979

The Writings of Thomas Hooker

Introduction

In 1586 Thomas Hooker was born into a period of dynamic growth and great turbulence in the English nation. It was an era made to order for the forging of great reputations, as the likes of Walter Raleigh, Francis Drake, and John Smith amply discovered. But, as in all periods of lasting change, it was not just dashing warriors and adventurers who would have the role of movers and shakers. Even such a man as Thomas Hooker, who chose the Church as his calling and spent some fifteen years in the shelter of university halls, would emerge as an important figure in the great events of the times. The very briefest sketch of his life suggests the degree to which he was involved in the turbulence of those times.[1]

Hooker was born in July of 1586 in the little town of Markworth in Leicestershire, where his parents were yeomen. He attended school in the neighboring village of Market Bosworth, eventually going from there to Queens College, Cambridge, where he matriculated on March 27, 1604. It was probably in October of the same year that he transferred to the predominantly Puritan Emmanuel College, where he remained some fourteen years, first as scholar, receiving his B.A. in 1608 and M.A. in 1611, then as fellow and catechist. During his stay at the college, he enjoyed the acquaintance of such fellow students as Zechariah Symmes, Nathaniel Rogers, John Cotton, and Cotton's cousin and a future Master of Emmanuel, Anthony Tuckney, and the tutelage of such able scholars as Emmanuel's long-time Master, Laurence Chaderton, and the Regius Professor of Divinity and future Master of Trinity College, John Richardson. The college's account books under the date of October 26, 1618, show a final payment to Hooker of only about three-quarters of the usual fellow's semiannual salary. This indicates his departure from the university in the early fall of 1618.

Relatively little is known of Hooker's English career after his leaving Cambridge in 1618 and before his going to Chelmsford in 1625. It is

3

assumed he went directly to the little village of Esher in Surrey, where he became a member of the household of one Francis Drake, serving as chaplain to the family, pastor to a small local congregation, and mainly counsellor to the emotionally and spiritually disturbed Mrs. Drake, who was convinced that she had committed the unpardonable sin and would burn in hell for it. Hooker, together with others—including the venerable John Dod and the young but noted John Preston—effected the cure of Mrs. Drake, who was converted and died content in 1625. The experience undoubtedly taught Hooker much about the ways of grace and had a lasting effect on his ministry.[2] Apart from his difficulties with Mrs. Drake's case, however, Hooker's years at Esher must have been rather quiet and uneventful, particularly for a man who while at Cambridge had gained a reputation for scholarship and disputation as well as for preaching. Still, he was apparently having his share of personal happiness. He married Mrs. Drake's maid-in-waiting, Susannah Garbrand, on April 3, 1621, and their first child was named Joan, after Mrs. Drake. Like England herself, he was enjoying his last years of peace and comfort for some time to come.

It was probably in 1625, the year of Mrs. Drake's death, that Hooker returned to fuller engagement in the affairs of the Church and nation by accepting the offer of the public lectureship at Chelmsford in the county of Essex, where there was a particularly high concentration of committed Puritans. His preaching in that market town gained him large audiences and a growing reputation as a moving preacher. He held forth in this location for some four years before he finally ran afoul of Bishop William Laud's campaign to enforce conformity to the forms of worship and attire among the clergy in the See of London, of which Chelmsford was a part. By late 1629 Hooker's preaching had been silenced, though he remained in the Chelmsford area running a school from his home, Cuckoos Farm, at Little Baddow, where John Eliot, recently graduated from Jesus College, Cambridge, and soon to depart for New England, lived in his home and served as the school's usher. The Hooker home served as a meeting place for younger clergy of the region, a fact which further angered the conformist Anglicans. Hooker forfeited bond when summoned to appear before the Court of High Commission, presumably went into hiding while considering his options, and finally, in the late spring of 1631, went to Amsterdam, where he hoped to be called as co-minister with John Paget to the English Reformed Church there.

He soon found himself embroiled in new controversies, however, stemming from Paget's unwillingness to have a pronounced congregationalist as his colleague. Though the Amsterdam congregation would have preferred to have him stay, Hooker left Amsterdam in November of 1631 for Delft, where he entered into joint ministry with the Scottish exile John Forbes. Even in this comfortable liaison Hooker was not out of reach of the English Church's dictates on the forms of worship and was caught in the middle of another controversy over the issue of his and Forbes's persistent nonconformity. He was otherwise dissatisfied with his situation in Holland, however, living away from his family and finding a troubling lack of "heart religion" in the Dutch churches. He returned secretly to England in the spring of 1633, remaining just long enough to make preparations for migrating to New England, and left with his family in early July.

Hooker was welcomed in Massachusetts Bay by a group of settlers who had followed his preaching in England and who were already living at Newtown, the village whose name would be changed shortly after Hooker's removal to its present Cambridge. Samuel Stone joined him in organizing the first church there, while John Cotton became the teacher at the Boston church. While at Newtown, Hooker was consulted on important colonial business by the governor and magistrates and established himself as one of the major figures in the New England experiment in the eyes not only of his fellow New Englanders but of those who had remained behind in England as well. His influence was certainly not diminished when a member of his own church, John Haynes, was elected governor of the colony in May of 1635. But members of his congregation, and apparently even Hooker himself, had become uncomfortable in their Newtown location soon after their settlement there; and as soon as Haynes's governorship was over, Hooker and Stone led a sizeable contingent through the wilderness to a still newer settlement on the Connecticut River which they named Hartford after Stone's birthplace in England. Again Hooker entered the taxing work of establishing a new church and a new community. Again he was a key figure, consulting with government officials on such matters as Indian policy, the legal code, and intercolonial cooperation, and such problems as drought and the consequent poverty and hardship. He was summoned back to the Bay on more than one occasion to advise on matters of controversy there in both church and state. Indeed, his reputation at home was still so strong that he was one of three New Englanders invited to represent the colonial viewpoint at the Westminster Assembly in the 1640s. When he died of an epidemic sickness at age sixty-one in July of 1647, he had lived a full and significant life in the midst of great change and great challenge. His reputation as a leader of the Puritan cause in England and especially in New England remained untarnished, and he continued to be remembered for decades by his successors in metaphors, analogies, and types suggesting strength, leadership, and high principle. He had been, said Cotton Mather in 1702, the "Light of the Western Churches."

At every stage of his career Hooker's commanding presence and instinct for leadership made him a highly visible and influential figure. Yet despite the fact that his career was a highly public one, his primary interest was the private spiritual life of his parishioners. He most enjoyed explaining the spiritual workings of the soul in the process of redemption. The *real* action, for Hooker, was in the invisible realm. In what strikes the modern mind as almost paradoxical, however, his ability to preach and to explain the ways of God and man in redemption was a primary reason for his emergence as a leader in the public events of his time. In his day, when questions of religion were uppermost in the minds of many—were, in fact, political questions—the powerful preacher was apt to find himself in the unsought role of leader of a semiorganized resistance movement. This was, at any rate, the case with Hooker, who became a leader, first in rebellion against repression at home and then in the work of building communities in the wilderness. He represents an unusual mixture of the often antithetical capacities for practical leadership and spiritual exploration.

This combination, however, did not seem at all odd to the seventeenth-century Puritans. Indeed, for them the realms of action and contemplation were integrally related. The few people who emerged as leaders in both the Old World and the New were able to embrace both aspects of life. Men like Thomas Hooker who insisted on spiritual contemplation but were equally committed to testing spiritual truths against the cold reality of the corrupt world were especially equipped for life in a New World. As Sacvan Bercovitch has recently argued, the participants in the Great Migration "took with them . . . a sacred and a worldly view of their errand," a sense of both the eternal and the temporal, the spiritual and the secular significance of their acts.[3] They envisioned a principle for life while maintaining a full awareness of the difficulty of making that principle work in actual experience. The writings of these Puritans, and of Thomas Hooker in particular, derived some of their energy from the fact that they emerged out of the events and movements of the Puritan era. Hooker was, of course, well aware of the great tensions in the Puritan's life—tensions born of the conflict between the individual's search for inner peace and the concurrent imposition of hardships and punishments by the political forces of the day. These conflicts forced many Puritans from their homeland into exile. But they also encouraged acceptance of the notion that the external world of challenges and conflicts was, after all, subordinate to the world of the spirit, where fulfillment was enjoyed without regard to one's condition in the outer world.

Because Thomas Hooker's recorded utterances reflect these tensions of his culture, this study of his writings is also a study of the Puritan mind and spirit in action. The "action" sometimes took the form of the actual deeds which Hooker performed in the world, but more characteristically it took the shape of an intellectual and emotional stance which rejected any tendency to stand pat, which envisioned the spiritual life as dynamically active. Pulpit literature and related ecclesiastical and theological theory in many ages tends to seem to the average layman deadening, dull, or at least uninspired. But in Hooker's work such materials acquire a language of action which in turn produces a story of heroics. Homiletics as practiced by Hooker and some of his contemporaries produced not just a rhetoric of persuasion but narrative art, even epic-scale dramatic action. And the speaker, when he is successful, manages to share his own sense of both the agony and the triumph of the religious life with the humble, simple souls who are with him in the English cathedral, the Dutch church, or the frontier meetinghouse.

This book attempts to recognize both the tension and the continuity between the two worlds of external and internal experience—a juxtaposition that was never far from Hooker's creative imagination. The first part of the book is mainly an examination of Hooker's "occasional" writings and of the occasions which produced them. Here we are able to measure Hooker's movement through a succession of crises of his time and through the process of transplantation from the Old World to the New. These several occasional works, for all the diversity of their causes, make a significant cluster of writings which represent the forceful response of Thomas Hooker to the challenges of his time and place in the external world. In the second and third parts of the book, Hooker's conversion preaching is the main focus. Here we see him confronting the ultimate realities of the spiritual world, realities which in his view transcend and supersede those of the mundane, the "carnal" world. In Part I, then, it may sometimes seem that I am writing mainly biography, while in Parts II and III it may seem that I am chiefly concerned with doctrinal explication. I hope I have not done either primarily, even though on any given page one or both of these may be precisely the goal. I have aimed at achieving a full understanding of the man's words as well as his deeds, taking up his several books more or less discretely in order to explore the differing contexts that led to their creation: I have assumed throughout that his imaginative response to the conditions which produced his works is fully as important as the intellectual positions described in them.

In fact, several purposes motivate this examination of Hooker's writings. In the first place, I have attempted to give substance to the many easy generalizations one sees in studies of the period claiming excellence and even superb mastery for Hooker as a preacher. This involves explaining the essential contents of his writings, which have never been widely available since the first half of the seventeenth century. It also involves demonstrating connections with the thought of earlier periods as well as his own and likewise suggesting some of the main connections with both English and American intellectual and literary traditions. At the heart of the study is the sometimes explicit but always implicit question of how Hooker attempted to solve the considerable problem of conveying spiritual truth to an audience of men and women who were very much of the world. The solution depended as much on literary skills as on intellectual power. My interests encompass both of these sources of Hooker's skill but probably tend more towards literary matters than have most other studies of Hooker or his contemporary Puritans. In making this examination, however, I have attempted to keep the discussion accessible to readers of broader backgrounds than those of specialists in colonial literature or history. Hooker represents an important point of departure for American history and culture and needs to be known in his essential qualities of mind and action to as broad an audience as possible. Yet the reader who ventures into such a subject must be prepared for complex issues. Insofar as possible, I have let Hooker point the way; I attempt to go where his writings lead.

1

Puritan Preacher, Sermon, and Audience

It is likely that no culture has ever been so profoundly influenced by a single literary form as was the early-seventeenth-century Puritan culture by the sermon. Certainly no literary form was so fundamental a part of Puritan life as this one. The sermon was a universally known and understood form of discourse. The illiterate and the college-educated were equally willing to admit the central importance of preaching in their lives. The sermon's potential for instruction and spiritual nurture was so obvious that it was a common practice for some auditors to take careful shorthand notes so as to preserve the preacher's words in detail and make them available for further thought and perhaps discussion at home. On both sides of the Atlantic it was the chief means by which the ministers "imparted" Puritanism to their hearers.[1] And it became, as Daniel Boorstin claims, "the characteristic institution of Puritanism in America."[2]

The devout Puritan's attendance at sermons and lectures was insured by his belief both in the ultimate importance of possessing saving faith and in the minister's ability to help him gain assurance of that possession. Most sensible Puritans did not persuade themselves that all who were admitted into church membership were legitimate saints, but the person who stayed away from sermons had little cause to wonder why he had no experience of saving grace. Given the Puritan clergy's acceptance of this weighty responsibility for effective teaching and guidance of the hopeful through their pulpit discourse, it is natural enough that, as one historian has put it, they "were preachers first and everything else second."[3]

But the sermon was more than a means of personal spiritual guidance. It became a means of stimulating and defining group identity.

9

The English Puritans of the late sixteenth and early seventeenth centuries sought a central role for preaching but found repeatedly that their most effective preachers were forced by the politics of the time into "an insecure outgroup status."[4] The Puritans were, after all, merely a minority group until they finally led a successful rebellion against the monarch and his party. Before that event, however, in the reigns of James I and Charles I, the persecution of the preacher and often the literal silencing of his words led to the the Great Migration to the New World, where the minister's preaching, given an unhindered opportunity to fulfill its potential, helped the Puritans more than any other influence except the wilderness itself to define their communal identity. They were a company of the faithful, and it was the minister in his preaching who again and again reminded them of this crucial fact. Thus, under the spiritual guidance of an effective, respected minister whose words could powerfully command attention, the people could believe in themselves as a truly chosen, convenanted community. Without such a minister, they were wanderers in a strange land. In all of America's history, no literary form has had the broad, profound impact on its audience that the sermon had in those early years of New England's colonization.

In the Puritan community successful preaching led to leadership status for the preacher. Thomas Hooker was certainly one of the most successful preachers and accordingly became a prominent figure in the success of the Great Migration. His joint role as preacher and community leader assured his prominence not just in his native England but also in the Netherlands and finally in two colonies in New England. Indeed, no clearer example of a minister's imparting identity to a community can be found than the story in Cotton Mather's biography of Hooker that before Hooker had made up his mind to emigrate, a group of English colonists from Essex established themselves at Newtown in the Bay Colony and were content to live without a minister for the time being, calling themselves "Mr. Hooker's Company" in anticipation of his arrival.[5]

This general acknowledgement of his role as leader attests to a respect for his ability as preacher and pastor which was just as strong after his death as at the beginning of his New English career. When he died in 1647 at Hartford, Connecticut, the community which he and his "company" had established some eleven years earlier, two members of his congregation wrote of their loss by saying, "The stroke is direfull and amasing, when such a stake is taken out of the hedge, such a pillar from the house, such a Pastor from his flock, in such a time and place as this." It was his preaching which they particularly remembered: "He was . . . one of a thousand, whose diligence and unweariednesse (besides his other endowments) in the work committed to him, was almost beyond compare. He revealed the whole counsell of the Lord unto us, kept nothing back, dividing the Word aright. His care was of strong and weak, sheep and lambs, to give a portion to each in due season."[6] His colleague at both his New England churches, Samuel Stone, wrote a sincere if sometimes prosaic elegy on Hooker's death, which pointed to his effectiveness as a minister: "Dark Scriptures he most clearly did expound, / And that great mystery of Christ profound." He was able to revive the hearts of the weak in spirit while "in reproof he was a sonne of Thunder. / He spake the Word with such authority, / That many from themselves to Christ did fly. / His preaching was full of the holy Ghost, / Whose presence in him we admired most."[7] And his fellow eminent preacher and sometime rival, John Cotton, summarized in a similar vein:

> Prudent in Rule, in Argument quick, full:
> Fervent in Prayer, in Preaching powerfull:
> That well did learned *Ames* record bear,
> The like to Him He never wont to hear.[8]

Years after his death he was remembered by a younger clergyman who had known him as "that great Elijah, that renowned man of God in his generation."[9] And modern historians have been inclined to accept these pronouncements as definitive. Babette Levy expresses a generally accepted opinion in saying, "Hooker as a preacher commands respect in any age."[10]

Hooker's excellence as a preacher, in fact, has become almost a cliché of modern Puritan studies, though until very recently little effort has been made to evaluate the particular nature of this achievement. For the present attempt to examine the major elements in the content and shape of his whole literary canon, most of the primary material is sermons. Given this centrality of the sermon to Puritan culture generally and to Hooker's career specifically, the place to begin the study of his thought and expression is with his expressed opinions on sermons and sermon audiences.

The Art of Preaching

Though his decade and a half at Emmanuel College, Cambridge, made Hooker particularly suited to address an educated audience in learned discourse, the usual preaching situation dictated plain talk and avoidance of both scholarly references and controversy. Accordingly, the bulk of Hooker's sermon canon represents as powerful a version of the plain style as the Puritan culture would produce. Hooker spoke to this issue in an early sermon in saying, "I have sometime admired at this: why a company of Gentlemen, yeomen, and poore women, that are scarcely able to know their A. B. C. Yet they have a minister to speake Latine, Greeke, and Hebrew, and to use the Fathers, when it is certaine, they know nothing at all."[11] This, of course, was a long-standing Puritan objection to the Established Church's approach. Hooker saw this disregard of the congregation's intellectual limitations as just a way of letting them go blithely along in their sins while failing to attack their hearts, where sin is lodged. Hooker therefore resolved: "For my self (being privy to my own weakness) it shall suffice in a familiar manner to accommodate my self (though it may be somwhat rudely) to the Capacity of the meanest. . . . We shall knit the whole frame [of a sermon] together by the joynts and sinews of distributions and divisions, that such as are attentive may never be at a loss, nor yet miss or mistake the Lord, but that it may be well seen (as *David* hath it) *How the Lord goes in his Sanctuary*, where the prints and footsteps of God be, in his proceeding with the Soul in this great Work."[12] No one from Hooker's congregation would go to hell for failing to understand his message.

One of Hooker's clearest characterizations of his audience comes in his *Soules Benefit from Union with Christ*, where he explains that "marriage" with Christ fulfills all the needs of the sinner, who need bring nothing to the match but faith. Citing 1 Corinthians 1:26–28 as his authority, he reminds his listeners that

> not many wise men after the flesh, not many mightie, not many noble are called, but God hath chosen the foolish things of the world, to confound the wise, and God hath chosen the weake things of the world, to confound the things that are mightie; why then to you fooles, why then to you weake things, *Christ is made wisdome, and righteousnesse, and sanctification, and redemption;* to you poore ones, to you weake ones Christ is made all this; nay, looke into the 28. verse, *God hath chosen the base things of the world, and the things that are despised;* nay, and *the things that are not, to bring to nought the things that are;* that is to say, the off-scouring of the world, the scrapings, as I may so say: looke as a man flings away the scrapings of things as nothing worth, why so the parings of the world, you that are nothing in the esteeme of the world, a company of poore base simplicians; *Christ is made wisdome, and righteousnesse, and sanctification, and redemption* to them.[13]

Here Hooker does not hesitate to address the poor and ignorant in his congregation as "fooles," "weake things," "the offscouring[s] of the world," even with full confidence that they will identify with such a view of themselves and be comforted and encouraged to faith by what the minister says.

Formal learning, he reassured these offscourings, is of no significance in spiritual struggles: "A dram of spirituall wisdome . . . is worth a thousand cart-loads of that dung-hill, carnall wisdome."[14] Worldly knowledge could even be a downright hindrance: "Men of the greatest ability for depth of brain and strength of understanding are most hardly brought to brokennes of heart." Hooker's verbal wit and his ear for a neatly balanced sentence are both evident as he presses this point: "It's the first step to wisdom *to become a fool,* and thats hard to him that is highly in love with his own wit."[15] The saints, whether they be university graduates or common day-laborers, "have the wisdom, and enlightening Grace of the Spirit in their Minds."[16] Hooker's audience could thus find reassurance in the fact that "true faith," the only attribute by which God judges men's worth, is God's gift, and as readily available to the poor and ignorant as to the high and mighty.

Having this full awareness of the nature of his audience, Hooker also became habitually concerned with the matter of prose style. In fact, in a sermon preached both early and late in his career he offered, in some seven paragraphs, one of the clearest and most effective justifications of the characteristic Puritan use of the plain style which his day produced. This plainness operates, he said, in both the language and the subject matter of a sermon. He takes up mainly the manner of speaking:

> The plainness of the Ministery appears, when the Language and Words are such as those of the meanest Capacity have some acquaintance with, and may be able to conceive; when the Preacher accommodates his Speech to the shallow understanding of the Simplest Hearer, so far as in him lies, alwayes avoiding the frothy tinkling of quaint and far fetched Phrases, which take off, and blunt as it were the edge of the blessed Truth and Word of God: Therefore the Apostle rejects *the wisdom of Words* as that which makes the Cross of Christ; that is, The Doctrine of Christ Crucified, revealed in the Gospel, to lose [its] proper and powerful effect when it is so Preached; where let it be observed that it is not only the vanity and emptiness of Words which is here condemned, but even that pompous gaudiness, and elegancy of Speech, which after an unsuspected manner steals away the mind and affection from the truth, and stayes it with it self, when it should be a means . . . to convey both Attention and Affection

from it self to the truth. He that puts so much Sugar into the
Potion, that he hinders the strength, and the work of it by such a
kind of mixture; though he please the Pallat of the Patient, yet
thereby he wrongs both the Physick, and his Health. So here in
Preaching.

For the excellency of Eloquence, and entising words of humane
Wisdom which in case were commendable to be used by him who
is an Orator, or a Declamor in the School, in the Pulpit becomes
ever Fruitless, and many times hurtful and prejudicial to the sav-
ing success of the Gospel. . . . And as all kind of Curiosity and
Niceness is to be avoided, so all obscure and unusual Phrases, dark
Sentences and Expressions, strange Languages are much more to
be rejected, as opposite even to the end of speaking, much more
to plainness of the Preaching of the t[r]uth. . . . He that hath a
Pastoral heart must be so affected in dispensing the Doctrine of
Grace, as *Paul* was in writing, *Rom.* 1.7. . . . *To all that be at
Rome,* so should he labor to reach out mercy and comfort to every
soul in the congregation, by every sentence he delivers, as much
as in him lies, whereas mystical cloudy discourses which exceed
the capacity and understanding of most in the assembly, its not
possible they should work powerfully upon their Consciences. That
which the Mind conceives not, the Heart affects not: Ministers
should be, and, if faithful they wil be as nurses to the people, they
will prepare milk for the meanest and weakest, and meat for all;
but never give dry crust or stones in stead of bread to any; for that
was not to feed, but to starve the Child.[17]

But when the "matter" is difficult, plainness is all the more necessary. "I have ever thought writings that come abroad, they are not to
dazle [*sic*], but direct the apprehension of the meanest, and I have
accounted it the chiefest part of Iudicious learning, to make a hard
point easy and familiar in explication."[18] And what was true of the
printed word, he felt, was even more true of pulpit preaching:

If Ministers will not be the Divels Brokers, . . . When they come to
Preach, they must make sin appear truly odious, and fearful to the
open view of all, that all may be afraid and endeavor to avoid it. Those
secret wipes, and witty jerks, and nips at sin, at which the most prophane are pleased, but not reformed; are utterly unsavory and un-
seeming the Place, the Person, the Office, of the Messenger of the
Lord of Hosts. What! A Minister a Jester! O fearful! to make the Pulpit a Stage, to play with sin; when he should terrifie the Conscience
for it? The Lord abominates the practice, he that knows and fears the
Lord should abhor it with detestation.[19]

To reach the consciences of his audience, said Hooker, a minister does
not need rhetorical decorations but rather "spirituall heat in the

heart."[20] "As it is beyond my skill, so I professe it is beyond my care to please the nicenesse of mens palates, with any quaintnesse of language. They who covet more sauce then meat, they must provide cooks to their minde."[21]

The prophets and apostles served as types for this plainness in preaching. And, of course, the Puritans learned from the examples of the great preachers in the generation preceding them, as well as from such indispensable textbooks as William Perkins's *Arte of Prophesying*. But Hooker defined the practice so well, both in his sermons on the subject of plainness and in his regular preaching habits, that he himself became an *exemplum* in his ministry, first in the Old World and then in the New. By example and reputation Hooker became an important teacher of his own and later generations of New England Puritan ministers.[22]

Plainness was thus for Puritan preachers a matter of rhetorical principle; their enunciation of the need for a plain style in fact represents the formulation of an aesthetic theory which governed their whole literary output. But it was much more besides. Such defenses of the plain preaching style as Hooker's emerge from the full context of political struggles between "Puritan" and "Anglican" factions within the English Church. Puritans often complained that Anglican preaching seemed to eschew plainness in favor of the self-indulgent "frothy tinkling of quaint and far fetched Phrases." It was through their united opposition to the more ornate Anglican preaching style that the Puritans derived an important dimension of their identity as a "purifying" element within the Established Church. In short, a Puritan minister preached as he did out of his own sense of both rhetorical and political necessity. In the practice of preaching in a plain style aesthetics and politics were inseparably conjoined.

Hooker's sermons took their form, not just from the dictates of such mentors as Thomas Cartwright, William Perkins, and William Ames, all of whose written instruction he gratefully acknowledged, but from his deep, inherent awareness of the proper role and importance of the minister as a means of grace to his congregation and from his own clear sense of the nature and capacity of that audience. His task, and that of all sincere Puritan ministers, was a monstrously challenging one. He had to convey the complex theology of Calvinism to a congregation of simple people who were often, despite our too-easy tendency to assign them a uniform godliness, less than enthusiastic about the task.

Hooker frankly admitted that not all ministers succeeded in their tasks. He occasionally took it upon himself to explain what the attributes of an effective minister are and to complain of the infrequency with which such men emerge in the Church. Mainly, two things are required. In the first place, a minister must himself be converted before he preaches conversion to others. "No Minister can convert another, who hath not stood in Gods counsell, that hath not beene sent by him." By the same token, one could draw an inference about the state of a minister's soul from the relative success or failure of his preaching: "Faith in a hearer doth argue a Teacher sent of God."[23] The danger of an unregenerate ministry was a considerable danger indeed to a community which placed such stock in the central importance of the preacher's function.[24]

The other major requirement for an effective ministry, in Hooker's view, was the desire and ability to preach "with particular application." Preaching in generalities would not help anyone. But unfortunately there were a multitude of preachers in Hooker's day who, he believed, were merely generalizers or, as he liked to call them, "dawbers." More than once he preached the sermon which has as its central doctrine the claim that "a plain and particular Application of special sins by the Ministry of the word is a special means to bring the soul to a sight of, and sorrow for them." Just as a doctor must prescribe the precise medicine for a particular ailment and as a shepherd must be attentive to each of his sheep individually, "the place and duty of a Minister" also requires this kind of particular attention to particular sins. Human nature, he punned, is such that "General Truths generally do little good. That which is spoken to all, is spoken to none at al."[25] "A sword in a childs hand, though never so sharp, will doe no harm; but if it be put into a strong mans hand, he wil make it cut deeply."[26] The secret is to avoid preaching in generalities; tell a man he must perish in such and such a sin, says Hooker, and "he then begins to bethink himself what to do."[27] This principle of specificity remained a fundamental characteristic of Hooker's approach to his audience in all his best sermons.

This direct approach was absoutely essential, he felt, because all too often congregations are sluggish in their listening. The following passage, likening the unrepentant sinner to a heavy sleeper, illustrates the vividness of his descriptions as well as his view of the minister's duty in the face of a congregation's resistance to truth:

> We here see the reason why there is so little good done by the Ministry of the Word upon the hearts of ungodly men: Many Hypocrites lie skulking under the covers of deceit, and are not discovered; many proud hearts not humbled, but go on in their sturdy distempers; many sleepers sit and snort in their security, and go hoodwinked down to destruction, and see nothing before they sink into the pit. We do not knock at mens doors, we do not bring the light to their bed-sides, we do not pinch them indeed

with sharp and part' ar roofs, and those set on to purpose; we do not put them h eir sence, we do not keep them under the arrest of sor tion, so that they cannot make an escape. . . . Oh w ev ot, we hit not, we apply not the Word so home, so part s the occasions, conditions, corruptions of men require: refore it prevails not with that power, finds not that su ss ch otherwise it might. Common Reproofs are like the co oise in the Ship when the Marriners were rowing *Jonah* to shore, notwithstanding all which, *Jonah* lies and sleeps under-ha.ches: But when they go down to him, and laid hold upon him, and awakened him with a witness, *Arise thou sluggard, and call upon thy God, lest we all perish*, Jonah, 1.5. He then began to bethink himself where he was, and what he had done. . . . So here, all the while we take up mens minds, and exercise their Ears and thoughts with some hovering Discourses, and common words of course, *We are all sinners, In many things we offend all, All flesh is frail;* but I hope better things of you, I hope there is none such amongst you.[28]

In a sermon such as this, where he directly addresses the clergy—the "we" who "hit not" and the "you" of whom Hooker hopes better things—he becomes a teacher of teachers, a leader of leaders, exhorting the ministers who hear him to imitate him and thus become "awakening" preachers. This is all the more obvious in the next paragraph of the same sermon, where he gives examples of various ways to address particular kinds of sinners in order to make them know that the preacher is, without doubt, speaking directly to them.

Those daubing discourses and roving reproofes, toothless, powerless dispensations, like arrowes shot cock-height, they touch not, trouble not, and in the issue profit no man at all. [The members of the congregation] come proud and stubborn and perverse and careless, they sit so and returne so, day after day and year after year. But you should shake up a sinner, go down under the hatches to *Jonah*[,] set upon the hearts of men in particular[,] *Awake thou sluggard.* Thou a master of a family and teachest not, instructest not those that are under thee? Thou a servant yet stubborn and perverse, and submits not to those that are set over thee in the Lord? Art thou a Wife and dost not reverence and obey with fear him whom God hath made thy head and guide? Art thou a member of a Christian Congregation, and hast the name of Christ called upon thee, and art thou treacherous to the Covenant of Christ, opposest the government and spirit of Christ, and despisest the ordinances of the Lord Jesus? Awake you careless masters and rebellious servants, perverse wives, treacherous and faithless members; Know that your Religion is vain and your selves also

> while these distempers rest in your bosom; cal upon your own
> hearts for Humiliation and repentance, and unto God for mercy
> that you perish not.[29]

Hooker concludes by citing a couple of types against whom the modern
preacher may measure himself as antitype, naming first the example of
Peter in his sharp accusation of the rulers and people of Israel for murder-
ing Christ (Acts 4:10–11) and then Thomas Cartwright, the sixteenth-century Puritan minister who, as many in Hooker's audience would have
known, was expelled from his posts at Cambridge in 1570 and 1571 for his
outspoken Puritan views and who was always a strong advocate of the importance of preaching in the Church.[30] "It's *Cartwrights* expression,"
says Hooker, that "when our saviour sent out *the sons of thunder then
Satan fel like lightening from Heaven,* the right levelling the ordinances of
Christ wil undoubtedly make battery in the kingdom of Satan."[31]

As the cases of Simon Peter and Thomas Cartwright show, aiming
directly "at the sins of the persons and people to whom he speaks" will
not make a minister popular, since the best and toughest preaching
"finds the least and worst acceptance at the hands of rebellious sinners." Given a choice, "Squeamish Stomachs had rather take Sugar-
sops a whol week together than a bitter Potion one day." But since "a
Chirurgeon may be most compassionate when he cuts most deep even
to fetch up the core," "all sharpness of rebuke and yet al meekness of
spirit do wel accord." The whole lesson is finally reduceable to a pithy
aphorism: "Sharp reproofs make sound Christians."[32]

An especially interesting testimonial to Hooker's own success in preaching with this "particular application" appears in the "relation" of the
troubled struggling to assurance of grace by John Collins, a 1649 Harvard graduate, teaching fellow, and later minister in London, whose
account of his conversion was preserved in the back of Michael
Wigglesworth's diary. Collins acknowledged that as a youth he had
been "moved" to greater seriousness in praying, reading, and attending
services by reading Hooker's *Soules Preparation for Christ,* but he was
subject to backsliding, so that when he later actually attended a sermon
preached by Hooker, he thought that he, John Collins, was the very
sinner to whom the minister was referring. Collins said, "Mister
Hooker preaching out of First Romans 18 here [Cambridge, Massachusetts Bay] I thought he certainly knew what a sinner I had
been[,] what convenants I had broke[,] and seeing I had held the truth
in unrighteousness I thought I was as good as in hell already[;] one that
had so grievously abused the light[,] there would be no other portion
for me."[33] This was just the beginning for Collins, and as he confesses,
it took the combined efforts of the Reverends Thomas Shepard,

Jonathan Mitchel, John Sherman, and Henry Dunster, in addition to Hooker, to make a sound Christian of him, but the personal identification with the sins to which the ministers—particularly Hooker— referred in their sermons played a major role in his conversion.[34] Whether Hooker actually knew any of Collins's sins we cannot say, but the point is that Collins *thought* he did. This was what Hooker meant by preaching with "particular application."

The Art of Hearing

The case of John Collins testifies that for the Puritans listening to sermons was not just an idle pastime. It was an activity in which the hearers ought to engage with a life-and-death commitment. As Hooker warned his congregation, "Every sermon a man heareth, he is thereby nearer either to heaven or hell, either he is made better or worse by it."[35] Such a warning clearly underlined the dual importance of an effective ministry and a responsive audience. For it was not merely the responsibility of the minister to bring a hearer closer to the throne of grace; the hearer had to do his or her part as well. Hooker more than once distinguished between good hearers and bad hearers. The good hearer's work begins the moment he enters the meetinghouse door: "I would have every Christian soule to look up to heaven when he commeth into the Congregation, and to say, speak Lord, thy servant is desirous to hear, and contented to hear and obey whatsoever thou shalt in this sermon make known to me. And if the Lord will have any thing, give it him, if he exact any thing from thee, yeeld to him."[36] Hooker here instructs his listeners with the advice which Eli gave to the young Samuel when he was being called by God (1 Sam. 3:9), telling him to respond, "Speak, Lord; for thy servant heareth." Hooker thought of this Old Testament story frequently in connection with his ideas about the proper attitude for a listener to have. Indeed, he more than once cited Eli as a type of the good hearer for his willingness to "hearken to" the ominous words which God had spoken to Samuel about His wrath against and intended punishment of Eli's house. Eli "would hear al, and know the worst of al: So it ought to be with every man, that in earnest, desires to know the evil of his sin."[37]

One of the major tests of the good hearer is his ability to profit from the preacher's prophesying of truth even though it indicts him directly for his worst sins. Hooker cited many "listeners" in both the Old and New Testaments as representatives of the type of the good hearer. A favorite was Cornelius, whom Paul tells of asking Peter to come to speak with him and a group of friends and relatives (Acts 10:33): "As

Cornelius said, *Wee are all here present* before the Lord to heare whatsoever thou art commanded us of God. So the humble Soule saith, Whatsoever trouble it brings, I yield to the truth, and desire to heare it."[38] Therefore, whenever you hear God's word, "you must come trembling, and submit to that good word."[39] The experience of the various prophets provided particularly good examples, since, like Hooker himself, they had in their audiences people who were both good and bad listeners. David, for instance, was a good hearer in that he "took hold of the reproof of the Prophet *Nathan.*" And Job listened and held his tongue while he heard the terrifying words of God.[40] On the other hand, Ahab's resentment of the truths spoken by both Micaiah and Elijah made him a notoriously bad listener, preferring as he did his "400 false Prophets . . . because they never disquieted him in his sins." And Isaiah's audience was like Ahab in that it wanted to "give the Prophet his Text, and tel him what points he should handle."[41] Jesus' own disciples, Hooker noted from John 6:66, "when he pressed Spiritual and searching Truths upon them," chose to avoid him. And in the early days of the Church Stephen's listeners turned on him for his preaching truth of self and sin.[42] The lesson borne by all these typical good and bad hearers is simply that God's true word, coming from his ordained messengers, is not comfortable for the sinner to hear; but hear it he must. Ideally, one should be discomfited in the manner of a John Collins. "Tinglings which come onely to the eare . . . are not sappy to nourish and affect the heart."[43] The Holy Spirit accompanies the word of the Gospel, so that the good hearer is apt to become a redeemed soul, while "the hearing of the Gospell without the Spirit, is nothing else but a beating of the ayre, and a dead letter."[44]

In just this way Hooker was consistently working to develop a receptive audience. Not relying merely on the force of his message to carry his audience to truth, he was helping them to see that their own receptive attitude as listeners was itself a sign of their election. It was no small part of Hooker's effectiveness as a preacher that he recognized the need to do more than preach from his heart with all the rhetorical skills his education, reading, and experience had taught him. He had to prepare his audience to receive the truth that he had to convey. Only then could the Spirit fully assist his preaching.

Structuring a Sermon

In the mechanics of preaching, the Puritan minister was greatly aided by precedent. The accepted sermon form laid down in William Perkins's standard text, *The Arte of Prophecying,* and later in William

Ames's important summary of Puritan theology, *The Marrow of Sacred Divinity*, dictated four main parts. The preacher was to begin by reading the "Text," a biblical passage, which he would then explicate to clarify difficulties in its meaning. Then he would quickly proceed to the "Doctrine," involving the statement and explanation of a thesis, an argumentative position. Next came the "Reasons," which were rational support of the Doctrine. Finally, the preacher laid out the "Uses," or "Applications," wherein, according to Robert Harris, who voiced the opinion of most Puritans, "a Sermons excellency doth consist."[45]

Thomas Hooker became known in his day as a particularly *affective* preacher—one who could especially reach the hearts of his listeners through his Uses. Some forty-eight years after Hooker's death Cotton Mather recorded that Hooker "had a most excellent Faculty at the *Applications* of his Doctrine; and he would therein so touch the *Consciences* of his Auditors, that a Judicious Person would say of him, *He was the Best at an Use that ever he heard.* Hereby was a great Reformation wrought."[46] His awareness of the different needs felt by the various elements in his congregation contributed to his creation of a great variety of intellectual and emotional appeals in his Uses. Perkins and Ames had already categorized various types of Uses, but Hooker did not limit himself to their preestablished categories.[47] They had listed in their textbooks Uses of information, confutation, instruction, reproof, consolation, exhortation, and direction; but he added Uses of humiliation, comfort, encouragement, thanksgiving, caution and advice, consolation, complaint, compassion, assurance, reprehension, trial and examination, wonderment, admiration, and terror, as well as occasional selective Uses, such as exhortation to believers, or advice to ministers. In this variety we see his earnest desire to bring some particular message to everyone. Not all of these were ever used in a single sermon, of course, since he usually did not include more than five Uses (eight is the maximum in his printed sermons) and often stated fewer. Still, he intended, while following the helpful guidelines of the traditional Puritan sermon form, to fill out that form with a personal and lively approach to those he knew to be in his congregation.

A full exploration of the characteristics of each of these kinds of Uses is impracticable and unnecessary here, but at least three are significant and characteristic enough to reward special discussion. Two of these, his Uses of trial and of wonderment, are examined elsewhere in this study.[48] The Uses of terror, however, represent an element in Hooker's sermons which clearly demonstrates his awareness of the various sorts of sinners in his congregation. Such Uses were a necessary part of his attempt to reach, not just the "poor, doubting Christians" who really wanted to come to Christ, but also the hardened, recalcitrant sinners in the crowd. Hooker was not willing to let the latter go their way to hell if there was any chance of reaching them. That he was sometimes amazingly successful in getting through to these tough-hided reprobates is clear from the anecdote (possibly apocryphal) told by Cotton Mather of "a profane person" in England who eventually followed Hooker across the Atlantic Ocean. This Englishman, intending "only an Ungodly Diversion and Merriment, said unto his Companions, *Come, Let us go Hear, what that Bawling* Hooker *will say to us;* and thereupon with an Intention to make sport, unto *Che[l]msford* Lecture they came. The man had not been long in the Church before the *Quick and Powerful Word* of God, in the mouth of His Faithful Hooker, pierced the Soul of him; he came out with an Awakened and a Distressed Soul, and by the further Blessing of God upon Mr. *Hooker's* Ministry, he arrived unto a true *Conversion;* for which cause he would not afterwards Leave that Blessed Ministry, but went a *Thousand Leagues* to Attend it, and Enjoy it."[49] To get this man's ear, Hooker may well have had recourse to a Use of terror. These Uses always told of the most dire results of continued waywardness and unconcern for godly matters. They make up a relatively small proportion of the Uses employed by Hooker, who, like most of his New England colleagues, was not characteristically a preacher of hell-fire.[50] But on occasion, when the text and his audience were suited to it, he could successfully terrorize the hardened sinners in the crowd with some mighty and fearful proclamations about the fate of unbelievers when they finally fell into God's hand at the moment of death. He explained this matter himself in a sermon which is primarily on the subject of Christ's atonement for the sins of faithful believers, when he paused in the second Use to comment, "This truth is like a thunder-bolt, and it is able to shake the hearts of all unbeleevers, and to dash them all in peeces: . . . every obstinate unbeleever is destitute of all hope of succour and pardon of his sinne: consider of this all you that are unbeleevers; you must pay your own debts, and beare your owne burthens."[51]

Hooker's particular power in giving teeth to his theoretical pronouncements is nowhere more fully proven than in his efforts to convince hardened sinners of the importance of the truth he was here proclaiming. On one occasion, he announced that the disease of sin cannot be hidden from God; those who *"continue in their sinful distempers"* are sure ultimately to feel sorrow, because at death the "filth and impostumate matter issues out of the ears and mouth and each man can see it."[52] On other occasions, he resorted purely and simply to challenging his listener to imagine his dilemma on the day of judgment: "When the Heavens shall melt, and the Goats shall stand on the left hand, and the Sheep on the right hand, and when ye shall see all the Heavens on a flame, and you shall heare that fearfull voyce, saying[:] arise you damned unbeleeving wretches, stand forth and heare your doome; what will bee your greatest misery in that day? even this, *Depart from me yee cursed, into everlasting flames:* this is the upshot of vengeance, and the sharpest sentence; would you not thinke this terrible, if you did heare it?"[53]

This is "hell-fire" indeed, but it would be wrong to characterize Hooker's preaching chiefly by a knowledge of Uses of terror, just as it is wrong to see Jonathan Edwards's *Sinners in the Hands of an Angry God* as a thoroughly representative Edwards sermon. Hooker's approach, like Edwards's, depended on his topic and his audience. When he did resort to "terror" tactics, he did so out of a sense of his responsibility as a minister on whom his congregation depended for guidance and out of the pastoral love which made him want to affect these listeners in whatever way he could. A passage in *The Paterne of Perfection* (1640) spells out the rational and theological justification for his Uses of terror:

> If a man in a good and healthfull constitution need opening diet, then much more, a body that is corrupt, hath need of strong physick. If *Adam,* that was in an wholesome condition, had need of a threatning, how much more need have wee, that have hearts overcharged with strong distempers, and clogged with venome and malice. This cheks the conceit of carnall persons, that think Ministers ought not to speak such terrible things; either they must bee wiser then God, or wee must bee better then *Adam.* Therefore wee should deale with our hearts as men do with the creature; though it be somewhat tame, it must have an ordinary sence; and if it be unruly, wee shackle it: So *Adam* had a well tempered disposition, yet he had a prohibition: but alas, our natures are like an untamed heifer, as they, *Jer.* 2. that *snuffe up the wind like the wild asse,* & are carried on violently into corruptions. What shall we say of these *wild asse colts,* as *Job* speaks? Ch. 11.15. for if *Adam* had need of a chek, a thousand threatnings are too little for such wretches as we are.[54]

Thus, human depravity loomed large as a motivating principle in Hooker's ministry, accounting for his ready reliance when occasion dictated on the Use of terror.

Hooker's approach to his listeners consistently indicates his wish that they share his sense of urgency about spiritual matters. Indeed, a recurrent motif in his preaching is a Puritan version of *carpe diem* thinking. Borrowing his imagery from the Bible Hooker occasionally waxes poetical on this subject: "Alas what is our life? a bubble, a flower, a shaddow, the bubble breaks, and the flower fades, and the shadowes pass away, thou art not certain thou shalt live til the evening."[55] Or he could put it more proverbially: "We should strike while the iron is hot, fashion the vessell while the clay is soft."[56] However expressed, his point is always that time is short. "The day of a mans life is very uncertaine, no man knoweth how long he shall live . . . many of us are in our middle age, nay some of us are in our old age, wee have one foote already in the grave."[57] To the young who feel no urgency about their spiritual plight, he warns: "O foole, O foole, I say unto thee as Christ did to the rich man in the Gospell, this night thy soule may be taken from thee, and then what will become of thy thoughts, plots, and projects, thy bed may become thy grave, and then what will become of thy poor soule, the divells may drag it into hell."[58] This is Augustinian thinking, straight out of the *Confessions*,[59] but one suspects it is also dictated by Hooker's own temperament. The urgency in this *carpe diem* message underlines and lends force to Hooker's whole ministry, both when he is preaching against evil public policies and national dangers in the "occasional" writings, discussed in the next four chapters, or against private personal sins which endanger the soul of a listener, as in the sermons discussed in Parts 2 and 3. This sense of urgency is surely behind his emergence as a major voice in the Puritan culture.

For all his urgency, however, Hooker was not a part of the millenarian school of Puritan preachers.[60] Whereas John Cotton preached at length on texts in Revelation, the major scriptural source of millenarian thinking, only two surviving Hooker sermons take their texts from that book.[61] For Hooker, the apocalypse came to every man at the moment of death. You are alive now, he said repeatedly, and thank God for that. Take advantage of life, therefore, for God's ways are mysterious, and tomorrow you may be dead. Or your minister may be dead or silenced ("the means may be taken from you"), which could amount to the same thing for you. So Hooker's hell-fire and terrorizing made up a small portion of his total philosophy of preaching and conversion. Some need cajoling, some need encouraging, some need brow-beating, but all need to humble their hearts. The powerful minister would see that each man had every opportunity.

It was a heavy duty to be a minister in Puritan England and New England. The minister was God's instrument for bringing the Truth to those who had a very great need to know. It is clear from what Hooker says about how the minister and congregation alike should go about their respective tasks that he felt he was entirely capable of performing this difficult duty. Whether addressing a special audience on a particular historical occasion or facing his familiar congregation to describe one of the many facets of the conversion process, Hooker always saw himself as the prophetic shepherd of his people. Late in his career Hooker approvingly quoted Calvin's *Institutes* on the minister's dual function vis-à-vis his congregation: *"Johannis Ministerium, nec plane Propheticum, nec plane Apostolicum, sed intermedium quoddam Ministerium fuit."*[62] He was the truth-bringer as well as the kindly guide, and his career would seek the delicate balance between the two functions.

PART ONE

THE OUTER WORLD
Occasional Writings

2

Troubles in the English Church and Commonwealth

Since the Puritan minister functioned both as a private spiritual guide and as a community leader, a dual concern is evident in the written product of the career of such an active author as Thomas Hooker. It is clear enough that most of the time Hooker felt his first priority was the spiritual nurture of individual souls, so that a large majority of his sermons were on his favorite subject of the stages of the soul's progress to heaven. These writings, which also bring out the resourcefulness of his imagination most fully, are the subject of the second and third parts of this study. The other writings—the written responses to occasions of public crisis or debate—provide the subject for our initial attention. Without a careful investigation of both types of writing, our picture of Hooker would be badly out of focus, since in the last analysis he was equally at home in two worlds—the spiritual and the temporal. He was, indeed, a prime example of the socially active idealist. He inherited the dual tradition of Reformation spiritual enthusiasm and Renaissance appreciation for the concrete as well as the ideal. These qualities, together with his humble family background, his schooling in the best educational tradition of Western Europe, and his personal traits, which Cotton Mather said included "a mighty Vigour and Fervour of Spirit" together with a "Heroical Spirit and Courage,"[1] gave the tools he needed to become a potent leader in both the Old World and the New.

For all of their well-known insistence on introspection, the Puritans had an immense impact on the external world. Not only did they overthrow a monarchy and establish a new, if temporary, form of government in England, but they were the chief engineers of what proved to be the most important colonial venture for modern civilization. And Thomas Hooker was particularly attuned to the momentous events in his social, political, and ecclesiastical world. His emphasis on the inner life in no way caused him to become myopic in regard to the events of history so rapidly building around him and his fellow Puritans. Indeed, the events occurring in the secular world seemed full of spiritual significance to Hooker and his fellow Puritans. To read aright the course of contemporary European history was to better understand the will of God for them.

Hooker first made a mark in public life with his intellectual, argumentative, and preaching skills at Cambridge. Later, his fame as a preacher and his commitment to ecclesiastical nonconformity made him notorious with the Anglican Church hierarchy in both England and Holland. Eventually he was instrumental in establishing the first churches of Cambridge and Hartford and served as adviser to the political leaders of both colonies. He probably had a direct influence on the drafting of a body of laws in the colony of Connecticut. He was frequently a participant or moderator at important synods, including both the Antinomian hearings and the Cambridge synod of 1643, and was asked to serve at the Westminster Assembly. He was, from the beginning to the end of his career, immediately involved in the turmoil of important events which were making for great change in England and America.

The surviving writings of Hooker do not give as full or as orderly a sense of his involvement in these external matters as they do of his depiction of the inner life of the elect saint. We know from his own occasional comments in sermons that he much preferred to leave controversy out of his pulpit literature. Yet he dealt enough in it to get himself expelled from the active pursuit of his calling in his homeland. Fortunately, we have a few sermons which give us an idea of why church authorities were so worried about this rabble-rousing preacher. And though we have no surviving sermons which we can be sure were preached in the Netherlands, his answers to the twenty propositions put to him by John Paget indicate precisely where he disagreed with the Dutch church authorities. His particular comments on matters of controversy in New England have also survived in the cases of the teapot tempest over John Endecott's cutting the cross from a local militia company's flag in 1634 and the more important disputes with English ministers over church polity and baptism. Less well known but also important in an attempt to trace Hooker's reaction to and involvement in issues of public moment are the doctrinal statements made in certain of his writings generated by such major events as the Antinomian controversy in Boston and the convening of the Westminster Assembly in London. From the surfacing in print of his writings on all these subjects—some intended for publication, others not—we can get a reasonably good impression of Hooker's unavoidable connection with crucial issues of his day. The fact is, men looked to Thomas Hooker as a leader in two worlds, the world of temporal events as well as that of spiritual concerns, and we are fortunate that, despite his apparent lack of interest in the publication of his writings throughout most of his career, samples of his comments on each of the public occasions just mentioned have survived.

In the early parts of his career, Hooker had little concern with publishing his writings. Nothing he wrote appeared in print until he was past the age of forty. His first publication, a brief preface to the second edition of John Rogers's *Doctrine of Faith* (1627), was probably published immediately after it was written. The next publication, *The Poor Doubting Christian*, which appeared anonymously in 1629, had probably been written a few years earlier, since it was apparently highly influenced by Hooker's experience at Esher with Joan Drake in the early 1620s.[2] His next work, a preface to William Ames's posthumous *A Fresh Suit against Human Ceremonies* (1633), appeared in print very promptly after completion. But between 1633 and 1645, a period which saw the first appearance of the great bulk of Hooker's sermon literature, publication of his writings was usually delayed well beyond their completion and was at best a haphazard enterprise. With only one clear exception (*The Properties of an honest Heart*, 1638) every Hooker book which appeared after 1633 and before 1645—some seventeen different titles—was probably published from sermon notes taken down in shorthand and later written out in detail by auditors of the sermons as delivered in England. Since shorthand was a much-practiced art among Puritan churchgoers, the texts, so far as we can judge, are surprisingly accurate.[3] In most cases, however, it is practically impossible to date the sermons accurately. Some of them could have been preached while Hooker was at the University in Cambridge; or later in his first parish at Esher, Surrey; or at his second assignment, the lectureship in Chelmsford, Essex. Indeed, since he was already in New England when most of the doubtful works appeared, it is even possible, though not likely, that some of them date from his Newtown or Hartford periods.[4] The reason for this dilemma is, in most cases, that his subject matter dealt with the inner world so entirely that there is little internal evidence as to when or where the sermons were delivered. In a few cases, of course, such details are present and the dates of delivery have been determined, sometimes with certainty, sometimes with at least a high probability of accuracy.[5] As I shall show, still further progress on this front is possible. But for the bulk of Hooker's sermon canon published before 1645, uncertainty as to date and place of origin will always remain.

The four remaining chapters in the first part of the present study deal with a number of works in the minority category in the Hooker canon, in that they speak to particular occasions in the external world of politics, law, family, and society. These works stand out in Hooker's career simply because they are so clearly occasional writings. They indicate his awareness of and involvement in the political complications of his day on both sides of the Atlantic. And they suggest a continuing commitment to a body of ideas and ideals which are both individually Hookerian and broadly Puritan. But above all, they help in shaping our understanding of this man who made such a firm impression on his own time and such a lasting contribution to religious literature.

"Public Dangers"

When Hooker moved from his Esher parish to become lecturer at Chelmsford in 1625, the lectureships so common in Puritan communities in England were supported by laymen and were not under the formal hierarchical control of the Church. Hooker probably enjoyed about three years of relative freedom from official church interference, time enough to establish himself as a major Puritan presence in Essex. But William Laud, in his exercise of power as the Bishop of London from 1628 on, was to show that continuance of individuals in particular lectureships would depend in large part on their ability to satisfy him in their adherence to prescribed forms of worship. In going to Chelmsford, which was in the See of London, Hooker was putting himself—to a degree he could not then know—directly in the path of conflict.

There were probably rumblings against him much earlier, but by the spring of 1629 anti-Puritan, pro-Laudean forces in Essex were actively agitating for Hooker's expulsion in the interest both of Bishop Laud's "owne future peace" and the peace and quiet of the entire region. Samuel Collins, the vicar of Braintree, who wanted his letters kept secret to protect his "creditt and fortune" in the neighborhood, and John Browning, rector of Rawreth, wrote letters, Collins to Laud's chancellor and Browning to Laud himself, warning that Hooker had great influence among the people—and especially among the younger ministers, for whom he was "an oracle and their principal library."[6] Perhaps most telling of the reports of these informers, however, was

Collins's claim that "all men's eares are now filled with ye obstreperous clamours of his [Hooker's] followers against my Lord [Bishop Laud] . . . . as a man endeavoring to suppress good preaching and advance Popery." On June 3, 1629, Collins could report that public attention was greatly attracted to the disagreements between Hooker's practice of nonconformity and Laud's principles of conformity. Because of Hooker's wide reputation, Collins warned, "this will prove a leading case, and the issue thereof will either much incourage or else discourage the regular clergie. All men's heads, tongues, eyes, and ears are in London, and all the counties about London taken up with plotting, talking, and expecting what will be the conclusion of Mr. Hooker's business."[7] "Cambridge disputes it *pro et con*," he reported elsewhere; and, again, "It drownes the noise of the great question of Tonnage and Poundage. I dare not say halfe of what I heare; paper walls are easily broken open. But hearing and knowing as much as I doe, I dare be bold to say that if he be once quietly gone, my Lord hath overcome the greatest difficulty in governing this parte of his diocese."[8] For much of 1629 Hooker was at the very eye of the storm that would in the next decade, long after his expulsion, drive the land into civil war.

That the clergy was split into factions over the case is evident from two petitions to the bishop regarding his actions toward Hooker. The first, dated November 10, 1629, and signed by forty-nine ministers from Essex, was a testimony in support of Hooker as a man "knowne . . . to be, for doctryne, orthodox, and life and conversation honest, and for his disposition peaceable, no wayes turbulent or factious," going on to commend "him and his lawfull suite to your lordship's honourable favour, and entreating the continuance of his libertye and paines there." Seven days later another petition was sent from "the conformable part of the clergy of his lordship's diocese," not mentioning Hooker by name but urging that Laud force the nonconformists "to conforme with us" to prevent the Anglicans' loss of "the credite . . . of our ministerie."[9] Though Hooker had told Laud's informants and presumably Laud himself, whom he confronted in June of 1629, that he was willing to depart quietly out of the diocese so long as Laud did not hale him before the Court of High Commission, which was very much under Laud's influence in silencing, imprisoning, and otherwise punishing nonconformist Puritans, about a year later Laud did have Hooker called before the court. Hooker understood the workings of the commission's form of justice all too well and elected to post bond, provided by a tenant of the Earl of Warwick, a friend of Essex Puritans. He hid out for a while at Warwick's estate and eventually departed for Holland.[10]

Given this personal involvement in the important political and ecclesiastical turmoil of the day, it is not surprising that several of Hooker's sermons from the 1620s refer ominously to "times of publike danger, such as these," times when "evill . . . befalls a Church or Common-wealth."[11] But in fact such references have a much wider context than just the persecutions of Laud and the High Commission. Hooker's arrival at Chelmsford very nearly coincided with the accession to the throne of Charles I. The next five years would be particularly agonizing for members of the Puritan and increasingly antiroyalist faction.

When James I died on March 27, 1625, England had enjoyed some twenty years of peace (though of late there had been much talk of and even preparation for war) at a time when nations on the Continent were involved in the wearying struggles of the Thirty Years War.[12] James, though he practiced a "feeble and inept" foreign policy,[13] had made peace in the first year of his reign and had sustained it until his death. Trade had prospered, while colonization in America had started to look more promising. But as Charles began his reign, the weaknesses of his father's policy of pacifism were telling; and under the very different approach of Charles and his chief adviser and instigator, the Duke of Buckingham, who was probably seeking personal glory and wealth as energetically as the good of England, armed hostilities with Spain and perhaps France were imminent. The years 1625–29 were years of war, and the English people, who had for some years favored England's going to war to rescue the Palatinate from Spain, soon became alarmed at the shocking ineptitude of the nation's military and at what this might mean for their own personal safety. The strenuously Protestant people—especially the wary, papist-hating Puritans—were especially fearful of the consequences of defeat, since England's enemies were Catholic countries and it was well known what bloodbaths followed Spanish victories. They took their warning from Buckingham's abortive attack on Cadiz in October 1625, which ended in defeat and disgrace, as did both the 1627 English attack on St. Martin on the French Isle of Rhé and the related attempt in 1628 to relieve the Protestant city of Rochelle on the mainland, which was blockaded by French Catholic forces. The battle on Rhé, politically ill-advised and crippled from the beginning by differences between the king and Parliament, resulted in what the standard history of the era calls a "massacre," with nearly 4,000—or more than half the total engaged British troops—killed.[14] The Court in general and Buckingham in particular were widely criticized, even despised, for these failures. Englishmen were extreme in their despair at the defeats on the battlefield, one calling the defeat at Rhé "the greatest and shamefullest overthrow received since we lost Normandy," and another concluding that "since England was England it received not so dishonorable a blow."[15]

Many of the English people were dismayed at King Charles's failure to appreciate the desire of the English people to control, through Parliament, their own financial and religious lives.[16] Charles's inability to cooperate with Parliament resulted in his three dissolutions of that body in the four-year period from 1625 to 1629. A contemporary Puritan diarist, Sir Simonds d'Ewes, referred at the time of the 1625 dissolution to "the great grief of all good subjects that loved true religion, their king, and the commonwealth." Just a year later, after the 1626 Parliament was also dismissed, the same diarist recorded that "infinite almost was the sadness of each man's heart, and the dejection of his countenance that truly loved the church or commonwealth."[17] The House of Commons rapidly clashed with the Duke of Buckingham, who became the symbol in their eyes of royalist arrogance and arbitrariness in law and religion. The Commons attempted impeachment of Buckingham in the spring of 1626, and though this failed, they increasingly despised him. Understandably, then, the alarm of Puritans was considerable when Buckingham was elected chancellor of the University at Cambridge in June of 1626, an election vehemently opposed by the Puritan colleges there, including Emmanuel.[18] Buckingham's popularity was not enhanced either by public knowledge that he had had a hand in the abortive efforts of James and Prince Charles to arrange the latter's marriage with the Spanish Infanta in 1623 and in the successful negotiations with the court of France to arrange the prince's marriage with Henrietta Maria, also a Roman Catholic. This was bringing the enemy to the very throne of England.[19] Buckingham's dominance of English political affairs continued from the last years of the rule of James I through the first three years of Charles I's reign, when England was shocked by his assassination in August of 1628.

In addition to these troubles we can add an increased stringency in the government's control of the press, greater intrusion into the affairs of the Church, and a growing opinion that the Court of High Commission, which dealt with religious offenders, was an unfair court. In June of 1628 a House of Commons committee drew up a "Remonstrance" to present to the king summarizing their grievances. It included eight points: "1. Innovation and alteration of the religion. 2. Innovation and alteration of the government. 3. Disasters of our designs. 4. Decay of trade. 5. Want of munition, powder, and shot. 6. Not guarding the narrow seas. 7. Unfurnishing of the forts. 8. Tonnage and poundage taken without warrant."[20] In addition, there were personal dangers and discomforts which threatened every Englishman in these years, begin-

ning with the plague of 1625—which, according to conservative estimates, took over 35,000 lives in London alone—and culminating in an
economic depression in 1629, "exactly timed to follow the failure of the
King's foreign wars."[21] By then, the English people had cause to be
discontented, aroused, and alienated.[22] Well might the preachers in
the countryside warn that England was in grave danger from within as
well as without. Certainly many in the congregations as well as in the
pulpits believed this to be so.

From the very beginning of Charles's reign, Puritans in England had
been aware of new threats to their liberty, particularly to the forms of
worship. For a short time, it is true, the popular preacher and Master
of Emmanuel College, John Preston, had held a position of considerable influence as the king's chaplain and friend of Buckingham, while
the Puritans—including such leaders as the Earl of Warwick, Lord
Saye, and the leader of the House of Commons, Sir John Eliot—were
hopeful that Buckingham would support them against the Anglican-
Arminian faction which Laud and the king favored. The Puritans were
finally disillusioned at two conferences on theological issues held at
York House in February of 1626, when the duke sided with the
nationalistic Anglicans against the Puritans' desire to establish in the
Church of England the strictly Calvinist doctrines of the Synod of
Dort.[23] From that point on Preston knew he was out of favor at court,
and the Puritans accordingly felt more and more threatened.[24]

What is perhaps most important here is that it was at just about the
time of Hooker's accepting the lectureship at Chelmsford that the Anglican party, led by the king himself, began to move formally to restrict
the freedom of lecturers.[25] The Puritans, following their emphasis on
the preaching of the Word as the primary function of the Church, had
established private funds which supported ministers to preach on Sunday and weekday afternoons, supplementing the usual Sunday morning
services conducted by the church-appointed vicars and rectors. The
lecturers were not immediately subject to the same restrictions as
other clergy because they were paid by private individuals or groups.
They considered themselves free from the necessity of heeding the
prescribed forms and ceremonies and could thus entirely satisfy their
consciences by avoiding such "ceremonies" as making the sign of the
cross, bowing to the altar, reading set prayers, and following a set
order of worship. As early as January 24, 1626, a week before his coro-
nation, King Charles issued a proclamation supposedly intended to be
used against Arminians but later used by Laud against the Puritan nonconformists: "The King will admit of no innovation in the doctrine,
discipline, or government, of the church," that was clearly "established

by law," further warning that "his majesty will proceed against all offenders against this order, with all that severity their contempt shall deserve, that by the exemplary punishment of a few, others may be warned against falling under the just indignation of their sovereign."[26] Though as yet no strong public animosity had developed toward Charles the issuance of his proclamation surely served as a red flag to the Puritans, coming as it did on the heels of the York House conference. The king's policy was consistent from the beginning, increasing only in intensity as he bestowed successive preferments upon Laud in the form of the bishopric of Bath and Wells, the bishopric of London, and finally the archbishopric of Canterbury itself, while all the time keeping him in charge of the Court of High Commission, which became a convenient legal tool of suppression. By 1629, with Laud installed as their bishop, the Essex County Puritans were feeling constant pressure to conform. Lectureships were suppressed, and in 1629 private chaplaincies, another refuge of Puritans from the Church's formal authority, were eliminated.[27] Under the High Commission and the Star Chamber, from the late 1620s through the 1630s, deprivation, excommunication, pillorying, mutilation, and forced exile became common. Some Puritans, such as Charles Chauncy, who was later to become president of Harvard College, gave in to pressures from the authorities and recanted previous defiant positions. Others refused to buckle, faced the courts, and paid the price of being branded on their faces or losing their ears, as did William Prynne, or even of losing their lives as a direct result of long imprisonment and refusal to bend enough to be released, as was the case with Sir John Eliot.

Given these conditions, it is not surprising to find occasional references in Hooker's sermons to "the publike evils of the times that wee complaine of so much."[28] Hooker was not averse to speaking out directly on what he saw as the central issues in need of reform by the people and the government. A few sermons in this vein help us to understand something of the causes of Laud's increasing ire with Hooker and his like. Before Hooker left England for Holland, he said his say against even the king himself, his most outspoken attack on the king, the nation, and the people coming in his well-known farewell sermon, *The Danger of Desertion*, a text to which we shall turn at the close of this chapter. But in earlier sermons occasioned entirely or in part by the troubles in the Church and nation, Hooker repeatedly stressed four main topics: the prevailing tendency to "oppose" God's "faithful ministers," the failure to maintain the Ordinances "in their purity," the need for renewed efforts by the faithful to cleanse their hearts and to avoid contributing to "publike evils," and the ultimate danger that God would finally desert the English people because of their infidelities.

Persecution of the Saints

The first of these recurrent themes sometimes crops up in the midst of a sermon on some other topic, while on other occasions it is itself the major concern of a full sermon. Hooker parenthetically introduces some strong words against those who persecute the saints of God in the first sermon in *The Soules Exaltation,* entitled *The Soules Union with Christ.* He does not define the saints of God simply as ministers but intends to include *all* saints and to condemn those who persecute them in any fashion. He introduces legal metaphors which suggest that there are two levels of law. Those who persecute Puritans do so under the guise of the law, but persecution of the saints is a "sin of a high nature," a veritably treasonous act, when considered in God's perspective.[29] He notes that even though civil law "provides not in this case to punish those that oppose the Lord Iesus Christ, and the power of his grace," those who "trample upon" God-fearing people are nevertheless earning condemnation in the higher court of God's justice. "Let all know that have beene professed opposers and dead haters of the Saints of God, let them know they are indited of high treason, and that in a most hainous manner against the Lord of Heaven and Earth, against the Lord Iesus Christ, the Redeemer of the world" (*SE,* pp. 11–12). This "high treason" earns "the greatest inditement at the day of judgement" because in persecuting the faithful saints, "they persecute Christ himselfe; they teare out the very eyes of Christ, and rend his heart in peeces" (p. 15). That Hooker knew he was taking sides in a volatile public issue is made plain in his disclaimer that "I speake not thus to countenance faction, my aime is at those that persecute religion and sanctity of life" (p. 16). He thus makes the radical point, without dwelling on it at length, that to obey the law of England is no longer necessarily to obey the law of God and that to oppose the English government's authority is not necessarily the worst form of treason.

The idea that this persecution of the saints is "treason" is again explicitly stated in a sermon much more directly addressed to the contemporary issue of governmental and Anglican harassment of the Puritans. On June 22, 1626, Hooker preached at the funeral of a young friend from Cambridge days, Robert Wilmott, the minister at Clare in Suffolk. The sermon, called *Spirituall Munition,* addresses the proper relation between a minister and his congregation. Overtones in the sermon suggest that all had not gone smoothly between Wilmott, "this

blessed Saint," this true "General" in God's army, and his congregation. The sermon's text, 2 Kings 2:12, describes Elisha's agonized cry
at the death of Elijah, "My Father, my Father." Hooker's first Doctrine is that "the ministers of God should be as fathers to the
people,"[30] a reverence which, he implies, was lacking at Clare and is
all too rare elsewhere in this day of political dispute over the forms of
religion. The background of governmental pressure on and persecution
of the Puritan ministers—especially lecturers—is implicit throughout
the sermon. Hooker forthrightly opposes these persecutions, for instance, as he says, "Brethren, is he a dutiful son that would cast his
father out of doors? A son? No, a slave to the devil, and a rebel against
the Lord Almighty, fitter for a prison to torment him than a house to
harbor him. It is a certain sign that the soul never had grace, which
opposeth the ministers of grace" (*SM*, p. 45). Ministers, after all, are
the "conduit-pipes of grace," and those who oppose them do not oppose merely "a poor weak man," but "the great God himself" (p. 45).

But Hooker is more to the point as he says, in his third Doctrine,
that "faithful ministers are the defenders of states, churches, and com-
monwealths" (*SM*, p. 47). At a time when the Puritans' refusal to observe the set forms of Anglican worship was being increasingly attacked
and punished as illegal by the High Commission court, Hooker insisted
that it is exactly the other way round. It is not the ministers who are
disloyal, traitorous, and treasonous, but their persecutors. Ministers,
after all, are interested in making men obedient to their earthly rulers
and "faithful to their religion and country" (p. 48). But loyalty to God
must come before loyalty to an earthly King.[31] Ideally, these loyalties
should not involve any conflict, but if they do, there can be no question about which object of loyalty must be in the wrong. "It is a certain
truth," says Hooker boldly, "he that is disloyal to the king of heaven
can never be loyal to the king of earth" (p. 48). Hooker does not say
any more explicitly than this that King Charles is out of step with the
will of God in allowing his functionaries to persecute Puritan ministers.
Rather, he makes his point ironically through preaching the rhetorical
assumption that things are as they should be—that the kings of heaven
and England are in agreement about what is right and good for England. This being so, it is clear that "those which are the enemies to
God's faithful ministers are the greatest adversaries that the Church or
State hath; for they spoil the munition of the land" (p. 49). Addressing
any in his audience who might side with the anti-Puritan forces, he
says that in opposing and undermining ministers, "thou art a traitor to
thy King and country, because thou persecutest him who labors in his
place to keep back wrath from seizing upon the land" (p. 49).

Thus, according to the way Hooker draws the battle lines, it is the opposers of the principled ministers who are traitorous, not the ministers themselves. These opposers, it would be well understood, were the bishops and any ecclesiastical informers who might reside in the community or be in the congregation at that moment. Such, surely, were Samuel Collins and John Browning, who would write to Laud and his chancellor, Arthur Duck, against Hooker in the fall of 1629; and such were the forty-one signers of the anti-Hooker petition sent to Laud in November of the same year. By that time, Hooker had preached enough sermons in the vein of *Spirituall Munition* to have earned Laud's punishment of silencing. In this early defense of the Puritan way of preaching and ministering, in fact, Hooker shows his awareness that it was an earnest battle—indeed, a war—in which he and his colleagues were involved. His rhetoric on occasion predicts the issues and tone of the Cromwellian era. Be prepared to pay the ultimate price, if necessary, he urges:

> It is wonderful to see what a good minister can do in a good war, how he can fight against 'principalities, and powers, and spiritual wickedness in high places' [Eph. 6:12], not fearing the face of man. The clear knowledge of this, that the battle he fights is the Lord's, assures him that the Lord will fight for him. Any coward will fight when he is assured of victory beforehand. A good cause will make men spend their dearest blood. When a man hath God to go before him, and the Word to warrant him in what he doth, he goes through thick and thin. We see with what joy and cheerfulness the martyrs sacrificed their lives to the flames. (*SM*, pp. 48–49)

Clearly, Hooker recognized the potentially revolutionary implications in his opposition to the Church's and Crown's—and even the civil law's—governance.

Purity in the Forms of Worship

It is, of course, common knowledge that the Puritans were called Puritans and were finally treated as outlaws in Tudor and Stuart England because of their uncompromising stance on the need to "preserve the purity" of the forms of worship. They vehemently resisted the intrusion into the English worship service of any vestiges of Roman Catholicism. It was just this threat which they saw in the Church's increasing desire to enforce conformity of practice in the worship service, whether in regard to the placement of the communion table, the stance of the worshippers in receiving the sacrament, or the garments worn by the minister. In sermons preached in England Hooker made occasional brief but highly charged remarks on the forms of worship. These remarks indicate that he stood firmly on principle, come what might. In *The Stay of the Faithfull* he expressed his opposition to the "superstitions" and "idolatries" of conformist churches. These objections are couched in the context of scripture quotation or explication, as when he quotes Exodus 32:30, where Moses fears that Israel's worship of the golden calf will bring God's wrath upon the nation—a typological analogy with England which was perfectly obvious to Hooker and not at all lost on his audience, especially when he said, "Thus you see, God leaves the Church at an uncertainty, at a hazard what hee will doe with them."[32] It is clear, according to Exodus 33:5, what God's instructions are: *"Pull off thine ornaments that I may know what to doe with thee"* (*SF*, p. 15).[33]

Hooker did not follow up this reference with more specific charges against the church authorities. But in a time when even the simplest auditors knew very well that nonconformity was getting local ministers into prison as well as official hot water, such subtle references to the subject would not have gone unnoticed. Hooker was being eminently clear, in fact, when he cited examples from Jeremiah or Revelation of God's punishment of the faithful: *"The Christian world,* Gods own servants, were growne devout in the *worshipping of images,* for yet saith hee, *they turned not from their gods of gold, and of wood, and iron, and of stone, wherewith they had provoked God,* and so hee caused a barbarous Nation to triumph over them, Revel. 9.14. So that you shall finde this ever to bee true, that the very sinnes of GODS Church, especially the Elect, have commonly shattered al the good that otherwise they might have found in their places where they be" (*SF*, pp. 33–34).

The minister relies heavily on examples from 2 Chronicles of good kings such as Jehosaphat and Hezekiah, who set all right in their kingdoms by setting all right in the church, sending "faithful *Levites* to teach the people the counsell of God" and "setting the Ordinances of God in their purity" (*SF*, pp. 48–50). This procedure, he points out, made their nations invulnerable to the attacks of strong enemy armies. The clear typological implication is that England, engaged as she is in frustrating struggles against the superior armies of Spain and France and with internal "enemies" in high places, also needs to restore the "purity" of the ordinances of God but as yet has failed to do so and is accordingly weakened. That the issue is in large measure one of purity in worship and in doctrine is made clear in the following passage:

> So long as ever the people of God did feare even the appearance of evill
> this way, and the skirts and circumstances of superstition in this kind,
> so long there was never any such feare of drawing on any such heresie
> in doctrine, any such superstition, and Idolatry, and false worship as
> since hath invaded the Church: but through the inclination of Gods
> people to tolerate themselves in this circumstance, and that circum-
> stance leading to superstition, to corruption in doctrine, or to the guid-
> ance and government of the affaires of the Church, from that hath
> sprung whatsoever danger and feare it is that any of you are now exer-
> cised with all. (SF, pp. 52–54)

Hooker made the same argument some ten years later in a sermon
delivered in Hartford, Connecticut, on October 4, 1638, where he
again repeated the same scriptural admonitions to "keep the ordinances
in the purity." The political climate was entirely changed for Hooker
by this time, but his commitment to the principle was unwavering:
"No brethren, it is certain the churches shall never prosper till there is
found seeking of God in humiliation, worshiping him according to his
. . . ordinances."[34]

Spiritual Cleanliness

As these passages indicate, for Hooker and his Puritan colleagues the
fate of the nation—or colony—was inextricably bound up with the condition of the Church. And both rested on the godliness and holiness of
the elect. As Larzer Ziff has explained, there was a "growth in England
of a new culture based on the pulpit as opposed to the altar, internalized authority as opposed to external, the superiority of the gracious
as opposed to the primacy of the anointed."[35] Hooker was very much
committed to this new emphasis. He related problems in the external
world to the condition of people's souls. If there are troubles in the
nation and the Church, look to yourselves, he said to his listeners. This
was a frequent chorus of the Puritan preachers in these years. John
Rogers was explicit about particular sins which he and his neighbors
knew about when he said from his pulpit in Dedham, "What should I
speak of the common sins of the times? The last assizes and every one
shows what state we are in, what horrible incests, the daughter being
with child by her own father, and the wife burning the child; another
ravishing his own daughter, being thereof accused by his own child and
wife; what cruel murders besides the common mother sins, ignorance,
extreme worldliness and that overspreading canker and leprosy of the
land, the contempt of good persons."[36]

Leprosy often served as a metaphor for sin—a spreading sore which
infects nations as well as individuals. Hooker uses it in just this way in

The Stay of the Faithfull when overtly speaking of the need for individual repentance and reformation, he means equally the need for redemption from the "publike evil" to which this work has constant reference: "If once a soule come in a sence of its owne leprosie, and lay open the nakednesse, and basenesse of the disease before God (the sinfulnesse of it, I meane) for the leprosie was but a type of the contagious spreading of sinne, let us come and show our contagion before God, our filthy, loathsome, spreading evills that our soules are corrupted with" (*SF*, p. 87). As he argues in another sermon which notices the "dangers" which "our country" is now subject to, personal humiliation and repentance are necessary if the nation is to be saved from disaster. England, he felt, was threatened by "a generation of Polititians" who follow Machiavelli's advice not to let their religion show.[37] Hypocrisy, he says, is rife in the world, and until this is cured, there is little hope for the nation. Whether you are a politician or a simple laborer, however, the rule still holds: reform begins with the individual soul but has ramifications in the general welfare. "Therefore, the body of this Nation, both all the meeke of the earth, and all the great spirits, and wise spirits of the earth too; behold, it behoves all to gather up themselves, and repent of their evill wayes" (*SF*, p. 100).

This whole line of argument is grounded upon the basic belief in God's Providence and the parallel insistence by the ministers of England, and later of New England, on the typological identification of their nation with Israel. They firmly believed that God's providential dealings with his chosen people are thoroughly evident and available to all in the Scriptures. Hooker makes the fundamental assumption that England's past sixty years of peace and prosperity have been due to God's favor toward the nation; "there is no nation that God hath dealt so mercifully with, as with us."[38] But there are limits to god's endurance of provocations from his people. Hooker reminds his listeners that "Israel provoked God to stir up *David* to take such a course, as should bring a plague that swept away seventy thousand of them: So that you see for the iniquities of *Iacob*, and for the sinnes of the house of Israel is all that evill that at any time befalls a Church or Commonwealth" (*SF*, p. 29). And behind all of the citation of Old Testament examples in Hooker's sermons dealing with the plight of the nation and Church is the fundamental assumption that "it is in every Common-wealth, as it was in *Davids* Common-wealth" (*SF*, p. 30). "He commands deliverance for them, that serve and obey him, . . . and plagues and destruction for them that disobey him, and rebel against him."[39]

These "plagues and destruction" are emphasized as a very real danger to England in Hooker's sermons of the late twenties, especially *The Faithful Covenanter*, *The Stay of the Faithfull*, and *The Danger of*

Desertion. They are, in fact, a sign of God's continuing concern. Richard Sibbes had taken just such a view of the devastating plague of 1625. Preaching in London on the topic, Sibbes had said, "You know how God hath dealt of late with this *Citie,* and with our selves indeed, for we are all of one body politike, and however God visited them, yet it was our sinnes also that provoked him. . . . A Physitian lets the arme blood, but the whole kingdome was in a distemper."[40] Hooker's occasional references to plague are more general than Sibbes's,[41] but he is quite explicit in warning of possible "destructions." Citing a verse in Deuteronomy, he warns, with obvious antitypical reference to England's battles with Roman Catholic France and Spain, "If the Lord should send the enemy upon us and lay hardness over us, and we should be made vassals unto the tyranny of wicked men, this will stick to your hearts. Had I served the Lord in plenty and such a time when I enjoyed the meanes of salvation, then it had been well with me."[42]

The Lord determines the fate of nations and entire peoples, Christian and non-Christian, Hooker believed, to the end of strengthening the life and health of the Church. History can be understood only in the context of this belief. The waywardness of "Gods owne people . . . may cause him thus to wheele about the whole fabrick of the State" (*SF,* p. 54). The relationship of God's chosen people with their Lord is *the* determining factor in the events of the world's history. If you read history, Hooker says, "you shall finde that the greatest Monarchies in the world have beene advanced, either for scourges to *Gods* Church, or else for the deliverance of his people. . . . The reason of all Gods Providence over the world is for his Church" (*SF,* p. 39). From this it follows logically that if there are troubles in the nation, there must be troubles in the Church; and if there are troubles in the Church, it is because the faithful, in their individual lives, have been wayward in some fashion. In the context of Anglican repressions of the Puritans in the late 1620s, the most obvious of all failings was near at hand: "The Lord is specially angry with a nation for the breach of his covenant, and neglect of his worship. The Lord doth hate it and is carried with great violence toward those people that worship God falsely."[43] It is not surprising, in other words, that a nation which permits unwarranted ceremonies in worship is also full of hypocrites and sinners.

Prophesying to the Nation

Since the feeling among Puritans was that the English nation did indeed have a special covenant with God and that all the signs of the times pointed to England's infidelity to that covenant, the main question became, What next? *Will* we suffer invasion by papist hoards with the consequent separation of families and loss of religious liberties? *Will* the "purity of the ordinances" be totally violated and outlawed, forcing the best of God's servants to the far corners of the world? Or will God relent and restore Christianity to its rightful place of dignity and influence in the kingdom? As Darrett Rutman has said, on this subject "Puritanism and nationalism came together."[44] Church and Commonwealth were bound to suffer a single fate. As a result, Puritan pulpits across the land resounded for a time to the rhythms of the jeremiad, sermons which held out hope for the nation but tended to overshadow the positive possibilities with the warnings of woe and misery to come if the people and leaders did not reform in time. And time was running out.

Hooker's most thoroughgoing jeremiads from this period are *The Danger of Desertion* and *The Churches Deliverances*. The latter, printed some twelve years after its delivery, as the second sermon in *Foure Learned and Godly Treatises* (1638), will serve to illustrate his success in this most bullying of all Puritan sermon styles. The sermon does not actually become a full-scale jeremiad until Hooker reaches his second Doctrine, where he states that "the estate of God's Church may be such that he may lend no further succour and deliverance unto it."[45] The sermon is a thanksgiving sermon, probably preached on November 5, 1626, a day of public remembrance of England's deliverance from the Gunpowder Plot.[46] Hooker is preaching, then, in the context of an awareness that God has been with England in the past, a truth which he stressed in his first Doctrine. But the main point in the sermon is that "when the sin of a nation comes to full ripeness and perfection" (*CD*, p. 76), the time for vengeance and destruction also arrives. The conditions for such actions are sketched so as to make clear that England has just come to that day of the Lord's vengeance when no further mercy can be expected. When sin becomes universal, common, and open, when affliction no longer profits the nation, when men do not love God despite peace, prosperity, and plenty, when preaching of the word is "unfruitful and unprofitable," "when a convenient company of godly men be taken away" and "the best of God's people" fail to oppose "the sins of the times," when all fail to see the fullness of their present danger and "sin outbids all means of reformation," truly then "men are ripe for desolation" (pp. 76–88 passim). Judea and Jerusalem found this to be all too true, he reminds the people. Take heed, England, or woe be unto you! "It is in every Commonwealth," after all, "as it was in *Davids* Common-wealth."

Despite intimation that there are *many* causes of God's destructive wrath in England at this moment, still the greatest cause is the persecution of ministers. This is so because if all else fails, God's Word can still correct the evils of the nation. But "when a man is not content to commit sin only, but he will oppose God's word, then the Lord like the lion of the tribe of Judah can help no longer, then 'the wrath of the Lord arose, and there was no remedy,' but he would lay waste the land" (*CD*, p. 83). The New Testament as well as the Old has ample evidence for Hooker's woeful predictions, as he shows in citing passages in Matthew 23 and Luke 19, where Jesus foretells the destruction of Jerusalem, where prophets are stoned and killed and the people "knowest not the time of thy visitation." Hooker observes that "they would not have the Word reform them, therefore they shall have the sword to plague them" (p. 84). The harassing and silencing of Puritan clerics was surely in Hooker's and his congregation's minds as he said, "When corruptions are grown so strong that good men are defiled and their hearts tainted and their mouths stopped, woe to that kingdom and people" (p. 85). Jeremiah is, after all, the most appropriate authority to quote for types of the present national antitype. Hooker plays the joint role of historian and prophet as he quotes Jeremiah 12:3: "They were as sheep fatted for the slaughter" (p. 87).

The ultimate alarming conclusion in all of this goes somewhat beyond even the thought that God will take vengeance on his people as a way of straightening things out in the kingdom. As pressure built on numbers of leading Puritan preachers to escape the wrath of the bishops, archbishop, and courts of the High Commission and Star Chamber, and as plans progressed in 1629 for the departure of a sizeable body of the faithful to establish the Massachusetts Bay Colony, the thought occurred to more than one minister that perhaps God was about to give up on England altogether. Perhaps the "vengeance" and "destruction" and "plague" which would next strike would take the form of the final departure of spiritual truth to a more congenial political and religious climate. Probably the most widely known statement of this possibility in Hooker's own day was George Herbert's couplet at the beginning of the following passage from "The Church Militant," a poem begun at least as early as 1623:

> Religion stands on tip-toe in our land,
> Readie to passe to the *American* strand.
> When height of malice, and prodigious lusts,
> Impudent sinning, witchcrafts, and distrusts
> (The marks of future bane) shall fill our cup
> Unto the brimme, and make our measure up.
>
> .   .   .   .
>
> Then shall religion to America flee.[47]

The modern editor of Herbert's poetry (which was very popular among Puritans in both England and New England) notes that "Herbert's idea was very much in the air at that time." A letter from Dr. William Twisse to Joseph Mede dated March 4, 1634, helps to document this claim: " 'And then considering our English plantations of late, and the opinion of many grave divines concerning the Gospel's fleeting westward, sometimes I have had such thoughts, why may not that be the place of the New Jerusalem?' "[48]

By 1634, one of Dr. Twisse's "many grave divines," Thomas Hooker, had already had his say on this subject and had himself joined the emigrées to the promised land. There was indeed much talk of this dire eventuality for England in Essex pulpits in particular. The metaphors varied, but the point was constant. What Herbert chose to imagine in the form of a man standing on tiptoe, ready to jump across a stream, William Fenner preferred to cast in the even more homely image of a householder's departure from his home: "God is now shutting up to be gone; and as we may justly feare, to remove away his Candlesticke, to take away the power of his Ordinances, and to withdraw his spirit from striving anymore with us, our stubbornnesse is so great."[49] And Hooker, knowing the mercantile enterprise of many of his Puritan listeners in the market town of Chelmsford, put it yet another way: "God is going. . . . England hath seen her best days, and the reward of sin is coming on apace; for God is packing up of his gospel, because none will buy his wares (not come to his price)."[50] The subsequent departure of Hooker, along with John Cotton and Samuel Stone, seemed a symbolic event to the younger Thomas Shepard, who commented on it in his *Autobiography* in the same vein: "I saw the Lord departing from England when Mr. Hooker and Mr. Cotton were gone, and I saw the hearts of most of the godly set and bent that way, and I did think I should feel many miseries if I stayed behind."[51] In fact, by 1628 the ministers' lamentations and jeremiads had already become characteristic enough that, when members of the House of Commons, in a particularly emotional reaction to King Charles's instructions to get on with their business and leave off criticizing him and his ministers, made dark predictions about the nation's destiny, a witness described them as "playing the divines, in confessing their own and country's sins," which drew God's "judgments upon us."[52]

Hooker's most outspoken statements about God's relationship with a disobedient England came in his farewell sermon to his Chelmsford congregation. His dire predictions are radical by any standards, no doubt made so both by his knowledge that this would be his last opportunity, in this location at least, to admonish his hearers to reformation and by his outright ire at having felt personally the repressive hand of the hierarchy's meddling in local church affairs. His life had been radically changed by the sentence of silencing pronounced unilaterally by Bishop Laud, and he could be expected to respond angrily to this penalty.

The Danger of Desertion begins calmly enough but soon becomes overtly prophetic and almost apocalyptic as he stresses repeatedly the great dangers which threaten England, desperately trying to shake his audience out of what he sees as their too great complacency in the assumption that God in fact will *not* desert England. The Text of the sermon is the last two clauses in Jeremiah 14:9: "We are called by thy name; leave us not." He begins by filling in the context of this verse, explaining how the Israelites had strayed from God's ways and were punished by drought and famine and finally by God's threat of disowning them. The typological assumption of England's similarity to Israel, and especially to Jerusalem, operates throughout. His ultimate intention is to stress the Israelites' response to God's threat—their prayerful plea, "leave us not." His first Doctrine, however, states theoretically that "God might cast off a people, and unchurch a nation" (*DD*, p. 230). He works quickly up to the immediate application of this theoretical truth, the likelihood of its now happening in England. First, the means of grace are removed; then God's protectors of the people, the faithful "magistracy and ministry," are taken away. And "when instead of counseling, there comes in bribing; and instead of true teaching, there comes in daubing, . . . then is God going away" (p. 231). Then Hooker moves directly to the tone and message of the jeremiad, which he continues through the rest of the sermon, as he says in his first Use:

> May God un-church or discharge a people, and cast a nation off? Oh, then let this teach us to cast off all security; for miseries are nigh at hand in all probability! When we observe what God hath done for us, all things are ripe to destruction, and yet we fear it not, but we promise to ourselves safety, and consider not that England is ready to be harrowed, and yet we cannot entertain a thought of England's desolation. When there are so many prophesies in it of its destruction, yet we cannot be persuaded of it. According to the conviction of our judgments, either it must not be, or not yet, as if it were unpossible that God should leave England, as if God were a cockering Father over lewd (and stubborn) children. God may leave a nation, and his elect may suffer, and why may not England (that is but in outward covenant with him)? (*DD*, pp. 231–32)

Hooker was always exceptionally good at puncturing the inflated, egoistic confidence of his hearers. He did it by getting them to see their gross need for cleansing their hearts in redemption, and he does the same thing here in undercutting the false confidence engendered by British nationalism. The climactic phrase of the above passage—"why may not England?"—is echoed repeatedly in the succeeding paragraph as Hooker molds it into an ominous chorus insisting that England, at this very moment, is "ripe to destruction." She has no permanent immunity from the wrath of God, being as guilty in her way as numerous other nations have been who have felt the full brunt of punishment, suffering, and finally desertion by God. Nor are these merely abstract sufferings. Hooker invites his listeners to imagine what it is like on the Continent, where war has been raging and the Catholic armies have resorted to the rack and other "cruel tortures," separating and destroying families. "Why may not England be thus?" he asks. "God can be God without England's prosperity" and may just decide to "go into Turkey"—the modern-day home of Antichrist—"and say unto them, 'Thou art my people, and I will be your God' " (p. 234).

This seemingly perverse speculation leads to Hooker's second Doctrine, which argues that "it is the importunate desire of the saints of God still to keep God present with them" (*DD*, p. 235). And this is done "in his ordinances" (p. 236). Preaching, above all, is crucial to the saints because in powerful, plain preaching men hear the voice of God: "It must be the God of peace that must speak peace to troubled souls" (p. 238). So for a time Hooker assumes his familiar habit of speaking to and for individual souls who seek assurance and salvation, but all the while he is also speaking in the larger dimension of the need for an entire nation's redemption from its gross and obvious wrongs. Thus, in the manner of the earnest prophet, Hooker posits as his main target the people just now before him, English men and women who remain complacent in the face of what he sees as dire personal and national dangers. In his Uses he condemns consecutively "2. sorts of people," first, those who have no real desire for God or his ordinances and, second, the saints of God themselves. On the first group—those bad listeners "that canst not abide so much preaching, but standest upon thorns whilst it is preaching" and say, " 'Too much of one thing . . . is good for nothing' "—Hooker trains his most fearsome bolts of hellfire for their "ill will to God and his ordinances" (p. 242). He tells them that "when the trumpet shall blow, thy ears shall tingle with that sentence, 'Depart from me.' Thou that art weary of God, get thee down to hell, I say; God will set his teeth at thee, and stamp thee down to hell with thy base lusts. Then will God say: 'For I have fed you on earth this twenty, thirty, forty, fifty, nay sixty years and upwards, and my mild word could not rule you, nor prevail with you, and therefore now get

you to hell, and there remain forever' " (pp. 242–43). This is the familiar Use of terror—now in a new setting. What makes it particularly
significant is what immediately follows. Hooker does not stop with
threatening just the common folk with damnation but cites Isaiah
30:33, where Tophet is said to be "prepared for the King," a warning,
as the marginal notation in the Geneva Bible indicates, that men's "estate or degree cannot except the wicked" from God's eternal wrath.
Hooker takes this passage as a warning to those in high places, including even the king: "But some may say: 'Surely kings and monarchs are
exempted, they need not fear that such torments shall come upon
them.' But God will say, be he a King that rules or reigns, yet as he
hath rejected God, so God will reject him. He is a King of Kings, and
Lord of Lords, and therefore such a one as will laugh at thy destruction" (p. 243). And Thomas Hooker, standing before the congregation
for the last time as their lecturer, for no other reason than the repressive edict of King Charles through his bishop, stood as living proof that
the king and the bishop were indeed rejecting God in the form of His
messenger, as Hooker himself went on to say. In short, he was charg-
ing that the king of England, by his actions toward the Puritan saints,
was earning eternal damnation for himself and perhaps for his obedient
subjects. This was an extremely daring assertion, even for a committed
prophet. Where other preachers and writers had assayed "general considerations" on the problems in England contributing to the Great
Migration,[53] Hooker was making dramatic announcements of the need
for a new view of the present historical moment. He was prophesying
that because of the difference of this present moment from all others in
history, special action was required.

The Use which follows is a sustained passage of prophetic preaching in
which Hooker explicitly tells his audience that he brings a message directly from God which they must heed, on pain of death and damnation to
themselves and to England. Here the literature of colonization reaches a
peak of emotional urgency. He uses his last public appearance in England
for a now-or-never message to his complacent countrymen, admonishing
them to pay better attention than they seem to be doing ("I marvel you
give no better attendance; I pray hearken what I say, and have to say,
stand up and hear, and the Lord give you grace to believe"):

> You see the gospel is going (brethren), Christ is departing, he is
> going to seek better entertainment. . . .
> I will deal plainly with you. As sure as God is God, God is going
> from England. Shall I tell you what God told me? Nay, I must tell
> you on pain of my life. Will you give ear and believe me? I am a
> poor ambassador sent from God to do his message unto you; and,

although I be low, yet my message is from above. . . . What if I should tell you what God told me yesternight that he would destroy England and lay it waste? What say you to this, my beloved? It is my message, by meditation in Gods word, that he bid me do to you, and he expects an answer from you. I do my message as God commanded me. What sayest thou unto it, England? I must return an answer to my Master that sent me, yea, this present night I must return an answer; for the Lord hath appointed a set time, saying, Ex. 9:5: "Tommorrow the Lord will do this thing . . . in the land." Why speak you not? An answer you must give. Do you think well of it? Will you have England destroyed? Will you put the aged to trouble, and your young men to the sword? Will you have your young women widows, and your virgins defiled? Will you have your dear and tender little ones tossed upon the pikes and dashed against the stones? Or will you have them brought up in Popery, in idolatry, under a necessity of perishing their souls forever, which is worst of all? Will you have these temples wherein we seem to worship God, will you have them and your houses burnt with fire? And will you see England laid waste without inhabitants? Are you well-contented it shall be so? (God bade me ask. Why do you not answer me? I must not stir without it, I must have it.) I am an importunate suitor for Christ. Oh, send me not sad away, but speak comfortably and cheerfully! What are you resolved of? Are you willing to enjoy God still, and to have him dwell with you? (You are, are you not?) It is well, I am glad of it if it be so.

But you must not only say so, but you must use the means, and you must plead importunately with your God; for, although his sword be drawn and in his hand, lifted up and ready to strike, yet suffer him not to destroy, but rather to sheath his sword in the blood of his enemies. (God grant it.) I would be glad to have England flourish still. (And so are you, are you not? You are.) But if desolation do come, thank yourselves for it, it is your own fault if you be destroyed, and not God's; for he delights not in the death of any. (*DD*, pp. 243–45)

In this remarkable passage Hooker is talking not just to a limited congregation but to all of England ("What sayest thou unto it, *England?*"). He is himself fulfilling the prophetic role that Jeremiah and Israel's other prophets had fulfilled; he is God's "ambassador," God's chosen messenger to his people, coming with one last warning before it is finally too late and all is lost, before the time for choosing has gone. He no doubt startled many of his hearers with his claim that the Lord told him "yesternight" of his plans to destroy England[54] and his insistence that he must return an answer tonight, as if he had nightly conversation with the "King of Kings." But he has come to the point of no return in his own ministry and startle them he must, once and for all. As he says a little later, "This is our day of atonement. This present day is ours. We have nothing to do with tomorrow" (*DD*, p. 246). Certainly his awareness that this was his farewell sermon affects his coloring of the moment in such a passage, but he uses his congregation's awareness of just this situation to heighten their sense of the moment's urgency as well. As was his habit in his nonpolitical conversion preaching, here in this highly charged, supremely political sermon, he urges his audience to be up and doing right now: "Our God is going, and shall we sit still (on our beds)? Would you have the gospel kept with [these] lazy wishes? Oh, no, no; arise, arise from off your downy beds, and fall down upon your knees, and entreat God to leave his gospel to you and to your posterity" (p. 247).

Throughout this passage and much of the rest of the sermon, Hooker bends his considerable dramatic and rhetorical skills to his task. In an image like that of God with raised arm grasping a sword, ready to strike the blow of annihilation at his favorite, England, we picture the tautness of a muscular arm, veins standing out, straining against its own impulse. The full psychological stress in Hooker's mind as he views the historical present is conveyed in this one visual image. And it is reinforced by his use of conditional clauses implying the hope that the blow may still be prevented ("*yet* suffer him not to destroy, *but rather*. . . ."). Even as he indulges in word play ("arise from off your *downy* beds, and fall *down* upon your knees") he compels attention and conveys the urgency of the situation. For, despite his hope that England can be saved, Hooker knows his own decision; as one historian has wryly observed, "It was Hooker, not the Gospel, that was departing."[55] He has discovered the absolute necessity of emigration, and every aspect of his rhetoric conveys the dynamic tension which such an unwanted decision has created—for him now, but, he knows, also for many others in the near future. No work of the Puritans' literature of departure so fully depicts the difficult inner tensions involved in a decision to leave their native land as does Hooker's emotional exploration of the truths which typology reveals in *The Danger of Desertion*.

Hooker ultimately tells his audience that they can give God His will by exorcising sin out of their souls and out of England—sins which they may spare "as well as I may spare water out of my shoes, or a [hot] coal out of my bosom" (*DD*, p. 248). And God's supreme will is that "we should worship him in spirit and in truth" (p. 249). Thus, again Hooker returns to the central issue in the churches of England: the purity of His Ordinances. You must "lay aside . . . all your superstitions, and erroneous opinions of God and his worship, and do it according to his will in his word revealed" (p. 249). One such superstition, the Puritans believed, was the Anglican practice of bowing or genuflecting and making the sign of the cross at the mention of Christ's name. He makes his position clear on this point even in the midst of his elevated prophetic message, as he says that "to give a bow with the knee, and a stab at the heart" when hearing the name Jesus is "idolatry" (p. 249).

The message of the sermon, though, is that England is in serious trouble and that no one seems to care enough to prevent disaster, a point condensed into a single sentence near the conclusion: "(O beloved,) there is a hard time ere long befalling England, if God in mercy prevent it not; but we do not consider it. Lamentable is our time" (*DD*, p. 250). And in a rare passage expressing Hooker's growing awareness of the significance of New England to spiritual history, he warns the people:

> England hath seen her best days, and the reward of sin is coming on apace; for God is packing up of his gospel, because none will buy his wares (not come to his price). God begins to ship away his Noahs, which prophesied and foretold that destruction was near; and God makes account that New England shall be a refuge for his Noahs and his Lots, a rock and a shelter for his righteous ones to run unto; and those that were vexed to see the ungodly lives of the people in this wicked land, shall there be safe. Oh, therefore my brethren, lay hold on God, and let him not go out of your coasts. (He is going!) Look about you, I say, and stop him at the town's-end, and let not thy God depart! Oh, England, lay siege about him by humble and hearty closing with him. (*DD*, pp. 245–46)

We know that Hooker had consulted with Roger Williams, John Cotton, and John Winthrop in July of 1629 regarding the plans for the Massachusetts Bay Company,[56] and his farewell sermon indicates that he still had the venture in mind, though for the time being he had probably already decided against his own involvement. It is possible, however, that John Eliot, who would precede Hooker to New England, was in the audience on the occasion of this sermon. And no doubt others were there who were also debating the question of emigration. Hooker indicates at the close of the sermon, in any case, that there is still a chance for England's redemption if the people strive for greater purity and godliness. If they do not, the outcome is certain: "The poor native Turks and Infidels shall have a more cool summer-parlor in hell than England shall have" (*DD*, p. 252). But even as he holds open the possibility of God's keeping his relationship with England, the whole subjective thrust of his sermon indicates that this eventuality is very remote indeed. While he is overtly urging "Stop God at the town's end," he seems connotatively and metaphorically to be implying that God has already set up shop in New England.

The Danger of Desertion is as good an example as there is of the jeremiad in England before the mass emigration of the 1630s got under way. It demonstrates dramatically the sometimes forgotten fact that this sermon form did not spring up spontaneously in American soil. It had been nurtured to full growth in the difficult times of Caroline England before the Great Migration and was even a major impetus, as we see here, to that migration. The typological parallel which had been assumed between the Israelites and English believers was later to be translated to an Israel–*New* England parallel and allowed to thrive almost immediately. The use of the jeremiad sermon form depends, however, on a sense of spiritual illness among the people at large as well as among the clergy. The feeling during the decades of the Great Migration that transplantation cured all these ills accounts for the jeremiad's falling into disuse for nearly a generation while the New Englanders conducted themselves to the relative satisfaction of the elders. These leaders returned to the form increasingly in the last four decades of the seventeenth century, as on the one hand they detected a faltering and backsliding among the people and on the other they anticipated a millennium in their very time and midst. The hiatus in the use of the jeremiad has caused some historians to imply, if not to claim outright, that the Puritan jeremiad had its birth in New England. Hooker's canon offers eloquent proof to the contrary.[57]

By the time he preached *The Danger of Desertion* Hooker had already, in sermons like *The Churches Deliverances* and *The Stay of the Faithful,* earned Bishop Laud's silencing. Suddenly free from fear of repression, therefore, he packed a great deal into this one brief sermon. Here he combined the several major themes of his other related sermons—the accusation of high treason against those who were persecuting the ministers of God, the necessity of maintaining pure forms of worship, the need for personal uprightness if the nation as a whole was to be saved, and the likelihood of God's giving up on England—while also making one last effort to jolt the spiritual consciences of the people to a new way of life. If Laud had not already taken action against Hooker, this sermon would have given him ample reason. Certainly *The Danger of Desertion* summarizes the radical Puritan sense of England's approaching spiritual tragedy as well as any other work of the period. In it we see Hooker himself, "that great Elijah of his day," making his last stand in England for the Puritan cause, reflecting as he did so the agonizing dilemma of the many Puritans who were being forced into exile. At the same time we see his sudden recognition that not England but New England was to be the antitype prefigured by Israel, the promised land. At this moment in his career, Hooker could not help regretting England's failure to fulfill the role. All too soon he would have to imitate the lonesome outlaw whom he had so often described in his redemption sermons and flee to the coasts to escape his pursuivants. The crucial difference, however, was to be that in his case the king would not appear at the last moment to bestow his mercy on the fugitive. He must flee "to the American strand."

3

Basic Questions
in the Netherlands

Exile was hardly a panacea. Hooker's decision to try Holland rather than New England carried him into the midst of new controversies and eventually returned him foursquare to the old issue of the forms of worship. His two published works from his twenty or twenty-one months in the Netherlands (1631–33)[1] reveal, however, that while he was unable to escape the tensions of disagreement with those in power, he did achieve a fuller definition of his Puritan-ness. Both of his Dutch works were sharply pointed responses to provocative challenges from adversaries much friendlier to the English Church establishment than was Hooker. In writing down his answers to twenty questions on his beliefs and practice in matters of polity and discipline posed by John Paget, the ejected English Puritan ministering in Amsterdam, Hooker grasped more firmly than ever his commitment to the principle of congregational church organization and to Congregationalism's fundamental confidence in the integrity of the individual human mind when properly guided by faithful ministers. And in joining William Ames in his protest against the English Church's enforcement of conformity in the use of "human ceremonies" in worship, he announced his unwavering commitment to the principles which defined the essential difference between Puritans and establishment churchmen. His expulsion from England clearly served to strengthen his commitment to the cause of congregational Puritanism rather than to wear him down. And beneath this intellectual self-definition which his Dutch experience produced, we hear a more subjective dissatisfaction, a restlessness, with his personal situation. In Holland he found much more contention than contentment. Separated from his family, troubled by the ague, hemmed in by creeping Pres-

56

byterianism, and aware of an absence of what he called true "heart religion,"[2] he soon discovered that Holland could be only a way station for him in his pursuit of a place where he could again become the prophet-shepherd to his people that he felt called to be.

Between the time of Hooker's decision not to appear before the High Commission court in July of 1630 and his arrival in Holland in June of 1631, a year during which he was probably under the protection of the Earl of Warwick, he was doubtless looking out constantly for a place where he could continue his ministry. Finally, in a letter from Stephen Offwood, he was invited by the English Reformed Church at Amsterdam to become co-pastor with John Paget, who had ministered there ever since the church's founding in 1607. He was to take the place of Thomas Potts, who had died in April. But what Hooker undoubtedly did not know when he left England was the degree to which the elderly Paget and his congregation were of different minds. This became evident enough soon after his arrival, when, in the first place, he was not given a clear-cut formal call to the church, as he expected he would be. Nor was his appointment approved, as required, by the magistrates or by the Dutch Classis (synod). Though the elders had invited him "to exercise his gift amongst us" and he had done so "to the good lijking of the church,"[3] the redoubtable John Paget was never in favor of Hooker's presence. And it was John Paget who single-handedly saw to it that Thomas Hooker should not become the new assistant in Amsterdam, despite the contrary wishes of the congregation.

On the very day that the lay leaders of the Amsterdam church decided to enact a more formal election of Hooker to the post, Paget declared that before this could be done, he would have to question the candidate. The elders objected, correctly, that such examination was the function only of the Classis, but Paget pressed on and got two elders to agree to listen to the questions which he would ask and to the answers which Hooker would give. Hooker, in turn, requested that Paget put the questions in writing, together with the questioner's own answers to them, apparently wanting to gain more time for composing his answers and to extract a little more information about Paget's positions on the issues, perhaps in the process learning more about Paget's motivation for creating this extra hurdle. It is debatable just how aware Hooker was of the reasons for Paget's raising the questions in the first place. But as he wrote out the required four copies of his answers, with Paget's answers also before him, he certainly became aware that on a few key issues he and Paget were far apart and that this exercise would serve admirably to disqualify him, in Paget's eyes, for the post he had come abroad to assume. Even so, Hooker expressed a willingness to compromise, if possible. Paget, it turned out, was not interested in compromise—nor did Hooker seem to expect it. After twenty-four years in Amsterdam, Paget knew how to manage church politics; and he promptly took Hooker's answers over the head of the local congregation to the Classis, which he knew would be fully as alarmed as he was at Hooker's patent congregationalist ideas and at his apparent softness—as Paget would have it seem—on separatism, or Brownism. The result was total victory for Paget. Hooker, aware of the firm opposition of the old pastor, elected to leave the city at the earliest opportunity. Indeed, the Classis left him little choice when it forbade Hooker's preaching in Amsterdam "now or in the future."[4] Though he already had in sight brighter prospects and a more comfortable situation at Delft, where he went to become the assistant to John Forbes, a Scotsman much more of his own mind on matters both of polity and doctrine, Hooker could not have enjoyed the experience of formal silencing in Amsterdam, having just freshly fled from a similar if more catastrophic experience in England.

As others have noted, "The questions put to Hooker by Paget in October 1631 were well suited to expose the differences between the Reformed Churches and the Non-Separating Independents, especially over polity."[5] Paget knew enough about Hooker's recent past in England to be sure that the answers he would give to the questions would make him *persona non grata* in the Netherlands church establishment. They did not disagree on all the questions, but several key points of difference made up for the rest. Paget began by asking three questions on the proper attitude toward and relationship with the Brownists. This had, of course, been a key issue in Holland for some years, and Paget was firmly opposed to accommodation with the Separatists. There were many former Separatists in the Amsterdam English Church's membership and Paget preferred to keep a tight rein on them, especially when there were active Separatist congregations nearby. But the issue of a congregation's relations with a neighboring Separatist group was apparently not one to which Hooker had given much thought before coming to Holland. His opposition to Separatism he firmly and categorically proclaims in answering the first question: "To separate from the faithful assemblies and Churches in England as no true churches is an error in judgment, and a sin in practice," so that "to communicate with [the Brownists], either in their opinion or practice, is sinful and utterly unlawful."[6] But he is willing to be somewhat liberal in particular cases, where the individuals concerned have clearly renounced the idea and practice of separatism. It is not "unlawful" to such people "to hear amongst them [the Separatists] occasionally and to communicate with them in that part of God's worship," though it might well be "occasionally offensive" if the Separatists saw such attendance as encouraging their practice. He admits that it might well be worth going to their service in order "to hear some savory point opened, and to benefit by the gift of some able minister, that may come amongst them," so long as there can be no mistaking one's intentions in going there. In this position Hooker's desire to trust the intellectual resources of the individual Christian is patently evident, as it would be in his other Dutch work. It was more trust than Paget thought permissible.

The second question asked whether those people who go to hear Separatist preaching are to be tolerated or censured by their congregation. Paget expressed the clear opinion that they should be censured, but Hooker was not willing to commit himself to this kind of undiscriminating rule, arguing that "moderation in things which are disputable" is the wiser course, especially since, as Hooker's awareness of psychological subtleties constantly reminded him, "the same degree of pains for convincing is not so sufficient in one disposition as in another" (*XXQ*, p. 279). And in answer to the third question, whether "Brownists as have not renounced their separation from the Church of England . . . may lawfully be received for members of our Church," Paget said decisively, *"Negatur,"* while Hooker just as decisively said that such failure to renounce Separatist opinions "can in no wise make a man unfit to be received a member of this congregation" (p. 280). Such questions were more than hypothetical. There was not an active Separatist ministry in Amsterdam in 1631, although there had been before and there would be again.[7] Any prospective assistant to Paget who disagreed on such fundamental matters of church discipline and membership would obviously make a poor match for him. Hooker's disagreement with Paget on these three questions alone was enough to guarantee the older man's obstinate opposition.

But there were still other major problem areas. The sixth question, for instance, raised an issue that was to be in the air throughout Hooker's lifetime and well beyond. The query was "whether infants whose parents are not members of the Church may lawfully be baptised according to the manner of these Reformed Churches" (*XXQ*, p. 281). Hooker admits that he does not yet know enough about the Dutch Reformed churches' practice to make an informed comment on it "nor in this short time can tell how to learn fully in all the particular circumstances thereof," but he does know his own mind on the matter, so that if the local church practice "be such as I understand by relation, I judge it unlawful for me to follow" (p. 281). In his refusal to baptise the children of nonmembers Hooker would remain entirely consistent, from this first written attestation through his final comment on the issue late in his career in *The Covenant of Grace Opened*. This was to be a distinct point of difference between the Presbyterians and the Congregationalists until well into the 1650s, when in New England the voice of compromise began to be heard foreshadowing the decisions of the Half-Way Covenant of 1662. But in any place and time it was hardly practicable for two ministers in the same church to have different opinions on such a fundamental matter as qualification for baptism.

The other major issue which the twenty propositions raise was also to become a basic point of difference between the Independents and the conforming churchmen. This was the relationship between the individual congregation and larger representative assemblies such as synods or, in the Netherlands, classes. Four questions, numbers eleven through fourteen, deal with this issue. In all four of his answers Hooker disagreed with Paget. The central question really was whether the congregation is subordinate to the power of a classis, or whether it can call ministers, decide controversies, and excommunicate offenders without or even against the counsel of the classis. As Hooker was to explain in the last section of his *Survey of the Summe of Church Discipline* and as all New England congregationalists were to hold, the essential power in these matters rests with the local congregation. Hooker's logic here and in *A Survey* is based on a simple historical observation. In answering question eleven, which inquires "whether a particular congregation hath power to call a minister, without the approbation of the Classis under which they stand," he begins by saying, "Before I answer this query I would ask one thing, which may give a little light to that which shall be said afterwards, namely, how the first Classis that ever was upon the face of the earth came to be constituted." Obviously, he says, it was comprised of congregations who had their power from Christ "and so did by that, their power, choose and call their ministers fully and completely before there was a Classis, and therefore had their power not derived from a Classis." Since congregations originally had their power from Christ, so it remains and always will. They may want to consult with a classis, but they could always "lawfully and without sin choose without or against the approbation of the Classis if they saw good reason" (XXQ, pp. 283–85). A congregationalist could be no plainer on the essential point of his difference from the presbyterian power structure. Hooker was fully as immovable in his position as Paget was in his. But Paget was able to use the classis structure to gain his ends in this very case, so that he had the last laugh in his debate with Hooker. Three years later, John Davenport, a candidate for the same post, would challenge Paget on the same ground, with more persistence than Hooker but with identical results.

Hooker grouped the twelfth, thirteenth, and fourteenth questions together. Observing that they required a very full answer which would be too tedious for him to write out in four copies "in this short time," he answered by noting his agreement with positions on the same matter discussed in works which he was sure Paget would know. He cites specific pages in Ames's *Cases of Conscience*, Robert Parker's *Ecclesiastical Polity* (Paget had already had debates with Parker in 1607–12), and Paul Baynes's *Diocesans Trial*, concluding with the observation, "How far they differ from you I doubt not but you fully know." He adds that he is willing to answer at greater length if Paget will "give me notice and time" (*XXQ*, pp. 285–86). Paget had what he wanted, however, and further debate would have been superfluous. Throughout Holland the relationship between individual English churches and the local Dutch classes was a popular subject for discussion; and, as it happened, Amsterdam was one of two cities wherein the English church belonged to the classis. It was obviously the wrong city for such a clear-cut congregationalist as Thomas Hooker to be seeking a church position.

While Hooker was consistent throughout his career on all three of the issues thus far discussed, there was another matter, raised in a single question, number seventeen, on which he would be inclined to change his perspective if not his opinion during the first few years in New England. Paget put the question this way: "Whether it be lawful for private members of the church to interpret the Holy Scriptures, at such set days and places, where sundry members of divers families do ordinarily assemble themselves together" (*XXQ*, p. 287). Hooker counters Paget's negative opinion by citing Ames's argument in his *Cases of Conscience*, the 1630 Amsterdam edition, where Ames notes three occasions in Acts where Paul advises such gatherings among laypersons. Hooker merely cautions that ministerial "direction and information" are appropriate, "as occasion serves, to teach men not to go beyond their gift" in this teaching. This was an issue which would be central in the trial of the Antinomian Anne Hutchinson just six years later. Hooker becomes almost prescient in qualifying his approval of these meetings in people's homes to the extent that "if there be any miscarriage in this, . . . as others of the church shall understand it, they are to deal with them according to the rule of discipline." Finally, he adds that "if any other distempers" occur, such as condemning the ministry, or wives demeaning themselves "disobediently and unwarrantably to their husbands," they must be dealt with (pp. 288–89). Thus, while Hooker held to a more liberal policy than did Paget on the matter of allowing assemblage in private homes for discussion of religious subjects, he also saw the possiblity of misguided leaders' taking their followers astray and requiring corrective disciplining by the congregation. The blueprint for New England's Antinomian heresies and trials was thus clearly present in Thomas Hooker's mind well before it required execution. He would later have to lay heavier stress on the qualifications to his approval of such gatherings of laymen.

Hooker's awareness that his positions were irreconcilable with those of Paget and that if he were to find a home in Holland it would have to be outside of Amsterdam is implicit in the final paragraph of this document. He did not like Paget's asking him these compromising, agitating questions, as is clear enough when he imputes to his questioner a desire to make trouble by concluding his fourth answer, "since there is no use of it [set forms of prayer] in this church, why it should be questioned I see not, unless men desire to find differences of opinion" (XXQ, p. 281). He is more docile in his recognition of his differences with Paget and what that means for him when he concludes the whole exercise by saying,

> These are my poor thoughts for the present touching all the opinions propounded and as my judgment so likewise my practice is like to be so far as conscience calls me hereunto, giving wiser and better [people] than myself, loving leave to think and do otherwise, being ever willing to hear better arguments and any converting reason, and to stoop thereunto.
>
> And because I do apprehend your opinion and affections to be so far settled that you apprehend there cannot be a peaceable concurrence in such distances of judgment . . . I am resolved contentedly to sit down and suddenly as I see my opportunity to depart, wishing that the God of Peace would provide so comfortable an assistant as might suit with you in all truth and godliness for your mutual comfort and the building up of the body of Christ. (XXQ, p. 291)

Obviously Hooker's desire to become Paget's assistant had by this time been removed, and he was willing to put Amsterdam behind him. The congregation, as it happens, was not willing to lose him, and they continued to argue with the Classis. Even more surprising, perhaps, is the fact that John Forbes, the minister at Delft with whom Hooker went to work next, called the Amsterdam Classis to account for their reasons for preventing Hooker from preaching further in that city. Before he was willing to let the matter rest, Forbes had called down the Classis's opprobrium on himself without in the least improving Hooker's position.[8] But at least Hooker's new colleague was his committed ally, not his antagonist. In teaming up with Forbes at the English Merchant Adventurers' Church at Delft, Hooker had good reason to hope that he had at last found a congenial situation in which to practice his gifts.

The timing of his arrival at Delft, however, put Hooker in the cross fire which was just beginning between the contentious Forbes and the English Church hierarchy. The catalyst of this trouble was Edward Misselden, the deputy of the Merchant Adventurers at Delft.[9] After some nine years of coexistence with Forbes in that city, Misselden in 1632 began to object to the patent nonconformist congregationalism in Forbes's church. After Forbes temporarily got the support of the Dutch States General, which asked their ambassadors in England to try to get Misselden recalled, Misselden appealed directly to the English Privy Council, which was easily persuaded that the abuses in Delft— and in all of Holland—required firm action. Hooker was again trapped in a controversy involving the question of local congregational autonomy as opposed to what he and Forbes saw as hierarchical repression. For at least part of the time during which the English authorities were investigating the situation at Delft, Hooker bore the brunt of the conflict, since Forbes was away for the last half of 1632 visiting Scottish relatives serving with the troops of King Adolphus of Sweden in Germany. But the new scrape with Laud and the English Church hierarchy—and the foreseeable dissolution of Puritan/congregational strength in Holland—apparently showed Hooker the need to get still farther away from Anglican officialdom. Indeed, shortly after Hooker's departure, Forbes would be relieved of his post and the English Church would require that only conforming ministers be assigned to the English churches in Holland. Hooker's presence in Delft, with his reputation as a nonconformist congregationalist, doubtless helped draw the attention of the authorities to the previously placid situation there, though Forbes's indiscretion in supporting Hooker's cause at Amsterdam so clamorously doubtless helped attract notice to him.

The pattern begun in the Chelmsford years had been continued in Amsterdam and again in Delft, as it would be in New England later on. Hooker repeatedly found himself defending the congregational way, with its emphasis on a decentralized power structure retaining essential authority in the local church and especially in the individual minister to modify the forms of worship as his light dictated for the closer following of scriptural example. Now he defended the rights of members to visit other churches, and as he had done at Chelmsford, he once again stood up for Independency against an established opponent whom he knew from the start he would neither persuade nor defeat. He was consistently opposing, in other words, an external power structure which sought undue authority over him and other individuals. This was not merely a political bias favoring the rights and abilities of the local unit or of the individual against a higher power; it was a theological conviction as well, as we shall see later in examining the dynamics of Hooker's preparationist preaching. He was firmly committed to ideas which were making it difficult for him to find a home in the world.

Hooker's Independency is also behind the only written work known to have come out of his years with Forbes at Delft. This was a preface of some seventy-seven pages written to accompany William Ames's third and last installment in his controversy with English Church authorities on the issue of set ceremonies in the worship service. When the full version of *A Fresh Suit against Human Ceremonies in Gods Worship* appeared, complete with Hooker's preface, Ames was already dead, and Hooker was in New England. A third party, probably Hugh Peter, attached a brief "Advertisement to the Reader" and saw the final portions of the work through the press. Although it was Ames who stated the case against the Anglican forms of worship, Hooker's involvement in the project indicated his continuing commitment to the Puritan principles which had caused his exile.

How Ames and Hooker came to collaborate on this work is not known. The acquaintance and mutual respect of the two men went back to Cambridge days. They were both at the university from the time of Hooker's arrival in 1603 to that of Ames's departure in 1610. Ames's admiration for Hooker's skills at disputation undoubtedly dated from their university days. Ames, according to Cotton Mather, said that *"though he had been acquainted with many scholars of divers nations, yet he never met with Mr.* Hooker's *equal, either for preaching or for disputing,"* while Hooker said in his turn that *"if a scholar* was but well studied in Dr. *Ames* his *Medulla Theologiae* and *Casus Conscientiae*, so as to understand them thoroughly, they would make him (supposing him versed in the scriptures,) a *good divine*, though he had no more books in the world."[10] Ames was on the faculty at Franeker, in the north of Holland—and a long way from Delft and Amsterdam—from the spring of 1622 until August or September of 1633, when he moved to Rotterdam to become an associate of Hugh Peter in the English church there and to establish a new school in the city, only to die in November of the same year.[11] Hooker, however, left Holland by March of 1633, stopping briefly in England to join forces with his family, John Cotton, and Samuel Stone before leaving for New England, where they arrived in early September. Despite Mather's claims, it appears that Hooker and Ames were never colleagues in the Rotterdam church. Keith Sprunger is no doubt correct, then, in his claim that Hooker and Ames carried on their collaboration on *A Fresh Suit* while Ames was still at Franeker,[12] probably through correspondence only. There is no reason why this could not have been the case, since their tasks were clearly separate, with Ames concentrating on the essential matter of church ceremonies and what enforced use of such ceremonies meant, and Hooker concentrating chiefly on attacking the work and qualifications of their opponent, John Burgess.

One wonders why Ames asked Hooker to write a preface to his work at all.[13] The preface, like the rest of the book, was published anonymously, so that it was not a case of Ames's wishing to gain strength for his book through the name of Thomas Hooker: indeed, Ames's own name carried greater weight than Hooker's, though it too was omitted from the published volume. And certainly what Hooker says is by no means an essential introduction to the work proper. The best guess probably is that Ames thought Hooker's ability at disputation and his firm opposition to enforced "ceremonies" in worship would make him just the man to deal with certain sticky aspects of the dispute which Ames preferred not to touch. For, despite the apparent objectivity which Hooker maintains, his work is a direct attack not only on the book which Ames is answering but on its author as well. Here, more than in any other of Hooker's controversial writings, he is willing to let his comments get personal, no doubt because he detected a heavy dose of hypocrisy in the attack of Ames's opponent.

To understand what Hooker is doing in his preface it helps to know something of the other participants in the controversy. The round robin of published arguments began with the publication by Bishop Thomas Morton of *A Defence of the Innocencie of the three Ceremonies of the Church of England viz. The Surplice, Crosse after Baptisme, and Kneeling at the receiuing of the blessed Sacrament* (London, 1618). Ames, already an exile for the cause of nonconformity, responded to Morton in two books, published successively in 1622 and 1623: *A Reply to Dr. Morton's Generall Defence of Three Nocent Ceremonies* and *A Reply to Dr. Morton's Particvlar Defence of Three Nocent Ceremonies*.[14] Eight years then intervened, during which time King Charles took the throne and Bishop Laud began to press urgently for conformity and use of the ceremonies. John Burgess, claiming that he was responding to the urging of the king himself to publish his thoughts, chimed in with a tome of over six hundred pages entitled *An*

Answer Reioyned to that mvch applauded Pamphlet of a Nameless Author. . . . A Reply to Dr. Morton's Generall Defence. . . . (London,
1631). This work was registered at the Stationers in London on March
24, 1631, and found its way subsequently into the hands of both
Hooker and Ames in the Netherlands.[15] Ames ultimately produced his
own longest entry in the series. *A Fresh Suit against Human Ceremonies,* as a response to Burgess's book.

When we note that John Burgess had once been William Ames's
father-in-law,[16] we realize that Ames's attempt to refute this particular
adversary, even in anonymity, was apt to be a tricky business. Ames
apparently did not wish to attack his former father-in-law on any personal grounds, though there were some likely bases for doing so in
Burgess's having once been a notorious nonconformist himself but having since become a thoroughgoing conformist and even a servant of the
Church's aggressive drive for conformity which had driven both Ames
and Hooker permanently out of England.[17] But the peculiar ironies in
Burgess's now appearing as the opponent of Ames probably seemed
worth pointing out, however subtly one might needs do so. So, in all
likelihood, Ames contacted Hooker about writing a preface.[18] Probably
glad to take on a task which would enable him to say a word against
the policies of the Church and government that had sent him out of his
homeland and away from his family, Hooker wrote the preface sometime in the latter half of 1632 or very early 1633, as we know from his
intriguing reference in the preface to deathbed comments of Arthur
Hildersham, who died in England on March 4, 1632.

Whether or not Ames told Hooker just what to write about is uncer-
tain, but it is true that the preface has one purpose: to discredit
Burgess's book, both on the grounds of its argument and rhetoric and
of its author's compromised career. Hooker leaves the substantive matter of the forms of worship in the Church of England almost entirely to
Ames, though his most significant comments in the preface may very
well be the few remarks which he makes on individual versus church
authority. Even here, however, he combines his statements of principle with biographical facts about Burgess in such a way as to keep the
attentive reader's mind on Burgess's somewhat checkered career.

Hooker's approach throughout is hardly vindictive or vicious. He is
subtle in his criticism of Burgess, maintaining for the most part a tone
of rational calm. Thus, he begins the preface in a seemingly impersonal
but concerned manner, observing that truth is on the decline. When
we consider that it was probably while he was writing this preface that
Hooker made his final decision to "go for New England," we discover
more than the usual depth of meaning in Hooker's opening analogy:

"They who put to sea, according to their several scopes and purposes, so do they steer [by] their compasses and proceed in their travels answerably." He explains that those who travel only for pleasure are easily sent scurrying back to harbor "when once the heavens begin to be beset with clouds," while those "who seriously intend to make a voyage of it" are "willing . . . to adventure the loss of their lives, but not willing to lose their voyage. Therefore on they will: Extreme necessities may overbear them, but no fears can discourage them in their course."[19] It is in traveling, says Hooker, as it is in professing the truth. The degree to which one is committed to his goal determines the seriousness with which he perseveres. Those who want mainly to "serve their own turns" are not willing to risk much in their pursuit of truth, though they put "fair colors" "upon all their proceedings." Since there is so much of the latter and so little of the true dedication to truth, Hooker proposes to examine the types of "decliners," listing four "sorts" and painting them with the efficient characterizing strokes which had already become one of the trademarks of his preaching. There are Temporary Professors, whose conviction is like the paint on the faces of harlots rather than like a "ruddy complexion which ariseth from good blood" (Preface, pp. 321–22). There are Elizabeth Professors who preach the truth when there is profit of some sort in doing so, whereas "the name of a prison, the noise of a chain, makes the truth so deformed in their eye that they dare not, and therefore will not own it." There are also those who witness to the truth for novelty's sake but desert it when its terms begin to be "somewhat high rated" (pp. 322–23). And there are those who are even willing to accept suffering for the truth so long as this brings them ultimate power and self-importance.

At this point we begin to suspect more than detached observation on Hooker's part, a suspicion that tends to grow as he describes the reasons which these decliners give for their actions. For instance, there is the "Statist," who affirms what the civil authority says he should affirm: "He crieth out for 'discretion' as that which would umpire and determine all doubts." Such "discretion" enables him to shift his religion with the times. "Authority is in stead of all arguments to this man" (Preface, p. 325). One can hardly avoid remembering—though Hooker makes no overt mention of it—that John Burgess's book was dedicated to none other than King Charles and that he described "the prime Question" between himself and his adversary as being "whether the wearing of a *Surplice* in Divine Service, *Signing* the forehead of the newly baptized with the signe of the *Crosse*, and *Kneeling* in the act of receiving the Bread and Cup of the Lords Table, being enjoyned by lawfull Authoritie to bee Vsed as indifferent Rites, may *lawfully* and

with a good Conscience bee so vsed and observed, or no? We hold
the Affirmative, others the Negative."[20] As Hooker describes the
Statist, in other words, the description seems to fit his opponent,
John Burgess, who argued the importance of living within the dictates "enjoyned by lawfull Authoritie" in order that one could continue to preach. And it was well known that Burgess—after having
been imprisoned by King James briefly in 1604 and having been a
nonconformist who was deprived of his living and who went abroad
for several years, where he became a Doctor of Medicine—
ultimately made it up to the English authorities, was reinstated in
1617, preached for a time at Bishopsgate, and later the same year
acquired a living at Sutton Coldfield in Warwickshire.[21] Then, in the
days of King Charles and Bishop Laud, Burgess became a staunch
supporter of the policy of knuckling under to church authority,
something which would always—but especially at this point in his
career—grate against Hooker's very nature.

While Burgess seems to fit Hooker's description of the Statist, he
also appears to qualify as a Temporary Professor—a conformist who is
swayed away from his early profession of truth by the example of
others or, better, by "some ecclesiastical canon." On this point Hooker
becomes urgently eloquent, mimicking the Temporary Professor's
reasoning and then scorning his lack of backbone: "The Church enjoins
it, and are you wiser than the Church? This strikes it dead. No man
must dare to dispute any further. Nay, they count it unreasonable once
to demur or doubt anymore, but expect that all men should captivate
their conceits presently and put off reason and pluck out their eyes to
see by other men's spectacles, which is in truth not only to cease to be
Christians, but to be men" (Preface, p. 327). Such reasoning, says
Hooker, "is the Romish tenet to a hair." The Church, he reminds his
readers, is the bride of Christ, but *only* the bride. In a good Hookerian
phrase, he asks, "What is it else but to jostle Christ out of his prophetical and kingly office, to resolve out faith and obedience lastly into the
determinations and commands of men?" (pp. 327, 328). The revolutionary Puritan boldness to question authority is everywhere evident in
Hooker's preface; and his disdain for such as Burgess, who cite the
authority of the Church as reason enough, is also pervasive, though
seldom does he directly point to Burgess himself.

One of Hooker's clearest slaps at Burgess comes in this context,
though again he relies on his audience's familiarity with Burgess's
reasoning to enable the application of the hypothetical example to
Burgess. Some, he says, "plead the love of their people, the necessity
of preaching, and [the] hope of doing good. . . . they are . . . willing to

bear all rather than to deprive the Church of the benefit, and the souls of God's people of the profit and comfort, of their ministry!" (Preface, p. 329). Burgess, in the preface to his own book, had taken just this stand: better to practice the ceremonies, which he claimed were not unlawful (though perhaps not prescribed by Scripture), than to deprive the congregation of all preaching. Hooker in the above comments is certainly thinking of such Burgess arguments as this: "Seeing . . . the observance of these Ceremonies is by his Maiesties Direction now more pressed, then of sundrie yeeres past; I conceiue that this Booke, by giving (if God will) satisfaction to some, may helpe to saue them from the lash of Authoritie, and keepe them in the Service of God and his Church."[22] To which Hooker answers: "But the doubt here is whether we may come to do lawful things by unlawful means, to sin that we may do service as though the Lord had need of my lie or else that he could not bring his servants to his own haven without the devil's boat, or that Christ could not uphold his own kingdom without the pains and preachings of some men" (Preface, p. 330). In direct disagreement with Burgess, Hooker and Ames both held that one had better *not* continue to preach if he had to use unlawful ceremonies in the process. The point is fundamental to the Puritan stand in England under the Anglican oppressions, and fundamental, in principle at least, to the way of the New England churches: allow the individual the integrity of mind and strength of faith to question and to depart from the dictates of an evil authority. The nonconformist position was valid, they claimed, because the Church's dictates could not stand up to the scrutiny of conscientious individuals who insisted on following scriptural rather than human authority. It is not the Church which must be listened to but the Word. This Word clearly shows that human innovations in God's worship are just that—thus, full of sin and corrupt. Burgess, early in his career, would have agreed with this principle; his conversion to "statism" needed a firm answer from the likes of Hooker.

Hooker's attacks on Burgess, veiled as they often are, actually respond to Burgess's seeming preoccupation with the awkwardness of his position as a spokesman for conformity. In the preface to his *Answer Reioyned,* Burgess had acknowledged some fourteen "Objections" which he thought his detractors were apt to cite to his writing such a book. He answered all these objections, but his doing so at all suggests that he was particularly sensitive to the persuasiveness of some of the objections, one of which is that "I haue been of another mind, and the blot of Inconstancie will sticke in my face. It is knowne that about 39 yeeres since, I was deprived of my place which I then had in *Norwich,* for Inconformitie."[23] In hinting at Burgess's flip-flopping on the matter of conformity and his now being entirely comfortable in his role of well-paid establishment spokesman, Hooker chafes the sore spot once more. And to Burgess's claim that in going from medical practice back to the ministry in England he had hurt himself financially, Hooker becomes outspokenly irate: "The bravado here vented by the Rejoiner is not to be borne, which observably [he] set down in the fourteenth objection: Doctor Burgess hath parted with more profit by taking up conformity and a benefice than any now in England hath done by his unconformity and loss of a benefice!" (Preface, p. 374). Hooker argues that all Dr. Burgess has given up is possible future gain and much hard work to reap the profit—work which he probably could not long have continued anyway. In contrast to what those who stood out for nonconformity have sacrificed, Burgess has lost little indeed. Hooker emotionally states the case for himself and other silenced preachers as he says,

> On the other side, ... what do men lose, by unconformity? Even all their means of living, all their liberty, not only of providing for themselves and their families but even of breathing in any air, saving only that which may be drawn out of stinking prisons. Nay, sometimes all the commodity of their country or national habitation being [taken from them, they are] forced to flee even unto the Indians for safety; to say nothing of their loss of life itself by cruel imprisonments. Now let our Savior judge betwixt us and Doctor Burgess. The poor widow, saith he, that parted but with two mites parted with more than they did who out of their plenty parted with many shekels because those two mites were all that she had [Mk. 12:41–44]. If this be true then, many and many a one hath parted with more profit for nonconformity than Doctor Burgess did for conformity, for so much as they have parted with all they had and he only with part of that which he had or might have hoped to get superfluous in comparison of that which others have lost. To conclude all, I suppose if we were willing to suffer, we should be more willing both to search and see the truth. (Preface, pp. 375–76)

This is as clear an indication as we find in any of Hooker's writing of his personal discomfiture and even anger at his unsought exile from his native country and of his leaning toward preferring the dangers of life among the Indians in the New World to his present near-but-yet-so-far location in Holland.

One reason for his increasing dissatisfaction with his exile in the Netherlands was probably his separation from his family. Others have speculated that Hooker left his wife and children under the protection of the Earl of Warwick in Essex when he left England.[24] This surmise seems to be borne out by another passage in the preface to *A Fresh Suit* which contains all the impassioned feeling of personal experience. Having requested Burgess and his readers to consider "how many poor ministers are under pressure, some fled, some imprisoned, many suspended, themselves and families undone" (Preface, p. 372), Hooker asks for an impartial hearing and fair dealing from the authorities, "that we may enjoy the use of our books, the liberty of the press, and if not the benefit of our charges, yet freedom of breathing in our native soil and with our poor desolate families." Since these conditions do not now hold in England, Hooker observes, "we are denied the benefit of the law and the courtesy of the court" (p. 374). Clearly Hooker had little patience for enduring the injustice of his exile while also separated from his family. Among the appealing aspects of this polemical defense of nonconformity are these occasional appearances of Hooker's personal involvement in the practical consequences of his ideas. He is not the stoic; he is an impassioned sufferer who is understandably impatient with those who defend an easier principle of action and at the same time seek sympathy.

In pursuing his intention to discredit Burgess's book as much as possible, Hooker concentrates on the language and logic of his opponent's comments fully as much as he does on personal innuendo and accusation. In fact, some thirteen pages of the central portion of the preface are devoted to a double-column format that provides quotations from Burgess in the first column and paired queries by Hooker in the second column, designed of course to expose extremities of language, absurdities of argument, or downright errors by Burgess. This method of refutation is spotty at best, though in its use we see Hooker the debater, willing to attack his opponent at his weakest points and to let it appear that the weakest points are typical of the entire work. Much more meaningful to a modern reader is a summary comment such as the following, which comes near the end of the preface and brings the issues and the emotions they aroused sharply into focus. Quoting Burgess's phrase, "civill warr about Ceremonies,"[25] Hooker points out that "in civil wars, the mischiefs ensuing on them are not wont to be charged upon one part alone, and that [the] poor [part], passive, overpowered, obnoxious to the suffering of whatsoever pressures their opposites please to lay upon them, which is the case of the nonconformists in these commotions. Tell us, I pray you: If in your conscience the prelates, canons, courses, courts, and proceedings have had no hand in working mischief?" (Preface, pp. 364–65). He depicts the situation even more precisely, describing the Puritan dilemma in England in the early 1630s as follows:

The state of this war is this: we, as it becometh Christians, stand upon the sufficiency of Christ's institutions for all kind[s] of worship; and that exclusively the Word, say we, and nothing but the Word [rules] in matters of religious worship. The prelates rise up on the other side and will needs have us allow and use certain human ceremonies of religion in our Christian worship. We desire to be excused as holding them unlawful. Christ we know and all that cometh from him we are ready to embrace. But these human ceremonies in divine worship we know not, nor can have anything to do with them. Upon this they make fierce war upon us and yet by the pen of Doctor Burgess lay all the fault of this war and the mischiefs of it upon our backs. . . . But the weakest must always go to the wall, and the lamb must die for troubling the water if it please the lion so to determine it. (Preface, pp. 365–66)

In appealing to the impartiality of his Christian reader, Hooker is propagandizing for the Puritan cause as best he can. Such books as this had to be smuggled into England, past the watchmen of the episcopacy.[26] That Hooker was aware of the seditious nature of the book to which he was contributing is clear enough in the brief "Rules for to Direct the Weak Reader How to read the book with profit" that he appended. The second of these urges readers who cannot follow the "maze of the multitude" of definitions and distinctions through which Hooker has had to pursue Burgess, to "crave the help of some judicious minister who is faithful not to betray him for having the book but willing and able to inform him how to conceive of it aright" (Preface, p. 376).[27] The book, as Hooker here pointedly warns his reader, will be a dangerous one to own in England.

For all of his efforts to retain a rational calm in his controversial writings in Holland, Hooker's dealings with the likes of John Paget and John Burgess apparently made his blood boil. The two men represented positions which he could only believe were wrong, yet both his opponents were politically astute enough to have their own ways. This seems to have been especially cloying to Hooker in the case of Burgess, whom he all but names a hypocrite for the convenient adjustment of his opinions to fit the new ecclesiastical climate in England.

Beyond this, the two works which Hooker's disagreements with Paget and Burgess produced have a somewhat different significance. The answers to the twenty propositions has become a classic document in the history of Congregationalism. Hooker defined his differences from the presbyterian system so capably and succinctly that he not only achieved a fuller self-definition but gave later Congregationalists opportunity for the same definition. There can be little doubt that the case did much to keep Hooker's reputation alive among other Independents in both Holland and England, just as Davenport's debate with Paget two years later would do in his case. Indeed, when the Westminster Assembly was convened a decade after Hooker's Dutch period, the chief congregationalist delegates returned from their exile in Holland and promptly wrote to New England inviting Hooker and Davenport to come as delegates. John Paget had given each of these two exiles lasting fame among their colleagues.

Hooker's preface to *A Fresh Suit* is by no means a classic statement. At times it is little more than haggling over minutiae in an ephemeral argument. But at its best the preface attests to Hooker's belief in the need for personal integrity in holding to one's convictions and for greater fairness and tolerance from political authorities toward those who hold strongly to their religious commitments. Indeed, as Hooker insists on the need for individuals to question and evaluate the laws of the authorities and the conduct of both prelates and magistrates he is showing the strength of character which enabled him to become and to remain a respected leader of the Puritan position throughout his buffeted career. It was his ability to live according to his own prescription—and not according to the compromised example of a John Burgess—which accounts for Hooker's profound influence on his young ministerial followers in England and would influence the magisterial John Winthrop to seek out his advice and assistance in the difficult days ahead in New England. For all of its relevance to the central Puritan issue of the forms of worship, then, the central significance of Hooker's preface to Ames's book lies in Hooker's attestation in it to the importance of personal integrity and unwavering dedication to that elusive entity, truth.

4

The Saints Dignitie and Dutie
HOOKER AND THE ANTINOMIAN CONTROVERSY

The decision to join the Great Migration to New England apparently did not come easily for Hooker. Approached by John Winthrop, Roger Williams, and others in the summer of 1629, while still in England, Hooker had decided against joining the Massachusetts Bay Company at its inception. This decision led him to search for preaching positions in Holland after his silencing. The abortive two-year stay on the Continent followed, leading in its turn to both personal and professional dissatisfaction. Finally, in early 1633 he reached the decision to "go for New England," which he may well in subsequent years have wished he had made some three years earlier. That group of English colonists under the leadership of William Goodwin who became known as "Mr. Hooker's Company" was apparently persuaded as early as 1632 that he would make this decision, since it was in that year that they had gone to Massachusetts Bay.

When he arrived in Boston aboard the *Griffin* in early September of 1633 accompanied by his colleagues John Cotton and Samuel Stone, at the advanced age of forty-seven and just emerging from some eight years at the eye of the storm of controversy, he doubtless longed for relief from squabbles and disagreement. While Cotton was called to be one of the ministers at the Boston Church, Hooker and Stone joined the Goodwin group a little farther up the Charles River and established the first church at what was initially named Newtown, though it would ultimately take the somewhat presumptuous name of Cambridge. Being committed to the challenge of building a community where none had existed until very recently, the Hooker company took pains to construct houses, clear and cultivate farmland, establish businesses and trades, and become involved in the political and social affairs of the larger colony. One of their number, the wealthy John Haynes, was elected governor of Massachusetts Bay in May 1635. Outward signs, at least, indicated that the Hooker company was well established in the mainstream of colony affairs. Yet discontent and disagreement seem to have pursued them across the Atlantic.

A little more than a year after Hooker's arrival, he felt impelled to enter a controversy, albeit reluctantly, which was attracting attention on both sides of the ocean. The impetuous John Endecott of Salem had carried the Puritan dislike of physical symbols and icons to an extreme when in the fall of 1634 he cut from the flag of the military company at Salem a part of the red cross of St. George, objecting that it was a relic of Roman Catholicism savoring of idolatry. Endecott's biographer sees this act as one of several in which he was heavily influenced by the opinions of Roger Williams, then still the teacher at the Salem church.[1] Throughout the winter of 1634–35 the matter was debated pro and con at various gatherings, including one reported by Winthrop in which all the ministers except Nathaniel Ward participated. A complaint had been brought to the General Court regarding Endecott's deed in November of 1634. The court next met in March 1635 and reached no decision, though at the meeting of May 6, they finally censured Endecott, forbidding his holding public office for one year. It was apparently at some point during these several months of inconclusive debate on the question that Hooker put his own opinions on paper. He protested that it was "most crosse" to his inclination "to express contrariety" in judgment from his brethren, "but beinge Importuned publiquely, privately by speech and Letter: and that by some to whom I owe much in ye Lord: and without whoes invitation it was in my Hearte never to sett penn to paper, on y^s point," he proceeded to argue in persuasively logical terms the reasons why "as yet I am not able to see ye sinfulnes of ye banner in a civle use."[2] His basic distinction was between the civil and religious uses of the cross; the cross appearing in a military banner, he argued, was nothing but a civil symbol, requiring no worshipful response and thus being in no way idolatrous. This view ultimately carried the day, though there was strong feeling on both sides of the question.

It may be that at this moment, coinciding as it did with the election of Hooker's friend John Haynes as governor of the Colony, Hooker was realizing the full influence which was at his power to command in the Bay.[3] But there were offsetting sources of dissatisfaction which ultimately drove Hooker and his congregation away from the Boston area. We cannot fully explain the exact nature of these discontents. But we do know that a mere ten months after the debarking of Hooker, Stone, and Cotton, the residents of Newtown were complaining of "straitness for want of land, especially meadow," and were talking about moving away. Just two months later, the town sent six people to Connecticut to reconnoiter, with the intention firmly in mind "to remove their town thither."[4] The Massachusetts Bay officials managed to discourage the Newtown residents from leaving for the better part of two years; but on May 31, 1636, with Haynes's term as governor just completed and not quite three years after the ministers' arrival, Hooker, despite the burden of his wife Susannah's infirmity, which required carrying her on a litter all the way, led his congregation and 160 head of cattle over the Indian path to the banks of the Connecticut River at what was to become Hartford, there to face all over again the difficulties of subduing a wilderness to a habitable condition.

There must have been powerful reasons for making such a change, and most commentators have been inclined to think that want of land, the chief reason publicly acknowledged, does not fully account for it. This is doubtless so, but we can easily dismiss this reason too carelessly. In fact, Winthrop recorded that one of the reasons advanced in September 1634 for the Newtowners' desired removal was "their want of accommodation for their cattle, *so as they were not able to maintain their ministers*, nor could receive any more of their friends to help them; and *here it was alleged by Mr. Hooker, as a fundamental error, that towns were set so near each to other*" (italics added).[5] The lack of sufficient grazing land and especially of hay meadows was thus a fact which had a direct bearing on Hooker's personal economic well-being, present and future. His congregation's ability to pay him adequately was a vital interest to Hooker, and he was obviously not above speaking out in his own behalf in this matter. He had not come this far, after years of difficulties, to suffer in such a roomy locale as the New World from an unnecessary and short-sighted lack of that essential commodity of America's future prosperity, land. It is noteworthy that he died some thirteen years later in comfortable circumstances.[6]

William Hubbard, the early Puritan historian, suggested that the essential reason for the move to Connecticut was a clash of opinions and perhaps of personality between Hooker in Newtown and Cotton in Boston: "Two such eminent stars, such as were Mr. Cotton and Mr. Hooker, both of the first magnitude, though of differing influence,

could not well continue in one and the same orb."[7] There were probably other reasons, perhaps including an incipient rivalry and clash of
governmental philosophy between John Winthrop and John Haynes.
Rumors were heard all the way back in England, however, that all was
not in agreement among the ministers in the Bay and that Hooker was
particularly opposed to the strict membership requirements at the Boston church of Cotton and John Wilson.[8] That he had fundamental disagreements with Cotton on the nature of the regenerative experience
and on qualification for membership is clear and will be more fully
discussed later in this study. On the whole, while proof is insufficient
to make an open-and-shut case, it does seem likely that Hooker's disagreements with Cotton contributed to his desire to be in a social climate where doctrine and church practice were not so thoroughly influenced by Cotton's eminence.[9]

While Hooker and Cotton remained such near neighbors in the Boston area, it may have been natural enough for observers to see their
relationship as one of personal rivalry. In fact, of course, Hooker was
by no means alone in his differences with Cotton, who was at the
center of a much larger storm than the one stirred up by Endecott.
David D. Hall, in documenting the progress of the Antinomian crisis,
has shown that Cotton's "differences of opinion" with the great majority
of the other ministers of Massachusetts were—even more profoundly
than Anne Hutchinson's ideas—"at the heart of the controversy."[10]
Certainly in the course of the seventeen months from October 1636 to
March 1638 during which the controversy simmered, came to a boil,
and was summarily cooled, Cotton himself discovered the surprising
extent to which the other ministers of the Bay and Connecticut could
not agree with his doctrinal views.

From August 30 to September 22, 1637, Hooker served with Peter
Bulkeley of Concord as one of the two moderators of the three-week-
long formal inquiry into the spread of Antinomian opinions. So his
abilities as theological interpreter, rational analyst, and observer of the
human psyche were all, no doubt, effectively harnessed at the outset of
formal proceedings in this controversy. The records of this synod were
not preserved so assiduously as were those of the General Court's inquiry later in the fall of 1637 or the court's final trial of the Antinomians in March 1638. The synod over which Hooker and Bulkeley
presided heard a great many witnesses in the course of its three-week
existence and compiled a list of some eighty-two "errors" to which one
or more of the pro-Hutchinson group subscribed. Thus, Hooker was
fully aware of all the conflicting positions in the case. As co-moderator

in this inquiry he must have had much to say to particular individuals and to the problem generally, but no statement by him on the case is known to have been recorded until after sentence was finally passed some two years later. Then he spoke with biting sharpness against Mistress Hutchinson: "The expression of providence against this wretched woman hath proceeded from the Lord's miraculous mercy, and his bare arm hath been discovered therein from first to last, that all the churches may hear and fear. I do believe, such a heap of hideous errors, at once to be vented by such a self-deluding and deluded creature, no history can record; and yet, after recantation of all, to be cast out as unsavory salt that she may not continue a pest to the place, that will be forever marvellous in the eyes of all the saints."[11] During the actual trial, Hooker was back home at Hartford, though his name was mentioned more than once in the proceedings. His well-known opinions must frequently have been in the minds of many as they heard Cotton present his very different ideas in response to direct and pressing questioning by the New England elders, magistrates, and deputies. Still, apart from the post facto statement quoted above, we have until now known of no major recorded public statements by Hooker on the controversy itself. But it is possible to show that Hooker did, after all, speak out on the issues of the Antinomian Controversy. An entire volume of sermons published after his death attests to this fact.

The first summary description of the proceedings of the Antinomian hearings and trial to be published was John Winthrop's *Short Story of the Rise, reign, and ruine of the Antinomians, Familists & Libertines,* which appeared in London in 1644 with a lengthy explanatory preface written by Thomas Weld, who had lived in New England from 1632 to 1641, when he returned to England. He had been, with Thomas Shepard, a prosecutor at Anne Hutchinson's trial, and so he knew the details of the case well. Weld told of six manifestations of God's providential response in the episode, the first of which was that God "stirred up all the Ministers spirits in the Countrey to preach against those errors, and practises that so much pestered the Countrey, to informe, to confute, to rebuke, &c. thereby to cure those that were diseased already, and to give Antidotes to the rest, to preserve them from infection."[12] Among these "Antidotes" were probably the seven sermons by Hooker published four years after his death as *The Saints Dignitie and Dutie* (London, 1651). There is no specific mention anywhere in the volume that these seven sermons came out of the 1636–38 disputes, but there is considerable internal evidence suggesting that this was precisely the case. The absence of specific explanation, together with the relatively obscure title, and the publication date some thirteen years after the controversy had been laid to rest probably account for the failure of anyone thus far to suggest that the sermons were preached at the time of the Antinomian controversy in the late 1630s.[13] Indeed, the comment in the editor's preface to the effect that the sermons in the volume have "no great dependence" on each other does not encourage one to see them as a series of related works on a single central issue. It would be wrong, in fact, to insist that these are single-minded answers to John Cotton, Anne Hutchinson, and John Wheelwright, in which all parts speak directly to the controversial issues. But since every one of the seven sermons does address issues of the controversy, some more insistently than others, it is worthwhile to examine the evidence for its relevance to the major dispute in the Bay colony in the first decade of its existence.

Two aspects of the book, though not sufficiently strong evidence to justify any conclusions by themselves, at least raise questions in the reader's mind about the possible conditions which produced both the sermons and the impetus for their eventual publication. In the first place, the book is preceded by a four-page epistle "To the Reader" which is signed by one "T.S." Readers who have considered the identity of T.S. have usually concluded that he must have been Thomas Shepard, no doubt a sound conclusion, even though Shepard died in 1649, two years before the publication of the volume.[14] Hooker and Shepard's affinity in matters of doctrine and polity gave the two men ample reason for a sympathetic relationship, a bond which was firmly cemented in 1637 when Shepard became Hooker's son-in-law. Surviving letters from their ongoing correspondence show that after Shepard arrived in New England Hooker occasionally sent him manuscripts at Shepard's specific request,[15] so that Shepard's possession of a Hooker manuscript at the time of the author's death in July 1647 is not at all unlikely. Since Shepard was not named as executor or overseer in Hooker's will,[16] we might not expect him to publish a posthumous book, though family ties and physical possession of the manuscript might well have persuaded him at least to prepare the work for the press. Whether Shepard sent it abroad before he died or whether it was found among his papers and sent to a printer after Shepard's death is simply unknown. That he had an abiding interest in the issues of the Antinomian controversy is well established, and that he and Hooker had continued to discuss with each other their differences with Cotton is indicated in their correspondence.[17] Indeed, the correspondence may even contain the explanation of why Shepard, in readying the manuscript for publication, did not explain the relevance of the sermons to the disputes of 1636–38. A September 17, 1646, letter from Hooker to Shepard speculates that during the struggle between the Independents and Presbyterians at the Westminster Assembly, the Scottish Presbyterians—most notably Robert Baillie, "a man of a subtill and shrewd head"—probably "had a secret hand to provoke Mr. Weld to set forth his short story touching occasions here in Mr. Vane his reigne" as part of their plot to bring public discredit on the New England Way.[18] Shepard, no doubt sharing Hooker's suspicions on the uses to which the enemies of Congregationalism were putting the documents of the Antinomian difficulties, might well in the late 1640s have preferred simply to say nothing in his preface to Hooker's book which would remind English readers of the disagreements among prominent New England divines in the preceding decade, while nevertheless letting them see what Hooker had had to say on the central doctrinal points. As it happened, however, by the time the book appeared in 1651, the assembly disputes were already ended.

Whether Shepard actually tried to edit the sermon texts so as to make them free from any taint of local controversy we do not know. They are almost purged of such references, at any rate—but not quite. And it is the exceptions which help to pique the historical curiosity of the reader of this volume. For instance, the first Use of the second sermon in the volume, a sermon entitled *The Blessed Inhabitant*, refers very directly to scandals. Hooker explains that God makes certain that scandals come in all ages. They are ultimately, he claims, for the good of the Church. He acknowledges that "the falls of holy men" result in many people attacking God, religion, believers, and ministers, but this is wrong, since those who fall away were usually not true believers to begin with. Possibly having reference to the "spiritual depression" of 1635–36,[19] just preceding the Antinomian controversy, Hooker notes that "usually where the ministry of the Gospell hath been any long time, and people have not been wrought upon by the preaching of the .Gospel, are not brought to a powerfull profession of religion, you shall usually finde it, that the Lord doth suffer some professors or other in these places to fall scandalously; Is it not so in many places in this city?"[20]

Though there is no certain evidence indicating the manuscript's origin in New England, the late date of its publication and Shepard's probable hand in it lead one to assume its origination in New England rather than England or Holland, a conclusion strongly encouraged by the book's ascription on the title page to "*that Reverend Divine, Thomas Hooker, Late Preacher in New England.*" Assuming a New England frame of reference, it seems much more likely that Hooker is referring to Boston than to Hartford when in the sixth sermon he twice mentions "this city" in a context suggesting that it is not the place in which he has his regular ministry. He would hardly be so egotistical, at any rate, to be referring to Hartford when he says, in an amusing piece of hyperbolic flattery of the local minister(s), "Certainly, had the Devill himselfe but any hope of receiving mercy, the sermons that are made in this City, were able even to melt his heart" (p. 214) or even in an earlier passage where he says that ignorance is rampant, "even in this City where the means of knowledge are more then ordinary" (p. 196). It seems quite possible, in other words, that at least some of the sermons in *The Saints Dignitie and Dutie* were preached in the Boston area. And it is clear that the audience was well aware of recent scandals or controversies involving prominent people in the Church. If, as also seems highly probable, Hooker stayed at Shepard's home in Cambridge during the synod in September of 1637—the year in which Shepard married Hooker's daughter Joanna—Shepard would have heard the sermons himself and perhaps retained the manuscripts or his own notes from the occasions.

All of this must be acknowledged for what it is: informed speculation. The matter becomes a bit less hypothetical, however, when we look at the themes of the sermons in the book. We need to remember that, as David Hall has shown, the central issues in the controversy were such matters as the relationship between faith, justification, and sanctification; the degree to which sancification is evidence of faith; the degree to which the human will is engaged in the process of justification; the differences between the covenant of works and the convenant of grace; the usefulness of self-examination; the manner of experiencing the Holy Spirit in one's soul; and the necessity of ministerial guidance in acquiring saving faith. Since Anne Hutchinson was the chief layperson charged in the proceedings, her conducting private sessions in her home with other laypeople, especially women, raised the additional issue of the ability of untrained laiety to teach the ignorant, and even the place of women in the Church and in society. Since Hooker addresses every one of these issues directly in *The Saints Dignitie and Dutie* and since every sermon deals, whether briefly or at length, with at least one of them, there is clearly a strong likelihood that the volume is a direct answer to the Antinomian heresies of Hutchinson, Wheelwright, and even John Cotton. Indeed, in Hooker's return from Connecticut to moderate this synod so soon after his departure, in the midst of hard times in Connecticut, and perhaps to preach some or all of these sermons during his stay, there is more than a little appearance of a return to vindication for his principles—a vindication implied in the thoroughness of Cotton's defeat as well as in the convictions espoused in the sermons of *The Saints Dignitie*.[21] If disputes between the two men lay behind Hooker's departure from the Bay, it seems likely that they also contributed to Hooker's return to active involvement in the Antinomian controversy.[22]

The title page of this book, perhaps prepared by T.S., perhaps by a knowing printer, gives the very first indication that a major topic in the book will be the relationship between faith and justification and the life of the justified when it provides as the epigraph for the volume Hebrews 10:38: "*Now the just shall live by Faith; but if any man draw back, my soul shall have no pleasure in him.*" The first clause, of course, indicates a fundamental tenet for all Protestants from Martin Luther on, but the entire verse speaks to a key issue in the Antinomian dispute. Believers, most Puritans held, do not "draw back" after acquiring faith; rather, they give visible evidence of their possession of faith. The efficacy of faith in producing or not producing good works in the believer became a central concern, as the records of the hearings and trial abundantly show. The first sermon in Hooker's book, called *The Gift of Gifts; or, The End Why Christ Gave Himself*, is on a Biblical text whose final phrase is one of the most highly charged phrases of the controversy: "*Who gave himself for us, that he might redeem us from all iniquitie, and purifie unto himself a peculiar people, zealous of good works*" (*SDD*, p. 1). The Antinomians, including John Cotton during the first round of the dispute when Hooker was moderating, held that "good works" are irrelevant to the question of whether or not one possesses saving grace. They felt that one's works—signs of his sanctification—should not serve to verify one's possession of grace, nor should ministers urge their hearers to be "active" in faith, since this was, as they saw it, preaching a "covenant of works." If any doctrine was anathema to Hooker, who had spent his whole career exhorting his followers to an *active* Christian life, it was this notion that one could be passive and still claim salvation. And it was on this issue that he was now called to do battle directly.

Cotton, answering the Massachusetts elders' response to his replies to sixteen questions which they had put to him, quoted the Jesuit Bellarmine to the effect that justification by works is not inconsistent with justification by faith. But then as Cotton states the necessarily differing view of the Reformers ("our Divines"), he seems practically to throw works out of the scheme altogether, going a good deal farther in this direction than Hooker and most other New England ministers cared to follow. After quoting Bellarmine, Cotton says, "Whereto you know our Divines are wont to answer, That Grace and Works . . . in the whole course of our Salvation from Election to Glorification, are not subordinate one to another, but opposite: so that whatsoever is of Grace is not of Works, and whatsoever is of Works is not of Grace."[23] Linking his opponents with the opinions of Bellarmine—the prototypical Roman Catholic controversialist whom scores of English Protestants, including King James himself, had been attacking for three decades—was of course no way for the usually circumspect Cotton to endear himself to them. Hooker, for one, had frequently cited Bellarmine to refute him. One book in which he did so contained an early reference to Hooker's annoyance with the willingness of the Antinomians to lay all the responsibility for a Christian life in the lap of Christ. Those Familists and Anabaptists, he complained, "thinke it is unprofitable for a beleever to trouble himselfe for his sinnes, and to goe up and downe with his heart full of griefe." They say that since Christ has accepted responsibility for their sins, why bother themselves? Hooker is frank about his annoyance, saying, "I have borne a secret grudge against this doctrine of theirs many a day, but I could not tell how to meet with it, neither do I love to meddle with it, till I meet it in my dish."[24] In the summer of 1637 it was served up in a plenteous portion, and Hooker was bound to meet it with a vengeance.

So, with his long-time awareness of the Antinomian tendency to look askance at the active role that he prescribed for the believer, Hooker uses the word *works* very knowingly in the first sermons of *The Saints Dignitie*. Cotton had cited the Apostle Paul to the effect that anything which is "of Grace" is not "of Works."[25] In selecting a text from the second chapter of Titus, Hooker, too, goes to Paul for authority. Significantly, that chapter is devoted entirely to Paul's ethical instructions to Titus: what to do and not to do as a faithful Christian. The sermon moves toward the culminating observation that, though there may be some backsliding, and though nobody, not even the most perfect saint, is free from sin, nevertheless, the believer will evidence his belief in the quality of his life. "Whosoever Christ hath redeemed from under iniquitie, he so works with them, that they shall never return to iniquitie again" (*SDD*, p. 37). But despite this fact, Christ also requires that we *work* at coming out from under the power of iniquity. Paradoxically, though our liberty has been given to us, we must constantly fight for it. As we shall see later in this study, a familiar refrain in Hooker's ministry is simply given a new application in this dispute: "Labour every day more and more to get from under that iniquitie under which we are" (p. 37). The Christian life as described throughout Hooker's canon is full of striving, tensions, and paradoxes, all of which would be largely eliminated if Cotton's way prevailed.

A principal aspect of this sermon, in addition to its concern for

clarifying the necessity of good works' following faith, is its consideration of the nature of faith itself. In thus analyzing faith, Hooker was
joining the general ministerial practice noted by Hugh Peter near the
close of the trial of Mrs. Hutchinson in March of 1638: "Some Elders
have made whole Sermons for fayth as if fayth should never hould up
her Hed agayne in this Cuntrye."[26] In the first part of his sermon,
indeed, Hooker sets himself the task of describing the qualities—the
"properties"—of faith. Knowing what we do of Hooker's joining of
theology and psychology to demand the active involvement of the believer in his working out of the spiritual life, it is no surprise that the
second property which he lists is its activity. Quoting first Galatians
5:6, he goes on to say that "where ever there is faith, it is working.
Faith is not an idle grace, it is not a fancie or an opinion that Christ
hath died for us, and there is an end, but it is a working grace, where
ever there is faith, there is work" (*SDD,* p. 5). The faithful are, as Paul
said to Titus, "a peculiar people, zealous of good works." It is significant that Hooker responds to the turmoil of this controversy by reminding the New Englanders that they are God's "peculiar people"
and that their lives should show it. It might well have seemed to him
that he had worked for naught through his entire career if he could not
make this central message stick now.

The reason why Hooker and the other ministers whom Hugh Peter
had in mind felt it was necessary to preach directly on the nature of
faith, and particularly on its active quality, was that the
Antinomians—and particularly Anne Hutchinson and her brother-in-
law, the Reverend John Wheelwright—had directly charged the New
England ministry with an undue emphasis on works. Wheelwright,
who had arrived in the colony only a few months earlier but had
promptly acquired a large following in the Boston church, was asked to
preach a sermon on a fast day declared for January 19, 1637. The sermon was boldly inflammatory, striking out with very clear implications
at the General Court as well as at the ministers in the Bay. His Doctrine was, "The only cause of the fasting of true believers is the absence of Christ." He leaves no doubt that he means there is an absence
of Christ in the government and churches of New England when he
says further that "those that do not know the Lord Jesus, they are
usually given most unto fasting." This is clearly a charge that those who
declared the fast—the members of the General Court—are unredeemed, a charge which Wheelwright knew could hardly pass without
notice. The main reason for this state of affairs is too much concern for
outward signs—works—and too little concern for the indwelling spirit
of Christ. Wheelwright exhorted the people to *fight* for Christ; other-

wise, "those under a covenant of works will prevaile." He goes so far as
to proclaim the present power of Antichrist in their midst: "Those that
are enimyes to the Lord, not onely Pagonish, but Antichristian, and
those that run under a covenant of works are very strong." He admits
his awareness that he is getting into hot water in all of this when he
says, "I must confesse and acknowledge" that "this will cause a com-
bustion in the Church and common wealth." His only answer is, "What
then?" Antichrist must be destroyed; "therefore never feare combus-
tions and burnings."[27] He could not have been very surprised, then,
when he was charged in the March General Court with sedition and
contempt, found guilty, and, in November, banished from the colony.[28] He had support from sixty petitioners from the Boston church,
but it was not enough to get him off. At the same session of the court,
one of the Antinomians, a merchant named Steven Greensmyth, was
fined the rather staggering amount of £40 and required to "acknowledge his fault in every church" for his imprudent remark that "all the
ministers (except Mr. Cotton, Mr. Wheelwright, and hee thought Mr.
Hooker) did teach a covenant of works."[29]

Hooker most fully developed his answer to the Antinomians' charges
that the ministers were preaching a covenant of works in *Grace Magnified,* the third sermon in *The Saints Dignitie.* In stating the Doctrine
he explains that "the difference between the Covenant of workes and of
grace, between the Law and the Gospel" is that in his *gracious* dealings with men, God enables them to do whatever he commands them
to do (*SDD,* p. 81). The difference between Hooker and his colleagues,
on the one hand, and the Hutchinsonians, on the other, was not on
this claim alone but on its conjunction, in the message of the voluntarist preparationists, with activism. Hooker, in saying God gives the
gracious believer a power to do good works, does not say that the
gracious man can sit back and ease up. His voluntarism is very much in
evidence as he argues that even under the covenant of grace, where
man receives from God a power to do, "indeavour" is still necessary.
He insists on the one hand that "there is no power in Gods children to
obey any Commandement" and on the other that God intends his children to obey His commandments "in some measure" (pp. 82, 81). This
paradox is resolved for the saints by the discovery that grace brings
with it enabling power—not the full power that Adam had, but power
to do God's will "in some measure."

One of the points which the elders of New England set out to clarify
in inquiring into the opinions first of Cotton, and then of all Cotton's
and Mrs. Hutchinson's followers, was just how great they thought to be
the power of a person not yet under the power of grace—still merely

"under the Law." This was one of Thomas Shepard's concerns in writing to Cotton to clarify his views in 1636, when Thomas Hooker had not yet left Cambridge.[30] And it was the doubt behind the formulation of "Error 12" in the list of errors compiled by the synod of September 1637. The synod ascribed in "Error 12" the belief that "in the covenant of workes, a legalist may attaine the same righteousnesse for truth, which *Adam* had in innocency before the fall." The elders answered this error in their "Confutation 12": "Hee that can attaine *Adams* righteousnesse in sincerity, hath his sin truely mortifyed, but that no legalist can have, because true mortification is wrought by the covenant of grace, *Rom.* 6:14. Sin shall not have dominion over you, for you are not under the Law, but under Grace."[31] It was this same text, Romans 6:14, which Hooker chose for the text of *Grace Magnified*, where he goes back over the familiar ground of the two covenants and of the difference between Adam's and the justified Christian's ability to do God's will. Through it all, from his sermons on the subject in England to his possible collaboration with Shepard in raising the questions with Cotton in 1636 to his leadership in the synod of 1637 and ultimately to his eventual sermon on the subject, Hooker was consistent in his arguments that a mere legalist could not approach the ability of the justified to do the commandments of God. Grace puts one in communion with Christ, who in turn gives the power. He could be no plainer in refuting the charges of preaching a covenant of works.

Hooker returned to the matter of the place of "works" in the life of the man of faith again as he preached a sermon entitled *The Activitie of Faith*, the fifth in *The Saints Dignitie*. In the manner of those other ministers whom Hugh Peter noticed, Hooker pursues the subject of the nature of faith and its effect on the life of the faithful. He begins by striking a note that the Antinomians also insisted upon: that "all outward priviledges, as the hearing of the Word, the partaking of the Sacraments, and the like, are not able to make a man a sound Saint of God" (*SDD*, p. 157). Salvation must be inward, spiritual, of the heart. Thus the sermon is in part an attack on those who put too much confidence in regular church attendance and a ritualistic observance of visible Christianity. With all of this the Antinomians would readily have agreed. But the crux of his sermon comes in the first of two "points" which he lists under this main doctrine. He observes that *"faith causeth fruitfulness in the hearts and lives of those in whom it is"* (p. 163). Faith in the heart of an individual "cannot be idle," he insists; it must bear the fruit of good works. Indeed, "if thou art fruitlesse, say what thou wilt, thou hast no faith at all" (p. 165). This issue was a major question in the exchanges between Cotton and the ministers as they debated the faithful person's degree of ability to do good works, finally reaching essential agreement with Cotton's statement in his "Rejoynder" that "we have power . . . by his [Christ's] help to use this help in bringing forth spiritual fruits," though he continued to quibble about the importance of Christ's constant renewal of the saint in order to make the fruits effective.[32] Cotton, in drawing back from the dangerous heresies of his Antinomian followers, gradually backed off from the logical consequences of their claim that one should not base spiritual conclusions on visible "works," namely, that even grossly profligate behavior is possible in the truly redeemed saint. He must eventually have seen that such a position, while fighting the pernicious power of "legalism," might also, in the minds of some, condone lawlessness and immorality. This imputation had always been a part of Puritan attacks on the Familists.

A closely related matter in the controversy was disagreement over whether or not faith comes to the soul before justification. Our examination of Hooker's treatment of the *ordo salutis* will show that Hooker unequivocally believed it did. Peter Bulkeley was of Hooker's mind here and said so to Cotton in his correspondence with him in early 1636 when he was just beginning to probe into Cotton's dubious doctrines. Cotton claimed that granting faith's precedence of justification was to make man's works in some sense a cause of his justification, something which he could not allow.[33] The second sermon in Hooker's *The Saints Dignitie*, entitled *The Blessed Inhabitant* (the sermon also referring to scandals "in this city"), is a direct attack on several of the Antinomian positions, including the notion that faith cannot precede justification. He says quite explicitly that Christ is in the justified believer, an indwelling which "in all justified persons, is the consequent of their union with him" (*SDD*, p. 49). This prior joining, he insists, takes place in the acquisition of faith. In so saying, Hooker is declaring the opinions expressed during and after the controversy by his fellow moderator, Peter Bulkeley.[34]

The same sermon makes very explicit comment on the Antinomians' position that self-trial—the examination of one's own deeds, emotions, and state of mind in order to determine the presence of grace—is useless. It is not good, said Wheelwright, to notice your own actions and conclude from them that you are in a "good estate." "If men thinke to to be saved, because they see some worke of sanctification in them, as hungring and thirsting and the like: if they be saved, they are saved without the Gospell."[35] Likewise, Cotton held that "we cannot take the assurance of faith of our Justification, from the sight and evidence of our sanctification."[36] But the whole thrust of Hooker's view of the approach to faith and the growth in it depended upon the sinner's constant self-examination, both to encourage the need for perseverance and finally to assure him of his acquisiton of saving faith. So he could not take lightly the views of the Hutchinsonians on the dangers of self-examination. Hold a mirror up to nature, he advises. "Here you have a cleer looking-glasse, wherein you may be able to judge of the faces, of the state and temper of your souls" (SDD, pp. 57, 58). "Now then (my brethren)," he urges, "be exhorted I beseech you in the fear of God, to put in practice, and to make use of this Touchstone, and looking-glasse" (p. 66). "To you that have the truth of grace in you, it is of great use to you to trie your selves by, for by often tryall you come to be setled and assured of the truth of your grace" (p. 67). Then, with clear reference to the doctrines of the Wheelwrights, the Cottons,[37] and the Hutchinsons, Hooker answers those who publicly oppose his opinions:

> Do not thinke that it is an irregular way to put people upon signs and tryals. I confesse there are some particular cases, wherein it is not safe for some particular persons, at that time, and in that case, to put them to try themselves by signs. But for the generall it is necessary, and it is the dutie of all people to looke to signs, and to try themselves by them. And if there were nothing more, but this that is in the Text, me thinks it is an unanswerable Argument, to confute them that crie out against Signs and Evidences of the truth of grace. Doth not the Apostle *Paul* as plain as any man in the world can, put them upon the tryall of themselves by Signs, telling them, that if they have such things in them, they are in a good estate, and if they have not, that they are in a dangerous and damnable condition? Therefore I say, put it not off, but make conscience to practice this duty, to view your souls in this, and the like looking-glasses. (SDD, pp. 67–68)

In such a passage we not only get Hooker's clear doctrinal message, but we readily perceive that he is speaking in a context of dispute over the doctrine—a dispute at the very heart of the differences between the preparationist Hooker and the nonpreparationist Cotton as well as between the Antinomians and the Massachusetts authorities.

Thus in the first, second, third, and fifth sermons in this posthumous volume Hooker addresses doctrinal issues which rested at the heart of the Antinomian controversy. The remaining three sermons in *The Saints Dignitie and Dutie* all approach issues in the dispute which are less purely doctrinal but which had important social and political implications. A major reason for the colony's great concern over the Hutchinsonians was the challenge that they posed to established authority, both ministers and magistrates. Hugh Peter, on the second day of the examination of Mrs. Hutchinson in November of 1637, put this problem succinctly in saying, "This is the main thing against her that she charged us to be unable ministers of the gospel and to preach a covenant of works." John Winthrop, whose enmity to Mrs. Hutchinson and the Reverend Mr. Wheelwright was a strong catalyst to the whole proceedings, spoke on the same matter in saying, "The ground work of her revelations is the immediate revelation of the spirit and not by the ministry of the word, and that is the means by which she hath very much abused the country that they shall look for revelations and are not bound to the ministry of the word, but God will teach them by immediate revelations and this hath been the ground of all these tumults and troubles. . . . this is the thing that hath been the root of all the mischief." To this speech by the governor, the court responded, "We all consent with you." Once ministerial authority had thus been questioned and reliance placed instead on supposedly suprahuman revelations, there was no telling what form the heresies might take. Deputy Governor Thomas Dudley, for one, saw plenty of reason for the elected officials of Massachusetts (such as himself) to fear the consequences. Some Germans, Dudley let it be known, have laid claim to revelations, and some of their listeners have been stirred up "to take up arms against their prince and to cut the throats one of another, . . . and whether the devil may inspire the same into their hearts here I know not, for I am fully persuaded that Mrs. Hutchinson is deluded by the devil."[38] Perhaps no speech in all the proceedings so fully shows the extreme fear of the threat of anarchy which the Antinomians inspired in the Massachusetts authorities.

However one saw the dangers, there was substantial agreement on the fact that the heretics posed a threat to authority. For many, indeed, this was "the main thing" in the whole dispute. It is no surprise, then, that Hooker's *Saints Dignitie and Dutie* contains two sermons, the sixth and the seventh, which address the matter of proper attitudes toward authority and the question of who the true authority is. A general assumption of the age was that to possess authority, one should be adequately possessed of knowledge and understanding. Hooker addresses this assumption in his sixth sermon, *Culpable Ignorance under Meanes*, taking as his text Isaiah 27:11, "*For it is a people of no understanding, therefore he that made them, will not have mercie on them, and he that formed them, will shew them no favour*" (SDD, p. 191). In outlining the context of this verse, Hooker explains that in the first part of the chapter, Isaiah talks of the Lord's dealings both with his faithful servants and with hypocrites. God, he points out, has a special care and love for those who are faithful, and he corrects those who are not sufficiently fruitful. But towards the hypocrites who live in the church, he is severe. The chief sin of these latter is that "they have no understanding." Such hypocrites pretend to knowledge which they do not have, refusing to recognize their own ignorance and lack of saving grace, which alone brings a real apprehension of truth. Anne Hutchinson was considered just such a pretender by the court, which was especially annoyed at her holding discussion sessions in her home in which the ministers of the church were frequently countermanded. Hooker's audience would have had no difficulty in reading local circumstances into his remark that "if a man should go from house to house, even in this City where the means of knowledge are more then ordinary, he should find a marvellous poor deal of sanctifying and saving knowledge, yea, I doe assure you, of any reasonable common knowledge in matters of Religion" (p. 196). Too many people are "mere naturall men," truant scholars, who turn a deaf ear on the means and on the ministers. In the examination of Anne Hutchinson, John Winthrop put this very matter of presumed knowledge and its challenge to the local authorities directly to her:

> Your course is not to be suffered for, besides that we find such a course as this to be greatly prejudicial to the state, besides the occasion that it is to seduce many honest persons that are called to those meetings and your opinions being known to be different from the word of God may seduce many simple souls that resort unto you, besides that the occasion which hath come of late hath come from none but such as have frequented your meetings, so that now they are flown off from magistrates and ministers and this since they have come to you, and besides that it will not well stand with the commonwealth that families should be neglected for so many neighbours and dames and so much time spent, we see no rule of God for this, we see not that any should have authority to set up any other exercises besides what authority hath already set up and so what hurt comes of this you will be guilty of and we for suffering you.[39]

Hooker agreed that those of "no understanding" in "the Bosom of the Church" were a great danger to themselves and to others: "Most either turn their back upon the Church, or turn a deaf eare to what they hear, and cast the Commandements of God behind them, and rather fleer [i.e., grin contemptuously or sneer] in the face of the Minister, and contemn what he saith, then be any wayes humbled for their sinnes" (SDD, p. 214). This is what comes of presuming to knowledge when in fact one is not redeemed. "There is such a knowledge as is peculiar to the Saints," he reminded the people (p. 208). "A man must have the work of grace within himselfe, before he can rightly understand the nature of it" (p. 209). It was precisely to this point that John Wilson of the Boston Church spoke in the trial of Mrs. Hutchinson when he accused her of *"the slightinge of Gods faythfull Ministers and contemninge and cryinge downe them as Nobodies"* and instead trying "to set up *your selfe in the Roome of God above others that you might be extolled and admired and followed after, that you might be a great Prophites . . .* and Undertake to expound Scriptures, and to interpret other Mens Sayings and sermons after your minde." The explanation for these carryings-on in the way of "culpable ignorance" is clear enough, and it took Thomas Shepard to say it in the trial: Mistress Hutchinson "never had any trew Grace in her hart."[40] The difference between the gracious person and the natural person, the true teacher and the false teacher, is great indeed, just as the danger posed to society by the false teacher is also great indeed. It is to this very point that the editor or author was speaking in selecting the epigraph for the title page of the first sermon in the book, Romans 5:15: " . . . if through the offence of one, many be dead, much more the grace of God, and the gift by grace, which is by one man Jesus Christ. . . ."

The final sermon in *The Saints Dignitie and Dutie* pursues still farther the issues raised in *Culpable Ignorance*. This sermon is called *Wilful Hardness; or, The Means of Grace Abused*. The Biblical text, Proverbs 29:1, pinpoints the preacher's desire to expose the danger of rebellious stubbornness: *"Hee that being often reproved, hardneth his neck, shall suddenly be destroyed, and that without remedie"* (*SDD*, p. 219). From the beginning of this sermon, as in the preceding one, there is much reference to rebellion against the authority and wisdom of ministers and magistrates. There is likewise a good deal of concern for "this congregation," which enjoys exceptionally powerful authority at its head. Hooker addresses the Doctrine that *"wicked men grow most rebellious under the best Means"* (p. 221). The context of strong exertions of authority against powerful and corrupt enemies is implicit in Hooker's choice of a similitude. He says that streams become deep and powerful if damned up. Every man has a stream of corruption within him. If the ministers and the magistrates dam up that stream, there will be a violent struggle. You quickly weary of your minister and "your spirits vex at him! And so sometime at the Magistrate, if he be more zealous to reform abuses amongst men then ordinary" (p. 228). The combat is between the Devil and Christ, and the prize is the soul of each individual in "this congregation." So Hooker exhorts his hearers to give up their stiff-necked stubbornness and haughtiness to cultivate instead what he calls "a melting heart." That is to say, be teachable by the ministers of God; use the means properly and use the proper means. "Have a tender, yeelding, melting heart, . . . a pliable, teachable disposition, . . . give way to whatever is made known out of the Word" (p. 239). The "quarrel" between the minister and the sinner, says Hooker, is simply over the sinner's unwillingness to leave his sin. Again warning against unauthorized teachings in the community, he says, "Take heed of admitting any carnall reasonings against the truth revealed, and the plain Word of God openly manifested to you" (p. 242). The means of grace are abundantly available, he reminds his listeners; use them diligently, since either Christ or the Devil must have every soul. Above all, be convinced of the authority of the Word and do not depart from authorized teachers and teaching of it. Here Hooker is very clearly preaching to a congregation exposed on the one hand to false teachers and on the other to civil and religious authorities who are forcefully exercising their power. Though final proof is lacking, the evidence strongly suggests that this sermon may have been preached to the Boston congregation of Wilson and Cotton, where many members were still leaning in the direction of the Cotton-Wheelwright-Hutchinson teachings. In any case, Hooker is obviously addressing a congregation close to the eye of the storm.

Hooker devoted the remaining sermon in *The Saints Dignitie* to the important matter of selecting one's teacher. *Wisdomes Attendants; or, The Voice of Christ to be obeyed* was printed fourth in the collection, at its organizational center. Whereas in *Culpable Ignorance* and *Wilful Hardness* Hooker stressed the proper attitude of the learner who is seeking knowledge, here in *Wisdomes Attendants* he addresses the question of who is the proper source of spiritual wisdom, of true knowledge. Here again he takes as his text a verse from Proverbs: *"Now therefore hearken unto me, O ye children, for blessed are they that keep my wayes"* (Prov. 8:32). The speaker of this passage, Hooker explains, is Wisdom herself—which is to say, Christ. It is by this essentially typological reading of the Old Testament proverb that Hooker is able to create a decidedly Christian Doctrine for his sermon: *"The voice of the Lord Jesus Christ ought onely to be attended to, and must be obeyed of all his faithfull servants"* (SDD, p. 126). This is hardly a startling or unusual claim, putting the emphasis on the Word as it does, but when read in the context of the Antinomian controversy and the issue of true versus false authority that the dispute raised, the Doctrine has a double-pronged applicability. A central point implied in this Doctrine is promptly and explicitly stated: depending on Christ for one's direction also means not relying on mere men. "We must not listen and hearken to any of those delusions and silly devises, wherewith Satan, by the ministery of his instruments, laboureth to draw us

from the truth" (p. 130). And once "our mindes [are] truly inlightned
with the knowledge of Gods will; we must resolve not to hearken to
any perswasions to the contrary, though they be backed with never so
many shews of Religion or learning" (p. 131). While these warnings
could have been made in any place or time in Hooker's career, it
seems most probable that they derived special meaning for the audience from its awareness of the Hutchinsonian troubles. This seems all
the more likely since Hooker points out that "all Heretiques" refuse to
hear any beliefs but their own. "This policie the Devill useth in Popery, and amongst the *Familists*, and *Anabaptists*, teaching them to resolve to hold whatsoever they have received, either from themselves or
others" (p. 131).

The sermon ends with five Uses, four of which have more than passing significance in the Antinomian context. The first four are Uses of
reproof, initially of those who listen to "any thing . . . but to the voyce
of Christ," and next of those who get their truth from men, thinking to
gain somehow from this (*SDD*, p. 137). The fourth Use is a direct
reproof of the godly for not going first to Christ but to the carnal and
being unnecessarily troubled as a result. Finally, he puts some pressure on those who are overly influenced by their friends rather than by
the minister or the word of the Lord. He suggests that they had better
hear and obey Christ's counsel now or they must obey his "horrible
sentence" hereafter. "Knowing the terror of the Lord, let that scare
you more then the anger and displeasure of all the friends in the
world" (p. 147). He insists on the danger of being influenced by one's
friends when they are unredeemed. "What ever carnall friends shall
perswade you to, nothing shall doe you so much good, as the hearing
and obeying the voice of Christ" (p. 148). What is demanded of the
faithful is *obedience*—but of Christ and his ministers, not ungodly
"heretiques." Shepard spoke directly to this issue in Anne Hutchinson's trial in attesting that "I account her a verye dayngerous Woman
to sowe her corrupt opinions to the infection of many and therefore the
more neede you have to looke to her." And since by the time of the
actual trial John Cotton had done a strong turnabout, even he could
admonish Hutchinson's female friends for just the weakness to which
Hooker's sermon refers: "Next let me say somewhat to the Sisters of
our owne Congregation, many of whom I fear have bine too much
seduced and led aside by her; . . . *Let not the good you have receved
from her, make you to reaceve all for good that comes from her*; for
you see she is but a Woman and *many unsound and dayngerous principles are held by her*." Nor did he mince words when he turned from
addressing the "Sisters" to Mistress Hutchinson herself: "And soe your

opinions frett like a Gangrene and spread like a Leprosie, and infect farr and near, and will eate out the very Bowells of Religion."[41] Thomas Hooker, who had differed with Cotton in much, could not have agreed with him more on this point. In this context, Paul's word to the Romans, quoted on the title page of the first sermon in *The Saints Dignitie*, is strikingly applicable: "Through the offence of one, many be dead" unless the offsetting power of Christ through the gift of grace may "abound unto many."

There are still other suggestions in *The Saints Dignitie and Dutie* that Hooker was speaking in the context of the turmoil of the Antinomian controversy. At the very outset of his volume, Hooker cites the scriptural passage in Titus 2:3–5, which deals directly with the role and place of women, suggesting they should keep at home, be subject to their husbands, and, as the Geneva Bible puts it, "Aboue all things shewe thy self an ensample of good workes with uncorrupt doctrine." Numerous comments in the trial and in the hearing before it indicate that Mrs. Hutchinson's seemingly unfeminine, headstrong carryings-on were part of what set the authorities against her. Not only was she ambitious of being a *"Prophites,"* as Wilson had charged, but, as Hugh Peter put it to her, "you have stept out of your place, *you have rather bine a Husband than a Wife and a preacher than a Hearer; and a Magistrate than a Subject."*[42] When asked what "warrant" she had for conducting religious meetings at her house, she adamantly insisted, in the face of arguments from the formidable Winthrop, on the authority in Titus 2:3–5, which says that "older women" should "teach what is good, and so train the young women." In citing the same passage, however, Hooker stresses its close, where Paul says the young women are to be instructed in proper ways of submission, love, and other homely virtues, whereas Hutchinson chose simply to stress the admonition to teach. But it is clear enough that the passage is central to the question of whether or not she overstepped her bounds. Hooker's citation of the passage, though made in passing, would seem to be one more indication that he and his audience alike had the disputes in church and state very much in mind as he spoke.

It bears repeating that the evidence for *The Saints Dignitie and Dutie*'s being a document reflecting Hooker's views in the Antinomian controversy—and probably produced immediately by that controversy—is far from conclusive. Nowhere in the book does Hooker specifically name Anne Hutchinson, John Wheelwright, or John Cotton, and nowhere does he explain without ambiguity just what these "scandals" involving ministers in "this city" are. But considering the fact that not just one or two of the sermons, but every one deals with doctrinal or political issues (or both) that were at the very heart of the dispute, considering the references to scandals in a city where the means of grace are "more than ordinary," considering the late date of the volume and its likely editing by Hooker's son-in-law Thomas Shepard, thus suggesting the manuscript's origin in New England rather than Old England, the circumstantial evidence is strong for their having been preached in the Boston area in 1637 or later.

The Saints Dignitie and Dutie represents a fair summary of Hooker's views on the place of works in the life of the saint, the value of self-examination, the relationship between faith and justification, the need for informed, knowledgeable teachers, and the necessity for using the means regularly and following the lead of appointed or elected authority. On all of these views, Hooker and his party were triumphant. And on those points on which John Cotton disagreed, John Cotton was the loser. Hooker had no taste for public controversy or for the imposition of strong punishment, but after returning to Hartford he urged that John Winthrop use the latter.[43] He was greatly concerned for the preservation of true doctrine as well as public order in New England. The closely related group of sermons in *The Saints Dignitie and Dutie* represents his judicious but firm declaration of these concerns and their scriptural basis. And since it is his full, outspoken commentary on the central issues in the greatest crisis in the first decade of life in New England, *The Saints Dignitie and Dutie* deserves inclusion in the main body of literature produced by the controversy.

5

Advocating the New England Way

From the time of their arrival on New England's shores, the Puritan settlers were well aware of a need to prove the validity of their approach to worship and church organization. They established a congregational, nonhierarchical church polity and a form of worship which they considered to be purified of scripturally unsanctioned ceremonies. Winthrop indicated, in a phrase drafted aboard the *Arbella* before he ever set foot on New England soil, that the colonists were aware of building "a citie on a hill"; they were being watched. By the early 1640s England was in turmoil over some of the same issues that had driven the colonists away. English churchmen remained in touch with their New England brethren, making frequent, often skeptical inquiries as to their methods and progress in organizing a church in the wilderness. Thomas Hooker had a sizeable stake in the success of this experiment and wanted to be sure that success was made known to the English Church and state. The decade of the forties, therefore, saw the appearance of several Hooker works which defend the New Englanders' practice in doctrine and in polity. With one major exception, these works are among the least known of Hooker's writings, but together they represent his deep commitment to the cluster of ideas and religious practices which gave the colonists a new identity: the New England Way.

Doctrine

In the summer of 1642 letters arrived in Boston from English Puritan ministers and members of both houses of Parliament inviting Thomas Hooker, John Cotton, and John Davenport to attend the

Westminster Assembly as New England's representatives. This invitation was a singular honor to the three ministers; both Cotton and Davenport were sorely tempted to go. The New Haven church decided, however, that since Davenport was its only minister, he could not be spared. Cotton's mind was made up for him when more letters came from England suggesting that because the relationship between the king and Parliament was so volatile it might be well for New Englanders to stay home for the time being. Already Hooker had informed the messenger from Boston who had brought the letters of invitation to Hartford that he "liked not the business, nor thought it any sufficient call for them to go 3,000 miles to agree with three men"—referring to the small nucleus of Independents among the English delegates to the assembly.[1] There was finality in Hooker's reaction, but it did not mean that he also gave up hope of having a voice in the proceedings, which began the next year and lasted through 1649.

There is, in fact, convincing circumstantial evidence which suggests that after declining the invitation to attend, Hooker still attempted to influence the assembly's deliberations on doctrinal issues. The evidence is largely bibliographic, based on three of the four books Hooker published in London in 1645. A close examination of these works and the available information about their publication leads to three significant observations: first, these are the only works of their kind among all of Hooker's published books; second, their form was particularly well suited to catch the eye of members of the Westminster Assembly; and third, unlike nearly all of the twenty full-length Hooker works previously published, these were specifically prepared for and sent to the press by the author.

One of the books in question, *An Exposition of the Principles of Religion*, is a catechism, while the other two, *A Briefe Exposition of the Lords Prayer* and *Heavens Treasury Opened in a Fruitfull Exposition of the Lords Prayer*, provide a phrase-by-phrase theological explication of the Lord's Prayer. The latter two are essentially the same work, though textual variations make *A Briefe Exposition* appear to be a later, more stylistically authentic Hookerian text than that of *Heavens Treasury*.[2] More important, these books are not sermons, as practically all of Hooker's books published previously had been.[3] In its careful analysis of a Biblical text and in its occasional use of a question-and-answer method of explication, the work on the Lord's Prayer contains elements characteristic of Hooker's sermons, but the Puritan sermon structure—Text, Doctrine, Reasons, Uses—typically employed by Hooker is conspicuously lacking. The subtitle published in *A Briefe Exposition of the Lords Prayer* accurately describes the book's purpose and contents: *Wherein the meaning of the words is laid open to the understanding of weake Christians, and what the carriage of their hearts ought to be in preferring each Petition.* The book is, in other words, a guide to the Lord's Prayer and is meant to be read, not heard.

The same is true of *An Exposition of the Principles of Religion,* which is a full-fledged catechism, apparently structured on the model of William Perkins's *Foundation of Christian Religion, Gathered into Six Principles* (London, 1590). Hooker uses the same six "principles" as organizational heads for the six sections of his work, with the phrasing of the headings often so similar as to suggest that he probably had a copy of Perkins's catechism at hand in Hartford when writing his own. The contents, however, while in clear doctrinal agreement with Perkins's work, are definitely Hooker's own. The 193 questions and answers represent a drastically abridged version of the theology of preparation and redemption which was Hooker's lifelong pulpit concern and which is the chief topic of most of the more than six thousand pages of his writings. The form of this book, like that of the work on the Lord's Prayer, suggests the author's clear intention that the text be printed and read rather than heard by a congregation.

Two of the main items of business for the gathered divines at the Westminster Assembly were the preparation for Parliament's approval of a new confession of faith and a new catechism. Hooker may have expected that the confession would contain a careful examination of the Lord's Prayer or even that the assembly would issue a separate document on the topic. Either assumption would explain his lengthy elaboration of the prayer in *A Briefe Exposition.* Perhaps even more likely, given the explicative, question-and-answer methodology of the book and the announcement in the subtitle of its usefulness to "weake Christians," it was intended to influence the new catechism's treatment of the Lord's Prayer. The assembly did not address the meaning of the Lord's Prayer in the final version of its confession, but it did include a section of questions and answers on it in both the Larger and Shorter Catechisms, as did Hooker's and most other catechisms of the day. Thus, Hooker's catechism finally proved to be more relevant to the work of the assembly than did his treatises on the Lord's Prayer.

The chances that members of the assembly would notice Hooker's publications were good, even apart from the appropriateness of form of the books. His earlier books, though nearly always published without his authority, had established an audience in England, certainly including many of the assembly's delegates. Three of his books had gone through four or more editions by 1645.[4] Two decades earlier he had earned a wide reputation at Chelmsford as a Puritan preacher of great power and influence which was by no means forgotten.[5] The voice of Thomas Hooker was still known in the homeland, and he had good reason to hope that his newest works, eminently adaptable to the work of the assembly, would command attention.

And then, as Larzer Ziff has pointed out, "Although no New Englander attended the Westminster Assembly, the way of the churches in New England became a matter of widespread interest to those assembled. . . . News from New England . . . was of prime importance."[6] Hooker was not alone in his effort to respond. Apart from his books, however, the New Englanders' publications were generally on the subject of church polity, the issue on which there were the clearest differences with the majority of clergymen in old England.[7] John Cotton's *Keyes of the Kingdom of Heaven* (London, 1644) was such a work, matched in importance only by Hooker's own *Survey of the Summe of Church Discipline* (London, 1648). The latter work, which will be discussed later in this chapter, was also aimed at the assembly, though Hooker wrote it only after urgings by his New England colleagues that he answer the Presbyterian arguments on church polity by Samuel Rutherford. Published posthumously, *A Survey* has far surpassed Hooker's other two assembly-oriented works in reputation; indeed, it is often the only book mentioned in brief descriptive references to Hooker's life as an author. Taken together, however, *An Exposition of the Principles of Religion, A Briefe Exposition / Heavens Treasury*, and *A Survey of the Summe of Church Discipline* represent a three-pronged attempt to sway the deliberations of the Westminster Assembly on three main projects: the formulation of the Catechism and of the Confession and the establishing of a church polity.

In addition to the fact that Hooker's catechism and his exposition of the Lord's Prayer were written in forms unusual for him but forms in which the Westminster Assembly could be expected to produce its documents, there is also evidence that he sent these works to London for publication himself, using the departure of his son John for Oxford as the occasion and the means for breaking with his own precedent and seeking publication abroad.[8] All of this evidence argues special concern that these books reach an English readership.

That the books were read, at least by some members of the assembly, is a virtual certainty; that they were important influences on the actions of that body is more doubtful. There is no indication that any parts of Hooker's works were directly transposed into the assembly's finished products. In the case of his work on the Lord's Prayer, the main reason is probably that the assembly prepared no statement of comparable length on that prayer. The last eleven questions of the Larger Catechism and the final nine of the Shorter Catechism, which deal with the Lord's Prayer, used the same organizational divisions as did Hooker's much longer discussion (i.e., a preface, six "petitions," and a conclusion), but this view of the prayer's structure goes back to Calvin and to Bucer before him. Most of the points made about the Lord's Prayer in the Westminster Catechism were also made by Hooker. The major difference aside from length is that Hooker was largely interested in explaining the appropriate "frame of the heart" for making the prayer's several petitions to God, while this interest in spiritual psychology was totally absent from the Catechisms, which were solely concerned with the prayer's doctrinal meaning.

There also were a great many competing catechisms already in print and in wide use by 1645. Among those challenging Hooker's for the attention of the divines, besides John Calvin's, was one by Herbert Palmer,[9] the man whom the assembly put in charge of preparing the new, authoritative catechism. Others that were especially influential were John Ball's *Short Treatise, contayning the Principall Grounds of Christian Religion,* Ezekiel Rogers's *Chief Grounds of Christian Religion set down by way of catechising,* and Archbishop James Ussher's *Body of Divinity.* In all, about a dozen members of the assembly had written and published their own catechisms by 1643.[10] In addition, an examination of the *Stationers Register* for 1645 alone reveals that no fewer than ten catechisms were registered for that year. This spate of new catechisms was bound to reduce even further the chances that Hooker's would carry any special weight.

Still, Hooker's *Exposition of the Principles of Religion* was doubtless among the catechisms known and even consulted in the final stages of the composition of the Larger and Shorter Catechisms. Alexander F. Mitchell, the most knowledgeable historian on the preparation of the catechisms, has pointed out that several "distinctly Calvinistic" catechisms ultimately became more important influences than Herbert Palmer's own, which had been the basis for the initial deliberations. It was in late 1646 and early 1647, especially after the completion of the Confession of Faith in December 1646,[11] that the most fruitful and definitive work on the Larger and Shorter Catechisms was accomplished. Also in that month Philip Nye, the famous and outspoken Independent who was later co-editor of Hooker's major posthumous publications, was added to the catechism committee of the assembly.[12] He would certainly have known of Hooker's new books. At this stage, according to Mitchell, "the doctrinal teaching" of the new work took on "a more pronounced Calvinistic character." "More strictly Puritan treatises rather than Palmer's" were being followed in creating, among other details, "the questions and answers as to the covenants of works and grace, . . . and the effectual calling, justification, adoption, and sanctification and perseverance of those who have been made partakers of redemption, and even the detailed and specific statements as to the sinfulness of the estate into which man fell."[13] Mitchell lists seven "distinctively Calvinistic catechisms" which contain the kinds of emphases present in the revised versions, implying that all or some of them were probably important influences at this crucial stage of the committee's work.[14] The influence of any of these is no more or less likely, however, than of Thomas Hooker's, which Mitchell might well have included in the list, since Hooker's catechism, consistent with his whole preaching ministry, makes a special effort to emphasize the stages of redemption and the sinful condition from which man is redeemed. As the deliberations of the catechism committee moved away from Palmer's text and increasingly stressed traditional Calvinistic points of doctrine, the group swung decidedly in the direction of Hooker's own emphasis in their ordering and explanation of God's nature and abilities, Adam's fall and man's inheritance of his guilt, the availability of redemption through Christ, and the several sequential stages of redemption, although the Westminster Catechisms lack Hooker's special emphasis on the preparatory stages of contrition and humiliation. These are similarities, however, which undoubtedly depend chiefly on Hooker's being largely in doctrinal agreement with most other Puritan leaders rather than on any thoroughgoing debt of the assembly's catechism committee to Hooker's *Exposition.*

There are, moreover, differences which are fully as important as the similarities. Hooker omits any consideration of the Ten Commandments and of the sacraments, both of which are discussed at some length in the Westminster works. Unlike the assembly's versions, Hooker's catechism ends—as had Ussher's, Perkins's, and others—with several questions and answers on the Last Judgment, a topic the assembly did not consider in the catechisms but treated in the Confession of Faith. Just as noticeable as the differences in doctrinal content, of which I have mentioned only the most glaring, are the pronounced differences in style and tone. Hooker's catechism bears his personal stamp in its roughnesses of cadence and sentence structure as well as in its helpful and lively metaphors, similes, and analogies, major sources of Hooker's rhetorical power that are completely absent from the comparatively antiseptic catechisms produced by the assembly's committee. A final distinction lies in Hooker's organization of his catechism upon the chronological progression of the soul from its first awareness of God to its final achievement of glory at the Day of Judgment, whereas the assembly seems to have been more concerned simply with converting the contents of its Confession of Faith into catechetical form. The Westminster Catechisms are chiefly doctrinal definitions, while Hooker's *Exposition* also conveys an impression of the author's personal concern for and involvement in the life of the individual Christian soul.

Hooker's impact on the doctrinal statements of the Westminster Assembly, despite his wishes to the contrary, was rather slight. Had he attended, it might have been a different matter, since his skill as a disputant could then have been more immediately brought to bear. The question, of course, is irrelevant since his decision was never in doubt. He felt instinctively what Davenport needed to be told: his place was in his New England pulpit. He was always a preacher first and, by his own choosing, never principally a publisher of books or a controversialist. What is remarkable is not that he should have declined to attend the assembly or that his writings should have had little demonstrable effect on that body's deliberations but that he should have chosen to send two books in his place. That he did is a sign both of his continuing concern for the direction of the Church in England and of his willingness to assume that his doctrinal contributions were both valuable and authoritative. Hooker's removal by some three thousand miles could not, it would seem, remove the tug of involvement in the central concerns of the Church of England.

Polity

If there was no drastic disagreement among the delegates to the Westminster Assembly on central points of doctrine, the same can hardly be said in the matter of church polity. They were all, of course, agreed that the episcopacy must go. The methods used in selecting delegates had insured that those friendly to traditional Anglican ways were almost entirely screened out. It was a largely "Puritan" aggregation, including the considerable variety of minds and attitudes which that broad term suggests. So as a group they had an essential unanimity in the belief that the excessive repressions and dictatorial attitudes of the Church under Laud and his bishops had demonstrated beyond question that fundamental restructuring was necessary. This eventuality was doubted by no one; when the assembly convened on July 1, 1643, Archbishop Laud had already been imprisoned in the Tower for over two years, some of his bishops were also in prison, and still others were in seclusion or hiding.

Parliament convened the assembly for the express purpose of revising and renewing the accepted doctrines, forms of worship, and organization of the Church; but the commissioners arrived for the task in varying stages of readiness to proceed, particularly in the matter of discipline. The group most prepared to prescribe a system was the delegation of four ministers and two laymen from the Scottish Kirk, who were apparently convinced that the events of the time—most notably the British Parliament's signing of the Solemn League and Covenant with Scotland, seeming to promise adoption of Scottish Presbyterianism in England in exchange for support by Scotland's army—had providentially conspired to enable them to carry the day.[15] Their confidence in their ability to set up Presbyterianism throughout England is summarized in the report of Robert Baillie to a Scottish correspondent that "we doubt not to carry all according to our mind."[16] They had the advantage of having recently established the Presbyterian discipline in the Scottish Church and, under this momentum, felt confident, as one historian has put it, of exporting their revolution.[17]

The English "Presbyterians" and the Independents were not nearly so prepared, it seems, to declare a fully blown system which, after acceptance by the assembly and Parliament, would become normative for the British Church. Oliver Cromwell himself could not be at all specific about what kind of church government could best replace episcopacy; and the leading Independents in the assembly stated, at the beginning of several years of prolonged debate between their side and the Presbyterians, that one of the three guiding principles of their congregationalist churches in exile in Holland, whence they had very recently returned, was to *avoid* making present practices binding on the future.[18] This cautious policy, however judicious, quickly proved inappropriate in dealing with opponents as positive as the Scottish Presbyterians, and the tone of most of the Independents' arguments thereafter is stiffer and more decisive. Since the assembly's very purpose was to make just such binding determinations on church organization and doctrine, timidity to pronounce the truth—for others as well as for oneself—had to be overcome.

The English Independents, however, seem not to have been given nearly so much to disputing in print as their Scottish opponents, who opened a veritable barrage of propaganda insisting on the truth and superiority of their discipline, while often attacking other systems—particularly that of the Independents—as the tools of the Antichrist. The Scottish offensive was not only loud and voluminous; it began early and lasted long. The Scots were already in high gear when the assembly convened, since they had really expected to convert the English Church to Presbyterianism in the winter of 1640–41, when the covenant was signed with the king agreeing on a uniform church system between the Scots and English. Directing their aim mainly at Laud and episcopacy, the Scottish Presbyterians had then produced Alexander Henderson's *Government and Order of the Church of Scotland* (Edinburgh, 1641), George Gillespie's *Assertion of the Government of the Church of Scotland* (London, 1641), Samuel Rutherford's *Peaceable and Temperate Plea for Pavl's Presbyterie in Scotland* (London, 1642), and several vehemently antiprelatical tracts by the fiery Robert Baillie.[19] So when the king failed to heed the Scottish wish for universal establishment of Presbyterianism and Parliament convened the Westminster Assembly to debate and settle the matter, the Scots already had their throats cleared and their arguments lined up. And they were impatient to boot. In accepting the invitation to send delegates to the assembly,[20] they dispatched Baillie, Rutherford, Gillespie, and two laymen, all under the leadership of Alexander Henderson, who at the time was probably the most eminent man in the Scottish Church, though he was also more willing to compromise on church discipline and less inclined to publish controversial tracts than his fellow commissioners.

The Scots quickly discovered that their major opponents on the issue of church discipline were the Independents, or, as they preferred to be called, the "Dissenting Brethren," a title which more clearly indicates their minority status in the gathering. It was not long before the Scots, along with some of the more aggressive English Presbyterians such as Charles Herle and Daniel Cawdry, began to spread the case for Presbyterianism before the public. In 1644 there appeared Henderson's *Reformation of the Church Government in Scotland Cleared*, Gillespie's anonymous *Recrimination . . . upon Mr.* [Thomas] *Goodwin, in Defence of Presbyterianism*, and Rutherford's *Due Right of Presbyteries*. Each of these books recognizes and refutes the arguments for congregational church government.

Thus, regardless of doubts regarding the wisdom of committing one's principles to paper, the Independent faction was forced to respond or be shouted down. Their first significant statement was issued jointly and called *An Apologeticall Narration, Humbly Submitted to the Honourable Houses of Parliament* (1643), in which they claimed that the congregational system comprised "a *middle way* betwixt that which is falsly charged on us, *Brownisme;* and that which is the contention of these times, the *authoritative Presbyteriall Government* in all the subordinations and proceedings of it."[21] Since the Scottish commissioners also claimed to represent a middle road between two evils— independency and prelacy[22]—the crunch was obviously on. Thousands of words were spent thereafter, both in floor debate in the assembly and in print, in the increasingly futile efforts to find grounds for accommodation between the warring factions. But after the *Apologeticall Narration*—which seems in large part an abortive attempt by the Independents to present the appearance of willingness to cooperate and be reasonable—we do not find Philip Nye and Thomas Goodwin, the chief debaters for Independency, rushing into print to answer the steady flow of printed attacks from the opposition. Nor do Sidrach Simpson, Jeremiah Burroughs, or William Bridge appear to have been particularly inclined to wage battle in the presses. They seem early on to have adopted the practice of arguing their case steadily and strenuously on the floor of the assembly and, when possible, relying on assistance in the form of political pressures from the House of Commons, where Cromwell and numerous of his followers comprised a stronger body of Independents than could be found in the assembly.

For the necessary task of debating and overcoming the Presbyterians in the press, the English Independents chose to rely mainly on their New England colleagues. Douglas Horton has suggested four reasons why the English Independents asked the New England pastors to answer the twenty-four questions put to them by William Apollonius.[23] Three of these reasons are applicable to the pattern of the entire debate: the time of the five dissenting brethren was too much occupied with the daily business of the assembly to write adequate answers to the numerous attacks on their position; the New Englanders had given the congregational structure a practical trial and were therefore the best informed proponents of its workability; and they were proven controversialists. Beyond this, of course, lies the fact that the New Englanders, fully as much as the Scots, felt that the time was now, if ever, for the prophesying of the validity and truth of *their* system to the reforming English Church, from which they had obstinately refused to separate, whatever their opponents might insinuate regarding their alleged Brownism. They had claimed from the outset of their colonial experiment that they would set an example which would show their English brethren the pure way of church organization. With the convening of an assembly at Westminster one of whose central purposes was the reformation of this very element in the nation's religious life, New Englanders could not help feeling, as Thomas Hooker said, that "the managing *of the outward kingdome*, unless my prospective much deceives me, is coming towards its last triall."[24] It was, in their view, nothing less than the time when God's prophecies for the perfecting of his church would be fulfilled and in that fulfillment New England had a special role to play. Alluding to the existence of New England's smoothly functioning congregational churches, Hooker held that "its a received rule, and I suppose most safe, *when Prophecies are fulfilled they are best interpreted,* the accomplishment of them is the best Commentary" (*A Survey,* sig. a). This view naturally made New England ministers entirely willing to be the English Independents' bulldogs despite their usual modesty in prefatory remarks to their treatises about their fallibility where truth is concerned. They did feel that they were appointed to a prophetic role in the important matter of English church reform.

In fact, all parties involved in the debate over church polity appear to have felt that they were engaged in no less a task than producing the final revelation of truth on this subject. Some of the participants, including both Hooker and Rutherford, used metaphors of childbirth and midwifery to underline their view of the historic consequences to which their millions of words would lead. Many "are travailing in paine," wrote John Spilsbery, "to bring forth that man-childe [truth]." Hooker agreed with Spilsbery's metaphor if not with his Anabaptist ideas.[25] The time has come, said Hooker, for the "delivery" of truth, which is why so many of God's "Worthies" have taken up pen "(midwife like) to lighten and ease the throws of the truth, in this sharp and sore travell for a safe delivery" (*A Survey,* sig. a2). Indeed, not the least of these worthies, Hooker points out, has been Samuel Rutherford, who has in the past valiantly opposed the errors of the Arminians.[26]

Hooker places his own chief contribution to the debate in such an historical perspective as to indicate his sense of the climactic importance of his and his fellow New Englanders' role in the history of Christendom. The preface to *A Survey of the Summe of Church Discipline* offers a brief sketch of the history of Christendom up to the present moment. Hooker views the history of the Church since Christ's ascension as having followed a sort of inverted bell curve. The decline of Christ's recognized stature at the head of his church began almost immediately, as the "hellish delusions" of a "wretched generation of Hereticks" took a foothold for some three hundred years, denying on the one hand Christ's divinity and on the other his humanity. "This made way for Antichrist, and did Midwife that man of sin [i.e., the pope] into the world." Gradually *men* encroached on the three "offices," or roles, belonging only to Christ, those of priest, prophet, and king. "The Spouse of Christ," the Church, was slowly but surely "taken aside by the slumber of Idolatry, till at last *she fell asleep*" (*A Survey,* sig. A2v, A3). Then finally, after Boniface III had managed to subordinate all churches in Christendom to the Bishop of Rome,[27] Hildebrand gave the pope power to confirm or refuse to confirm the emperor himself. At this point, with the pope established as superior to all, the truth of Christ and man's love for this truth had fallen into the deep decline in which they remained for some eight hundred years until the first stirrings of the Reformation, when truth began to climb back towards ascendancy. First, Hooker says, the combined efforts of the Waldensians, Armachanus, Wycliffe, and Jerome of Prague restored Jesus "as the only PROPHET of his Church." Then Luther eliminated the financial rewards of indulgences and "wonderfully cooled and quenched the fire of Purgatory, and the Popes kitchin" (*A Survey*, sig. [A4]), thus restoring Christ to his rightful priestly office. Finally the pope's assumption of "KINGLY POWER" was attacked and eliminated by, first, the actions of the Councils of Constance and Basel, and then in England, King Henry VIII's assumption of the leadership of the Church. Henry, in the Puritans' view, did not go far enough, however, since "he *cut off the head of Popery, but left the body of it* (in *Arch-Bishops, Primates, Metropolitans, Archdeacons*) yet within his realm" (*A Survey*, sig. [A4v]). Further progress was made in England with the establishing of a "Parity in the Ministery" (presumably referring to the abolition of episcopacy in the Interregnum), thus eliminating the arbitrary power of bishops over ministers. Now it remains to decide where "Ecclesiasticall power" shall rest, with presbyteries or with individual churches.

Having no doubt what the correct answer is, Hooker is willing to offer his views in favor of power to the people simply because the time—the moment in the long history of Christendom—is so propitious for the final establishment of the people's liberty. It would be wrong, he says, for the saints to "loose their cause and comfort" merely because they remained silent. It would be "not selling but casting away their inheritance, and right, by a carelesse silence, when the course of providence, as the juncture of things now present themselves, allows a writt *Ad melius inquirendum*" (*A Survey*, sig. a). Whereas John Cotton in *The Powrring out of the Seven Vials* (1642) had cited Revelation 16 to show the special importance of the present day, Hooker cites a variety of scripture passages, including Revelation 11:15, where the sounding of the seventh trumpet signifies the bringing together under Christ of all the kingdoms of the earth. Not being as inclined to apocalyptic, visionary interpretation of Scripture as John Cotton, he is no less sure than his fellow colonist that New England's strenuous argument for congregational polity is a divinely appointed duty in the climax of Christian history.[28] And he sees himself and his New English co-defenders of congregationalism as the prophets to whom is appointed the climactic function of bringing truth into the ascendancy for the first time since the ascension of Christ.

If Hooker and Cotton presented the historical context of their present enterprise most comprehensively, their colleagues in New England
rallied to the cause whole-heartedly, producing a formidable body of
literature on church polity during the 1640s. The year 1643, when a
synod at Cambridge fulfilled Hooker's dream in establishing a formal
confederation of the several New England colonies,[29] was the date of
the first concerted efforts by New England ministers to answer questions and criticisms from abroad, some of which had begun before the
Westminster Assembly was convened, but all of which after July 1,
1643, became relevant to that body's deliberations. In that year,
Richard Mather's chief work on polity, *Church-Government and
Church-Covenant Discussed,* appeared, as did John Davenport's *Answer of the Elders . . . unto Nine Positions* and the consensus paper
called *An Apologie of the . . . Elders in New-England for Church
Covenant.* Also in 1643 Charles Herle, an English Presbyterian member
of the assembly, attacked the New England Way in his *Independency
of Churches.* This was answered promptly by Mather and the pastor at
Braintree, Benjamin Tompson, in *A Modest & Brotherly Answer to Mr
Charles Herle his Book, against the Independency of Churches* (London, 1643). John Cotton published several works on the subject, beginning with *The Doctrine of the Church* (1643), followed by the more
definitive *The Keyes of the Kingdom of Heaven* (1644), and finally *The
Way of the Congregational Churches Cleared* (1648), the last answering Robert Baillies's *Dissuasive from the Errours of the Time* (1645)
and addressing particular issues raised by Daniel Cawdry's *Vindiciae
Clavium* (1645) and Samuel Rutherford's *Due Right of Presbyteries*
(1644). The well-known Dutch Presbyterian minister and theologian at
Middleburg, William Apollonius, sent a set of twenty-four questions to
the New England ministers which were answered by John Norton's
Responsio ad totam quaestionum syllogen. . . . (1648).[30] All of these
books were written, if not published, in the years 1643–45, before the
clear numerical superiority of the Presbyterians in the assembly had
been conceded and prior to the political developments of 1647 and
later, when Cromwell's forces temporarily gave the day to the Independents in spite of the assembly's recommendations.

Hooker's major contribution to the cause of congregationalism, *A
Survey of the Summe of Church Discipline,* also dates from the same
period, even though it was not published until 1648. When the Cambridge synod of 1643 was doling out duties in the coming anti-
Presbyterian war of words and policy, Thomas Hooker was asked to
write a refutation of Samuel Rutherford's *Peaceable and Temperate Plea
for Pavls Presbyterie* (1642); though reluctant, he accepted the assign-

ment, presumably because he felt a duty as a church leader in New England to help to defend the congregational system against all charges. After Hooker's return to Hartford, Rutherford's second volume appeared under the title *The Due Right of Presbyteries; or, A Peaceable Plea, for the Government of the Church of Scotland* (1644), which Hooker, by then working on his own book, also refuted, finally giving more attention to Rutherford's later than to his earlier book.[31] Before Hooker was through, in fact, Samuel Hudson, an English Presbyterian, published *The Essence and Unitie of the Church Catholike Visible* (London, 1645), which Hooker also refuted in the fifteenth chapter of Part I of his work. He was apparently finished with "this so hard a task" by late 1645, and at "a common meeting" of the New England elders on July 1, 1645, "*was desired by them all, to publish what I now do.*"[32] The manuscript was put aboard a ship but went, with its cargo of saints, to the bottom of the ocean. Hooker then had the unenviable task of sitting down and writing the book again at a time when his letters to Shepard indicate that he was increasingly infirm. He died before the book was ready to be sent off the second time. The "overseers" of his will, Hopkins and Goodwin, mention in a one-page prefatory "epistle" that he had not finished the final section on synods, and they add some notes "found in his study" on that subject as the final pages in the book. But the work, in its four hundred octavo pages, was essentially complete—enough so to stand for centuries as one of the major explanations of the earliest form of non-separatist New England congregationalism. In Congregational circles, in fact, Hooker's fame has long rested largely on this book, despite its being a product of a partisan dispute that was already a dead issue in England if not New England by the early 1650s. To the modern reader, this persistent fame of *A Survey* contains abundant irony, since the book is, of all Hooker's works, the one most a product of his rational faculty alone and most a product of ephemeral circumstances. Relying as it does throughout on the syllogistic method of argumentative refutation, the book surely represents more fully than any other his familiarity with the methods of the Schoolmen and his thorough grounding in Aristotelian-Ramistic logical principles. For this chore he laid aside his pastoral concern with psychological and emotional complexities.

Yet *A Survey* was written to fulfill a very explicit requirement which Hooker's New England colleagues laid on him: to answer the arguments for Presbyterianism and against congregationalism published by the formidable Samuel Rutherford. Hooker nevertheless managed to use the publications of Rutherford as a workable excuse for presenting both rational and scriptural defenses of the central tenets of congregationalism. This was no small achievement considering the comprehensive scope of Rutherford's arguments and the multitude of scholarly references in Rutherford's two books, which total just under twelve hundred pages. Rutherford was one of the foremost men in the Scottish Kirk; after Alexander Henderson's death in 1646, in fact, he is said to have been "by far the most eminent man in the Church of Scotland."[33] He was a professor of divinity at St. Mary's College, St. Andrews, and relied on his broad familiarity with theological and ecclesiastical scholarship to embellish his arguments in *A Peaceable and Temperate Plea* and *The Due Right of Presbyteries*. Thomas Murray, an early biographer, commented very much to the point in observing that Rutherford's tomes are characterized "by great, though probably unnecessary, erudition."[34]

Hooker's answer is much more restrained than Rutherford's assertions in this respect. He was particularly conscious of the seemly virtue of plainness, as he explained in his preface: "I have ever thought writings that come abroad, they are not to dazle, but direct the apprehensions of the meanest, and I have accounted it the chiefest part of Iudicious learning, to make a hard point easy and familiar in explication" (*A Survey*, sig. b). He reminds his reader that his treatise comes "*out of the wildernesse*, where curiosity is not studied. Planters if they can provide cloth to go warm, they leave the cutts and lace to those that study to go fine" (*A Survey*, sig. [a4v]). Yet despite these claims of New World stylistic rusticity, he felt a need to mention his insistent use of tight logical reasoning, excusing himself by saying he had no choice, given "the nature of the subject"; the tool of the syllogism, he says, was ready-made to his purpose, as anyone else who attempted the same task would readily see. And he by no means avoids references to previous authorities, though he relies much more heavily on scriptural than on secular proofs. In fact, he cites or quotes the works of over fifty authorities on various aspects of his subject, ranging in date from Aristotle to Ames. He depends most heavily on the several anti-Roman works of controversy by two men: William Ames—especially his *Medulla* but also his 1626 attack on Bellarmine, *Enervatus Bellarminus*—and William Whitaker, the important Calvinist master of St. John's College, Cambridge, in the generation of William Perkins. These two authorities are each cited at least a dozen times, while Beza and Bucer among the Reformers, and Parker and Junius among the moderns, are also frequently helpful to Hooker. The additional authorities cited give full evidence of the ample range and depth of the leading Puritans' scholarship and undoubtedly offer insight into the contents of Hooker's personal library in Hartford,[35] which we know to have been valued at the considerable sum of £300 at his death but the exact contents of which can be told only by inference from such evidence as this. In his earlier works he occasionally shadowed forth his familiarity with early and late authorities, but here we find a wealth of references to authors of the likes of Thomas Aquinas, Duns Scotus, Augustine, Chrysostom, Bellarmine, Origen, Peter Martyr, Ambrose, Durand, Zanchius, Calvin, Paraeus, Plesseus, Zepper, Piscator, Musculus, Cajetan, Vasquez, Chamierus, Robinson, Perkins, Ainsworth, Cartwright, Ball, Lord Brooke, Bishop Bilson, and many others. Yet even with all of these references to his reading, Hooker's treatise is much less weighted down by scholarship than are Rutherford's, which often strike one as simply pompous in their display of learning. Hooker indicated well enough that though a mere "Planter," as he claimed, he was equipped not only with a long exposure to the libraries and public debates of Cambridge but also with a good knowledge of current publications, so that Rutherford, writing several years after Hooker's death, though not about to concede as much as a single point of debate, at least felt obliged to "give testimonie to his Learning, his dexterous Eloquence and Accuracy in Disputes."[36] Coming from an unbending man like Rutherford such grudging acknowledgement might have seemed almost satisfactory enough to Hooker.[37]

Hooker approached his argumentative chore as one requiring, first, a sorting out of the grounds on which the New Englanders and Rutherford agreed and disagreed and, secondly, answering Rutherford on the points of disagreement. He did the sorting with admirable succinctness in his preface, listing there twelve points of agreement with Rutherford and mentioning that there are "severall other particulars" on which he sees no need to argue. Then, as he lists some seventeen major points of disagreement which he will explore in his text, he argues for liberality on both sides in approaching issues over which men differ. His understanding of the healthy spirit of debate, inbred in him by his Cambridge experience as scholar, tutor, and fellow, is reflected in his observation, pointedly aimed at the unbending Scottish Presbyterians: "He that will estrange his affection, because of the difference of apprehension in things difficult, he must be a stranger to himself one time or other. If men would be tender and carefull to keep off offensive expressions, they might keep some distance in opinion, in some things, without hazard to truth or love. But when men set up their sheaves (though it be but *in a dream,* as *Josephs* was) and fall out with every one, that will not fall down and adore them, they will bring much trouble into the world, but little advantage to the truth, or peace" (A Survey, sig. [a4]). He further expresses the hope that learned men may, as a consequence of his work, point out deeper truths than he or his New England colleagues presently perceive so that they may judge of their value, adding the necessary point that *so far*, the arguments against the New England Way have been too weak to convince them to change their practice or beliefs. He had not so whole-heartedly entered into public debate in the press since his preface to *A Fresh Suit*. Though the writing of *A Survey* was no doubt a burdensome assignment in the midst of his other work, one is frequently struck by his resonant tone of obvious enjoyment in the exercise of his argumentative powers, after keeping them in check for many years. At one point, in discussing what he sees as the confusion of the Roman Catholic Schoolmen on the subject of ordination, he admits to "sporting" self-indulgently in this exposure of Protestantism's arch-foes (A Survey, pt. 2, p. 52). He resorts to tricks as well as fair play in his arguments, often incriminating Rutherford and the Presbyterians by associating their views with popery, as he does in discussing their stand on ecclesiastical power and the nature of the Church at large. It is fair to say that, in giving free play to his mastery of the methods of debate, even though he might have preferred not to have had to write the book, he did enjoy himself.

In reducing Rutherford's lengthy discussions to manageable terms and size, Hooker divided the subject into four parts, devoting a separate section of his book to each. The first and longest of these deals with the essentially theological subject of the "rise and essence" of the Church. Here he considers such questions as, What makes a church? Is there such a thing as an organized Church Universal? With whom does the power of a church reside? What does church membership signify? Such questions expose the central distinctions between the Presbyterian and Congregationalist viewpoints. It quickly becomes obvious that the basic point of Hooker's argument is that "power" (i.e., the ability to call ministers, ordain officers, and discipline or excommunicate other members) belongs to the church members at large rather than to church officers and presbyteries, as the Presbyterians would have it. This is an essentially democratic thrust in Hooker's message and is consciously intended as such. The observation that "the power of the Keyes is committed to the Church of confederate Saints as the first and proper subject thereof" is, says Hooker, a "truth" which is "of greatest worth and waight" (A Survey, pt. 1, p. 192). Each member is thus "a judge of his brother" (p. 195), having equal power and responsibility with all other members. Hooker readily acknowledged that there is considerable variation in the spiritual and rational abilities of church members, but he insisted that all members who have received the grace of God—even the simple—also possess at least a minimum level of rational discernment enabling them to make necessary distinctions such as identifying heresies, for instance (pp. 204–5). In making his case here Hooker quotes Rutherford in order to refute him, highlighting the reputed Presbyterian desire to reserve power to the privileged few (and making them in the process sound rather like the Anglicans). Rutherford: "That which maketh the government of Gods house Democraticall and popular, is not to be taught."[38] Hooker: *"The Government of the Church, in regard of the Body of the People is Democraticall: in regard of the Elders Aristocraticall; in regard of Christ, truely Monarchicall.* And its such a compound of all these three, as that a paralell [sic] example to the like perfection, is not to be found on earth" (p. 206).

This sympathy for the integrity of the individual soul carried over from Hooker's thoughts on church organization to his ideas on political theory and practice. His famous sermon in Hartford on May 31, 1638, usually credited with having had a formative influence on the soon-to-be-drafted Fundamental Orders of Connecticut, focuses on just this point. He preached on the Doctrines that "the choice of public magistrates belongs unto the people by Gods own allowance" and that "they who have power to appoint officers and magistrates it is in their power also to set the bounds and limits of the power and places into which they may call them."[39] Just as the people select a minister, so should they select their magistrates. And these officers should not be given arbitrary power but clearly assigned prerogatives and limits of power. As this sermon states, Hooker fully agreed with Roger Williams that "the foundation of authority is laid 1stly in the free consent of people." Thus, in both realms, the secular and the ecclesiastical, Hooker was committed to the basic principle of democratic government which gives the governed power to select and to restrain those over them.[40] It is very likely that his opinion on secular political power and its origin derived from his long consideration of the issue in church politics.

At the heart of much of the debate over church polity was the fundamental disagreement over what a church is. Rutherford argues that until a congregation could partake of the sacraments it was not a church at all. Hooker disagreed, saying that it was indeed a church, in essence if not in full practice, since the existence of a church in no way depended upon a minister's presence or the existence of higher legal bodies. There are, he explained, a "Materiall Cause" and a "Formall

Cause" involved in effecting a church. The material cause is a group of visible saints. Several scholars have recently made this concept abundantly clear, but what is perhaps not quite so clear is the willingness with which the New Englanders—and Hooker in particular—admitted that *all* churches contained false saints—hypocrites who were able to pass for visible saints, join the church, and enjoy all its benefits. Visible saints are the only "fit Matter" to constitute a church; but, as Hooker says repeatedly, the elders and membership judge a candidate "according to the rules of reasonable charity" (*A Survey*, pt. 1, pp. 15–16),[41] which is simply the best that can be done by fallible men acting in fairness and retaining their own humility before God. Necessarily, hypocrites will get in. This does not particularly concern Hooker. The damage such hypocrites do is to their own souls, not to the congregation. So while in principle the church is composed of visible saints, in practice it is less than pure. These saints establish a church in the first place by declaring a mutual covenant with each other, which is their "Formall Cause." This *"free consent and mutuall ingagement . . . is as it were the sement*, which soders the whole together: or like the mortising or brazing of the building, which gives fashion and firmnesse to the whole." It *"gives constitution and being to a visible* Church" (pt. 1, p. 46). Once a church is established in covenant, all new members must subscribe to the covenant, thus keeping the church a true community of saints pledged to each other's spiritual welfare. "The *bond of Church-confederacy*," he wrote, "engageth the one to the other more then any other Christians in the world" (pt. 3, p. 2). The strength of a church is thus determined by the individuals' commitment to a covenant rather than by the power of a ruling authority.

Another theoretical issue of some importance which Hooker debated with both Rutherford and Hudson was whether or not an "invisible" catholic church "as Totum integrale," consisting of all individual churches as its members, exists at all. Hudson's book argues that such a church does exist and that it has a primary power over individual churches. Hooker simply disagrees on both points, insisting that "the true Church of Christ," and the only one supported by the Scriptures, is the *"particular congregation."* To claim the contrary looks like a *"Popish Tenent."*[42] It is also thoroughly impractical since, in a system where membership includes power to admit and excommunicate members and to call a minister, every church would presumably have to consult all the others in taking any such routine actions. The obvious impracticality of such a procedure is enough to point up the absurdity of the opposition's argument. Hooker's method is a convincing *reductio ad absurdum.*

The second, third, and fourth parts of *A Survey* deal with more clearly pragmatic questions relating to the operation of the church. Part 2 explains the structure of individual churches, what officers are required, and what their duties are. The first chapter of this section gives an admirably clear explanation of the duties—all quite distinct—of the pastor, teacher, ruling elder, and the deacon, omitting only a description of the function of the widows, a church office now long since assumed by the deacons but once kept separate. Since Hooker includes the office in his table of church offices, the omission of any discussion of it may be one sign of the incompleteness of the manuscript which went to press. Of special interest today because seldom noticed is the distinction which Hooker makes between the duties of the pastor and the teacher. Whereas the pastor's job was "to work upon the will and the affections" (*A Survey*, pt. 2, p. 19), the teacher, or doctor, was expected "to informe the judgement, and to help forward the work of illumination, in the minde and understanding, and thereby to make way for the truth, that it may be setled and fastned upon the heart" (p. 21). Whereas the teacher, then, delivers the fundamentals of faith, "the principles of Religion," handling textual interpretation and doctrinal controversy, the job of the pastor is to "endeavour by heat of exhortation to quicken . . ., strengthen and incourage the soul in every holy word and work" to "speak a good word for Christ, make up the marriage, and betroth the soul to our Saviour" (pp. 19–21). Nowhere in all the Puritans' writings are we apt to find so clear a demonstration of their insistence on the separateness of the various faculties in man's psychological makeup. In actual practice, of course, it was well nigh impossible for a preacher to avoid one or the other of these functions and to limit himself entirely to working on his hearers' minds or will and affections. Hooker, in his sermons, certainly did both. But in keeping with this division of labor he may well have left the catechizing and Biblical instruction to his congregation's teacher, Samuel Stone. Faculty psychology was the intellectual assumption which most thoroughly pervaded all aspects of the Puritans' religious lives, and in thus making it the basis for distinguishing between the duties of pastor and teacher, they were insisting on its importance to the public as well as private dimension of their faith. Indeed, in the disagreement with the Presbyterians which produced *A Survey*, the Congregationalist/Independent faction had distinguished themselves from their opponents early in the proceedings by holding out for two ministers in every congregation.

Hooker's disagreement with Rutherford becomes even more pronounced as he continues in part 2, discussing the theory and practice of ordination and the concept of Independency. And in part 3, where *"the Government of the Church"* is duly considered, he takes up an issue which is still more interesting and more important for modern readers. English critics had persistently inquired and complained about the New Englanders' seemingly exclusive membership requirements, whereby they demanded a confession and statement regarding one's possession of grace before admission and whereby they withheld the sacraments of baptism and communion from all nonmembers. The lists of questions from England typically contained requests for clarification and/or justification of this practice. Hooker, therefore, approaches the subject of admission to membership with some deliberateness in *A Survey,* and the result is one of the clearest descriptions of procedure in admitting applicants to membership produced by his generation. It has been argued that Hooker was somewhat more lenient in his enforcement of membership requirements than other of his New England colleagues, especially John Cotton.[43] This claim is borne out by his comments here and in scattered remarks in published sermons, though the system he prescribes is certainly intended to discourage those who may be in doubt about their readiness for membership. In brief, he says that the person wishing to apply for membership must make this known, not to the minister necessarily, but to the ruling elder, a layman duly elected to the office by the congregation. This elder then informs himself, both through questioning the person and through conducting a sort of local inquiry or investigation regarding his or her uprightness, conversation, knowledge, and acquaintance "with the things of Christ and his Kingdom." The ruling elder must determine, in other words, whether the individual is "a visible Saint to the judgment of reasonable charity" (*A Survey,* pt. 3, p. 4). The elder has the power and duty to stop the application himself if he sees cause. If not, he takes the application to the entire congregation, "that *they* also may *use their best information . . .* touching the unblamablenesse" of the candidate. If the people have well-grounded objections, they tell the elder, "and that is sufficient to stay the proceeding for the present." If, however, there are no objections, then "the person doth shortly *give some reason of his hope* in the face of the Congregation, & is admitted," pledging himself to the church covenant (p. 5). Hooker adds that some women are "not able to express themselves in the face of a Congregation," due to their "feeblenesse . . ., their shamefac't modesty," and even their "melanchollick fearfulnesse," though they "yet have the precious work of saving grace in their hearts." In such cases, "we are forced to take the *expressions of such in private,* and *make report of them to the Congregation*" (p. 6).[44] Among the women who availed themselves of this privilege were Mrs. John Cotton in 1633 at Boston and, because of illness rather than timidity, Thomas Shepard's first wife in 1635 at Cambridge.[45] Presumably, however, many women overcame the threat of these various forms of stage-fright in order, for once, to exercise the right of speaking out in church, which on all other occasions was reserved to men alone.

A related matter, the censuring of church members, is taken up in the third chapter of part 3, where Hooker offers a comparable description of the several stages of procedure in such actions. The New Englanders' thinking on the imposition of church censures was that it could serve to "purge out what is evill." In this regard, *"each particular Brother"* is "a skilfull Apothecary," able to initiate church action against a member in order to cure him of his faults (*A Survey*, pt. 3, p. 33). Hooker urges caution and moderation at all stages of disciplinary action. A person seeing a fault in another which no one else knows about should approach the wrongdoer privately and, unless the offense is blatantly obvious to the witness, *inquire* rather than *tell* the person about his actions. Be sure you have evidence before you accuse, he warns. Most sins which are known to others are, in some sense, public, however, and Hooker provides a fuller description of procedure against these sins (drunkenness, swearing, stealing, lying, etc.). First the witness must bring it to the elders, who will decide if it is worth taking to the congregation. If it is, the elders will reduce the issue to simple terms so that the "meanest" in the congregation can understand it. As Hooker warns that the complainant must be both sure and exact in his charges and have "direct" and "pregnant" proofs—at least two witnesses to support each charge, or a confession by the offender—his caution suggests that he may have learned the need for this care the hard way, through having to deal with too many flimsy charges. The elders are admonished to record the accusation exactly and immediately, together with the accused's answers to it. All discussions with the accuser and accused must be limited to the point in hand. Finally, if the case holds up, it can be taken to the congregation and, thanks to all this preliminary preparation by the elders, "may easily be determined in half an hour, which cost many weeks in the search and examination thereof" (p. 38). When the case is presented to the congregation, the elders are to *"lay open the rule"* in such cases and *"to expresse their judgement and determination."* Then, "unless the people be able to convince them of errour and mistakes in their sentence, they are *bound to joyn their judgement with theirs, to the compleating of the sentence."* Then the ruling elder pronounces the sentence, "whether it be the censure of *admonition* or *excommunication"* (p. 38). If it is the latter, Hooker advises that, since the people are required "to renounce all *voluntary and unnecessary familiarity with him, even in civill converse"* in order to make him ashamed, they ought to make the sentence unanimous (p. 39). This procedure means, in effect, that the elders conducted their hearing in private and decided on guilt or innocence. If they determined the person was guilty, they declared their view publicly to the congregation. Only those assumed guilty were haled before the congregation, in other words; and the burden of further proof was laid on those who believed in their innocence. So while it is unlikely that the congregation very often reversed the deliberately determined judgment of the elders, it is also unlikely, given Hooker's stringent requirements for certainty, that many dubious cases came before the congregation. He reminds his readers that the congregation has the advantage of being able to take action against the elders if they feel for any reason that the elders are using partiality in these cases.

It was certainly through trial and error in his own churches at Newtown and Hartford that Hooker evolved this orderly system for handling both applications for membership and censure proceedings. In his description of each, what strikes the reader (and is not so evident in secondary comment such as this as it is in Hooker's own words) is both a willingness to admit hypocrites if necessary in order to avoid barring timid saints and a concern for proceeding only with "much *moderation, pitty, patience and long-sufferance"* in administering censures (*A Survey,* pt. 3, p. 39). It is neither arbitrariness nor "democraticall" anarchy which emerges through this description, but a highly systematized method for insuring, if possible, both the preservation of the brotherhood of saints and the exercise of compassion.

Hooker's final attention in *A Survey* goes to the subject of synods. His view and that of New England Congregationalists generally was that synods are appropriate and, in fact, necessary tools for the clarifying of dubious and difficult points of doctrine. But he insisted that they carry no authority to dictate their decisions to individual churches. They are merely advisory. Rutherford and the Presbyterians held a different opinion, believing that the conclusions reached by a synod were binding on the individual churches within the jurisdiction of that synod. New England had, of course, already used "consociation of churches" on several occasions and would continue to do so. While its synods did generally reach conclusions which individual churches supported, as in the Cambridge Synod of 1648, there was nothing mandatory about this acceptance, as the Half-Way Synod would so thoroughly demonstrate. Each church retains the last decision, said Hooker. In this matter he could argue all he chose without much success in converting the opposition, since for the Presbyterians to deny the authority of synods would be for them to cease, in a large measure, to be Presbyterians. Likewise, for congregationalists to allow for subordination of individual churches to the dictates of synods would be for them to compromise their very definition of a church.

In fact, this is the case on most major points of disagreement between the two sides. Both argued strenuously for the "truth" of their views and of their interpretation of the Scriptures on which they based their polity, and both were committed to standing firm. From the first, the chances of accommodation on some middle ground were slim, since neither side, despite its protestations to the contrary, was prepared to compromise. Though there were a few defections on both sides, such as John Owen's conversion from a Presbyterian to a congregationalist bias and the intrepid Philip Nye's apparent modification of his Independent position to something closer to the much-talked-of middle way, on the whole there was little of this sort of movement. Most ended where they began. This is demonstrated by the way the exchange between Rutherford and Hooker continued to reverberate down through the years. Hooker's death in 1647, the year before the appearance of *A Survey,* was of course no more guarantee of acquiescence by his opponents than was the end of the Westminster Assembly in 1649 or the rise to full power by Cromwell and, under him, of the Independent church polity.

The first of Hooker's two main opponents to answer the arguments in *A Survey* was Samuel Hudson, who published *A Vindication of the Essence and Unity of the Church Catholike Visible* (1650). In this work Hudson actually devoted more space to vindicating himself from the charges of one John Ellis than to answering those of Hooker. Ellis, in *Vindiciae Catholicae* (1647), had accused Hudson of sounding like a Catholic. Hudson excuses the supposed tardiness of his reply on several grounds, including his having been caught up in the seige of Colchester in the Civil War. Perhaps more significant is his remark that "I desired to see some of my betters go before me, in vindication of their own Tractates of the same subject."[46] Since he also says this is "a subject wherein I can find so few going before me," his remark about hoping his "betters" will answer first is a clear allusion to Rutherford, calling attention to the Scot's silence. Rutherford himself, after delaying a great while, finished another lengthy expostulation sometime before the end of 1655 on the same subjects he and Hooker had already handled. By this time, however, a lengthy book on church discipline was hardly a hot item for the booksellers; Andrew Crooke, the London printer who had published theological items by Hooker and numerous others in the past, was not at all anxious to print Rutherford's manuscript, which, in print, would run to over five hundred pages.[47]

Finally, in 1658, ten years after Hooker's *Survey* had appeared and over a dozen since it was originally finished, Crooke published Rutherfords's answer in London. A recent critic observes, in regard to Rutherford's delay and his ultimate answer to *A Survey*, that Hooker's book "was too much for Rutherford, who was spurred to write a reply, but without producing any fresh arguments."[48] The fact is that neither Hudson nor Rutherford did much but stir the muddy waters of controversy once more, though Hudson's is the clearer work and, from a philosophical standpoint, the more interesting book. But these two publications were by no means the only contributions to the argument which Simeon Ashe could say in early 1656 "lyeth dead among us." If the issue was dead, the corpse was not yet buried. Daniel Cawdrey, who in the fifties was the major arguer for Presbyterian ways, attacking John Owen and John Cotton, had much to say against Hooker as well in his *Inconsistencie of the Independent Way* (1651), which John Owen then answered in *A Defence of Mr. John Cotton from the Imputation of Selfe Contradiction, charged on him by Mr. Daniel Cawdrey* (Oxford, 1658). Other entrants in the controversy included Samuel Stone, who came to the defense of his deceased colleague Giles Firmin, and William Lucy. In the long run the New Englanders seem to have been far less willing to continue the debate than their English counterparts, no doubt because internal problems in their system were increasingly evident after the Cambridge Platform. Besides, once the Westminster Assembly was disbanded, the New England clergy knew that the opportunity for affecting the future of the Church in England had been greatly reduced. By 1650, in fact, rather than seeing their "prophecies" heeded and followed in the homeland, they were finding their divinely ordained discipline challenged from within. In just the next two decades the system so carefully established and protected from corruption in the 1630s and so fully and convincingly defended and codified in the 1640s would crumble and fall in the face of the challenge from a new generation not inclined to discover grace in the same clear and identifiable way as their parents but just as inclined to have babies who, they understandably believed, needed baptizing.

Hooker's definition and defense of the congregational principle of church organization was achieved by responding to his opponent's contrary views and imitating his form of argument. Yet in doing so he managed to create a work of lasting merit and validity. Responding to Rutherford did not, in the last analysis, inhibit this achievement as much as some church historians such as Walker and Horton have

claimed. Hooker continued to dwell on the major principles of local autonomy and the individual member's significance while also defining the exact
roles of various services, sacraments, and officers. If the book lacks the dynamic sense of immediate inspiration which characterizes earlier, more
clearly prophetic writings such as *The Danger of Desertion*, it is still a major
prophetic work in that it is a telling-forth of the truth of God as understood
by His messenger in a particular place and time. Hooker said, in fact, that
his book introduced and defined the New Englanders' view of *Truth* in the
matter of church polity. It did so with authoritative logic and persuasive
power, refuting the opposition and touching the essential points of theory
as well as practice. Hooker's "midwifing" was capable enough, with or
without the supposed inhibition of Rutherford's books, to last until now as
one of the classics of Congregational literature.

Baptism

The determination apparent in Hooker's writing such a monumental
work as *A Survey* not just once but twice must have rested on his
declared sense that the moment of truth was truly at hand, that the
great cycle of history commencing at the birth of the second Adam was
about to be completed by the establishment of a true and pure church.
This being so, it is more than a little ironic that the seeds of a divisive
issue—an issue which would ultimately abort the birth of the new
purified church were abundantly sown in the several explications of
congregationalism by first-generation ministers. In the face of pointed
questions about their practice from abroad, the New Englanders responded uncompromisingly that the sacrament of baptism was "a
brand-mark, and a separating note of the sheep of God's fold and *such
as are without*" (*A Survey*, pt. 3, p. 8). In *A Survey* Hooker argued
this position against his opponents and even against the inclination of
his own heart. In an interesting passage showing his pastoral compassion for those who must be denied baptism, he said that "the pinch
. . . of the Question" comes when we ask whether nonmembers have a
right of baptism for their children. In order, as he says, "that I may
shrive my heart to the Reader and Master R. I shall nakedly professe,
that if I should have given way to my affection, or followed that which
suits my secret desire and inclination, I could have willingly wished,
that the scale might have been cast upon the affirmative part, and that
such persons (many whereof we hope are godly) might enjoy all such
priviledges, which might be usefull and helpfull to them and theirs."
But because of the "main pillar principle"—the church covenant, which
implied the acceptance into membership only of professing visible

saints—he cannot give in to his affections. His "understanding" balks
and must carry the day (pt. 3, p. 12). He states explicitly the very
tenet of the first-generation New England church which the Half-Way
Synod of 1662 finally had to overturn when he writes, *"The Predecessors cannot convey this right* [baptism] *without the next Parents"* (p.
14). Thus, the church membership of grandparents does not give
grandchildren the right to baptism since the parents' "apostacy takes off
the *federall holinesse* of the Children, *I Cor.* 7. 14" (p. 14). Though an
astute first-hand witness had publicly observed as early as 1642 that
this policy would surely lead to disastrous declines in membership,[49]
most New England divines—Hooker among them—were not yet prepared to admit it. Richard Mather was an important early exception to
this rule, having seen as early as the mid-forties the ultimate need for a
policy of broader admission to the sacrament of baptism. Gradually
others came around to his position, as Hooker might have done had he
lived longer, since even by 1650 his Hartford colleague, Samuel Stone,
had announced his awareness of this need. But in writing *A Survey* in
the mid-1640s, Hooker was accurately describing present New England
practice, since no church actually began baptizing the children of nonmembers (or of "federal members," as those baptized but not regenerate and fully covenanted were called) until at least 1656.[50]

Hooker's fullest consideration of the issue of baptism and its relationship to church membership came in an important work contemporaneous with *A Survey,* the now all-but-forgotten *Covenant of Grace
Opened.* This work, published posthumously in 1649, was completed
sometime before the end of the summer of 1646, probably having been
composed after the first writing of *A Survey* but before the rewriting.
Hooker did not intend to publish the work, but it circulated in New
England before his death, as we know from his comment in a letter of
September 17, 1646, to Thomas Shepard, wherein he states, apparently in response to his son-in-law's desire to see the manuscript, "My
notes of Paedo-baptisme are out of my hand, else you might have had
them."[51] His use of the term "paedo-baptisme" indicates the controversial context of this work. Though it is tempting in viewing this
period retrospectively to associate any controversial works dealing with
baptism with the debate leading to the Half-Way Covenant, another
concern was uppermost in the mid-1640s. This was the debate over
toleration, which focused especially on the increasing numbers of
Anabaptists in the colonies as well as in England. This sect was entirely
opposed to infant baptism, holding that one must be of age and able to
declare his faith before deserving baptism. New England Congregationalists, whatever their views on baptizing the children of nonmem-

bers, were unanimous in favoring infant (paedo-) baptism. Nathaniel Ward spoke for orthodoxy in New England when he wrote, probably in 1645, this passage in his famous *Simple Cobler of Aggawam*: "I dare take upon me, to bee the Herauld of *New-England* so farre, as to pro-claime to the world, in the name of our Colony, that all Familists, Antinomians, Anabaptists, and other Enthusiasts shall have free Lib-erty to keepe away from us."[52] In fact, the Massachusetts General Court was sufficiently conscious of the threat to orthodoxy that in 1644 it passed a law banishing obstinate Anabaptists.[53] By 1646 the matter was still of concern to Hooker, since he said in September that "I like those Anabaptists & ther opinion every day worse then other."[54]

To this concern about the general threat of Anabaptist ideas and practices was added a specific incentive which drove Hooker to write his *Covenant of Grace Opened*. This was the appearance in 1643 of a book by an English Anabaptist, John Spilsbery (or Spilsbury), entitled *A Treatise concerning the Lawfull Subject of Baptism*. Hooker's *Cov-enant of Grace Opened* begins as a general consideration of the doc-trines of baptism and the church covenant but it becomes fully as much a work of argumentative controversy as *A Survey* in its final two-thirds, where the author cites or quotes Spilsbery's book, often noting specific page and line references, at least a dozen times. The essential point of disagreement between Hooker and Spilsbery is on the meaning of bap-tism itself. To the Anabaptists, baptism signified the full adult recogni-tion of the person's acceptance of grace. The baptized individual neces-sarily possessed faith at the time of baptism. This could not be the view of any who argued for infant baptism. So Hooker and his fellow New Englanders held that baptism is an initial sign and "seal" of a child's "incision" into faith. Hooker resorts heavily to the typological analogy of the Christian believers with the ancient Hebrews, claiming that what circumcision was to Abraham's tribe, baptism is to modern Christian believers. Just as Abraham's children were able, without the power of reason, to receive and benefit from their "sacrament," so are Christian children, to an even higher degree, able to receive and bene-fit from baptism. But in baptism the child is passive, whereas in receiv-ing the other sacrament, the Lord's Supper, the believer must be ac-tive. Between one's baptism as an infant and one's adult participation in Holy Communion, he or she had to grow in the faith. Baptism, then, "is a seale of our first entrance; and the Supper is our nourishing in the family of Christ."[55] Between these two events, presumably, one would experience regeneration, publicly announce his faith, and submit to the church covenant.[56]

It is important to note that Hooker is not arguing that baptism has a causal relation to faith. In fact, he takes pains to refute "the Papists," who say that the sacrament of itself has the power of grace. One does not acquire faith *because* he has been baptized, he insists, nor does one *have* to be baptized as a child in order to receive grace as an adult. Faith must be present for baptism to work any good as a seal of the covenant. Presumably this means that faith in the parents of a baptized child is a necessary starting point for that child's growth into grace. But Hooker always insists that while baptism, like the sacrament of the Lord's Supper, when "used by the holy Ghost," has "spirituall efficacy," it is merely a "Morall instrument," having no power in itself. His analogy makes the point clearer: he says that some herbs have an inherent power to cure, whereas tools require art in the user in order to be effective; the sacraments are like the tools rather than the herbs (*CGO*, pp. 13–14).

The common term for the spiritual state of a baptized person who had not yet experienced and declared his possession of true faith was "federal holiness."[57] Having been baptized as an infant, one had received "a spirituall priviledge, but not a saving grace, nor a spirituall work of sanctification." It is a "relative holinesse" only, since "there be many persons that enjoy federall holinesse, that shall not have glory" (*CGO*, p. 42). Not even all the baptized children in a given family will necessarily be saved. "Sanctification cannot be lost," but "federall holines" may be lost (p. 49). The former can never be conveyed by the parent to the child; "to say that holinesse is by generation, it is a dreame" (p. 56).

By the same token, a constant refrain in this work is Hooker's well-known belief that admission to full church membership was itself a flawed method of separating the sheep from the goats. Many members, he frequently observed, are only "federally" holy and will never be saved. The "judgement of the Church," in admitting or not admitting individuals to membership, can be based only on outward and visible signs of holiness (*CGO*, p. 60). The Church could do no more than act in "rational charity" in admitting professing saints. Better to admit doubtful cases than to keep out possible saints, in his view. And once persons were admitted to the Church, they were eligible for all the benefits of membership, so that if they should sin secretly and become hypocritical professors of the faith, such people "come & eat and drink their own damnation, and the Church in no fault because she proceeds not against them, because she knowes them not" (pp. 58–59). Hooker makes no attempt to gloss over the number of those who slip by and gain membership wrongfully, either, since he estimates that "there are hundreds of those that are men of yeares, that are close and grosse hypocrites, that never had any communion with Christ, and yet they are in the Church, and the Church cannot hold them back" (p. 59).

It is important to notice in this connection that, while Hooker held diligently to the orthodox New England Way of baptizing only children of full church members, it was somewhat easier to gain admission to membership in his congregation than in some others where "rational charity" was not so actively invoked. The dilemma which ultimately developed, forcing the Half-Way Covenant in order to replenish the youthful stock in the Church, was one answer to the problem. Another answer, which involved less compromise of original ideals, was that practiced by Hooker and continued by his son Samuel at Farmington, Connecticut, until practically the end of the seventeenth century. The son, like the father, believed in a broad exercise of "rational charity" in admitting adults to membership. This necessarily served to give more people the right to infant baptism than a policy of rigid exclusion of doubtful cases would have.[58]

Hooker, of course, never relaxed his insistence on the need for his parishioners to seek grace. His *Covenant of Grace Opened* apparently began, not as a controversial work answering John Spilsbery, but as a sermon on baptism and its relationship to the church covenant. It opens with a formal statement of the Doctrine and ends with a series of Uses, while along the way it addresses Spilsbery's points directly. In its published form it is neither fish nor fowl—neither sermon nor tract— even though it is a thematically unified work. The final Use in the work, which clearly addresses, sermon-fashion, the children and youth in his congregation, particularly indicates Hooker's clear grasp of the practical threat to the strength of the New England Church in the falling away of the younger generation from the active spiritual life which their parents had pursued. He exhorts the children "to lay hold of the covenant; keep it, and lay hold of it, and never let it goe, maintain your interest by that means of the covenant of your Parents; God is the God of your Parents, keep the passage open and maintain it, know the God of your Fathers, and that God pardoned their sin, and from whom they received their good, that God may pardon your sins, and you may receive good from him by that covenant" (*CGO*, p. 84). Rather surprisingly, Hooker aims words of terror at these young people at the end of his treatise, reminding them to "take heed; if thou have a godly Parent, father and mother; if thou remaine in a sinfull estate and condition for all this, it shall be easier for *Pagans* in the day of judgement then for you" (p. 85). So, in the end, this argumentative tract returns to the thrust of a conversion sermon, admonishing the young to renew the vitality of the covenant between God and His New England chosen people before it is too late. Having in the earlier portions of the discussion proved the legality and propriety of admitting the children of believers to the sacrament of baptism, Hooker now urges those children not to defect. He seems here to come down to practical cases, acknowledging the danger—or at least the potential danger—to the Church if the younger generation lets them down. In a sense, he is forecasting the very problem that, in the decade and a half after his death, gradually brought a majority of New England Puritans to a formal modification of the baptism practices Hooker had, in his two works of the mid-forties, so meticulously set forth. It is rare indeed that we find Hooker addressing a Use to children and extremely significant that it is this particular Use, at the end of a work on baptism, which is so addressed. In the final years of his life Hooker was clearly aware of the developing changes in the New England Church which he would not live to see.

The Covenant of Grace Opened, like *A Survey of the Summe of Church Discipline* and all the other occasional writings considered thus far, was intended as a constructive analysis of crucial questions of Hooker's age and culture. In writing each of these works Hooker was giving firm definition to his latest frame of mind on the issues. Some of these works, such as *A Survey* and the jeremiads, are supremely successful examples of the genres which they represent. Others, such as the preface to *A Fresh Suit,* and *The Covenant of Grace Opened,* have faded with the passing of the issues which gave them birth. But all of these occasional writings are important elements in understanding this "Elijah" of his people because they show Thomas Hooker taking his stand on what to him and his contemporaries were crucial issues, again and again basing his stand on principle rather than on expediency. These works reveal a worldly dimension of the man which lends substance to our picture of him as preacher of those works of psychological, spiritual probity for which he is mainly remembered and to which we now turn.

PART TWO

THE INNER WORLD
Struggles of the
Unredeemed

6

The Anatomy of the Soul

It is perhaps too easy an assumption to claim that the greatest Puritan preachers were successful because of their mastery of the word—because they could manipulate style in a commanding, literate, persuasive manner. Although stylistic command is certainly a large part of Hooker's success as a conversion preacher, the style itself was a response to a more basic set of givens with which Hooker was operating. Perhaps no single consideration so thoroughly influenced the pattern of his preaching and the larger outlines of his career as did his ready acceptance of faculty psychology, the version of human psychological anatomy long since established and taught by European Church fathers.[1] For all the intellectual ferment of the early seventeenth century, one area which was not to see major changes in basic assumptions for several decades was that of the anatomy of the inner self, the soul, or what we consider the psychological components of human nature. Without these assumptions, Hooker's work could not have been what it was. The total organization of his lifelong *magnum opus*, the long series of sermons guiding his congregation through every minute stage of the redemption process, is based upon his understanding of human psychology. And every individual sermon preached by Hooker was also structured to take advantage of the known inner workings of the human soul. Anyone who would understand Hooker's achievement as a conversion preacher must first understand his conception of the human soul.

Christians have always used the term *soul* to describe the spiritual essence of man. The concept is pre-Christian, though such views as Aristotle's—that the soul and body are interdependent and "inseparable"—were of little use to Hooker or any other Puritan. Knowing the value of definitions in philosophical discourse, Hooker was careful to define the fundamental term *soul* concisely. He said the soul is "a spirituall substance in every man, which is immortall, and

129

hath two faculties, Understanding and Will."[2] He usually also mentioned the third component, the affections, thus agreeing with most of his contemporaries in conceiving of the soul as a tripartite entity, though there was general agreement, as William Perkins had said, that the understanding and the will are the "two principal faculties," while the affections are subordinate to the will.[3] A minister interested in influencing, even changing, the inner life of the members of his congregation would have to be skillful in manipulating these three elements of the inner man in the proper sequence. It was with just such a calculated goal in mind that Hooker organized and preached every sermon in his canon.

As Perry Miller has explained, the sermon's division into four main parts was really a twofold division. The first section of the sermon, including Text, Doctrine, and Reasons, was chiefly argumentative, addressing itself to the reasoning powers of the audience; while the second part, the Uses, was more apt to appeal to the hearer's emotions, or affections, intending to elicit a practical reaction.[4] William Ames put it this way: "A doctrine must first be rightly found out, and then afterward hand[l]ed. The finding it out is by Logick Analysis, unto which Rhetorick also and Grammar serveth," whereas "a use is a theologicall principal deduced from a doctrine which shows the use, goodness, or end of it."[5] The sermon's structure was thus especially fitted to the Puritans' understanding of the way man's inner nature responded to the stimuli which could lead to faith: work on the understanding first, then proceed to have the heart accept what the mind has perceived. Remembering the Puritans' recognition of the heart as the key to the inner man, it is not surprising that the preachers of Ames's and Hooker's generations were inclined to feel the final part of the sermon was the most important.

The Antagonistic Self

The Puritan view of the nature of man had its roots in the Biblical account of the creation of Adam "in God's image." This account was, in Hooker's view, the logical place to begin the work of conversion, since the original Adam figured forth an example—the only one in history until Christ—of ideal humanity. His most direct approach to this subject is in *The Paterne of Perfection* (1640), where Adam is examined as the type with whom every modern is to be compared. After quoting Genesis 1:26 ("*And God said, Let us make man after our owne image*"), he sets up a dichotomy after the manner of Peter Ramus in remarking that "religion, being the Doctrine according to godlinesse, is referred to two heads: The knowledge of God, and of our selves" (*PP*, p. 1). He then makes the prompt and characteristic announcement that he will deal with the most "available" (most experimentally accessible) subject first: "My purpose is not to begin with the knowledge of God, but with the knowledge of our selves, because it is most available to make us see our misery, and the need of a Saviour" (p. 4). The essence of this self-knowledge is that we are the children of Adam, in whose soul "God imprinted his image . . . in his Understanding, Will, and Affections" (p. 41) but who, in breaking his covenant of works with God, fell from "the pinnacle of perfection," his creation in God's image (pp. 5–7). Now men characteristically have Adam's image in that they inherit, not the perfection of Adam's original condition, but the corruption of his fallen nature. Thus, the aim of all men ought to be to become, in Paul's words, "new men." It was to the realization of this goal in the lives of those whom God had chosen that Hooker dedicated his ministry.

Hooker's listing of Adam's faculties in carefully ordered sequence—understanding, will, affections—is consistent with the long-accepted view of man's thought processes. According to this view, thought typically begins with the understanding, which receives and analyzes information and passes a judgment on to the will, which reacts to the judgment by accepting or rejecting it, thus activating the appropriate affections, such as fear, desire, love, hate, or anger. The affection produces a speech or act which concludes the sequence. If one were to follow the correct order, "the mind and judgment should only have attended God; the Will attend our Judgment, the Affections wait on the Will, the Actions issue as the execution of al."[6] The conditional phrasing is as much a part of the explanation as the subject matter itself, since Hooker is always the Calvinist religious analyst, never the secular philosopher. His interest in human psychology is dependent on his commitment to the Calvinist understanding of the nature of man and his view of himself as a redemption preacher, the one insisting on man's inability, the other on his need for effort. He is consequently much more inclined to focus on the likelihood of difficulty in getting one's faculties to function properly than were his predecessors outside the Calvinistic tradition, with some of whom he otherwise had much in common.[7] For Hooker it is clear that because of Original Sin and the consequent natural depravity of all men, the ideal order of thought to action is not usually followed. Even when it is, there is no guarantee that some malfunction by one of the soul's components will not cause an individual to go astray. In fact, it usually does. This unreliability of our governing faculties is the major reason that the work of redemption is so difficult. The Puritan preacher was well aware that it is one thing to say, "This is the way a man should proceed if he is to be justified," but quite another thing for that man to follow instructions. Yet the preacher was entirely committed to proclaiming the lesson again and again.

The notion of a combat between body and soul, flesh and spirit, had been nourished in the considerable body of pseudodramatic or debate literature in the Middle Ages and early Renaissance. This sense of struggle was one of the fundamental assumptions of the first settlers of New England. "The world," often a synonym for flesh or temptation, was the aggressive opponent of the upright Christian.[8] Man's sense-oriented desires were always pulling against his wavering desire for spiritual uprightness. The two tendencies in man's nature dated back to Adam's creation in God's image on the one hand and his fall on the other. Anne Bradstreet's allegorical character, Spirit, confronts the problem in addressing Flesh:

> Sisters we are, yea, twins we be,
> Yet deadly feud 'twixt thee and me;
> For from one father are we not,
> Thou by old Adam wast begot,
> But my arise is from above,
> Whence my dear father I do love.[9]

The idea that it was indeed Satan who had control of "the world" and its people was fundamental to Hooker and his fellow Puritans and accounts for the thoroughgoing dualistic mode of thought that runs throughout his writings, which posit God, Christ, righteousness, and the road to Glory as the chief components of the life of the elect, while Satan, the world, sin, and the road to hell are the chief elements in the life of the damned.[10]

It had been characteristic of the medieval and Renaissance scholastic mind to think of realms of knowledge and experience in a dualistic framework. Thomas Aquinas divided wisdom into two types: metaphysical, which is grounded in sense experience, and theological, which is based upon revelation.[11] This kind of division is characteristic of Paul and Augustine as well as of Plato before them. Peter Ramus's dialectical theories of logic were an integral part of the curricula at Emmanuel and other colleges by the end of the sixteenth century. And Hooker's contemporary Francis Bacon, even while he was insisting on a reexamination of the channels in which man thinks and the things which he thinks about, held to the necessary distinction between two kinds of truth, the truth of religion and the truth of science.[12] This notion of dichotomies, of dualistic opposition between parts of the same whole, provided the fundamental dynamics of Hooker's account of the soul's struggle towards grace and heaven. There was always something for the sinful soul to struggle against, and that something was inside himself. The self was, in fact, an "archetypal Puritan protagonist-antagonist."[13]

Head

In Hooker's understanding of the tripartite sequence of the soul's activity, it was at least certain that mental activity came first. The mind could engage in various kinds of activity, such as understanding, reasoning, or judging, but as soon as any of these cognitive processes began, man's fallen nature asserted itself, threatening to make things run amok. There is no stage in the sequence of mental activity at which the eternal battle between flesh and spirit does not become manifest, as Hooker implicitly recognizes by quoting Romans 8:7 to the effect that "*the Wisdom of the flesh, is Enmity against God, it is not subject to the Law, neither indeed can be.*"[14] Man, that is, is most comfortable in denying truth and even in fighting lawlessly against it. Since the understanding is the eye of the soul, it is crucial that it see with a true sight and with the aid of full mental light. "That which the eye sees not the heart rues not, that which is not apprehended by the understanding, is not affected by the will."[15] Self-knowledge illuminates the soul and is bound to expose corruption.

Most men are satisfied with the general awareness that they are sinful and cannot help it. But this kind of knowledge is not knowledge at all, in Hooker's view, being an *escape* from real insight. "It's one thing to say sin is thus and thus, another thing to see it to be such; we must look wishly [*sic*] and steddily upon our distempers, look sin in the face, and discern it to the full."[16] Hooker's unwillingness to compromise or to let his listeners compromise on spiritual matters is fundamental to his character. He speaks to us through his published words as a tough-minded, demanding spiritual taskmaster, thoroughly honest in his recognition of man's weakness and relentless in his desire to help individual men change. Spiritual lassitude was anathema to Hooker, and accordingly, his career involved an implied war on this kind of self-excusing apathy. "We do not single out our corruptions and survey the loathsomness of them, as they come naked in their own Natures," he said. "This we ought to do."[17]

When God created Adam, he gave him the tools for "the right discerning of sin" by putting into his understanding "wisdom and knowledge," or, as Hooker prefers to say, "wisdom and prudence." Wisdom is the spiritual light which enables the perception of truth. With this ability, Adam was able "to pierce into the nature of things, and perceive them with . . . perfection," while his "prudence," which is practical wisdom, enabled him to know how to do the work required (*PP*, p. 42). Hooker does not cite "the Philosopher" at this point, but this theoretical-practical division of man's powers of reason is an important distinction in Aristotle's writings on the mind, and Hooker's explanation here probably indicates his reliance on aspects of Aristotelian psychology.[18] The basic terminology which Hooker uses to describe the elements of the soul suggests that he gave the study of Aristotelian physics its due while he was at Cambridge. But his Aristotelian physics was merged with a Calvinistic view of the origin and nature of man. Hooker the Calvinist insists that the essence of man's problem now is that he can no longer do what Adam could do. The sinner's yearning for justification is a struggle to regain, in part, Adam's God-given capacities.

This identification of one's understanding with the problem of seeing sin and the self clearly would seem to give an advantage to the man whose mind is unusually sharp. Hooker says elsewhere that the power to reason is essential to acquiring faith: "Though faith be above reason, yet it is with reason; it is not that collier faith of the Papists, that put out his owne eyes to see by another mans."[19] It is through reason that the soul of a man is "inlightened," in other words;[20] and Hooker does not say to his congregation, "What I tell you of yourselves and God is true; believe it," so much as he says, "What I tell you is true but you will never believe it until you *experience* its truth." This experience is not to be found by taking a walk around the village square or a trip to the Continent or even to the New World, but by learning to look into one's own soul with intellectual precision.

This stress on the intellect makes Hooker's system begin to sound like a doctrine devised *by* graduates and students of Cambridge *for* graduates and students of Cambridge—a spiritual favoring of the intellectually superior. In fact, however, throughout his career Hooker was outspoken against any such inference. "If wisedome, and prudence, and skill in arts and sciences, would have carried men to Jesus Christ, the Scribes and Pharisees would then have gone to him."[21] Not only do such men usually *not* go to Christ on their own; they are much the hardest sort to convince to do so. *"Men of the greatest ability for depth of brain and strength of understanding are most hardly brought to brokennes of heart."*[22] It was not book learning which counted, he felt, so much as the diligent searching of the recesses of one's own soul with whatever powers of reason and honest perception one might have. In Hooker, as in Shakespeare's *King Lear*, it is sometimes the fool who has the most essential kind of wisdom. Hooker takes his cue from Paul, however, in paraphrasing 1 Corinthians 3:18: "It's the first step to wisdom *to become a fool,* and thats hard to him that is highly in love with his own wit."[23] But the simplest ignorant soul that is *humbled,* "that is almost a naturall foole, that soule knowes and understands more of grace and mercy in Christ than all the wisest and learnedst in the world."[24]

Thus, while faith depends upon a proper and active use of reason for its existence, this reason is fairly elemental and can be mustered up in sufficient degree by men of even the weakest intellectual capacity. It is comprised of the theoretical understanding's capacity for spiritual insight and the practical understanding's ability to seek actively for God's help. Without the assistance of God, the knowledge of man's corruption would be frustrating and could lead only to despair. But together with the man who will look to Him, and who will heed the words of the minister, God actively engages in the struggle. We need not expect the kind of miraculous revelation that Saul received on the Damascus road, says Hooker, "but when the word is brought home to the understanding, the soule will thinke those strange things, such as he never heard or thought of." His choice of verbs stresses God's active involvement in bringing the sinner around: "The Lord knockes at the doore of the soule, findes him out behinde the Pillor, awakens him asleepe in his Pue, finds him out his sinnes, and discovers his abominations." Hooker, perhaps having Jacob's struggle with the angel in mind, becomes still more dramatic in imagining the confrontation between God and the sinner's mind in terms of physical combat: "God deales like a Wrastler, first catches hold then comes in, and at last throwes a man upon his back[,] makes him yeeld and confesse, I am the man. Thus the Lord causeth the minde to attende the word."[25] In such cases as this, God is using more than persuasion; He is forcing the mind into line. But Adam's fall made God's aggression necessary, as does the accepted theory of the sequential functioning of the faculties. Without proper perception of one's own personal evil, spiritual redemption cannot occur. And this full intellectual perception can come only with God's active help.

Heart

If in the first place "truths come to the understanding to be judged," the next stage begins when they are "presented to the heart to be beleeved."[26] The understanding, as Hooker put it, "is the inlet of the heart, so that nothing can affect the heart, but so farre as reason conceiveth it, and ushers it home to the soule."[27] He defines the term *heart* in several places in his writings. Perhaps his clearest explanation of it occurs in *The Soules Preparation*, where he says that the heart "is the will it selfe, and that abilitie of soule, whereby the heart saith, I will have this, and I will not have that. As the understanding is setled in the head, and keepes his sentinell there, so the will is seated in the heart, when it comes to taking or refusing, this is the office of the will, and it discovers his act there."[28] In *The Vnbeleevers Preparing for Christ* he gives much the same definition of *heart*, this time including the affections among its characteristics: "A heart in Scripture, besides that which it signifieth naturally; is applied to the will of a man, or to that ability which is in a reasonable soule, whereby he willeth or rejecteth a thing, this is put for a heart in Scripture, together with love, delight, joy, hatred, and griefe, which are attendants upon this will."[29] Later, in *The Application of Redemption*, he cites four places in Scripture where the heart and particular affections are linked: *"The heart shal fear*, Deut. 28.67. *Joy of heart*, Isa. 65.14. *Sorrow of heart*, Levit. 26.16 &c. And *out of the heart comes murders and adulteries*, Matth. 15.19. All which carry undeniably the work of the Will and Affections."[30]

The importance of the concept of "heart" to Puritan thinking has seldom been properly underscored. Even those who have discussed "the heart" as a key element in Puritan thought have not always given the meaning of the term itself adequate attention.[31] This can probably be partly explained by the fact that there was inconsistency among the Puritans in the degree of precision in their uses of the term. Its meaning is sometimes broad, sometimes limited. William Perkins seems to have thought of *heart* as synonymous with *soul*, thus making it in his case the "metonym for the inner man" which Norman Pettit calls it. Perkins uses *heart* to include precisely the faculties which Hooker prefers to include in his definition of *soul*, when he writes, "The place or mansion of the spirite is the heart, that is, the mind, wil, and affection," adding that "the beginning of our new birth is in the heart, when a new light is put into the minde, a new and heavenly disposition into the will and affection."[32] John Cotton is much closer to Hooker's usual view of the heart as separate from the mind and as particularly associated with the will when he writes:

> The heart is the way of the entrance of God into the soule, or into the whole man. . . . *Psal.* 24.7, 9. *Be yee lift up you everlasting doores*, and what are those doores: but the hearts of men? They are not the doores of a mans house, nor the gates of a city, for they will bee consumed, but these be everlasting doores, and such as

into which the *king of Glory must enter*, and they must be inlarged, this is certainly meant of the heart of man, and of the will
of man which dwels in the heart. . . .

It is called the doore of the soule, because of that authority that
the heart and will hath over the whole soule, and the power it
hath to rule both soule and body.[33]

Hooker agrees that the will is the soul's ruler, calling it variously "a
wise king" (*PP*, p. 167), "the Queene of the soule," "the great commander of the soule," "the great wheele of the soule," and the "root"
of both belief and unbelief.[34] This consistently held view that the will
is man's preeminent faculty puts Hooker in a more unequivocal position on the matter than some of his predecessors and followers, who, as
in the case of John Preston, defended the will's role as "queen" of the
soul at one time and denied it at another,[35] or who, as with Samuel
Willard, held to the belief that the will is decidedly subordinate to the
understanding. Hooker's position on the will's supremacy proves an
important point of differentiation, setting him between, on the one
hand, Pelagians and Antinomians, and on the other hand, the more
conservative majority of his brethren who talked somewhat less about
breaking man's heart and the difficulties thereof and somewhat more
about simply coming to Christ. In Hooker's view conversion ministry
involved more than mere teaching; it involved persuasion. If a sinner's
spiritual movement involved only his intellect, Hooker said repeatedly,
that person was a lost soul for certain. Since the will was capable of
disagreeing with the mind, it had to be won over to divine truth, just
as fully as did the understanding.

This outspoken commitment to a voluntarist position harks back to
Augustine and, after him, Anselm, Bernard, Bonaventure and Duns
Scotus, all of whom emphasized the importance and power of the will
and, in some cases, related affections, more than the intellect.[36] The
Italian Renaissance humanist, Coluccio Salutati (1331–1406), was following Petrarch in staking a clear voluntarist position when he said "that
the will rules the intellect because it is active and the intellect is passive."[37] Despite this background, however, the voluntarist position was
not a dominant one in late sixteenth- and early seventeenth-century
English Puritan circles. Most were content with the dictates and practices of the long-standing scholastic tradition, which—following Aristotle, who made little effort to distinguish the will as a separate faculty,
and Aquinas, who gave a clear priority to the intellect—had a highly
rationalist, intellectualist understanding of the workings of the inner
man. Hooker was like his friend William Ames in espousing the voluntarist position. Norman Fiering, in the best discussion of the relative

roles of will and intellect in English and New English Puritanism in the seventeenth century, has said that "Ames's program was revolutionary within reformed Protestantism and even within Puritanism itself, which in the course of the sixteenth and seventeenth centuries had become deeply scholasticized and intellectualized."[38] Hooker was quick to join Ames's revolution, and he spent his career furthering it.

Hooker's voluntaristic stand is important because it puts him firmly in a position of leadership among those preaching the need to take preparative steps before grace would be revealed. Perry Miller observed that giving the will this power to disagree with the understanding was crucial, since "unless the will were granted some degree of independence, unless it were free to act or refuse of its own power, there could be no moral responsibility."[39] This statement is, of course, perfectly true insofar as the issue is one of morality. In fact, though, Miller states only half of the implications of the importance of granting the will preeminence over the intellect—and the half which Hooker felt was the less important.

To understand Hooker's sense of the major issue here, we need to return to his discussion of the concept of Adam's creation in God's image. We have noticed Hooker's statement that God constructed Adam's soul of understanding, will, and affections. In *The Paterne of Perfection*, as we have seen, Hooker explains that the understanding reflects God's image in its possession of knowledge and prudence. Then Hooker asks, "What was the image of God in the will?" (*PP*, p. 61). The answer is that God put "holiness" and "righteousness" into Adam's will. In discussing these qualities, Hooker reveals again the tendency of the Puritan to see the world as a composition of dualities or dichotomies. These are the qualities by which the will can relate properly, on the one hand, to God, and on the other, to self and fellow man. Holiness, says Hooker, is "a spirituall power, or frame put into the nature of *Adam*, inabling him to doe Gods will, and fitting him to love God above all"—to "close with God" (*PP*, p. 63). Righteousness, however, is "the second part of the spiritual image put into *Adam*, whereby hee could love himselfe as hee ought, and his neighbour as himselfe" (*PP*, p. 84). Thus, holiness and righteousness have an incipient life within men's wills, but both require cultivation. First and foremost, he advises, pursue holiness so that you may come closer to God and make His will your will. In a Use of trial Hooker asks, Can you "love God above all?" If so, he answers, you have holiness (*PP*, pp. 80–81).

But this holiness fits a man to go to God, not to his neighbor. When righteousness is properly developed in the soul and adequately supported by God's assistance, man can often—certainly not always—respond to the dictates of right reason by taking right moral action. In a rare and beautiful passage in *The Paterne of Perfection*, Hooker reminds his congregation that man "was made a sociable creature. . . . Love is the sinewes of society" (*PP*, p. 104). Love and will are frequently related in the thinking of Renaissance voluntarists, who are, on this point as well as in their basic preference for the power of the will over that of the intellect, faithful to Augustine's example. In fact, as Eugene Rice has said, an "emphasis on the will and love is a traditional characteristic of those medieval thinkers who kept their Augustinian fervor undampened by Aristotle's intellectualism."[40] The voluntaristic hierarchy of will over intellect, according to Rice, led in the Renaissance to the "secularization of wisdom." Hooker and Ames both, however, provide preeminent examples that secularization was not a necessary result of voluntarism, even for one in the Calvinist tradition. In Hooker we find that, in addition to the preeminence granted to the will, and in addition to the identification of will with the emotion and act of love, the entire process has significance chiefly because it is central to man's working out of his relationship with God. The *Puritan* version of Augustinian voluntarism, in other words, is primarily a function of a *theological* rather than a "metaphysical" or secular perspective on existence.

Thus, Hooker shows the will to be centrally involved in what modern theologians have called man's "vertical" and "horizontal" relationships—those with God and with men. Without God's help in both of these relationships, one gets nowhere. Simply put, "the children of God are the children of love, the children of Satan are the Children of hatred" (*PP*, p. 106). These children of Satan, Hooker kept insisting, are far more numerous than the children of God; most men do *not* become regenerate. This is particularly important to remember in connection with the power of the will to choose what it will do in response to understanding's advice. Typically, it chooses poorly. The will's freedom to select a course of action, then, is a built-in guarantee of immoral, as well as moral, action, a point to which Miller fails to give adequate emphasis. Adam's sin is a powerful poison. Hooker late in his career defined Original Sin as a "running wrong of all . . . the Faculties of the Soul of man"[41]—a description which he knew was amply supported by empirical evidence.

The importance of the belief that the will's function is of a higher order than the understanding's should not be underestimated. Fully one quarter of Hooker's published writings are directly concerned with the spiritual task of "breaking" and humbling the heart, of pounding the stony heart into impressionable powder, of turning the heart of cold stone into a heart of warm flesh. Above all, Hooker was concerned with getting his listeners to realize that the judgment of damnable corruption which the enlightened understanding passes on their individual souls must be "brought home" to the heart with such conviction that the sinner would vehemently wish to change his condition—would dispose his will to choose to pursue the "narrow path" to justification which the minister was pointing out. The point to which he wanted to bring all of his congregation was that climactic moment in the arduous process of self-examination at which Saint Augustine turned finally away from himself and said, " 'How long, Lord? . . . How long, how long? Tomorrow, and to-morrow? Why not now? Why is there not this hour an end to my uncleanness?' "[42] Hooker cites this event in Augustine's life in urging his congregation to come to this ultimate commitment of *will*, which forces an acceptance of Christ and enables the faithful finally to say "Amen to the businesse."[43] In a sense, this is the ultimate moment in one's spiritual pursuit of grace, since at this point he has literally done all he can and God must do the rest. If he becomes a "new man," of course, it will not be because of anything he has done on his own but because God has chosen him and has given him the necessary divine assistance. Nevertheless, it must be added that he is actively, even aggressively, *willing* to be saved. Hooker and his contemporaries agreed that divine ambushes, Damascus road miracles, just must not be expected any more. Salvation had become a more orderly—and more intricate—process.

This elaborate orderliness appears in Hooker's explanation of the way in which the judgments of the clear-seeing mind were said to be brought home to the will. Two important aids to this process were available: meditation and the conscience. Both of these tools could help the will adopt a correct reaction to the dictates of understanding. The collaborative relationship between meditation and conscience is clearly explained in *The Soules Preparation,* where Hooker urges that "serious meditation of our sinnes by the word of God, is a speciall meanes to breake our hearts for our sinnes." Meditation, he says, "brings home sin more powerfully to the heart"; it goes out of church with the congregation and "fastens sinne upon the consciences of those to whom the word of God is spoken." Meditation should include reflections on the mercy and justice of God as well as on the heinous nature of one's own sins and the potential "endlesse torments" that they will cost the sinner. One must never cease meditating until the heart feels the evil of sin as much as the mind has understood it.[44]

If meditation is to result in gaining power over the soul, says

Hooker, the conscience must bring its power to bear. "Understanding and reason are but the underlings of the wil," since the will can reject their dictates, but the conscience can actually affect the will. If the conscience so directs, the heart will give way.[45] This is no easy process, but an agonizing one, often involving "desperate discouragements" and *"Hellish provocations."*[46] Hooker addressed this subject repeatedly in his sermons, and it is significant that the earliest published comments on it in *The Soules Preparation* (1632) are, though briefer, essentially the same as the remarks in his final, posthumously published work, *The Application of Redemption, The Ninth and Tenth Books* (1656). In each, he uses metaphors of physical confrontation to suggest the pain and suffering involved in making the will accept the conscience's insistence on the grievous need for a savior.[47]

Part of the inheritance of Adam's sin, then, is our inclination to resist grace. The eighth book of *The Application of Redemption* is devoted to "proving" the Doctrine that *"God the Father by a Holy kind of violence as it were, plucks his out of their Corruptions, and Draws them to Beleeve in Christ."* The will's obedience to right dictates of the understanding is enabled by *"a Double Drawing, or Constraint,"* by which the soul is severed from its thoroughgoing union with sin and the will is "attracted" to Christ.[48] Without this "drawing" by God, the soul would perish simply as the result of one's own "natural" inclinations.

Given the aid of conscience and meditation, however, the matter is somewhat altered. When these weapons enter the fray against sin, man's chances improve noticeably. It is not that their functioning removes man's corruption in some miraculous way but rather that their forceful operation is a sign that God is willing to see the individual saved—that, in other words, the sinner is "His" and He is initiating the "Double Drawing" action, without which men are helpless to come to grace.

While thus striving to get the heart to say amen to the judgments of reason, the sinner must be wary of another power of the mind that can prove extremely dangerous: the imagination. Perry Miller has commented on the Puritans' sense of this danger.[49] But while Hooker comments on the potential evil of the imagination in a very decisive and colorful way, he does not return to it and give it the kind of insistent emphasis that characterizes, for instance, his concern for the need to see sin clearly and convictingly. Futhermore, his use of the term *imagination* should not be confused with our own (a danger not sufficiently guarded against by Miller), since in Hooker "imaginations" usually means simply "thoughts," though sometimes more particularly "wandering thoughts"—thoughts, that is, which have gotten out from under the organizing and refining power of reason. A man's imaginations, he says with his customary metaphorical exuberance, are "the forge of villany," "the Ware-house of wickedness," "the Magazine of al mischief and iniquity," and "the Sea of abominations." "The Imagination of our mind is the great Wheel that carries al with it."[50] If the imaginations of the mind are "the womb where wickedness is conceived; So are they also the breasts and dugs where [evils] are maintained and nursed up."[51] Thus the imagination, like other attributes of the mind, is potentially very powerful, requiring proper harnessing if it is not to destroy its possessor.

But even if the imagination is properly controlled and such mental functions as meditation and conscience do their chores well—if, in other words, the findings of the understanding are effectively "fastened" to the will—the will is entirely unable to will any lasting spiritual good without the intervention of God Himself. As we have already noticed, Adam's fall insured our possession of limited abilities of soul and made a "running wrong of all . . . the Faculties of the Soul of man" the norm. Whatever stage on the road to redemption an individual sinner may have reached, he *always* needs God's help to continue on the "straight way." Even in the regenerate, "there is two men . . ., a heart and a heart, a will and a will"—one of the spirit, which is willing, and one of the flesh, which is weak. *"The Faculty of the Will attended only in its natural being and ability, cannot Will a spiritual or supernatural good; but must have a spiritual and supernatural power put into it, to enable it to put forth a supernatural work."* God's guidance to the will typically comes as a "holy kind of violence" which strikes, not at the will itself, but at the corruptions which inhibit the right action of the will. Again Augustine's description appealed to Hooker: "that old Sentence of *Austine,* which all Divines embrace and follow, and I desire no more for the cause if it be rightly scanned and considered; *God makes of an unwilling will, a willing will."*[52]

Implicit in the idea that the will can either reject or accept the dictates of the understanding is the sticky matter of freedom of the will, which Hooker carefully defines as "a speciall priviledge proceeding from the image of God in *Adam,* whereby he was able to chuse any good without any impediment, yet after a mutable manner" (*PP,* p. 116). Since it was a "priviledge," Adam's freedom "to chuse any good" did not necessarily lead to such a choice, though since it was "without any impediment," nothing either inside or outside of Adam could actively *prevent* his choosing good (p. 123). Also, "freedome is not seated in the understanding" (p. 119). "It is easie to convince a mans understanding, all the difficulty is in the will" (p. 120). But *freedom* is properly expressed only in a certain *kind* of choice: the choice of good. For "it is no liberty for a man to be carried on headily to evill" (p. 121). Despite what men think when making the choice, the selection of evil is merely a persisting in one's enslavement to sin—a condition he has naturally, regardless of the attributes of his will. Yet, as Hooker says, Adam's ability to choose good was "mutable"; only God is immutable. This mutability gave him equal ability to do good *or* evil. Without freedom to do good or not to do it, Adam's service to God would not have been acceptable: "All Gods servants must be Volunteers, not prest" (p. 133). Adam's freedom, however, is lost to the reprobate, while it is partially regained in the regenerate, to whom Christ has restored it. The gracious soul, Hooker argues, hates evil and eventually "gets the upper hand of evill" (p. 144), though never complete power over it.

Thus, freedom comes with grace. Without grace, man is a slave. And in *The Application of Redemption*, Hooker, apparently desiring to correct any tendency to read his earlier works on the preparation for grace as smacking of Arminianism, vehemently and directly argues against the heresies of the Arminian doctrine of freedom of the will. It was Hooker's avowed policy to keep dispute of any kind out of his redemption sermons, but here he makes an exception to his policy in order to argue, for about seven pages, what he felt was a crucial matter. He had earlier said that "the Lord in his word saith, it is not talke, it is not wishes, but it is the willing of Christ and grace that will obtaine grace."[53] This text—which may or may not reprint the preacher's words faithfully—makes the process sound a bit easier than Hooker would have wished, particularly when cited out of context; we must remember his constant refrain that grace comes only from God's mercy, so that if it is man's willing of Christ and grace which obtains them, this willing would have to be the result of God's creating it out of man's unwillingness, a point on which Hooker followed Augustine explicitly. The Arminian doctrine that implies that man, by his own doing, can in effect force God into justifying him "makes Gods free grace lackey after mans free wil." "*It cuts the very sinews of the Covenant of Grace, and the freedom thereof*" and "plucks the Crown from Christs Head, the Glory from his Work, the Praise from his Grace, and gives it to the will of man."[54] This strikes Hooker as both absurd and heretical, since to him—and anyone else in or near the mainstream of the Calvinist tradition—there is simply no way that man can deserve or earn grace. Man's possession of freedom of will certainly implies no such power. Grace is God's to bestow, while the free choice of good is a privilege enjoyed by the gracious alone: it is an effect of God's grace, not its cause.

Affections

The final stage of Hooker's discussion of the image of God in Adam in *The Paterne of Perfection* deals with the affections, which are usually identified as being in the heart and thus an important function of the will. In answer to his own rhetorical question, "What was the image of God in the affections of *Adam?*" (*PP*, p. 149), Hooker responds that His image appeared in the submission and perfection of the affections to the will and understanding. When man's faculties are rightly ordered, as they were in the prelapsarian Adam, there is an uninterrupted congruity between the thought of God and the acts of men: "Here was the right order in which we were made, and we should have kept Rank and File; the mind and judgment should only have attended God; the Will attend our Judgment, the Affections wait on the Will, the Actions issue as the execution of al." In its original harmony, the Creation was full of ordered progressions and hierarchies of government like this one, by which man's favored position in God's universe was demonstrable. The cataclysmic event of Adam's fall threw the divine harmony into discord. The straight line of progression from the mind and will of God through the mind and will of man and into man's deeds was broken. Misdirection, imperfection, and downright wrongheadedness became typical of all stages of man's thought processes and, of course, of his speech and acts. In the psychological system which the Puritans accepted from an earlier day, the affections were placed nearest to man's actions. They immediately preceded an act or speech by which the affection was made evident to the world. Yet Puritans of the late sixteenth and early seventeenth centuries recognized that if the affections were wrongly disposed—if, for instance, a man hated the saints of the Church and desired his neighbor's wife rather than hating sin and desiring the mercy of Christ—it was a symptom of a deeper spiritual illness. The Puritans of this age did not, therefore, merely appeal to their congregations to reform their affections. They knew the disposition of the affections reflected the disposition of the will, and they therefore typically concentrated their energies on reforming the whole heart. As John Cotton said, "Let not men satisfie themselves in giving God any part of their lives in the whole course of their conversation, or any affections, but give him the heart, and when hee hath that then hee will take the rest, with-hold that and give him all the rest, and hee makes account you give him nothing."[55] The "Heart-religion" of early New England could hardly be expressed more concisely than it is here.

The saint is always anxious to bring his affections to the degree of speedy, dedicated obedience to "wisdom and holiness" that typified Adam. One of the signs of a gracious heart is that its possessor is greatly troubled by his inability entirely to control his unruly affections, whereas a corrupt, unregenerate man "beares all with a Pish" (*PP*, p. 169). Man's control, or lack of it, over his affections is thus a "measure" of his possession or lack of grace. In a Use of examination, Hooker advises his listeners to look inward to "see what tractablenesse there is in thy affections, to submit unto the authority of holinesse" (p. 162). "Art thou able, when [jarring affections] would transport thee, to allay them, and bring thy soule to a calme frame? Then it is a signe thou hast grace" (p. 165).

The apparently simple structure of man's psychological anatomy, when properly used and acted upon, could bring a person a long way. It could also, of course, carry him or her just as far in the wrong direction. It was this inner makeup of "the soule" that determined Hooker's emphasis on experimental religion throughout his entire career. Had he not understood the human mind's operation in terms of the precisely designated and logically sequential order which we have observed, he could never have developed the equally precise and elaborate series of stages through which an individual had to go to "apply" redemption to his soul. Even in this preliminary examination of Hooker's understanding of the anatomy of the soul it is apparent that man's constitution provides obstacles aplenty to the work of redemption. Heroic effort by minister and parishioner alike would be required to bring the soul to even an imperfect imitation of Adam's example.

7
Preparation for Grace
THE DOCTRINAL PREMISES

No doubt the voluntarist stance taken by some Puritans in their interpretation of faculty psychology was an important element in the development of the doctrine of preparation for grace. The essentials of Calvinist dogma, involving joint belief in God as the sovereign elector of the faithful and in the base depravity of Adam's descendants, would seem to have dictated against the individual sinner's playing a significant role in the working out of his own destiny. But Calvinists were not fatalists. Some of those who affirmed the will's supremacy among the soul's faculties pressed on to the granting of an active role for the will in the search for spiritual regeneration. They did not ignore or change the tenets of God's sovereignty and human depravity, but they did insist that an individual's role in the face of these realities should be something other than benign passivity. In Thomas Hooker's view, preaching, for all its importance, was a futile exercise unless the listener intended to put the minister's truths to work for him when he left the meetinghouse. He was quite serious in remarking, "All that I have said, is but a speech of a little time, but it is a taske for all a mans life."[1]

Calvinist thinkers, understanding the world as a place where God's order is everywhere manifest even though His will is not everywhere triumphant, had early devised a very orderly explanation of the progressive stages through which the soul proceeds on its way to union with God and eternal glorification. The major parts of this progression had been described in Calvin's *Institutes*, but English Puritans of the late sixteenth and early seventeenth centuries elaborated Calvin's outlines. In particular, the great English codifiers and simplifiers of Calvin's theology, William Perkins and William Ames, made some progress toward full explication of this step-by-step progression of the life of

146

the elect soul. But it remained for others of Hooker's generation to expand it, both doctrinally and rhetorically, in their sermons intended for "the weake." Hooker's own sermons on redemption were so detailed and yet so clear that Perry Miller did not overstate their importance in claiming that they "constitute the most minute and searching analysis of the soul and the process of spiritual regeneration, the most coherent and sustained expression of the essential religious experience ever achieved by the New England divines."[2] These writings on the stages of redemption constitute the heart of Hooker's achievement as a preacher.

Calvinists had always held that, in acquiring grace and thus drawing nearer to a perfect union with God, the individual believer would as a matter of course go through certain spiritual stages. They usually listed four such stages: calling or vocation, justification, sanctification, and glorification. Calvin discussed each of these stages, but his English followers—especially Perkins and Ames—were more inclined to stress their immutable sequence in the spiritual progress of the regenerate Christian.[3] John Phillips, an English contemporary of Hooker, summed up the common view: "There are certain graces, *that accompany salvation,* which . . . may be all included in these foure, that is, the grace of *Election,* the grace of *Vocation,* the grace of *Iustification,* and the grace of *Sanctification;* all which, ioyntly and inseparably haue their period and end in *Glorification.*"[4] The usual opinion was that grace came to one in conjunction with vocation, though there was not universal agreement about whether this influx of divine favor was immediate at the very beginning of the process of vocation or whether it came fairly late in this stage, after one had had an opportunity to come a little way towards God on his own. This slight difference of opinion gave way to a larger one which became a major distinction among Puritans who could otherwise live contentedly together.

The fundamental question in the late sixteenth century and much of the seventeenth was a theological one: Does the sinner who desires salvation have anything to do with whether or not he possesses it? More basically, can one actively *prepare* for grace—invite its coming by certain acts or thoughts while still in an unregenerate condition? The issue, as Norman Pettit has explained, became a major source of disagreement among divines at the 1618–19 Synod of Dort.[5] It remained a potentially divisive matter. Puritans who emigrated to New England stood on both sides of the controversy. John Cotton answered the question unequivocally in the negative, saying, "For our first union [with Christ], there are no steps unto the Altar."[6] Hooker and a few other New Englanders disagreed profoundly. So insistent was Hooker on this point, indeed, that his contemporaneous fame seems to have rested in part on his desire to see people exert themselves strenuously before they became assured of grace. That sometime lawyer, minister, and humorist Nathaniel Ward, who was in New England for very nearly the same years as Hooker, suggested Hooker's position was extreme when compared with that of others: "Mr. Hooker, you make as good Christians before men are in Christ as ever they are after; would I were but as good a Christian now as you make men while they are but preparing for Christ."[7] One can understand Ward's amazement, perhaps, by noticing that when Hooker revised his published work on contrition, he ended up with a book of some 600 quarto-sized pages in *The Application of Redemption, The Ninth and Tenth Books.* And this was only the half of it, since he did not live to revise his work on the next preparatory stage, humiliation. He was thoroughly committed to the vast importance of preparation for grace, and he stood by this commitment to the end.

Hooker was aware that the preparationist message was not accepted as being in the mainstream of orthodoxy by many of his colleagues. John Calvin himself discusses humiliation only briefly, making the point that the meaningful life of the redeemed begins with faith. Calvin gives his main attention to the crucial stage of justification. The absence from the *Institutes* of any detailed comment on the stages of contrition and humiliation, which the preparationists put before justification, was repeated a century later in the Westminster Confession of Faith, where no mention is made of either. Even Thomas Goodwin and Philip Nye, friends of Hooker in England and sympathizers with him on most doctrinal and ecclesiastical issues, were in some disagreement with his insistence that extensive preparation of the soul takes place before grace is received. In their introductory essay for the posthumous first edition of *The Application of Redemption, The Ninth and Tenth Books* (1656), they said that he "urg[ed] too far, and insist[ed] too much upon that as *Preparatory,* which includes indeed the beginnings of true *Faith.*" But, as Pettit has shown, there was ample precedent for Hooker's position among English predecessors such as Richard Greenham, Richard Rogers, William Perkins, William Ames, and Richard Sibbes, all of whom had, with varying degrees of emphasis and always with less elaborate insistence than Hooker, taught their congregations and their reading audiences that the corrupt human heart is in no condition to experience grace without some degree of preparation.[8] Hooker, of course, became more energetic than any of these predecessors and contemporaries in arguing the need for preparation.

If the freedom—psychological as well as theological and social—to preach truth as he knew it was not present in one location, he was willing to subject himself, his sometimes invalid wife, and his entire congregation to the seemingly unnecessary hardships of a long ocean voyage or wilderness trek to a location more suitable for the preaching of his message. For Hooker and his immediate followers the frontier certainly offered the freedom which he needed. His doctrine of preparation took firm root in the wilderness settlement of Hartford. The active involvement of the individual was a fundamental principle in the practice of this doctrine, just as it was in the other aspects of his thought noticed in Part I of this study. Indeed, a full understanding of Hooker's message on redemption, especially the early stages—contrition, humiliation, and vocation—enables an appreciation of both his personal character and his role in the development of American theological thought. We hear in these sermons the voice of a man uncompromisingly dedicated to the Christian ideal of personal salvation and deeply compassionate toward the individual sinner's weakness of will and misdirection of energies. And we can hear the voice of the religious idealist that was to be echoed in the writings of successive generations of Americans.

Hooker's account of the *ordo salutis* enlarged the process not just by adding two preparatory stages (others had done this before him) but also in the sheer volume of his explanation of the whole history of the soul's redemption—contrition, humiliation, vocation, justification, adoption, sanctification, and glorification. His writings on this subject total more than 4,000 pages, or about two-thirds of his published writings. We know from Goodwin and Nye that Hooker preached the entire series at least three times at different stages in his career and to different churches: "He *Preach'd* more briefly of this Subject *first*, whilst he was *Fellow* and *Chatechist* in *Emanuel Colledg* in *Cambridg*. The Notes of which, were then so esteemed, that many Copies thereof, were by many that heard not the Sermons, written out, and are yet extant by them. And then again, a *Second time*, many yeers after, more largely at *Great Chelmsford* in *Essex;* the Product of which, was those Books of Sermons that have gone under his Name. And *Last* of all; *now* in *New-England*, and that in, and to a *setled Church* of Saints."[9] Cotton Mather, writing less than fifty years after Hooker's death, also pointed to his special emphasis on the theology of redemption: "Although he had a Notable Hand at the Discussing and Adjusting of *Controversial* Points, yet he would hardly ever handle any *Polemical Divinity* in the Pulpit; but the very *Spirit* of his Ministry, lay in the points of the most *Practical Religion*, and the *Grand Concerns* of a Sinner's *Preparation* for, *Implantation* in, and *Salvation* by, the Glorious Lord Jesus Christ."[10] To a large extent, in other words, Hooker's reputation was based on this dominant thematic emphasis in his sermons on the stages of grace.

But more striking than the physical bulk of these sermons is his characterization in them of the way it feels to be a sinner engaged in such a soul-searching enterprise as the pursuit of grace. His predecessors had often tended to treat the sinner's progression through vocation, justification, sanctification, and glorification as an operation which, in effect, happens *to* the elect saint, willy-nilly, by the grace of God. Perkins, for instance, speaks of the first stage of redemption—for him, "calling"—as resulting from the "sauing hearing of the word of God" through preaching. This hearing surprises the sinner, who is "both dead in his sinnes, and doth not so much as dreame of his saluation."[11] Perkins goes on to describe the process as something in which the sinner seems to have a largely passive role. This is implied in Perkins's tendency to cast his verbs repeatedly in the passive voice. For instance, in vocation, "inwardly the eyes of the minde are enlightened" and "the heart and eares opened that he may see, heare, and vnderstand the preaching of the word of God."[12] The standard Calvinistic emphasis on the sinner's inability to do anything about his own salvation explains this comparatively dispassionate treatment of the process. Perkins goes on to deal in this manner with all the stages which he discusses: "In the worke of faith, there are foure degrees, or motions of the heart, linked and vnited together. . . . The first, is knowledge of the Gospell, by the illumination of Gods spirit. . . . And after the foresaid knowledge in all such as are enlightened, commeth a *generall faith.*" While Perkins occasionally notices that the sinner must do something in all of this, such as "approaching to the throne of Grace, that there flying from the terror of the Law, he may take hold of Christ, & find fauour with God,"[13] the reader familiar with Hooker's writings on the subject is struck by the relative absence of the real sense of active adventure on the part of the sinner seeking grace which so thoroughly characterizes Hooker's works. For Hooker, the sinner is desperately involved in the process: "Arise, arise, therefore ye secure and dead hearted Sinners, and come away. . . . Come to him who so kindly invites you, who promises to accept you, who is able and willing to save you."[14] Though God is always the prime mover, the sinner's whole mind and all his senses must be focused on the task before him. Hooker aids his listeners in this effort by frequently describing the process of redemption from the perspective of the sinner himself. While with Perkins, God's role as initiator and bestower of grace so thoroughly influences the way the redemptive process is described that it tends to sound like an inevitable course of events through which the soul is safely carried by the Holy Spirit, Hooker pictures, from ground level, a rocky road full of pitfalls over which he is forever urging the poor doubting souls in his congregation to clamber. Perkins, of course, usually saw his role as that of instructor and codifier. His fame and authority among his own and later generations depended on this stance. He was, as Larzer Ziff has said, "the man whom Cambridge recognized as her greatest theologian,"[15] and the difference in tone and urgency between Perkins's and Hooker's accounts of the redemptive process is accountable largely in terms of the difference between the theologian and the pastor. Ames, too, in reducing the subject to textbook formality, tends to describe the stages of redemption abstractly as a procedure to which the elect soul is subjected rather than one which he is actively guiding or encouraging.[16] Hooker's achievement is based largely in his ability to bring the doctrines dynamically, dramatically alive.

The distinction among these presentations of the doctrine of redemption is thus one more of color and tone than of substance, based more on psychology than theology. Hooker, though he seldom mentioned the writings of other men in his sermons, several times named Perkins as an astute and reliable authority on fundamental theological tenets, and the last thing he would have wanted was to seem or actually to be in major theological disagreement with that great preacher on the important points of their mutual doctrine. Likewise, as we have noted, Hooker was a great admirer, emulator, and friend of William Ames. So Hooker was attempting no break from traditional authority in his detailed discussion of the way to salvation; he was, rather, building on the foundation laid by his predecessors from Calvin to Ames, attempting to simplify by dramatizing and personalizing the difficult intricacies of Calvinism. Hooker's ease in identifying with the frustrated sinner's dilemma in desiring salvation but feeling unworthy of it caused him to stress the difficulties in earnestly seeking God's grace. His tone, as a result, often seems to resemble Augustine's more than that of his own immediate predecessors. Whereas Calvin, Perkins, and Ames were inclined to say, "This is the way redemption happens . . .," Hooker preferred to say, "If you would achieve redemption, this is what you must do. . . ." Though he never said, "Follow these steps and I guarantee that you will be saved," still, his writings do not hold much hope for the passive Christian who is willing merely to be carried along by the tide of predestination. The man who thinks getting to heaven is easy, Hooker insisted, is fatally deceived. But so too is the man who thinks there is nothing to do but hope. For instance, the character whom Hooker calls the "judicious professor" actually has no saving faith; he fails to realize that gaining faith is *difficult:* "This man hath found out a shorter cut, and an easier way to heaven."[17] But there are no short cuts. Hooker was convinced the road to heaven was an arduous one: "You must not thinke to goe to heaven on a feather-bed."[18] As a result of this awareness of the challenge which the search for grace presents, Hooker's sermons are filled with verbs in the active rather than the passive voice and figures of speech based upon the principle of action. He wanted his parishioners to be up and doing, to be particularly lively in their minds and spirits. The "gracious man" would, as a function of his desire for and acceptance of faith, make every effort. It was a demanding assignment to be a regular member of Thomas Hooker's congregation, as Nathaniel Ward obviously knew.

The message of the New England preparationists—including especially Thomas Shepard, who in some respects was Hooker's protégé, and Peter Bulkeley, the first minister of Concord, Massachusetts[19]—appeals to modern readers in its insistence that the individual man has a role to play in working out the final disposition of his soul. The sinner, as described by the preparationist preacher, does not save himself, of course, nor does he so much as influence God's decision in the matter, since that has been made long since. But he does not sit on his hands, waiting for the angel of the Lord to embrace him and lead him away. If he responds as Hooker repeatedly insisted he must, he constantly and diligently "labours" to "fit" himself for union with God, never ceasing to hope that, desperate as his condition is, he might be found acceptable by his Lord. This laboring and fitting oneself comprises the central motif in Hooker's lengthy series of sermons on redemption.

The Application of Redemption: Preliminaries

Since Hooker had spent his career working out fuller and fuller accounts of the *ordo salutis*—the stages of redemption—it is understandable that as he approached the age of sixty he determined to write down his explication of the process as it then stood in his mind. His intention, apparently, was to publish the full account when it was completed. Due to some ambiguous statements by those involved in the publication of some of his posthumous works, it is unclear how far he actually got in his final revisions of the series. As we have seen in the case of *The Saints Dignitie and Dutie* (1651), not all of his posthumous publications were gotten to the printer so expeditiously as was *A Survey of the Summe of Church Discipline*, which was published in 1648, the year after Hooker's death. The Brief *Covenant of Grace Opened* saw timely publication in 1649, while the baptism controversy was still very current. Then, after two more years, came his book on the issues of the Antinomian controversy, followed by a five-year hiatus before the appearance of three major volumes, each containing parts of the redemption sermon series. When they appeared in 1656, Hooker had been dead for nine years. This delay may be ascribable partly to the fact that those charged in his will with seeing to publication of suitable manuscripts were involved in divisive squabbles in the Hartford church in the years following Hooker's death.[20] It was finally the two English divines Thomas Goodwin and Philip Nye who edited and saw to the publication of the final three volumes in Hooker's canon: *The Application of Redemption, The first eight Books*; *The Application of Redemption, The Ninth and Tenth Books*; and *A Comment upon Christs Last Prayer*, which was numbered "Book Seventeen." The editors, obviously interested in making a strong case for the importance of their editions of these writings, argued in the best editorial hyperbole that in them Hooker had corrected errors in the "imperfect Editions" previously published under different titles "without his privity or consent" from notes "taken by an unskilful hand," which "utterly deformed and mis-represented . . . multitudes of passages."[21] Hooker clearly intended the new books to refine and expand the subjects treated in the earlier ones. From the standpoint of doctrine they are certainly to be preferred, though the differences are usually more in clarity and precision than in substantial theological differences. Yet, for the modern reader interested in studying Hooker's oral style, the earlier volumes are invaluable and often preferable.

Since the three volumes published in 1656 in London by the printer Peter Cole are numbered Books One through Ten and Book Seventeen, appearances strongly suggest that Cole also intended to issue Books Eleven through Sixteen. In fact, an advertisement in each of the published volumes announces that "there are six more Books of Mr. *Hookers*, now printing in two Volumes." One is inclined, however, not to take this claim too literally. The same advertisement lists the biblical texts for the eleven books actually published but does not include this information about those still unpublished. It seems likely that the other works were at least not "now printing," if indeed Peter Cole ever had them in his hands at all. Cole apparently believed that they would be published, however, and no doubt said so in good faith. Why they never appeared is one of the lasting mysteries of Puritan studies.

The contents of the missing volumes can be surmised from the editors' comments about what was left uncompleted in Hooker's task. The two volumes given the title *The Application of Redemption* actually treat only the first of the several separable stages of redemption, namely contrition. This is the subject of Book Ten. The preceding books, as we shall see shortly, deal with essential theological background to the entire series. Book Seventeen, *A Comment upon Christs Last Prayer*, treats the last stage, glorification. The six books which Cole claimed were "now printing" apparently dealt with humiliation and vocation, since Goodwin and Nye regretted that "the other *Great Points*, as *Union with Christ, Justification, Adoption, Sanctification*, and *Glory* (which Subjects, as he was able for, so his heart was most in them) he hath left unfinished." Fortunately, most of the unauthorized volumes of which Goodwin and Nye complain give full and reliable accounts of the later stages of the redemption process, so that the entire sequence can be reconstructed, if not as Hooker would have wanted it at the time of his death, at least as it was recorded from sermons actually delivered at one point or another during his career.

It is of some significance that in beginning his revisions Hooker did not throw himself immediately into an explication of contrition, but spent nearly an entire 400-page volume discussing what are essentially crucial points of theological background to the *ordo salutis*. The first volume of *The Application of Redemption*, as a result, is a much more theoretical treatise than the second. Its title page summarizes the argument of each of its eight books:

1. Christ hath purchased all spiritual good for HIS.
2. Christ put all HIS into possession of all that Good that he hath purchased.
3. The Soul must be fitted for Christ before it can receive him: And a powerful Ministry is the ordinary means to prepare the heart for Christ.
4. The Work of God is free: And the day of Salvation, is while this Life last, and the Gospel continue.
5. God calls his Elect at any Age, but the most before old Age.
6. The Soul is naturally setled in a sinful security.
7. The heart of a Natural man is wholly unwilling to submit to the Word that would sever him from his sins.
8. God the Father by a holy kind of violence, plucks His out of their corruptions, and draws them to beleeve in Christ.[22]

The contents of these eight books can be reduced to four essential subjects of Calvinist theology: (1) Man's corruption and need for help in achieving any degree of spiritual purification, (2) God's merciful nature, (3) predestination, and (4) the need for men to prepare for Christ's possession of their hearts. Hooker's elaboration of the first three of these topics clearly demonstrates his orthodoxy on the main points of Calvin's theology, while the last point indicates his powerful and consistent stress on the responsibility of the individual sinner in the redemptive process to a degree which clearly distinguishes him from many of his contemporaries in the Calvinist camp.

The corruption of man and his need for divine assistance if he is to be saved is one of the most consistently recurrent themes in all of Hooker's works. It is stressed particularly in the first eight books of *The Application of Redemption* and in *The Vnbeleevers Preparing for Christ*, which was an earlier version of the main substance of Books Four, Five, Seven, and Eight of *The Application*. Hooker says that man puts up a "hellish opposition" against all good, including his own salvation. *"That power by which the Lord works in Application is an Almighty power"* (AR, i, 128), as it must needs be, since the unregenerate man's will is thoroughly corrupt and occupied by the power of darkness. The full contrast between God's miraculous powers and man's helplessness is implied in Hooker's further comment that "it's beyond the power of darkness to bring light" (AR, i, 131). Only God, the opposite of darkness, can bring this light, and Hooker looked to nature for an analogy which helped him say so: Christ "must apply himself to us, before we can apply him to our own hearts. As the beams of the Sun must come down to the waters, before it can draw up the water in clouds and vapors: So here" (AR, i, 90–91). As he puts it elsewhere, "The very same power that raised Christ from the dead, the same power must worke repentance in the heart of a man." If you have the power to resurrect Christ, you can repent of your own accord. If not, look to God.[23] In this personalized syllogism, Hooker rebukes the proud man deftly and unanswerably. He reminds his listeners both literally and metaphorically who and what they are: "a company of poor, miserable, sinful, and damned Creatures, sinful dust and ashes, dead dogs" (AR, i, 200).

Given this characterization of man, it is especially fortunate that God is a merciful being. That He is indeed merciful is one of the joyous refrains in Puritan literature and in Hooker's writings especially. He makes no demand that sinners earn His love. "The offer of grace from God is altogether free"; "from the beginning of election, to the end of glorification; from the beginning of conversion, to the end of salvation, all is grace and mercy."[24] Similar passages extolling the mercy of God can be found in practically any of Hooker's works, but the theme is particularly significant in the first eight books of *The Application*, where he is laying the foundation for the elaborate edifice which was to comprise his full system for redemption. In the second book of *The Application*, after explaining how the eternal good of spiritual redemption is "applied" to God's chosen, Hooker, in a Use of admiration, becomes rhapsodic in rejoicing at the riches of God's mercy and the freeness of his grace. In this passage of exceptional rhetorical force, Hooker expounds a theme which is recurrent throughout the entire canon. He is telling the redeemed sinner how to approach God:

That thou mayest forever each day that passeth over thy head, remember it to the Lord, and leave it upon record in thy own Conscience; say, Hadst thou (blessed Lord) given me the desire of my heart, and left me to my own will, its certain I had been in Hell long before this day, when in the days of my folly and times of my ignorance, when out of the desperat wretchedness of my rebellious disposition, I was running riot in the wayes of wickedness, *When I said to the Seers, See not; and to the Prophets, Prophesie not,* to Christians, to acquaintance, to Governors, Admonish not, Counsel not, Reprove not, Stop me not in the pursuit of sin . . . I would not have that Word of thine reveal or remove my corruptions, I would none of thy Grace that might humble me and purge me, none of that Mercy of thine that might pardon me, none of that Redemption of thine that might save me, hadst thou then taken me at my word, and given me what I wished, and sealed up my destruction, saying, Be thou forever filthy, for ever stubborn, and for ever miserable, thou wouldest neither be holy nor happy, thou shalt have thy will, sin with Devils, and take thy Portion with Devils, Lord, it had been just with thee, and I justly miserable.

But to bear with all my baseness, to put up all those wrongs and provocations, to strive with me for good when I took up Arms against thee, and strove against my own good; nay, when I resisted Mercy, and then to take away that resistance, and to cause me to take Mercy, and make it mine, when I used all the skil I could to hinder my own salvation, Oh! the height, the depth, the length, the breadth of this Mercy! (*AR*, I, 97–98)

In such a passage, Hooker's consistent view of the utter folly of human nature and the supreme blessing of God's active mercy are put into the juxtaposition that the orthodox Puritan preferred, giving all the praise to God and showing man for the dead dog that he is when left to himself. It is the existence of these two opposing natures which makes the application of redemption both necessary and possible. The devout Puritan lived earnestly by the truth of this disparity of God's and his own nature, as Hooker himself proved on his deathbed in Hartford on July 7, 1647, when "one that stood weeping by the Bed-side said unto him, Sir, *you are going to Receive the Reward of all your Labours,* he Replyed, *Brother, I am going to Receive Mercy!*"[25] No truth, apparently, was any more thoroughly ingrained in the man than his own undeserving nature and the great "height, the depth, the length, the breadth" of God's mercy.

But with all of the insistence on God's possession of mercy and His willingness to pursue its recipients in order to bestow it on them, another truth of Puritan theology is always implicit and so fundamental to the doctrine of redemption that it is easily overlooked: the doctrine of predestination. Samuel Eliot Morison's mistaken conclusion that, "after reading some hundreds of puritan sermons, English and New English, I feel qualified to deny that the New England puritans were predestinarian Calvinists,"[26] is understandable, since writers like Hooker seldom found it necessary to insist upon the predestinarian premise of their theology of redemption; it was simply there, an implicit part of God's plan for men. The doctrine is fully implied in Hooker's frequent use of such highly charged words as "the faithful," the "in-lightened," and "believers." It is what is meant on the title page of the first volume of *The Application* when Hooker says that "Christ hath purchased all spiritual good for HIS" and that "Christ puts all HIS into possession of all that Good that he hath purchased." "HIS" are the Elect, those predestined through God's prior election to be saved and glorified.

Yet Hooker has a rather special problem here. He is laying the groundwork for his lengthy presentation of the theology of preparation for and redemption by grace, a theology which, as he preaches it, insists upon the active involvement of the individual at all stages of the redemptive process. With this in mind, he draws some distinctions that would undoubtedly have seemed unnecessary to a man like John Cotton, who took a somewhat harder line on predestination, or one like William Twisse, moderator of the Westminster Assembly, whose line was even harder than Cotton's.[27] Hooker, in discussing the meaning of the claim that "Christ hath purchased all spiritual good for HIS," makes two important points which are not exactly qualifications but which do serve partially to pave the way for the following energetic sermons urging the would-be saint's active pursuit of grace. He first observes that *"this precious blood of Christ was shed for Sinners, BUT NOT AS SINNERS."* If Christ died for sinners as sinners, then he died for all men, an absurd idea in any pure Calvinist's view, since "Christ died for none but the Elect, and none but they shall receive any benefit from Christ" (*AR*, I, 12). The people he died for are, rather, "such sinners as are, or shall be made sensible of their sins in a right manner, being lost in point of pardon, and grace and peace" (p. 12).

But if Christ did not die for the sinners *qua* sinners, neither did he die for the elect *qua* elect. God, after all, could have put a new covenant of works into effect and given His elect the power to obey it. But they would not then have needed or benefited from Christ's sacrifice. Instead, God made it necessary to "partake of his spirit in *effectual Vocation and Faith*," which is made possible through the covenant of grace. Thus, Hooker says, "A sinner . . . under the Covenant of Grace, the seed of the Covenant . . . for him Christ dies, and this I chuse rather than that consideration of Elect as Elect" (*AR*, I, 13). Here the covenant and Christ are given that centrality which characterizes the

Puritan view of man's relationship with God. It is easy to forget that for them predestination was not a mechanical, impersonal, legalistic operation simply imposed on men by a distant Power. Their Christology brings Jesus—the second Adam, the exemplary man—front and center, where he serves as both the supremely imitable type and as the immediate cause of grace's availability to the elect through his establishment of a new covenant.

These views enable Hooker both to encourage the sinner that he needs to "labour" to ready himself for grace and to conclude that anyone who does not receive grace and dies unregenerate simply gets what he deserves. On the one hand, Hooker made the point that election and vocation are two separate stages, the one preceding the other, thus suggesting that the elect still had to work their way to vocation. On the other hand, he pointed out that the covenant of grace not only provides help to the regenerate in reaching Christ but makes men "justly faulty and guilty of their own death in not beleeving nor relying upon a *Mediator* thus graciously offered in the second Covenant, through their own corruption and hardness of heart neglecting their Savior: Though it be as impossible to beleeve as to fulfil the Law, yet because that comes through their own original sin, whereby they refuse beleef in the one as obedience to the other, they are punished for both" (*AR*, i, 14). There is paradox here with a vengeance, as there must be if the arguments on one side are not to negate those on the other. Men are saved because God saves them, through Christ and the Holy Spirit, but they are damned because of their own guilt. The fact that belief is "impossible" does not allow one to "refuse beleef." While the preacher gives the reason for discouragement, he warns against it. Incredibly, in the midst of this tension between the impossible and the unlikely lay hope for the person willing to focus on Christ and the covenant. In addition to this dilemma, when we remember Hooker's *carpe diem* message that time is desperately short for the unredeemed, it is not surprising that he repeatedly stresses his belief that the hardest thing to do in the world is to get to heaven. "No, no, narrow is the way and exceeding straight is the gate; wee must not thinke to goe to heaven with our hands by our sides."[28]

The essential point of all of this preliminary material is that the soul of man is unfit to accept grace without some kind of preparation. This is the burden of the Doctrine which leads off Book Three of *The Application: "The Soul must be fitted for Christ before it can receive Him, or Salvation by Him"* (*AR*, i, 144). He discusses this notion at some length, using most frequently two tropes, one suggesting that the soul is like a branch from a tree which must be grafted on a new tree and thus receive new life, the other likening the soul to a disorderly house which must be set to rights before a visit from the king can be expected. Though the former figure is the more consistently recurrent in Hooker's works, the latter is probably the more apt in his hands. Certainly the "weake" in his congregation could readily grasp his meaning when he said, "Imagine you saw Christ standing and knocking at the door of your hearts, as indeed he doth, and say, Hoe all you within there, all you proud hearts, all you covetous and malicious hearts, Have you no regard to a Savior? a Crucified Savior?" (p. 204). Since Christ has said he will come "into our souls, if we humble them," "therefore sweep your hearts, and clense those rooms, clense every sink, and brush down every cobweb, and make room for Christ" (p. 201). Just as it is unnatural for a child to be born while the mother sleeps, so is it unlikely that Christ will enter a totally unprepared heart (p. 299), a heart "dead asleep in the security of a sinful condition" (p. 285).

Of course, the combination of man's degeneracy, God's mercy, and predestination need not lead infallibly to Hooker's conclusion that earnest endeavor is required. There were those Puritans who consistently held to the idea that there is simply no way to prepare for grace; it will come or it won't. Hooker, however, not only sensed psychological dangers to his listeners in such a line of reasoning but was also constitutionally averse to it. As in the outward world, where his career carried him from place to place, so in his understanding of the inward world of the soul, vehement activity was a central component of the life of faith. One of the most appealing aspects of his work is that he recognized the alternatives of belief regarding man's pursuit of grace and took up his stand on the grounds of belief in man's need for preparative action, always supposing that if one prepared, he *might* become assured of salvation. In Book Four of *The Application*, in explaining a Use of encouragement to his congregation, he urges everyone to "plead for thy self" with God. He recognizes an objection which might be posed to this in the argument that "if the Dispensation of Grace depend upon Gods Free Will, he may fail us, as well as help us; he may deny it, as well as give it" (AR, I, 238). But he answers this objection with a characteristically optimistic reply: "The Answer is, He may give it as well as deny it, and thats Argument enough to sustain our hopes, and to quicken our endeavors" (p. 238). The other attitude is liable to lead to "desperate discouragement," something Hooker always fought against on behalf of his congregations. If discouragement should raise the thought of suicide, he warns, fight it off. Discouragement is a tool of the Devil, he said at various points in his preaching of preparation.

Hope, not despair, is on the way to heaven. The conundrum that while there is life there is hope was thus good theology. Hooker's psychological understanding of his people's weaknesses and his humane desire and considerable ability to encourage them in hope, despite his belief that the condition of many undoubtedly *was* hopeless, argues strongly for his greatness both as a pastor and a preacher. This positive approach to predestinarian beliefs, moreover, makes him a prime example of that "cosmic optimism" which Perry Miller reminded us was a major characteristic of Puritan thought.[29]

It is clear enough from all of this that Hooker forcefully opposed the Antinomian position which allowed that man can be involuntarily ravished by the grace of God, thus minimizing the importance of the means and the significance of the saintly life. But he did run the risk of being charged with Arminianism, which allowed that man could earn salvation through his deeds and attitude. Hooker, like any careful Puritan, kept well offshore from each of these treacherous shoals. They were the Scylla and Charybdis between which the heaven-bound voyager had to navigate. The doctrine of preparation, granting to the sinner as it did some responsibility for exertion in his pursuit of grace, *could* sound as if the sinful supplicant could somehow force God's hand. Perry Miller has argued, in fact, that Hooker's position on preparation established a tradition which, in triumphing in New England over a period of several generations, ironically led to the transcendence of Arminianism over pure Puritanism.[30] Seen as an explanation of intellectual-theological currents which ran in increasingly liberal directions as the colonial period grew towards its climax in the Revolution, the theory has persuasive strength, though it does oversimplify American theological history. For understanding the first twenty years of New England history, however, the theory is not particularly helpful, since Hooker, Cotton, Shepard, and their colleagues were unanimously and outspokenly opposed to the "damnable heresy" of Arminianism. They all insisted, whether they held a preparationist view on redemption or not, that grace comes only from and by the will of God, which it is beyond the ability of corrupt man to influence. In no way could man oblige God to save him; in this, they all agreed.[31]

In his tenth book of *The Application of Redemption*, Hooker digresses from his principal subject to make the fullest, most vehement attack on Arminianism in all his writings. It is interesting to speculate that in his enlarged revision he may have been answering insinuations from theological opponents that his theology of preparation leaned too much toward Arminianism in its sometime emphasis on men's responsibilities in the pursuit of grace. He devotes twelve pages to a single

Use which argues that the breaking of one's heart (i.e., achieving true contrition) does *not* depend "upon any preparation a man can work in himself."[32] "We may learn from hence," he says, "for ever to fear and avoyd that haeretical doctrine of the Arminians so deeply dangerous to the salvation of mens souls" which holds that self-reliant actions will lead to God's saving one's soul. Not so, says Hooker; this belief "destroyes the whol frame of grace in the carriage of it."[33] He then lists four specific objections to this heresy. First, this Arminian doctrine "makes Gods free grace lackey after mans free wil," thus both binding God to an obligation and making it possible for man to miss "his Good." Second, *"it cuts the very sinews of the Covenant of Grace, and the freedom thereof."* This takes the disposal of mercy out of God's hands and puts it in man's; the covenant of grace becomes a covenant of works. Third, "The end of the Covenant" is "to set forth the glory of the Riches of Gods Grace in the Eyes of all," but the Arminian view "plucks the Crown from Christs Head, the Glory from his Work, the Praise from his Grace, and gives it to the will of man." And fourth, our "improvements of Abilities" "cannot deserve Grace," nor can they "dispose the soul" to be fit to receive grace. God does not make promises to man to do anything.[34]

Throughout these arguments, Hooker makes effective use of Scripture to support his refutation of the Arminian heresy. In concluding this Use, he raises a very pertinent rhetorical "objection": if my endeavor will not save me, says his imaginary objector, "why should I endeavor any further, any longer, or attend the use of the means, or practice answerable thereunto?" He answers this crucial question by saying that, despite that fact that "thou thy self, and al thy services . . . are as a menstruous cloth, both in themselves, and in the sight of Gods pure eyes," nevertheless, neglect of God's means *"will undoubtedly damn thee."* The law given to Adam still holds; man is still the debtor, and the bond is in force. While you cannot "purchase" grace, God does work effectually through the means. "If thou canst not avoid al sin, avoid as much as thou canst."[35] The effect on Hooker's listeners, then, is still to encourage their earnest actions in pursuing the means of grace, if not because their actions will be directly efficacious, at least because they may help in the struggle to keep off the Devil. Hence, the effort to engage man's will in the quest for grace is present in an essentially negative argumentative context, subordinate to Hooker's chief aim in the Use, which is to refute Arminianism. Elsewhere, as we shall see, the need for man's action is more positively presented and argued but always with the necessary qualification that, of itself, it is not efficacious.

In all of this lies the crux of an interesting and crucial problem in the thought of Thomas Hooker. The spiritual activity and striving of the Christian, he both says and implies throughout his discussion of the preparatory stages of contrition and humiliation, is always necessary. "You must not think that Christ will pardon all, and you doe nothing."[36] But at the same time, your doings will not get you grace. This presents to the modern reader an apparent logical inconsistency which Hooker insists upon sustaining. An exploration of his specific positions on the two major stages of preparation—which are detailed chiefly in *The Soules Preparation;* the expanded revision of that book, *The Application of Redemption, The Ninth and Tenth Books;* and *The Soules Humiliation*—will show how he molds these complexities into a forceful message of Christian adventure. In these books, the message and the style advance the assumption that the Christian life must be active, never passive, if one is to make the necessary progress along the road to grace. Yet for all the activity on the part of the Christian, the process was above all an orderly one, following certain precisely mapped-out stages: "Its as impossible to be Justified before we be Called, as it is for a man to be Glorified before he be Justified" (*AR*, 1, 27). Sometimes Hooker spoke of the stages as points on a road, sometimes as rungs on a ladder ("The foot of *Jacobs* Ladder is here on Earth, though the top of it reach unto Heaven") (p. 241).[37] There were great numbers of scriptural examples in addition to Jacob for the sinner to follow in molding himself into the contemporary antitype of the persistent and successful pilgrim. What all such pilgrims had in common was the vital energy of the laborer in Christ's vineyard; they were aware of their own weakness and unworthiness but insistent on making the exertion nonetheless. The tension between this assumption of the need for activity and Hooker's clear anti-Arminian position that one cannot earn grace or force God's hand created the intellectual and stylistic demands that made his sermons on the preparative stages some of the most dynamic in Hooker's entire canon. His methods of getting this message across deserve close attention.

8
Preparation for Grace
A TALE OF ADVENTURE

Thomas Hooker was a man of great energies—not a passive spectator of the world's events but a compulsive participant. We have noticed his willingness to put himself in political as well as physical danger, whether among the Anglicans in England, the Classis establishment in Holland, the Antinomians in Massachusetts Bay, or even the Indians in Connecticut.[1] Cotton Mather quotes the first-hand impressions of the Reverend Henry Whitfield, who knew Hooker in Connecticut and called him "incomparable," "a man in whom learning and wisdom were . . . tempered with zeal, holinese, and watchfulness." Whitfield also noted Hooker's firm "command of his own spirit," which was especially important in his success in the world because he had a "cholerick disposition, and . . . a mighty vigour and fervour of spirit, which as occasion served, was wondrous useful to him, yet he had ordinarily as much government of his choler, as a man has of a mastiff dog in a chain; he *could let out his dog, and pull in his dog, as he pleased.*" Mather tells of another who "observed the heroical spirit and courage, with which this great man fulfilled his ministry." Hooker, he added, "was a person who while doing his master's work, would put a king in his pocket."[2]

This joint possession of an energetic, even impassioned spirit and the ability to restrain and control the expressions of it is thoroughly evident in the way Hooker tells the story of redemption. It is a story told in the framework of rational discourse but appealing to its audience's larger awareness of the contradictoriness of human nature and the struggle and conflict so persistently a part of human life. Hooker's view of his fellow men and their potential is doubtless colored by his view of himself and his own life. He was a man of very humble beginnings who, after achieving increasingly wide recognition as student, teacher, and preacher, had challenged great odds in helping a company of colonists to settle a new world in the midst of what he and his colleagues named quite literally a "howling wildernesse." His achievements were undeniable and have been duly noted by generations of historians; yet on his deathbed he denied having *earned* any rewards, and hoped only for mercy. All the conquering of worlds, within and outside the self, led back, not to man's prowess, but to the sovereignty of God. This personal attitude was of a piece with his preaching and shines forth in his sermons through the way he characterizes the life of the Christian.

The interest in spiritual psychology and the thoroughgoing belief in basic Calvinist principles noticed in the preceding chapters, together with his overriding desire to reach his audience in an accessible language and preaching manner, all came together with his dynamic personal character to produce that "masterpiece" of analysis of the motions of the soul in "the essential religious experience" to which Perry Miller admiringly refers.[3] Like an major literary work, in other words, Hooker's sermon series on the personal history of redemption in the soul of a representative sinner/saint arises from a complicated combination of elements in the author's mind and experience. But the modern reader needs especially to note that the series is not abstract reasoning or airy theological discourse but an interpretation of life, a product of a whole man.

Hooker's "masterpiece" deserves closer attention than it has received, since in it Hooker set himself his greatest challenge. In his extended description of the morphology of conversion he focused his mind and energies on the invisible realm of the spirit, the subtle windings of the human psyche, while showing what the usual relation of man to the sovereign God of the universe is and what it might, in any individual case, become. Here he fully reveals his sympathy for and connections with the humanist tendencies of his age, for he takes an approach to his topic which stresses the point of view of the individual sinner/saint. On a subject which is implicitly theological and which predecessors from Aquinas on had explained more or less abstractly, Hooker insists on following "the motions of the heart" of sinful men and women from the perspective of their limitations as fallen human beings.

While Hooker certainly relied heavily on the tools of logic—especially as described by Ramus and Aristotle[4]—he did not see his essential task as one of rational argument or explication so much as one of impressing his listeners with the fact that the truths he was preaching must be applied to them personally if they are to have any practical meaning whatever. His central problem, then, was to convey scriptural truth and its spiritual "application" by capturing and holding the imaginations of his hearers. Hooker, we must remember, was a man for whom even an explication of the Lord's Prayer provided an opportunity not so much for abstract doctrinal definition as for tracing "the frame of the heart" of the person offering the prayer.[5] Thus, to understand Hooker's achievement, we must focus not only on the message itself but also on the way that message is conveyed. In doing so, we discover a Puritan artist in masterful control of his medium as well as his message, an artist who predicts future literary methods and concerns while he extends old literary and intellectual traditions.

For Thomas Hooker as for every Puritan minister the sermon was an instructive, hortatory medium, so that the "Doctrine," the message of truth, the *logos*, is always stated first and remains uppermost. But Hooker was more inclined to cultivate the pastoral than the doctoral or teaching role of the ministry. Aware of his congregation's weaknesses, he knew the need to capture its attention. With this in mind and knowing that his audience could appreciate a good story so long as it had an appropriate purpose in the sermon, he proceeded to demonstrate that a narrative dimension in preaching could aid in bringing the people's souls to Christ. Naturally, he resorts frequently to narrative episodes from both the Old and New Testaments to illuminate particular points. He also occasionally chose a scriptural text which provided a ready-made plot line for his sermons, as he did in using the parable of the prodigal son as his text in *The Soules Humiliation*. But beyond these predictable and common sermonic methods is the more fundamental fact that he saw the redemption of the individual soul as an eminently fit subject for something very like narrative description. His account of the soul's progress from the earliest stirrings of self-awareness to the climax of heavenly glorification follows a clear plot outline. It becomes a story, orally communicated, in which the listener is invited to become desperately interested in the fate of the central character—a figure in whom he is meant to see his own image reflected.

So, molded by Hooker's energetic imagination, clarified by examples from Scripture and the contemporary world, and underlined by Hooker's own obvious strength of character and personality, the potentially cold and objective description of theological doctrines on redemption became in Hooker's ministry a veritable saga. In his view, *the* great adventure story was the soul's odyssey through the temptations and dangers in the world all around to triumphant safety in the Lord.

Requiring as it did all the vital mental energies of the hero, and occupying the entire earthly tenure of that hero, giving him the worthiest and most elusive of goals toward which to struggle, this story has at least some of the central elements of epic.[6] As Hooker communicated the story to a listening audience, he was inviting his listener, the man or woman on the bench in front of him, to *become* the hero. As he spoke of the difficulties and challenges to be experienced at the various stages of redemption, Hooker was asking his listener to share those experiences, not just vicariously as one does in reading of distant or imaginary people and events, but *actually*, in the here and now of one's own spiritual life. Ames had said that the central action of one's life was the process of working one's way "to salvation as to an end"; Hooker invited the individual sinner to enter this quest, the outcome of which, as Hooker preached the message, was not entirely out of the individual's control. But it involved heroic exertion, heroic commitment. He gave his audience the ultimate challenge: to transfer the hypothetical details of his oral narrative into their lives. Insofar as he successfully appealed to his culture's willingness to dramatize the process of redemption, he was contributing to the creation of a myth.[7] At the same time, Hooker's practice necessarily helped to loosen the traditional Puritan admonition against the use of the "feigned history" of fictions. A wide enough latitude would eventually be created on this issue to admit *The Pilgrim's Progress*, which would in turn point to such a descendant as *Robinson Crusoe*.[8] In Hooker's case, of course, the stretching of this guideline was not fully intentional but a direct result of his dramatic use of his materials.

The narrative quality of Hooker's redemption preaching quickly becomes apparent as we examine *The Application of Redemption, The Ninth and Tenth Books*, where, having laid the doctrinal groundwork in the first eight books of *The Application*, he looks at the first of the several stages of "Gods order" in applying redemption to the sinner's soul. This volume is an enlargement of *The Soules Preparation* (1632), bearing the stamp of the author's final approval.

Hooker, in telling the story of redemption, often employs as an aesthetic tool the notion of the juxtaposition and balancing of opposites. Redemption reconciles these opposites or at least keeps them in constructive tension. Among these opposites are such notions as grace and damnation, holiness and depravity, the new man and the old man, beauty and ugliness. The initial sermon in the volume—the only one in the very brief Book Nine—is based on a biblical text which emphasizes just such a dramatic juxtaposition of opposites. The text is Isaiah 57:15: "Thus saith He that is the High, and the Lofty One that inhabiteth

Eternity, whose name is Holy; I dwell in the High and Holy place, with him also that is of a contrite and humble Spirit."[9] This verse sums up much of the theology of man, God, and election that Hooker has outlined in the preceding books of *The Application*, while it insists on the possibility of a happy outcome in the sinner's spiritual history. Here the high and lofty God dwelling in the high and holy place is both contrasted with the lowly, contrite, and humble soul and joined with him. The ultimate hope of the sinner—that he may some day dwell with God in the holy place—is offered as a real possibility at the very outset of Hooker's treatment of the long and arduous process of getting to that point, while the odds against it are implied in the terminology suggesting the vast gulf between God and man.

Hooker's more immediate purpose here, however, is to point to the qualifications necessary for this ultimate spiritual success: the possession of a contrite and humble spirit. Since the typical sinner is not contrite and humble, Hooker's first task was to show how one acquires these attributes. Dealing with contrition alone would take him the full 600 pages of the tenth book of *The Application*. It was thus clearly a work of monumental scope, especially when one considers that the work of preparation is only accomplished after humiliation has been added to contrition. But the unavoidability of this "work" is stated unequivocally in Hooker's first Doctrine: *"The Heart must be broken and humbled, before the Lord will own it as His, take up his abode with it, and rule in it"* (AR, II, 5). Hooker directly indicates that he is talking within the presumed limits of the doctrine of predestination when he says he will consider at length "the Frame and Disposition which is wrought in the Hearts of such as the Lord hath purposed to save" (p. 2). He never forgets this prior selection by God of His elect, and the reader who does necessarily distorts the meaning of Hooker's message on preparation.[10] One does not force God's hand by acquiring contrition and humiliation and giving God no option but to save him. Rather, one acquires these prerequisites only through the underlying assistance of God, however much the sinner may exert himself and thus seem to be doing it himself.

At the very outset Hooker makes a statement which not only declares his theme but carries with it important evidence of his recurrent tendency to present key segments of his message in a narrative mode. The passage begins with an argumentative statement of his theme but quickly resorts to several literary tools, all of which either implicitly or explicitly encourage the listener/reader to conceptualize the process dramatically, as an ongoing adventure which has important biblical and historical precedents. He writes:

There must be Contrition and Humiliation before the Lord comes to take possession [of the heart]; the House must be aired and fitted before it comes to be inhabited, swept by brokenness and emptiness of Spirit, before the Lord will come to set up his abode in it. This was typified in the passage of the Children of Israel towards the promised Land; they must come into, and go through a vast and roaring Wilderness, where they must be bruised with many pressures, humbled under many overbearing difficulties, they were to meet withal before they could possess that good Land which abounded with all prosperity, flowed with Milk and Honey. The Truth of this Type, the Prophet *Hosea* explains, and expresseth at large in the Lords dealing with his People in regard of their Spiritual Condition, *Hos.* 2. 14, 15. *I will lead her into the wilderness,* and break her heart with many bruising Miseries, and *then I will speak kindly to her heart, and will give her the Valley of Achor for a door of hope;* the story you may recal out of *Jos*[hua] 7. [5–26] when *Achan* had offended in the execrable thing, and the hearts of the Israelites were discomfited and failed, like water spilt upon the ground. (*AR,* ii, 5–6)

In the story to which Hooker refers here Achan had secretly stolen some of the silver, gold, and "Babylonish garment" from Jericho after it had fallen to Joshua, despite Joshua's instructions not to meddle with these "accursed things." This forbidden plunder caused the Lord's anger so that the Israelites were routed in their next battle. Ultimately, Achan's sin was discovered, the "execrable thing" destroyed, and he was stoned and buried under the stones, after which "God supported their hearts with hope." This recollection of Old Testament history leads Hooker to cite a New Testament passage which helps to explain the references to the Valley of Achor in the books of Hosea and Joshua, which valley Hosea describes as "a door of hope": "So it shall be Spiritually, the Valley of Consternation, perplexity of Spirit, and brokenness of heart, is the very gate and entrance of any sound hope, and assured expectation of good. This I take to be the true meaning and intendment of the place, and part of the description of a good Hearer, *Luke* 8. 15. *Who with an honest and good heart receives the Word, and keeps it, . . . and brings forth fruit with patience*" (p. 6).

There is much in these passages that is representative and instructive regarding Hooker's sermonic approach to both his subject matter and his audience. As usual, he relies on a variety of metaphors to illuminate his meaning. The heart is imaged as a house which must be swept and aired before the noble guest will enter and reside there. Then the same tenor is given another vehicle as the heart is compared to that "vast and roaring wilderness" through which the Israelites had to go before possessing the land of milk and honey. This metaphor derives immediately from the biblical context, since Joshua has just completed Moses's work by bringing the people across the Jordan into Israel and taking Jericho from the enemy. The pairing of the passages from Joshua and Hosea creates a neat unity of place since both refer to the geographical Valley of Achor, which was part of the Israelites' first experience after possession of the promised land and is therefore a symbol of hope. The experience which is "typified in the passage of the Children of Israel" through the "vast and roaring wilderness" is repeated antitypically in the hearts of each of the redeemed. The unfaithful Achan threatens the entire community of faith, and only after he is brought to justice do the faithful people of Israel regain stability and full possession of "the valley of hope." It is entirely possible, of course, that Hooker is implying still another typological dimension here, since the wilderness figure had by the 1640s long since become a recognized metaphor for the experience of God's people in crossing from the Babylon/Egypt of England to the promised land of New England where hardships had to be endured—a veritable "Valley of Consternation"—before the promised fruitfulness would be theirs. Hooker thus may well be extending his message here beyond individual heart-religion to his people's cultural consciousness of themselves as a chosen people of God forced for the time being to endure a wilderness, both metaphoric and actual, and even to deal with some Achans in their midst. Typological significances, as with effective literary symbolism in any age, here speak to the listeners in more ways than one. But whether the passage is interpreted by a given listener personally or culturally or both, he or she is encouraged to see in the biblical example a "type" of his or her own situation.[11]

The passage reveals Hooker's thoroughgoing acceptance of the typological method of biblical exegesis. The experience of the Israelites in the wilderness is primarily an historical type of the spiritual experience of the sinner who would be redeemed. "So it shall be Spiritually": one must pass through the wilderness of "perplexity of Spirit," which he names allegorically "The Valley of Consternation," before he may have "expectation of any good." In the traditional manner of the typologist, Hooker gives heightened meaning to the Old Testament passages by explicating them through their parallel to the passage in Luke which holds out the promise of fruitfulness for the patient heart. Old and New Testaments thus speak alike to the need for patience and endurance in the spiritual struggle. In this insistence Christ is not explicitly mentioned, but his role as antitype is implied in the wilderness/suffering/patience imagery. He is the culmination of the Old

Testament prophecies, the antitype to Joshua's type. Furthermore, it needs to be noticed that Hooker implicitly extends the typology to contemporary times by citing the prophet Hosea and the Gospel writer Luke as bringers of the same message as he, Thomas Hooker, is now bringing to a new generation of listeners. The implication is that the minister is prophesying a truth long since proven valid by its appearance in the Holy Scriptures. He himself becomes an antitype of the types mutually represented by Old and New Testament leaders and prophets.

Even more, however, he suggests a way in which the typology extends to the hearer himself or herself. It is no accident that here at the outset of the long series of sermons on contrition, Hooker quotes "part of the description of a good Hearer." He offers first the example of Achan, who failed to heed his leader's instructions and stole the "execrable things" which in turn brought his own destruction. Achan, the bad listener, is implicitly contrasted with Luke's "good Hearer," who in turn becomes the type of every good hearer in contemporary life. Since there are good and bad hearers in every congregation, Hooker is urging on his audience the crucial need for them to become good hearers as well as patient bearers of doubt and affliction as they enter the work of contrition. This subtle instruction on how to listen to his message, mentioned above in Chapter 1, is especially appropriate here at the beginning of his sermons on preparation for grace, since at this point the audience must become good hearers or regret their failure for all eternity.

This typological method helps to give a narrative thrust to Hooker's description of the process of redemption. If the sinner in the congregation can envision himself as in some sense the protagonist of the saga Hooker is describing, that listener will identify all the more readily as the antitype of figures whose stories are already known and which Hooker knows his audience "may recall." The central, rather abstract, but eminently logical argument for contrition before grace is given a supplemental dimension as the listener's memory of the biblical stories of Joshua, Achan, and Hosea is prodded. He is reminded of examples of those who followed the Lord's will and those who did not and is invited to identify with one or the other. In identifying with Joshua and his obedient followers or Luke's good hearers, the listener in Hooker's congregation is given hints of his own possible future. Those who survive their experience in "the Valley of Consternation"—the stage of contrition—may anticipate entering the Valley of Achor, which stands for the beginning of hope.

In thus using typological exegesis Hooker is able to give the story that he is telling—the adventures of the souls of those people just now before him—a ready-made narrative framework. The known story of Achan reverberates in the consciousness of the listener to serve as a warning that he must not permit his life to follow the same misguided line of action. The biblical parallels thus call the listener's attention to himself. In following this practice Hooker contributes to the significant development in Protestant typology in the seventeenth century which Barbara Lewalski describes as "a shift of emphasis, modifying the medieval focus upon Christ's life and death as the primary antitype to which all the Old Testament types refer by developing a further focus upon the contemporary Christian as an antitype." Sacvan Bercovitch, who has written extensively on this subject, speaks directly to this point: "It became the task of typology to define the course of the Church . . . and of the exemplary Christian life. . . . Every believer was a *typus* or *figura Christi*." Typology "proceeded to impose the scriptural pattern upon the self."[12]

Yet the resourceful redemption preacher, primarily concerned with the "selves" of all those in his congregation, did not rely solely on typology as a means to the primary end of regeneration. Hooker found other, related tools equally helpful. He made extensive and stimulating use, for instance, of metaphor, analogy, and the extended simile. The character sketch was also a technique for which Hooker became especially well known, and though the old free-wheeling application of allegorical significances to scriptural passages practiced by Origen and other Hellenists had largely fallen into disrepute by Hooker's day,[13] a more exact and limited form of allegory proved a very effective method for him on occasion when he wished to enliven the doctrinal thrust of his message with still another kind of narrative method. Dialogues between imagined characters or actual figures, sometimes including the listener, were also frequent elements of his sermons. In examining the outlines of his message on the application of redemption we shall find opportunity to notice his skillful reliance on each of these methods, separately and in combination.

Contrition

The essential argument of Hooker's sermons on contrition is that the individual must be made aware of his dire spiritual condition before anything can be done to change it. Only when the soul actually desires a change in itself can it hope to acquire saving faith. And it can only possess that desire by first acquiring knowledge of itself. The effect of contrition is to begin to free a man from bondage to sin by making him aware of the grave danger he is in because of sin and making him want to free himself from this bondage. "Haughty and hard-heartened sinners" need to have their hopes dashed immediately, for only when the stony heart is reduced to "powder" can it be reformed in a more perfect shape (AR, II, 11). As the Puritans loved to point out, the stony heart cannot receive the impression of God's seal.

Following the Ramist logical principle of dichotomy, Hooker first divides preparation into contrition and humiliation, then divides contrition into two "causes" and two "effects."[14] The causes which enable one to absorb contrition into his own heart are the "sight of sin" and the consequent "sorrow for sin," while the effects are "detestation" of sin and "sequestration" from it (AR, II, 21). These follow each other in an orderly sequence in the elect Christian's experience, though none of them is easy to come by. Since Hooker takes up each in its turn, they provide the organizational sequence for the sermons on contrition. For the sinner, contrition is largely a matter for the mind to handle. The preacher needs to influence the rational apprehension of the listener enough so that he will perceive his danger and the need for change. The initial (unsuccessful) efforts towards change occur in the next stage of the preparatory process, humiliation. Hooker is here carefully adhering to his knowledge of the operation of the human faculties. One must start by reaching the understanding, which means clearing his mind of the prejudices and special considerations which prevent impartial perception of the destructive force of evil within oneself. "That which the eye sees not the heart rues not, that which is not apprehended by the understanding, is not affected by the will" (p. 36). God assists in this process, as He does at all stages of the progress of His elect, shedding a "new light" which enables the sinner to come to a fuller internal acceptance of the weight of God's law in his particular case. The mind is turned heavenward, and the understanding is given a new "sett" (pp. 37–42), the first stages of the process that, if followed to its conclusion in true faith, will result in a new and "harmonious combination of the faculties."[15]

But there is throughout Hooker's treatment of the stages of grace the prior assumption that all must be done in its proper sequence. And contrition, he is careful to remind his listeners, is just the beginning. It is crucial to get the right beginning, of course, and to do that one must "strive to enter in at the straight Gate of Contrition and Humiliation, and then you will hit the right way to Christ and eternal Life" (AR, II, 14). Entering at the strait gate is a standard scriptural phrase (Luke 13:24), perennially popular with conversion preachers, but Hooker uses it here and in later references in The Application to stress the dramatic significance of this moment of beginning. It is a crucial event in itself, and its accomplishment implies a whole sequence or process that is to follow. In developing the symbolic significance of the moment, Hooker compares the opening of the gate to the moment of childbirth, which involves pain and violent motion but results in new life and joy. "This great worke of contrition," he said, "is nothing else, but the child-birth of the soule."[16] This pivotal point in the life of the sinner destined for justification is a moment of high archetypal significance—such a moment as numerous later American writers have rendered in symbolic terms. What Cooper suggests, for instance, in Deerslayer's emergence from the woods to look at pristine Lake Otsego for the first time, what Melville dramatizes in Ishmael's going to sea in a whaler, what Faulkner symbolizes in Ike McCaslin's entering the woods in a flatbed wagon, Hooker's sinner experiences on entering on the road to heaven at the "straight gate." It is, like those other moments of rebirth, the event which signals the initial act in the hope-engendering creation of a "new man." To go with Hooker from the first gate into the realm of toil and danger beyond, which at times seems a wilderness to the man on the path but which, to the true seer, always reflects God's order, is to begin that epic adventure of the soul in which the unlikely hero/ listener actually becomes, in the Puritans' meaningful use of the term, conqueror of "the world."[17]

Because the command to enter at the strait gate is followed by a promise ("then you will hit the right way to Christ and eternal life"), this concept and the terminology in which it is phrased go far towards determining the thrust of Hooker's message from this point on. He employs the word *way* intentionally and precisely, suggesting a road or path along which it was necessary for the sinner to walk.[18] This useful metaphor establishes two things which Hooker will hereafter take for granted: first, exertion is necessary on the part of each hopeful soul, and second, his audience will have firmly in mind a visual image of a pilgrim walking on a road which leads to heaven eventually but is, in a related metaphoric sense, the road of life. He would later remind his audience that "this is the way that God hath appointed"; there is no "shorter cut" (*AR*, II, 111). "Dost thou walk in the common road according to the course of the world? thou art in the kingdome of darkness, and art ruled by the Prince of darkness and shall go to everlasting darkness. Dead Fishes Swim down the stream. Thou art a dead man if thou goest with the stream of the world" (p. 121).

Though it took on new popularity in the era of the Reformation and Renaissance, this road metaphor for the Christian life had a long history dating to Augustine, Paul, and Jesus himself ("I am the way; whoever . . . ."). Numerous scriptural sources supported the idea, including passages in Genesis and Exodus telling variously of Enoch's walk with God lasting three hundred years after the conception of Methuselah and of Moses's walk with the people of God out of the land of bondage. These biblical types provided examples capable of manifold duplication from Old and New Testaments alike, all suggesting daily struggle and exertion to the end of spiritual improvement. Hooker was thus developing what was already a commonly accepted metaphor for the spiritual life. No doubt undue credit has gone to John Bunyan for creating this metaphor, though certainly it is his allegory of the travels of Christian which captured in the most detailed and lasting form the implicit drama in this notion. But we wrong both Bunyan and his predecessors when we try to read every occurrence of the metaphor—whether before or after Bunyan's work—in the light of *The Pilgrim's Progress.*[19] Perhaps one example from this pilgrim literature will serve to illustrate the existence of the tone as well as the metaphor which both Hooker and Bunyan would later employ. John Hopkins had addressed England's queen in the following terms in 1609:

> The life of a Christian is compared to running a race, set out by the words of labouring, *striuing, indeauouring,* & here by *walking:* for the passage to heaven is painefull on foote in the worke of mortification, not riding at ease in following the pleasures and lusts of the flesh. *In my bed by night I sought him that my soule loued, I sought him but I found him not,* saith the spouse of Christ [Canticles 3:1], teaching that such as will find Christ, must arise from their bed, (by which is meant, pleasures and delights of the flesh) and seeke him in the exercises of fasting and prayer, and such like duties of holines. The way to heauen could neuer have been called a narrow way, nor the gate a straight gate if it were sufficient, in words to professe true religion, and in our workes to denie our hearts no pleasure.[20]

Thus, no more did Hooker create the metaphor than did Bunyan after him. Hooker found especially useful its implying of the need for energetic toiling. When he did not explicitly tell his listeners of the difficulty of the spiritual journey which they were on, his imagery did. Whether the journey was described as leading along a road, up a stream, across a river or ocean, or up a ladder—all images Hooker used—it represented a progressive journey-quest characterized by laborious, struggling, forward movement. And Hooker made sure that this image of the burdened pilgrim was so firmly fixed in his congregation's imagination at the outset of his narrative of the story of redemption that they lived with it constantly in mind thenceforth.

In another important way Hooker's work is a not-too-distant ancestor of

Bunyan's. Hooker gives us glimpses, usually only fleeting but sometimes extended, of his affection for a method familiar enough to narrative artists of the day and most elaborately developed into popular art by Bunyan. Hooker's account of the soul's journey, of course, never achieves the level of full-scale, consistent allegory that Bunyan's story represents. But the allegorical temper of mind is decidedly a part of Hooker's complex aesthetic sense of how to interest his audience in his central story. Here again his tendency to employ the techniques of narrative art to support those of rational argument is thoroughly evident.

Having begun his description of the soul's odyssey by having his central figure enter at the "straight gate," just as Bunyan was later to do, Hooker takes occasional opportunities to provide a landscape over which this itinerant must journey. We have already noticed that before he goes very far he must journey through "the Valley of Consternation" (*AR*, II, 6). The phrase ideally represents the allegorical tendency to picture experience in terms both of the outer, visible world ("Valley") and of inner feelings or states of being ("Consternation"). The degree to which such a way of treating simultaneously two dimensions of experience might well lend itself to a preacher with Hooker's subject is easily apparent. Having once posited the notion that each soul is on a "way," a path with intricate, difficult windings, it would follow, especially to one with a tendency to resort frequently to dramatic metaphors and analogies, that the speaker would begin to paint certain points on that roadway in the recognizable colors and shapes of external reality. For instance, a particular sin or temptation in the life of the sinner may be described as a key landmark on the horizon: "The house of the Whore is the way to hell, and none that goeth with her, returnes againe, neither take they hold of the path of life, *Pro.* 2. 19."[21] Or a visual image of the Gate of Heaven may help to correct a listener's theological misunderstanding: "These sensual self-deceiving men make the gate of Mercy and Salvation so wide, that so they find room not only for themselves, but to carry their sins to Heaven with them also."[22] Or the inner characteristics of one's personality may take on the visible shape of adversaries who drastically slow one's progress on the "road":

> As it is in a Road, the Traveller is fitted to go his Journey, but he is hindered because the crowd is so great and strong, that they cross him, and oppose him, and are ready to carry him another Way against his Will; just so it is with a Soul thus troubled with tumultuous Thoughts, especially Melancholy, and those other Enemies of the Soul, as vain Imaginations, sinful Fears, sinful Sorrow, distemper'd Tho'ts and Cares; that tho' the Heart is willing and able to believe, yet those stirrings of boisterous Affections, they cross *Faith* in the Way, and bear it down.[23]

This method of rendering invisible particulars as parts of a comprehensive, visible landscape is precisely the method of the Renaissance allegorist and later of the symbolist.[24] It is one of Hooker's most indispensable techniques.

Living when he did, Hooker was writing almost midway between the creation of two of the greatest of all allegorical works, Spenser's *Faerie Queene* and Bunyan's *Pilgrim's Progress*. As Rosemary Freeman has shown, the movement from Spenser to Bunyan is a movement from an allegory grounded in realism of the external world, an allegory in which figures are sometimes recognizable from the Elizabethan court but in which the figures are typically drawn with much attention to the visual and the concrete, to a still "realistic" allegory but one in which a heavier stress is on experience in the intangible world of the spirit. Indeed, "as the seventeenth century progressed allegory found a less public and more psychological sphere."[25] Allegory, as it stood in the view of artists and of the public in the 1620s, 1630s, and 1640s, was thus ideally suited to the psychological purposes of Hooker. He weaves it in and out of his sermons, never getting as concretely elaborate as Spenser but often momentarily predicting the new style of Bunyan. It was one more method by which Hooker could give substance to the slippery matters of the spirit and drama to the labors and movements of the soul up and down the road to heaven.

The notion of the difficult journey which Hooker thus adumbrates is thoroughly appropriate to his treatment of the preparatory stages of redemption. What he wants most to emphasize at this point in his series is the difficulty of it all. Two metaphors which convey this idea are fundamental to his discussion of contrition, while one of these remains perhaps the dominant figure of speech throughout all the volumes on the *ordo salutis*. The first of these is the image of piercing, lancing, or wounding; the second refers to the process of physical labor.

Both of these figures of speech are derived from the scriptural passage which Hooker chose as the text for his book on contrition, Acts 2:27, "And when they heard this, they were pricked in their hearts, and said unto [Peter and the other Apostles], Men and brethren, what shall we do?" The text is naturally suited to a preparationist message and to the aims of a preacher wishing to render the process of preparation for grace in dramatic terms. It emphasizes the sinner's desire and responsibility to "do" something for himself, and it shows the central importance of affecting, "pricking" one's heart. Thomas Shepard chose the same text for his sermons on preparation in *The Sound Believer*, and John Bunyan in the very first paragraph of *The Pilgrim's Progress* told of Christian looking up from reading a book and breaking into a "lamentable cry, saying, 'What shall I do?' "

The main appeal of the passage to redemption preachers is of course that it presents a moment of dramatic realization that something must be done to alter one's inner condition. The cry is uttered in desperation: "What shall I do?" It strikes the exact degree of urgency and personal realization that Hooker was trying to impress upon his audience. It is the very moment of the start of redemption, a moment of self-awareness that simply could not be circumvented for any who really desired spiritual regeneration. Calvin had summarized the text's fundamental relevance for Hooker's message in observing that "this is the beginning of repentance. . . . the entrance to godliness, to feel grief for our sins and to be wounded by an awareness of our evildoing."[26] Hooker gives elaborate emphasis to these concepts of beginning and pain.

Hooker picks up on the "piercing" and "wounding" metaphors, stressing his point that getting started on the right road is a painful business simply because the affliction which must be cured is so deeply ingrained in man's nature. True "piercing" of the heart, he insists, is "more than bare pricking." It is "so to prick as to pierce and enter, dig on every side, to pierce not overly, but quite through the soul, as some of the Antients render it" (AR, II, 323). As with a woman's travail in childbirth, a "passage" is made, after much sorrow, "that corruption . . . may be drawn out" (p. 324). The worse the sins, the greater the sorrow and pain. The piercing metaphor is particularly appealing to a Calvinist preacher because it relies heavily on the assumption of "corruption" or disease within the self which needs to be "drawn out." Natural corruption of spirit must be broken and turned aside if the beginnings of redemption are to take effect. So Hooker does not mince words in reminding his hearers where they are starting this process. They are in their natural condition, and what could be worse? When a natural man dies, he says, "filth and imposthumate matter issues out of the ears and mouth and each man can see it" (p. 331). Metaphors of disease abound here, with the medical cure prescribed generally being piercing of the sore, lancing, or in some contexts administering an emetic.

In the manner of the true physician of souls, Hooker urges ministers in his audience not to be "too hasty to heal the wound" in their listeners, since old sores take long to heal. At the same time they should not be "slight in the searching" (AR, II, 355). One must get to the bottom of the infected area before he can purify it. At this point "pity is unseasonable and [the] greatest cruelty" (p. 355). Whether the separation of a sinner from his past sins and attitude towards them is sudden, so that the heart is pierced "at one thrust," or whether it is slow and gradual, working "insensibly," this separation of the victim from the affliction must be sure and thorough. Only "when the heart and the power of corruption are parted" is the heart "pierced quite through" (p. 370). When this is the case, the sinner has acquired true and thoroughgoing sorrow for sin. He has passed well into contrition and has made a "good beginning" on redemption, though nothing is certain yet; in the preparatory stages nothing can be guaranteed.

In preaching this message, Hooker is at his best in his metaphoric resourcefulness. Especially conscious that he must use "the easiest and openest way to help the weak" (*AR*, II, 380), he resorts to a variety of parallel analogies from the common life experience of the people in his audience to bring home the point that it is not only an honor to be "battered" by God in this work but also the surest course for self-preservation:

> *In regard of the sinner himself, it's safest for him that he may be throughly recovered from his corruption for the present, and preserved against it for the time to come.* Recovered for the present, he needs heavy blows, or else he is like never to have any good by them. As with Trees that are rooted deep, and of long time & continuance, ordinary winds have setled them, it must be a Herricano that must pluck & tear them up from their roots. So when the sinner is rooted in these wretched distempers: the wood that is knotty, there must be sharper wedges, & the heaviest beetle,* and the hardest blows to break it: So it is with the hard, and stupid, and knotty heart of a scandalous sinner. As with the stomach filled with stiff and noysom humors, easie Physick, and gentle Receipts may happily stir the humors, but it must be strong Ingredients, and a great quantity that must remove it. So with a corrupt heart.
>
> This is a means also to preserve him from it afterward; if once he have throughly smarted for his sin, he will fear to meddle with it; if he have felt the danger of the Surfet, he wil tast the Sweet-meat no more. (*AR*, II, 342–43)

In such passages, fed as they are by Hooker's analogic resourcefulness, we see proof of J. Paul Hunter's assertion that "the Puritan mind had a rather desperate commitment to pictorialness."[27] In all of this description of internal, essentially nonvisible aspects of spiritual self-examination, Hooker presents his point in spatial imagery which forces his listener to visualize, to feel, the possibility of *separating* his striving soul from the burdensome weight of his sins. The pricking and piercing of the heart is to let the infectious, abscessed matter of sin out. The

---

*A heavy wooden hammer used to drive a wedge.

easing of the womb through the birth of a child and the easing of a sick stomach by the vomiting of noisome "humors," unlike though they are in some ways, both represent the concept of relief through separation which is precisely what happens, according to Hooker's vision of the process, when the sinner sorrows for his sin so thoroughly as to put it away from him. Hooker's multiplication of metaphorical examples forces the listener to form a visual, sometimes even tactile impression of what happens in his heart as the process of redemption begins.

Part of the implication of these metaphors, of course, is that the sinner is a patient, a victim of affliction, who is treated by a physician with skills greater than his own: the minister with the powerful curative words. Hooker is implicitly the antitype of the powerful preacher in the biblical text in the second chapter of Acts. Just as Peter moved his hearers to ask the crucial question, "What shall I do?" so does Hooker hope to move his present audience. The thrust of such a parallel comes home chiefly to the listeners in their antitypical relationship to Peter's audience, who proved to be "good hearers." Calvin's commentary on the passage stresses this point: "They alone profit from pricking of this kind who are willing to be made sorrowful and are prepared also to seek a remedy from God."[28]

This emphasis on the need for his audience to heed what he says, to be good hearers for the good of their souls, becomes a matter of more than mere implication, however. As we noticed in Chapter 1, Hooker sees part of his responsibility to be teaching his audience to listen. He does this by citing examples of listeners from both contemporary life and Scripture. Preaching on the necessity of seeing one's sins "convictingly," Hooker points out that unwillingness to hear the truth about one's sins reveals unwillingness to reform, a deadly preventative to grace. He then recalls a case which he knew and perhaps even some of his audience would recall of a "Formal Knight [who] once professed (in the Country from whence we came) he would not come to the Assembly until the Minister had made an end of such a Text" (*AR*, II, 106). He cites several supplementary cases of biblical figures who resisted the truth of prophecy to the end of their own destruction, beginning with Ahab's disapproval of Micaiah's prophesying (1 Kings 22:8), and going on to mention the audiences of Isaiah, Jesus, and Stephen, all of whom disapproved of their messages. Against these examples of truthtellers whose words were ignored by hard-hearted listeners Hooker poses other figures who were good listeners to the truths of God, men such as Eli, Job, and David, all of whom heeded the voice of truth (pp. 106–9, 117–18). This extensive listing of types of good and bad hearers returns him to the topic with which he had begun the discussion of preparation, the lesson of Achan. God, Hooker reminds his listeners, "makes *His* see their sins, and that cleerly, before they ever see his pardon of them, or power against them: if he never convinceth, he never converts" (p. 117). Given the historical examples which the preacher cites from both Testaments, there is powerful persuasion in this piling type upon type. Since Hooker implicitly paints himself as the antitype of Joshua, Isaiah, Micaiah, Samuel, Nathan, Stephen, even Jesus himself, there is no avoiding the point that the present listener, hearing the voice of the modern-day prophet, Thomas Hooker, is a potential antitype of the scriptural listeners. The listener's recollection of the stories being cited in the sermon would tell him clearly enough: better to be the antitype of an Eli or a Job than of an Ahab or an Achan. Better to pay heartfelt attention to the message of one's own prophet than to lose the chance for redemption forever. The known narratives of history carried their own weight with an audience well-read in the scriptures. And Hooker, through this typological emphasis on the speaker-audience relationship, was giving his hearers indirect but fair warning of the grave importance of the present preaching-listening experience. Any person who "setts himself against the truth," said Hooker, "is very neer to the sin against the Holy Ghost," which is the one unforgiveable sin (p. 111).

At this point Hooker's other major figure of speech in the contrition series of sermons, and even in the entire *ordo,* becomes especially relevant. Having been awakened to the point of asking what they must "do," the listeners are given a first introduction to a motif that will recur again and again. They must "lay out their labour & that unto the utmost of all their abilities never to give the Lord rest, nor rest unto their own souls, before they get this true sight of sin" (*AR,* II, 111). No admonition is so frequently recurrent in Hooker's ministry as this one. As he moves from mood to mood in his preaching, he threatens, cajoles, terrifies, informs, but always returns to this admonition to "labor." There is a characteristic rhythm from downbeat to upbeat in his most effective sermons, a rhythm characterized especially by the repeated return to this exhortation to put out one's best energies on one's own behalf.

Exactly *how* one "labours" to "affect the frame of the heart" can be a frustratingly abstract notion, of course, and so at this early point in Hooker's treatment of the first stage of redemption he expands a Use of exhortation from its original preaching length in *The Soules Preparation* to a self-sustaining discourse of some 81 pages, or 30,000 words, in *The Application,* the sole function of which is to explain the how and why of spiritual exertion. The very scope of his expansion of this point indicates Hooker's realization of the crucial importance of instructing his people in the practical matter of "laboring." Nowhere is his interest in spiritual psychology more evident than here, where he analyzes through the use of a diagrammatic breakdown of men's evasive mental tactics their wily ways of skirting their responsibility for serious exertion. In the course of this explanation he sacrifices the shape of the sermon to his concern for thoroughness in the written version by dividing and subdividing his explanation, starting with enumeration of the chief "motives" and "means" to spiritual labor, then citing typical "cavils" used to avoid responsibility, each of which in its turn is caused by several "excuses," all of which have several "answers." This elaborate breakdown of the psychological tactics of unredeemed men serves to stress the point that he had established in *The Paterne of Perfection:* Adam's image of perfection was not totally washed out of man in the Fall; there are still faint glimmerings of his abilities in modern men. Though Hooker and his audience understood that the number of people who could make constructive use of these latent abilities was very small, they recognized that not to try was to fail to respond to the divine challenge to faith. They simply had to toil, to stagger ahead under the seemingly insupportable burdens that one feels all the more after attaining a "true sight of sin" and being fully repulsed by one's careful meditation upon it. Hooker reminds those in danger of being "overwhelmed with the unsupportable weight of the wickedness of their own souls" that the path through the "vally of tears" is "the right way to Zion" (AR, II, 438, 439). At this point suffering is necessary because the fundamental characteristic of contrition is agonizing self-appraisal and the consequent wounding of the soul. No one, however, should rest until he comes "to the right pitch of this saving sorrow." Otherwise, "we shal lose our labor, and our souls and all" (p. 447). Still more incentive came from Hooker's reminding his audience that "thousands" have "miscarried" here. If you miss the way here, "thou art undone forever" (pp. 451–52).

Thus, Hooker never loses sight of the odds against acquiring saving faith. He darkly acknowledges that there is "very little saving sorrow . . . in the world, and therefore . . . little saving grace" (AR, II, 417). He makes full exploration of this fact, enumerating and briefly describing some "five sorts of people" on whom this truth falls especially heavily, who are in fact served with a "bill of inditement" by the doctrine of the need for "saving sorrow" that runs throughout Hooker's treatment of contrition. At this point Hooker employs still another of his special preaching skills, a modified form of the "character," a method popular up to and including the early seventeenth century.[29] In this technique the author draws a word portrait—sometimes it is close to being a moral caricature—of a human character type. He usually names the character after his dominant trait and then explores that trait by describing certain typical acts or speeches. Usually the efforts at physical visualization are minimal, though the technique is inherently dramatic, embodying a major aspect of Hooker's anticipation of Bunyan's popular allegory. He introduces in turn five characters who are without saving sorrow for their sins but who want to appear righteous anyway. We meet "heedless and fearless professors," "the treacherous formalist," "your self-conceited Pharisee," "your complaining Hypocrite," and "the discouraged Hypocrite" (pp. 417–28). Of the "treacherous formalist," for instance, he says in part:

> He carryes the face of religion, the garbe and guise of Godliness in outward appearance and would be counted a friend to the truth, so far as he may serve his own turn of it, and he is content to be at league with the Gospel, provided he may make his own terms, and attain his own ends; namely that he may have allowance in some lusts and *yet be honored also among the people*, with the title of *an honest Godly and good man*. But when his carnal ends are not answered, and the word requires more than he hath, and commands more than he would do, and would pluck away his beloved lust that he is loath to part withal; he then begins to set up secret conspiracies in his heart against the evidence of the doctrine. (*AR*, II, 419)

In such passages Hooker's aim was to hold a mirror up to his audience. Many of his listeners were doubtless struck with considerable force in recognizing similarities to themselves among these characters who, unless they change, cannot possess saving grace.

By studding his sermons with an array of these character gems, Hooker, always the devout Puritan, plays the role of incipient dramatist, substituting narrative description for the actions and speeches of full-fledged stage character creations. For the Puritans, the imaginative, creative preacher could provide—probably without either his or his audience's realization—a substitute for other available forms of entertainment which for them were outlawed. Whether indulging in allegorical scene painting, the character sketch, dialogues between the sinner and Satan or other imagined figures who could serve the doctrinal point of a sermon, or typological exegesis which called up familiar biblical stories, the skillful minister played on his audience's love of fictional dramatization while also making the fiction seem very much a part of one's immediate life. Since the stress was on the latter rather than the former, he could safely circumvent the Puritan prohibition against fiction. His aim was instruction and alteration of the life of the listener. An entirely suitable approach to this end was through the imagination of that listener, an avenue which Hooker was inclined to exploit with all the considerable resourcefulness at his disposal. On the basis of Hooker's example, we may well observe with J. Paul Hunter, that "it is no coincidence that the first major English writers of prose fiction were steeped in Puritan tradition." Hunter is correct in speculating that "the novel as an art form owes a great debt to Puritan modes of thought and to the Puritan response to significant ideological developments of the seventeenth century."[30]

One of the "Puritan modes of thought" which Hooker exemplifies is implicit in his concurrent stress on the two metaphoric clusters which we have examined, the "piercing" of the corrupt soul and the "laboring" of that same soul to its own benefit. In this dual emphasis lies a partially contradictory sense of man's nature which provides Hooker's preaching message with much of its liveliness. He exemplifies the Puritan belief both in man's total depravity and in the possibility for something better than the damnation one deserves. So he exerts every effort to impress both ends of the story on his hearers. In doing so, he creates a continuing awareness of man's peculiar dilemma between heaven and hell, grace and damnation, the Word and the world. In both his matter and manner, Hooker manages to convey the eternal truth that while there is life there is pressure and tension between these opposing forces. His words give a feel for as well as a literal analysis of this tension.

This tension is nicely captured in a sermon which comes towards the end of the series on contrition and which develops the Doctrine that "he that is truly pierced by the Ministry of the word, he is buisy to enquire and ready to submit to the Ministers of God making known his mind therein" (*AR*, II, 560). Parts of this sermon—most notably the first Use—have the clear force and tone of the jeremiad, being directed against those regular members of the congregation who, in spite of periodic reminders and opportunities, never seriously ask the question, "What shall I do to be saved?" They are very careful to ask all necessary questions regarding self-betterment in worldly affairs, but similar questions in the far more important realm of their souls' eternal destinies never occur to them. In dealing with this subject, Hooker refers to those who have travelled from Massachusetts Bay to Hartford with him but have still not found "the way to Sion," then goes on in jeremiad fashion to indict "the present Generation" for its waywardness and casual attitude in spiritual matters. Although Thomas Shepard was also engaging in this type of preaching on occasion, for the most part we tend to assign it to a later period in seventeenth-century New England history. The fact is, of course, that the demanding preparationist preacher probably ran into the spiritual recalcitrance of New Englanders before his fellow ministers became quite so aware of or troubled by the problem. Hooker, at any rate, did not consider his generation of New Englanders to be quite so exemplary as their descendants, looking through the tinted glasses of the providential historian, were to consider them. He quotes the comment of the Lord's angels in Zechariah's vision (Zech. 1:11), *"We have walked to and fro through the Earth, and behold all the Earth sits still, and is at rest,"* then picks up the passage's terminology and elaborates:

> Walk we from one Plantation to another, from one Society to another; nay, which is yet a further misery, from one Assembly to another, *all the Earth sits still, and is at rest;* there is no stirring, no trading in Christianity; men cheapen not, enquire not after the purchase of the precious things of the Gospel, what shall I do to be quit of my self? what shall I do to be severed from my sins which have pestered me so long? prejudiced my peace so much, and if it continue, wil be my ruin? As though Christ were taking the Charter of the Gospel from the present Generation, and were removing the Markes, there is no stirring, Trade is dead, men come dead, and sit so, and return so unto their Habitations, there is deep silence, you shal not hear a word. What spiritual good they get, what they need, or what they desire; men are willing to do nothing, and therefore they wil not enquire what they should do; certain it is, the Word never wrought kindly upon thee, nor prevailed with that carnal and hard heart of thine to this day in any saving manner for thy spiritual good: thou never knewest what it was to be lost, if thou never had'st a stir of heart to enquire the way to Sion, it's made an Argument of a man in the bonds of Iniquity, in the depth of his Natural distemper, *Rom.* 3.11. *They have no understanding, neither do they seek after God;* and it's made an evidence of Satan's Rule. (*AR*, II, 565–66)

In this startling characterization of his society Hooker envisions a death-in-life wasteland, where the absence of spiritual activity produces people who are "dead" and an environment in which "silence" reigns, conditions which were anathema to an activist prophet such as Thomas Hooker.

Thus does Hooker indict his fellow Christians and his generation of hardy settlers of the new land for already being too much occupied with worldly and personal affairs and too little concerned with the essentials: "Every man is seeking after the things that may suit his own carnal heart, and yet seek not after the things that concern their peace"

(*AR*, ɪɪ, 567). They are concerned with protecting their colonial charter but forget to safeguard the "Charter of the Gospel." In passages like these, the combination of spiritual idealism with stern criticism of society's dominant values makes a bridge by which, despite the differences of the speakers' theology and the societies' shape, the Puritan Hooker makes intellectual contact with such later writers as Ralph Waldo Emerson and Henry David Thoreau. He did not see social criticism as being entirely irrelevant to spiritual admonition. He felt, as did later idealists, that men's inner condition determines the level at which they pitch their system of values.

This dynamic tension in Hooker's vision of his congregation's dilemma—his awareness of the difference between what is and what should be—created the conditions in which his forceful mixture of prophecy and pastoral guidance could flourish. Since his awareness of this tension is most fully felt in his treatments of the earliest stages of the redemption message—the stages at which the sinner is most closely bound to sin—it is natural enough that his fame must rest chiefly on his preparationist sermons. In the very length and detail in which he treated contrition in his final revision of the topic, Hooker conveys an immediate notion of the difficulty of the chore, the length of the journey. It is indeed a Hill Difficulty but one which will never permanently discourage the true Christian, for whom labor is the way of life. Hooker's greatest accomplishment lies in his ability to reduce this brilliant psychological dissection of man's spiritual life under evangelical Calvinism to terms which are not merely understandable to the simple folk in his congregation but which are, by anyone's standard, dramatically compelling and engaging. His psychological breakdown of the ways of the human heart is not merely a clinical analysis—though it is a more detailed analysis than any of his contemporaries made—but it is a call to adventure, a challenge. He was thus explicator and exhorter, teacher and pastor, fixing the imaginations as well as the understandings of his listeners on the spiritual task before them. His considerable flexibility in the use of figurative language and his skill in selecting supportive biblical passages contribute substantially to his success. But perhaps most fundamentally, his certainty that he is both narrator and guide of a true adventure for his listener gives these sermons the supple psychological force essential to the creation of myth. And as he unfolds the tale of adventure for the sinner preparing for grace, the story evolves into a myth which offers the listener a new definition of himself and a new understanding of his destiny.

9
Preparation, Stage Two
HUMILIATION

At the end of his sermons on contrition, Hooker urges his congregation to labor in two specific ways: to hope and to confess. Both of these are possible for the elect at that point because one's mind has become sufficiently aware of the soul's dangerous alliance with sin to want earnestly to destroy that alliance. Hope is necessary in order to avoid the defeatist frame of mind which can lead to that killing "desperate discouragement," a state of mind against which Hooker repeatedly warns his people. And confession is the most overt result of one's gaining a truly contrite heart. As Hooker explains in some detail, the confession may be to God alone, to an offended party, to a minister, or to an entire congregation, depending on the nature of the offense, but in some form it is necessary, sometimes to satisfy wronged parties but always to satisfy God and to quiet the sinner's conscience.[1] There are many who are unable to perform these labors, including such characters as the "fearless Christians," the "NEUTERS in religion," the "lazy hypocrites," and the "treacherous hypocrites," none of whom hates sin sufficiently to get him past the stage of contrition. Yet, Hooker concludes, "if thou wilt part with thy sins the Lord will set his love upon thee" (AR, II, 702).

This being so, one might logically suppose that the very next step in the conversion process would be the influx of God's grace. But as he moves on to the next stage, Hooker reminds his listeners of the text in Isaiah 57:15 with which he begkn his sermons on contrition: it is only the contrite *and humble* who dwell with the Lord in the High and Holy place. Contrition is just the half of it; only with "true humiliation" is preparation for grace completed.

Had Hooker's career not been cut short at age sixty-one, he would undoubtedly have written a companion volume to *The Application of*

Redemption, The Ninth and Tenth Books. Just as the completed volume was a revision and enlargement of his earlier work, *The Soules Preparation,* the next large volume would have been a revision of *The Soules Humiliation* (1637), a book comparable in size, style, and popularity to *The Soules Preparation,* with which it shares simplicity of form and immediacy of style. Both works often give more sense of Hooker as speaker than do the two volumes of *The Application of Redemption.* By comparison with the revised work on contrition, *The Soules Humiliation* has a simpler and crisper outline, explaining the individual's progress through three successive stages within the larger stage of humiliation. These stages all involve arrival at successively deeper levels of understanding of the problem facing a person in search of grace. Having emerged from his successful struggle to achieve contrition, the broken-hearted sinner first relies on his own resources to put sin behind him. Secondly, realizing at last that he is thoroughly unable to relieve his own misery, he is utterly at a loss and near despair. Finally, rebounding from this inaction, he "fals downe at the throne of grace,"[2] submitting to Christ and his offer to help. In the final act, self-sufficiency is totally abandoned, being in direct conflict with faith. As Hooker said in a sermon on self-denial, "Hee that will be a servant, must do two things: first, he must renounce all other Masters, secondly, he must renounce his owne liberty, so we must renounce the masterdome of sinne and the world, and be content to be commanded by Christ, and then follow him: you cannot serve God and Mammon. Renounce all, and serve Christ."[3] Humiliation brings total reliance on Christ, so that Christ's role as the only source of strength for the redeemed is the central theme of the volume. But all the while Hooker stresses the importance of the soul's "labor." One must struggle to free oneself from bondage to one's worst enemy: self. Once again, the flux between exertion and submission provides the dynamics of the work.

Self-Reliance

It is this thrusting and parrying between Christ and the soul that must hold the listener's attention as Hooker sets forth another lengthy description of a single stage in the process of redemption. Hooker's special ability at engaging the hearer in the process at a stage which proves, above all, the sovereignty of God is put to an extreme test here. He leads off the discussion by returning to two favorite metaphors, both of which describe the pursuit of grace as an ongoing *process,* engaging the energies of both man and God, rather than as a mere series of inevitable occurrences. He writes:

> Therefore *Iohn Baptist* was sent to prepare the way, that all those
> mountaines of pride might be laid low, and all the ditches filled
> up, and all the crooked things might be made streight and all
> rough things might be made smooth, that there might be a way for
> Christ. The meaning is this: The heart of a man is the high way
> wherein Christ comes. Now there are mountaines of pride and un-
> toward stoutnesse of heart, and many windings and turnings, and
> devices which the heart hath, by reason of many lusts that are in
> it. This fitting and preparing, is nothing else but the taking away of
> that knotty knarlinesse of the heart, and that pride, and all such
> cursed corruptions, that the doore may be set open, and the heart
> made ready that the King of glory may come in. (*SH*, p. 2)

Thus pride, man's cardinal sin and the opposite of humility, is the
great adversary in the stage of humiliation. The mountains on the internal "high way" are the peaks of pride, and he who would imitate the
great preparationist John the Baptist must level those mountains. The
effect of this preparation is to open the door of the heart so that—
echoing David's lyric in Psalm 24—the King of Glory can come in.

   The Soules Humiliation depends heavily in both its theme and its
organization on the biblical text in Luke 15:14–19, which is the portion
of the parable of the prodigal son telling of the son's spending all his
wealth and experiencing famine and poverty, and finally deciding to
return home in order to put himself entirely at his father's disposal,
asking nothing except to be a servant in his father's house. As Hooker
presents the story, it is wonderfully adaptable to his treatment of
humiliation. The prodigal son, motivated by self-interest and pride,
goes through the three-stage process, learning that his natural ways
bring only disaster and despair and that a full turnabout in his destiny
is possible only through selfless dependence on the love of his father.
Throughout these sermons, Hooker makes effective use of Old and
New Testament typology, in fact, reminding his listeners frequently of
the case of Job in the Old Testament, the original type of whom the
prodigal is the New Testament antitype. Their subsequent reception of
God's abundant riches and mercy is the very point at which Hooker's
redemption message is driving. God *will be* merciful to the truly humbled sinner. Thus, the final mental attitudes of Job and the prodigal
must serve as models for the modern Christian. Lest this sound too
easy—too much as if the sinner can, by going through certain prescribed acts, force God's hand—we should constantly realize the importance of the adjective in the phrase "true humiliation." As there are
not many truly contrite people in the world, neither are there many
truly humble ones. The elect are, after all, a small minority, and the

winnowing process described by Hooker exposes to a great many their failure to achieve spiritual triumph.

Hooker's wayfaring man, freshly emerging from the acquisition of true contrition, looks around him and wonders where he ought to go for the help he needs to keep clear of sin. He does not at this point go to Christ because this would seem to his still befogged perceptions a reflection of pride, an assumption that he has a right to expect Christ's mercy, when common knowledge tells him he has no such right. So he relies on things he can do himself, such as using the means of grace— hearing sermons, praying, and fasting—and on worldly duties—"almes, and building of hospitals" (*SH*, pp. 9–10). But Hooker observes that these means are insufficient in themselves. This desire to do for one-self, says Hooker, is a holdover from Adam's original nature. In Adam's innocence, man was endowed with full self-sufficiency to accomplish good, and man inherits enough of Adam's innocent nature to *want* to be self-sufficient. But, like Samson after his hair was shorn, we find that we can no longer do what we once could. In concluding the first sermon, Hooker advises his hearers that even though God *could* reject the formerly self-sufficient sinner when he finally sees the light and goes to him for help, He never does: "But here is the wonder of mercies, that whensoever we come, hee casts us not of[f], yet if we would but come to him . . . he would receive us" (p. 16).

Self-reliance, then, will not get the sin-burdened wayfarer where he wants to go. The illusion of self-sufficiency is a trick of the devil; "hell is full" of self-sufficient people, says Hooker (*SH*, p. 17). Even such acts as sermon-hearing, fasting, and prayer can become "idols," ends in themselves which a sinner practices for his own comfort. Hooker says, "I doe not dishonor these ordinances, but I curse all carnall confidence in these." "The divell slides into the heart this way unsuspected and unseene, because he comes under a colour of duties exactly performed" (p. 17). The unredeemed soul all too easily subverts the use of the means and performance of duties into Phariseeism. Having mistakenly turned to self in order to pursue contrition efficaciously, the individual finally learns that self and duties provide "no saving succour" (p. 21).

Self-Examination

This perception of the limitations of self-reliance comes through a process of careful introspection, of self-examination, an exercise which is much belabored in the whole experience of humiliation. One can be

humbled only when fully aware of one's inner shortcomings. The "distemper" of pride, Hooker says, "is mervailous secret, yet a man may
take a measure and scantling of it" by examining his heart according to
the preacher's full instructions (*SH*, p. 171). Hooker's refrain, repeated
at all stages throughout his redemption message, "often to examine
thyself" was a characteristic Puritan emphasis which stemmed from
Paul's admonition to the Corinthians: "Examine yourselves, whether ye
be in the faith; prove your own selves" (2 Cor. 13:5). Before emigrating
to New England, Hooker's acquaintance Henry Whitfield preached
that a Christian's business "hath speciall, and primary relation to a
mans selfe"; "his faculties, members, and powers of soule and body
are, as it were, the tooles and instruments by which" spiritual gains
and losses "are wrought and framed."[4] Like Whitfield, Hooker frequently chose metaphors related to physical labor and crafts to clarify
his meaning on the subject: "As the Carpenter laying his Rule often to
his work, makes it the more even and straight, so comparing thy selfe
with the *Word*, and framing thy whole conversation to that rule, will
make thy heart, though as false and slippery as *Gehazi*, to become
faithfull and honest unto thee."[5] Hooker, in fact, singled out this subject of self-trial for explicit treatment in an entire sermon in which he
urged that *"everyone that lives in the Church is bound seriously, and
with great diligence to try and examine his estate, how it stands betwixt God and himselfe, in respect of the worke of saving grace
wrought in his soule."*[6]

It goes without saying that self-examination when properly practiced
requires a very difficult combination of critical detachment and involved commitment to one's own spiritual good. Hooker frequently
admits that he is fighting human nature in asking that the sinner see
his sins for exactly what they are. His staunchness in this aspect of his
practical theology of redemption caused some of his listeners and readers more than a little grief. The young Richard Baxter was one such
person, as he tells in his *Autobiography*: "And as for those Doubts of
my own Salvation, which exercised me many years, the chiefest Causes
of them were these: 1. Because I could not distinctly trace the Workings of the Spirit upon my heart in that method which Mr. *Bolton*, Mr.
Hooker, Mr. *Rogers* and other Divines describe! nor knew the Time of
my Conversion, being wrought on by the forementioned Degrees. But
since then I understood that the Soul is in too dark and passionate a
plight at first, to be able to keep an exact account of the order of its
own Operations."[7] That Hooker was as demanding as Baxter claims
about one's responsibility for keeping the "exact account" of what was
going on in the soul at every stage of progression up to and beyond

regeneration becomes clear as we read in each of his sermon volumes the numerous Uses of trial to which he admonishes his hearers. The recurrence of this strain in the sermons is a sure sign of his steady assumption that the exercise of the intellectual faculty in this painful business of gaining self-knowledge was not only necessary but possible for every believer. Hooker consistently felt he *could* ask those simple people in his congregation "who know not their ABC" to be perceptive as well as rigorous in acquiring self-knowledge.

As Baxter implies in grouping Hooker with Bolton and Rogers, this kind of rigor in the psychological and spiritual demands placed upon individual sinners was a common approach. The year before Hooker's departure from England, for instance, one of his Essex colleagues and supporters, Adam Harsnett, published a book of nearly four hundred pages on self-evaluation entitled *A Touchstone of Grace* (1630). The book may have been encouraged, directly or indirectly, by Hooker, who often made the point that "a searching and *examining Heart*" is one that "takes much paines with himselfe, trying his estate at Gods touchstone."[8] Not only the book's metaphoric title, however, but its tone, style, and ideas closely resemble Hooker's preaching characteristics. Recognizing the existence of both "true and counterfeit grace," Harsnett insists that "we haue all need to be skilfull, because of the deep imposture, and deceitfulnesse of our owne wicked, wretched hearts, which (like vnto lying spirits) will flatter, and deceive vs, telling vs that we are in a good way, and that all is well with vs, when as it is worse than nought."[9]

Hooker himself wrote two handbooks to aid his congregation in these inner searchings. He probably circulated them in manuscript, leaving them to find their separate ways into print after his emigration, one under the title *The Properties of An honest Heart*, which was bound with *The Stay of the Faithfull* when that work was published in 1638, and the other as a three-part collection of *Miscellanies* printed as an appendix to *The Paterne of Perfection* (1640).[10] The awareness of this emphasis in Hooker's ministry and writings probably had a direct influence on John Higginson, who had in his youth been Hooker's student at both Newtown and Hartford. In 1652 Higginson, then the minister at Guilford, Connecticut and later at his father's former church in Salem in the Bay, drew up "Some Helps to Self-Examination" which he finally published some thirty-four years later.[11]

This widespread emphasis on self-trial is based on the assumption that an earnest Christian's uncompromising exploration of his own soul for the signs of grace would offer him enough encouragement— whether from actual hopeful indications that he was making progress or from the fearful absence of such signs of hope—to pursue his spiritual aspirations with more energy than ever. At the preparatory stage of humiliation, Hooker coached his audience in this exercise by explaining that the humbled person ceases to rely on his own abilities but lies in the dust and looks up to God in total supplication, asking that Christ be his sole help. To do this is to pass through a period of despair or discouragement but not to remain there. The humble person has every reason for discouragement but instead retains the hope that will lead eventually to faith. So as one looks within, one must remember the important difference between a humbled and a discouraged heart. Humiliation, Hooker explains, seasons the vessel, while discouragement cracks it; humiliation stretches the tent cloth, while discouragement tears it (*SH*, p. 187). Again, the thrust of his message is positive. The way leads through dismay but issues in reassurance.

In this respect, the plot outline of the parable of the prodigal helps Hooker to control his material. The prodigal had every reason to be totally discouraged, being trapped as he was by his initial self-reliance and subsequent failure. But he is the ideal example for the present-day Christian because, after coming to full self-knowledge, he got up off the husks and turned to his father, swallowing both pride and self-sufficiency in the process, and asked only to be taken in as a lowly servant. There is a kind of still point in the sinner's experience, as Hooker describes it, where his attitude of self-renouncing humility is followed by an exertion of self which brings him "to the foot-stool of mercy." At this juncture an inherent logical contradiction in Hooker's message becomes apparent. It is present throughout his sermons on the preparatory stages, but discussion of this moment in humiliation makes it especially apparent. How can one be truly humble and still make the spiritual exertion which will bring him to grace? How, that is, are "labor" and "self-denial" compatible?[12]

The answer would seem to rest in the fact that humiliation, as Hooker sees it, is chiefly a recognition of God's sovereignty. Having admitted that God will destroy him if He chooses, the sinner elects a course of action which is far preferable to its alternative. He "fals at the footestoole of mercy, and lyes grovelling at the gate of grace, and submits himselfe to God that he may do what he will with him" (*SH*, p. 81). But this act, for all of its selflessness, is a more proper exertion of one's will and energies than is the maintenance of pride and self-sufficiency in the manner of "all the stout ones of the world," the Pharaohs and the Nimrods, who "thinke to goe to heaven . . . bolt upright" (p. 92). By totally releasing one's fate into the hands of another—Christ—the sinner makes further progress down the road to salvation.

Through all of this there runs the subtle persuasion offered by typological examples. As the prodigal was to his father, so the sinner should be to God. In the latter half of *The Soules Humiliation,* Hooker locates numerous scriptural *exempla* to support this primary one. Besides Job, others were brought low and finally submitted entirely to God's will and the saving mercy of Christ. Even great heroes, doers of wonderful deeds which might at first seem sufficient of themselves to bring a heavenly reward, owe their eternal happiness not to themselves but to the active mercy of Christ: "If I could looke up to heaven, and speake to *Abraham,* and *Paul,* and *David;* and say, how were you saved; they would all make answer, and say, oh, away to the Lord Christ, it is he that saved us, or else we had never come here" (*SH,* pp. 30–31). All the didacticism in the world could not make Hooker's point more clearly than do these scriptural *figurae.*

Everett Emerson has made the perceptive observation that one of Hooker's special skills as a speaker was his uncanny ability to address a question at just the moment when it seems to present itself to his listeners/readers.[13] This skill comes into play at just this point in *The Soules Humiliation* when he anticipates his audience's question, "How may a man goe beyond himselfe in all his duties?" (*SH,* p. 71). He admits that "this is a skill above all skills," and then offers "three directions" for the soul's assistance. All three directions are admonitions to inward "labour." For instance, the hopeful sinner must "labour to see an absolute necessity of a Christ in all these priviledges that thou hast," and also to "see a greater beautie and excellencie in the Lord Iesus Christ, th[a]n in all [God's ordinances]" (pp. 71, 72). These instructions are followed by a final admonition to "labour in the use of all meanes, as to see the beauty of a Christ surpassing all meanes" (p. 73). All of this is an increasingly intense, abstract, and paradoxical message to seek higher realms of spiritual perception. The directions are meant to be practical aids, but they have to do entirely with the yearning sinner's creation within himself of higher and higher levels of perception, an ascent which the weight of his natural depravity would seem to prevent. In each case, the sinner must "see" something more clearly and fully than he has "seen" it before. His labor to do this will presumably be successful if he is among the elect because then he will have God's help. If he is not, he may be foiled at this stage as well as at another. But the whole package is paradoxical in that Hooker's basic message is that you *cannot* labor to any advantage unless you have God's help. You cannot reflect, think, pray, "see," (all of which Hooker is urging his listeners to do with greater intensity than they have ever done before) to any purpose on your own. Man's actions are to no avail unless God intercedes, but woe be to the man who sits on his hands. Such a spiritual loafer's doom, it is perfectly apparent, is sealed. The sum of the message, then, is perseverance despite seeingly overwhelming odds and despite the seemingly obvious theological fact that it is fruitless. So long as man does not assume self-sufficiency but always remembers the superhuman magnitude of the job ahead of him, he can keep moving ahead *if*—and this condition is present at all steps of the way—God chooses to let him. Should this be the case, the reward, of course, is worth all of the agony. So, Hooker urges, use the means but do not consider them sufficient in themselves.[14]

This passage is followed by some five pages of metaphorical analogies, some scriptural, some from the world of secular experience, but all indicating the transporting power of the means when one uses them without forgetting that it is Christ who activates them and makes them potent. The man on the road to grace makes a timely reappearance here: "When a poore travelling man comes to the Ferry; he cryes to the other side; Have over, have over; his meaning is, he would goe to the other side by a Boat; he onely desires the use of the Ferryman to convey him over. So, Christ is in heaven, but we are here on earth (as it were) on the other side of the river; the ordinances of God are but as so many Boats to carry us, and to land us at Heaven where our hopes are; and our hearts should be. Therefore you would be landed: Have over, have over (saith the Soule). The Soule desires to bee landed at the Staires of Mercy, and saith, Oh, bring me to speake with my Saviour" (*SH*, p. 75). The recurrent message which we have seen thus far is thoroughly evident at this point: higher and higher aspiration is always required in the journey to the ultimately desirable goal. Don't be foiled by the rivers and valleys along the way but procure the necessary help. A successful end to the journey depends upon this last point: "See a need of Christ in all, and see greater beauty in Christ then in all, and be lead nearer to Christ by all, or else you get nothing by all that you do" (p. 77).[15]

There is nothing easy about any of this. In humiliation the self is so thoroughly subdued that one is content to have God do whatever He will with the soul. But this is directly contrary to human nature, which is why Hooker can say that "the worke of renovation, is greater then the worke of thy creation" (*SH*, p. 37). To subdue the dominance of pride and the devil in the soul is to follow the guidance of truth. It is to this effect that Hooker is speaking in a Use of instruction, pointing out that a truly humble soul is "mervailous teachable and tractable," responding to any impetus that the Lord provides (p. 95). Once again, it is the good hearer—the one who "hearkens" properly and follows the minister's guidance—who has the promise of the ultimate reward.

Meditation

At this and every point on the road to glory there is an implicit understanding that the listener who is truly sincere in his desire to grow towards and beyond faith will work hard at absorbing the truths which the minister is laying out. What the mind had recognized the heart still needed to absorb. Self-examination, as we have seen, often produced a new intellectual awareness of one's need for change. This change could be fostered by the sinner's meditating on scriptural truth. Such meditation, wrote Richard Baxter, opens "the door between the Head and the Heart." He offered an aphoristic summary of a generally accepted truth among Puritan thinkers: "He is the best Scholar who hath the readiest passage from the Ear to the Brain, but he is the best Christian, who hath the readiest passage from the Brain to the Heart."[16] Thus, as we have seen Hooker saying, it is one thing to convince a man rationally of a truth, but it is quite another to get him to absorb the truth into his inmost nature. In a book which Baxter was to cite in his own later work, Joseph Hall had tied the intellectual-psychological process together specifically with the need for meditation in the life of faith: "Our Meditation must *Proceed* in due order, not troubledly, not preposterously: It begins in the vnderstanding, endes in the affections; It begins in the braine, descends to the heart; Begins on earth, ascends to heauen; Not suddenly, but by certain staires & degrees, til we come to the highest."[17] The terminology was standard; this passage, in fact, could easily have been written by Hooker himself, including especially the "staires" metaphor, with its suggestion that the spiritual life is a forward and upward progression. Hooker certainly agreed with Hall that at every step of that movement meditative reflection was absolutely essential. "Besiege the heart with daily meditation," he urged, "that so you may cut off any ease and refreshing, that the heart may seeme to have in any sinfull course." Diligent meditation and "nothing else" brings "sorrow and compunction for sinne."[18]

Louis Martz has traced the long tradition of formal Christain meditation from the Middle Ages to the seventeenth century, showing its relationship to devotional poetry in the latter period.[19] As he had demonstrated, formal meditation as a private devotional exercise was primarily a continental and Roman Catholic practice until the late sixteenth and early seventeenth centuries, when a great increase in interest occurred in England. This interest began in Roman Catholic circles, in whose continental counterparts meditation as a formal, structured part of private devotions had long been standard, especially among the Jesuits. Later, however, Anglicans too began to show an interest in such devotions. Martz underlines this early division of interest, noting that "John Heigham . . . reproached the 'deceaved Protestants' of England with having no knowledge of the contemplative life because their doctrine is all definition and speculation." This was true, Martz believes, mainly because Protestant publications were largely in the nature of discussions or examples of scattered aspects of worship—prayers, sermons, fragments of liturgy[20]—as opposed to the extended devotional works outlining step-by-step procedures for meditation which were an important product of the Counter-Reformation.

One likely reason for the greater popularity of meditative exercises among Roman Catholics than among Protestants was the formal arrangement of the meditative experience into a set sequence. For the Reformation Protestant, it probably smacked too much of popish ritual, even in the privacy of one's own closet, though it is true that "set forms" of prayers were considered helpful to "the weak" by some Puritan ministers, so long as the "forms" were supplemented by personal application.[21] Certainly, too, its popularity among the Jesuits made it for a while a very suspect practice among Protestants and particularly Puritans. As Martz has explained, at any rate, from Ignatius Loyola on, the meditation devotions outlined in numerous books took the form of a three- or four-part sequence of reflections, beginning with intellectual concentration on a personal recollection or a scriptural text, followed by an extended consideration of this subject which was usually divided into several "points," and finally succeeded by a colloquy with God—a mystical elevation of the whole experience to a spiritual climax.[22] A fourth stage included by some involved a private review of the experience to determine its specific worth to the meditator. In general this sequence followed the sequence in which man's faculties were thought to operate. The text or incident which was to be the impetus and subject of the meditative experience was introduced by an act of the memory, after which the understanding went to work on it, analyzing it first and then taking it to heart personally, with a final outgoing of spirit and will to God in colloquy. In the final stages, too, one came to see the way in which this experience might be made useful—one considered, that is, what its meaning to his affections and thus its effect on his actions might be. Saint Bernard saw the process as an ascension through three "degrees of truth."[23] The first degree involves the use of reason for self-analysis, a process entailing severity toward the self. The second degree was reached as one rose beyond this severe self-criticism to a stage where one was able to perceive similar struggles in others and to feel for them a loving sympathy and pity. This stage, of course, involved a going out of the self in concern for others and thus

engaged the heart and affections in the process. A final degree of truth
was achieved when one's concerns and insights took one out of the
realm of human considerations to an enraptured vision of purity. This
last stage goes beyond the normal, expected duties of man, but it is
clearly a result of the two preceding stages.

It will already be apparent from all that has been said about the
typical organization of the Puritan sermon that its structural patterns
are generally consistent with those of private meditation. Both are built
on the assumption that the advancement to spiritual awareness and insight must be gradual and progressive. And both also assume that in
order to make this advance one must begin in the head and work
through to the heart. These assumptions consistently provide a
rationale for organizational structure, then, whether one is practicing
the Jesuit form of meditation experience, listening to a Puritan sermon,
or following the "taske for all a mans life." These parallels do much to
clarify Thomas Hooker's relation to the meditative tradition.

For a number of years after Martz's studies of the meditative tradition and English devotional poetry, it was common to accept his claim
that it was only with Richard Baxter's *The Saints Everlasting Rest*
(1650) that we could see "a sign that English Puritanism [was] entering
a new stage."[24] In this work, Martz argued, the individual worshipper
was exhorted to "methods" of meditation involving all three powers of
the human soul: mind, heart, and affections; Baxter was making a "plea
for the integration of the whole man in the service of devotion." This
dating has recently been shown to be much too late. In fact, several
Anglican and Puritan writers and preachers over a period of two generations were "preparing an audience for Richard Baxter."[25] These were
precisely the years of Hooker's ministerial career. Indeed, just as
Hooker's preaching practice was helping to prepare the way for John
Bunyan's allegory of the "way" to heaven, so it was also helping to
make possible the great and sudden popularity of Baxter's famous work
on meditation. By reviewing Hooker's regular practice and especially
his description of the Christian life as a series of progressive advances
towards a heavenly union with Christ, it is possible to supplement our
knowledge about the connections between Puritan preaching and Puritan meditation.

In the first place, we need to remind ourselves of Hooker's and
other Puritans' recurrent admonitions to their parishioners to "use the
means" at home as well as in church. Devotional practices involving
the immediate family as well as servants in the household were a standard part of Puritan family life.[26] "Using the means," of course, involved reading the Bible and praying, activities which one immediately

imagines in connection with home devotional practices. But hearing sermons was also an important use of the means. We perhaps tend to overlook the fact that this too was possible, through the exercise of one's memory, in the privacy of one's own home. It was a common practice for the people in Puritan congregations to take notes on the sermon. This not only helped the note-taker to follow more closely the development of a particular sermon at the time of its delivery, but it served him or her as a concrete reminder of the major points of the sermon during the week.[27] It was a way church members had of taking the sermon home with them, and for many it served as an aid to daily spiritual reflection and devotion. That this was a particularly suitable tool—one, in fact, compatible with the traditional format for meditation—is easily perceived if we recall the logic of the seventeenth-century sermon form. It was based, as we have seen, on the head-to-heart theory of the acquistion of knowledge. The Doctrine was followed immutably by the Reasons, appealing to the understanding, and the Uses, asking for both further understanding and activation of the will and affections. The faculties were thus exercised in their natural order, first as one listened to a sermon when in attendance and later as one returned to study and ponder his sermon notes.[28] So, not only were the aims and forms of sermon and meditation identical, as Barbara Lewalski says, but the one became the actual substance of the other, thanks to the individual's shorthand notes. Note-taking was not simply a form of mental discipline or an encouragement to careful attention to the preacher. It was itself the source of one's subsequent meditation.

Martz credits Baxter with making this connection in 1650 between sermon and meditation:

> Declaring that "*Soliloquy* is a Preaching to ones self," [Baxter] says
> that "Therefore the very same *Method* which a *Minister* should use
> in his Preaching to others, should a Christian use in speaking to
> himself." That is, one should follow the usual divisions of a
> seventeenth-century sermon: Explication, Confirmation, Applica-
> tion, Use of Information, Use of Instruction, Use of Examination,
> and so on. . . . And thus we find a Puritan sermon intercalated in
> the higher reaches of the method of meditation; nothing, I think,
> could pay higher tribute to Baxter's shrewdness and dexterity in
> bringing together the best that both sides could offer in the service
> of devotion.[29]

"Shrewdness" and "dexterity" are the wrong terms here, since it did not take extraordinary manipulation at all to say what Baxter was saying. It is in fact a statement of a generally accepted congruence of

Puritan sermon form and Puritan "meditation" form. Sermon notes had for generations provided the assistance that "the weak" needed in order to "preach" to themselves, or at least to help them to "hear" the minister's sermon over again and thus to have their faculties activated in the same sequence encouraged by both the sermon form and the traditional meditation form. "That man that will not regard the preacher in his bosome," wrote Edmund Calamy, "will never regard the preacher in the pulpit."[30]

A second major use of the pattern of meditation and sermon in Hooker's career stems from the first. Just as each person took the sermon home with him in order to reactivate the head-to-heart-to-affections process in his daily reflection on it, so did Hooker's description of the entire lifelong process of redemption and faith provide a long-term repetition of the same sequence. There is a significant similarity between the stages that Hooker describes in the *ordo salutis* and the three "degrees of truth" that Saint Bernard perceived. As Hooker insistently proclaimed, the whole process of regeneration begins with one's critical perception of his own degradation and his related need for improvement. This, as Hooker and his preparationist colleagues told it, was cause for considerable severity with oneself—piercing, lancing, wounding—since one had to despise the sins which often seemed an inextricable part of oneself. Initially, in other words, one reacted rationally, understanding the need for change before such change was actually possible. In humiliation and then in vocation, one gradually activates the will by setting aside self and accepting the aid of the Lord. And finally the affections are constantly activated as one puts one's faith to work in daily Christian living. Indeed, in the later stages of the saint's journey, as we shall see in succeeding chapters, the approach to glory gradually increases the mystical possibilities in the spiritual life of the saint.[31] Since Hooker's understanding of human mental and psychological process is essentially the same as that of the early formalizers of meditation practice, it is not surprising that his whole sequence of sermons describing the growth of the soul away from sin and towards communion with God is very similar to their prescription for the stages in the meditative process. This becomes clear as we remember that Ignatian meditation involves the sequential stages of rational consideration of a limited topic followed by a bringing home of that aspect of the meditation to the heart followed in turn by a more highly wrought and emotional colloquy with God employing the will and affections. This sequence of stages is present not only in the form of an individual Puritan sermon, as Lewalski has shown, but in the framework of the entire Christian life as Hooker describes it.

Hooker's structuring of his sermon sequence is the ultimate expansion of the head-to-heart, earth-to-heaven, sin-to-glory progression, since it occupies not just an hour on occasional days of the week but the entire earthly life of his listeners. Following Hooker's road map, the spiritually diligent individual would necessarily come to see "meditation" as the central activity in life. If his private devotional experience did not always follow the traditional form of the meditation, his entire spiritual life did.

For the dedicated Puritan, then, the end of the meditative experience was the end of life, for that was the point at which the ultimate union and communion with Christ would occur. As Martz, again quoting Baxter, has said, the Puritan had a "heart set upon heaven." The Puritan's interest in the incarnation tended to be centered on the question of what that crucial event would mean to him in the long run—at the far end of the stairway to heaven—rather than on what it meant to him in the present moment's efforts to achieve mystical communion with the divine.[32] So it was appropriate for Hooker to establish the most elaborate framework offered by any Puritan minister for a life dedicated to the achievement of that ultimate goal for those elected to it. His sermon series is neither fragmentary nor highly intellectualized. It offers his congregation both a subject and a method for meditation. It is a personal project for each believer and "a taske for all a mans life." Insisting that one must always be of a meditative frame of mind, he thus offered a framework for a life of meditation in the sermons that he preached.

Concluding Humiliation: Contentedness

Hooker challenges the would-be saint to the practice of meditation at all the points on the journey to glory. But its importance to his purposes is particularly evident at the early stage of humiliation, since it is here that a sinner begins to sense that his early insights into his own nature and his efforts to free himself from self are parts of a much longer process of spiritual evolution into a new being. Without constant recourse to "meditation," "contemplations," "reflection," one cannot even get to stage two in the process, much less all the way to the end.

The final sermon in *The Soules Humiliation*, occupying more than half the volume, is on the theme of contentedness. Here Hooker argues that the truly humbled soul is content to take however much or little mercy the Lord might give. It is here that he adds his oft-cited claim that "the heart truly abased, is content to beare the estate of damnation" (*SH*, p. 112). Anyone who can be "content" to bear the ultimate bad news is obviously a humbled, truly self-less person. Hooker does not really suppose that such knowledge is bearable to the truly hopeful Christian, but by imagining the situation, he is able to dramatize the extreme degree of selfless acceptance that the thoroughly humbled soul is able to manifest. Mercy may come in various shapes, he insists, painting a picture of Mercy as a rather tough taskmaster in the process. The contented soul will be perfectly well satisfied, even though Mercy takes away "friends, and meanes, and ease, and liberty, and credit, and whatsoever it is that the heart hath loved most" (p. 117). When one is as content as this, one is properly prepared for faith, since faith requires total reliance on another.

Hooker finally insists that the *whole* man is humbled in this stage, not just his mind or will or affections. In explaining this he expostulates on the opposition of pride to the process of humiliation, a point which he had mentioned at the very outset of this work but which now receives his full attention. Pride opposes the covenant of grace, redemption, and even God Himself: "A stout hearted man is a thousand miles from righteousnesse" (*SH*, p. 199). Consequently, the high and mighty, the rich and powerful, those of "greatest parts and gifts and meanes, and places, abilities and honors," are the ones "most hardly brought home to the Lord Iesus Christ" (p. 133). It is doubtless meant as a sort of backhanded encouragement to the weak and lowly when Hooker says rather begrudgingly, "Indeed, blessed be God, there are some great, some wise, and some noble men converted. But, not many" (p. 135). Such an empirical observation obviously had roots in Hooker's immediate awareness of the Puritans' relative political impotence in the face of Royalist power as well as in his psychological knowledge that power breeds pride.

The Soules Humiliation ends with three paragraphs in which Hooker drives home the value of the rewards and comforts made available to the humbled soul who receives God's grace. He begins by speaking directly to the congregation before him, in whose faces he sees evidence that his message is having an effect. "Me thinkes your hearts begin to stirre, and say, hath the Lord engaged himselfe to this? Oh then (Lord) make me humble. Mee thinks your countenances say so" (*SH*, p. 220). He then puts a question to the people before him, the answer to which is obvious to all, and follows it with several more rhetorical questions, with equally obvious answers, ending with a clause which is a simple summary of the message of this whole series on preparation for grace. The passage conveys with great clarity the rhetorical forcefulness and almost hypnotic potency of the oral manner of this great preacher in the plain style. He has begun, we should recall, by observing encouraging signs in the countenances of his listeners. They know, in other words, that he is both speaking directly to them and carefully watching their response. Having their full attention, he proceeds:

> Let mee make but this one question to your Consciences, and give mee an answer secretly in your soules; when the Lord shall close up your eyes here, and put an end to your pilgrimage, would you not be content to dwell with Christ in heaven? which the Apostle did account his greatest happinesse, to be ever with the Lord; we shall be ever with Christ to comfort us, when we shall be no more with sinne, to vexe and trouble us: would not you be content to be with Christ? mee thinkes your hearts say, that's the end and up-shot of all, that's the end why we live, and pray, and heare, that we may be ever with him. And doe not you meet with many troubles, while you are members of the Church Militant? I know you have sometimes distempers without, and troubles without, would you not have comfort against them all? And what would you give, that Christ would looke in, and asked how your Soules doe, and say, thou art my redeemed, and I am thy Redeemer. No, you know, all flesh desires it. Would you not be content to have some honour in the Church? and to leave a good name behind you, that the disgraces which wicked men cast upon you, may not be as a blot upon your names? and when you shall bee no more, and you shall bid adue to friends, and honours, and meanes; would you not be blessed, and though you would be content to be the meanest in the Kingdome of heaven, what would you give to be the greatest in heaven? let mee put a condition to you; get but humble hearts and you have all. (SH, pp. 220–21)

The simplicity of statement here reduces the entire arduous business of inner struggle to the simplest of terms: "Get but humble hearts and you have all." Christ looks into the individual's home, into his heart, the soul's house, and asks how his soul is doing, implicitly answering the question by saying he has come as Redeemer, so all is right with the soul from now on.

With all of this, the rest of the way along the road to Glory looks a good deal easier. Indeed, the sinner has a new guide and companion: "If there be any Soule here, that is content in truth and sinceritie to be humbled, and to be at Gods disposing in all duties to be done, do not you make too much hast to goe to heaven, the Lord Iesus Christ will come downe from heaven and dwell in your hearts, hee will sit, and lye, and walke with you; his grace shall refresh you, and his Wisedome shall direct you, and his Glory shall advance you, and as for happinesse, take no thought for that" (SH, pp. 221–22). Thus, the journey continues, but Christ's indwelling presence in the soul makes the way easy by comparison with its previous difficulty. Hooker's able manipulation of this tableau makes it all seem very tangible at this crucial moment.

Hooker takes pains here to add that the humbled man ought to make it a central task of his life to see that his wife and children are also humbled so that when he comes to die, he can, regardless of worldly poverty, be content in leaving Christ with them. "When you are gone this will bee better for them then all the beaten gold, or all the honours in the world" (*SH*, p. 223). This brief comment is significant in that it seems to assign a brand new "taske" to the humbled man just when he seems to be getting to the end of his labors. He must not think, in other words, that his job is done just because he has opened his own heart to grace. He must—and will want to—go to work on the hearts of those he loves. A desire to do so at this stage in one's spiritual odyssey is thus a further test of the validity of his humiliation.

In the last paragraph in this treatment of preparation for grace, Hooker again reminds his hearers of the two ways the sinner can go, urging them one last time to go the right way:

> Where are all those *Nymrods*, and *Pharaohs*, and all those mightie Monarchs of the World? The Lord hath thrown them flat upon their backs, and they are in hell this day. Therefore be wise, and be humbled under the mightie hand of the Lord. It is a mightie hand, and the Lord will be honoured, either in your Humiliation and conversion, or else in your damnation for ever. Let all the evill that is threatned, and all the good that is offered prevaile with your hearts, and though meanes cannot, yet the Lord prevaile with you, the Lord emptie you, that Christ may fill you, the Lord humble you, that you may enjoy happinesse, and peace for ever. (*SH*, p. 224)

Appropriately, both theologically and psychologically, the final phrasing is positive, looking hopefully and confidently far into eternity. It is a benediction, lacking only the Amen.

10

Becoming Faithful
THE AFFECTIONS AND THE
WILL IN VOCATION

At the end of his treatment of humiliation, Hooker had assured his congregation that if they could but "get humble Hearts" they would "have all." Saving faith, bringing grace and salvation, was sure to follow. This sounded easy enough. But nothing is automatic in Hooker's depiction of the evolving life of the soul on the way to grace. Another stage of the process intervened before full assurance of grace belonged to the sinful penitent. Having minutely examined the successive processes of self-knowledge in contrition and of self-rejection in humiliation, he now turned his powerful magnifying lens on the period between humiliation and the knowledge of one's sure possession of faith. This stage, depicted mainly in *The Soules Effectuall Calling* (1637), reissued the next year with the title *The Soules Vocation*, involved chiefly an activation of certain affections whose action preceded the will's acceptance of Christ. Hooker relied very heavily on his audience's common earthly experiences to provide the correlatives which would give a tangible character to the motions of the soul at this climactic point. Metaphor and analogy, with a skillful if only occasional use of allegorical technique, make for Hooker's success in this unrevised but still highly refined analysis.

In keeping with his awareness of the need both to instruct and to persuade, Hooker in this book merges his description of Calvinist thought on the theology of faith with psychological analysis. Vocation involves the joint operation of a call from God and a hearing of the call by the believer. As Calvin put it, calling "consists not only in the preaching of the Word but also in the illumination of the Spirit."[1] The Reformers based their notion of calling on the passage in Romans 8:30,

"Whome he predestinate, them also he called, and whome he called, them also he iustified, and whome he iustified, them he also glorified" (Geneva Bible). Calvin comments on this verse by saying that "although in choosing his own the Lord already has adopted them as his children, we see that they do not come into possession of so great a good except when they are called; conversely, that when they are called, they already enjoy some share of his election."[2] At this stage, then, the individual recognizes that God has chosen him—that he is indeed among the elect. Vocation is thus the process by which one finally acquires faith and assurance. Only after this glorious discovery does the believer begin to experience the *indwelling* spirit of God.

Early seventeenth-century Puritan definitions of faith imply this close interrelationship with vocation. Hooker's Essex County neighbor and friend John Rogers, for instance, said in his popular treatise on faith, "To say that Faith is a particular Application of Christ to a mans owne soule, or a particular apprehension or laying hold on Christ, as John 1.12, is a true and safe definition thereof." Ezekiel Culverwell, another contemporary, said simply that "Iustifying Faith is a beliefe of the Gospell, whereby I receive Christ offered vnto me in the same." William Ames in his turn said that "faith is the resting of the heart on God," while also being "an act of choice, an act of the whole man." "By faith," said Ames, "we first cleave to God and then fasten on to those things which are made available by God." And Ames's teacher, William Perkins, had earlier said that through faith "the elect are truly *joyned* vnto Christ, and haue an heauenly *communion* and fellowship with him."[3]

Hooker was quite conscious of all of these prior definitions of faith when he offered his own variation in his preface to Rogers's *Doctrine of Faith.* There he tells of "Faith being nothing else but the going out of the soul to God through Christ to fetch a principle of life which in Adam we lost and now need."[4] The achievement of faith, in Hooker's description as in the others quoted, is a climactic coming together of the sinner and Christ which radically alters the nature of the man's inner being, so that, having been made a "new man" in grace, he is capable of things which his "natural" condition had prohibited. The difference is, in short, that the "gracious," the "faithful" person has begun to partake of the actual benefits of Christ's love. But what once again distinguishes Hooker's definition of faith from all the others just quoted is his depiction of the act of faith as an energetic movement. The soul, in Hooker's imagination, "goes out" "to fetch" faith and the new life it brings. Ames, too, speaks of faith as an *act* of the whole man, but Hooker gives the act an actual character, making it easy to compare—in all but the degree of difficulty—with familiar efforts such as fetching in the cows from the field or drawing a bucket of water from the well. While the passive voice is common in the definitions of Calvin, Perkins, Culverwell, Rogers, and even Ames, Hooker insists on the active voice. Hooker's spiritual activism asserts its strength even in the unlikely form of his definition of terms.

In his seven-page prefatory epistle to Rogers's book, Hooker observed that "much more might be said of this particular, and shall be when occasion shall require." This was in 1627. It is very likely that in his lectures at Chelmsford Hooker was then about to begin the series of sermons on vocation which were published a decade later as *The Soules Effectuall Calling*, which may be the fullest analysis of the process from the sinner's perspective and for his benefit published by any man in the Reformed tradition, including Calvin himself. Shorter works such as *Spirituall Thirst, The Soules Ingrafting, The Poor Doubting Christian*, and the final sermon in *The Soules Implantation* are important supplements to Hooker's treatment of vocation, but *The Soules Effectuall Calling* is the central work.[5]

Effectual Calling

Hooker makes the transition from his descriptions of contrition and humiliation to vocation in a short work of some thirty octavo pages entitled *The Soules Ingrafting into Christ*. The activist stance of a preparationist preacher is everywhere evident in this sermon. The text of the sermon is Malachi 3:1, which tells of a messenger who is coming to prepare the way for the Lord, who will then come "suddenly" into his Temple. Two dimensions of figural interpretation come into play here, since the "temple" is clearly a symbolic representation of the human heart into which Christ will quickly come when it is properly fitted out for him. As a king on entering an inn does not expect the humble innkeeper to provide all of his retinue's needs without help from the king's larder, so Christ never expects a corrupt sinner to do everything himself in getting to heaven. Christ occupies his heart and then brings "provision enough of Vocation, Adoption, Justification, and Sanctification."[6] At the same time, the text in Malachi suggests the role of the preparationist preacher in the spiritual life of those under him. The passage, says Hooker, is "a Prophecie of *Iohn* the Baptist" (*S Ing*, p. 5), who is in turn a type of the later prophets of God, men like Hooker himself, who must prepare the hearts of the humble for their occupation by God.

At the beginning of this description of effectual calling, Hooker gives a nodding acknowledgement to those people who experience a "passive receiving" of grace, which leaves them unaware of their possession of it. There are a variety of reasons for this failure to recognize the very event for which the sinner has been preparing himself for such a long time: we may have false preconceptions about what the coming of Christ to us individually will be like; we may be too preoccupied with worldly things to notice Christ's "quiet" coming; Christ may find it better to hold back partly at this stage so that one does not become self-righteous and censorious in his grace. Whatever the reasons, "many men have smoken out their dayes in sorrow, and at their death have great assurance" (*S Ing*, p. 22). In these cases, the soul receives Christ's grace as an empty vessel receives a liquid. Predictably, these passive receivers do not interest or challenge Hooker nearly so much as those more ordinary people who are conscious of an "active calling," whereby the soul, "having received power, by vertue of that power returnes an answer to the call of God, as it is with an eccho. . . . Its the same voyce that ecchoes, the same beame that reflects from the wall: So it is the same spirit that returnes the voyce: and this answer of the Soule, wee tearme faith" (*S Ing*, pp. 29–30). Here the transaction is reciprocal, involving a response—an echo or reflection—as well as a reception. After thus stating the case in terms of a Ramist dichotomy between passive and active receiving of faith, the preparationist Hooker opts for concentration on the active function.[7] It was this same preference for the active over the passive Christian life which contributed to Hooker's energetic sermons on the "activity of faith" aimed against the New England Antinomians. As it was for his fellow colonist Richard Mather,[8] the special insistence that the affections have an active role was fundamental to Hooker's preaching ministry. Where there was difficulty, tension, struggle in the inner man's spiritual experience, there Hooker would nearly always focus his attention. No one in his congregation was apt to acquire faith either casually or unawares.

Hooker's consideration of vocation is an orchestrated, progressively structured discussion of the role that the affections play *before* one acquires the full assurance of grace and faith. In this respect he is part of a philosophical tendency in England noticed by Vernon J. Bourke, who points out that up to and including John Locke there is in British philosophy "a gradual but persistent tendency to place some sort of feeling before the movements of the human will."[9] Knowing that the affections also operate after the will has responded, Hooker insists that this prior role of the affections is different. Yet it is not a sudden entrance of the affections into the process, since he points out that in getting the soul through contrition and humiliation such affections as fear, sorrow, and hatred have already helped to carry the soul away from sin. After these affections have responded to one's own sinfulness and the need to alter that condition, their opposites—hope, desire, love, and joy—carry the soul to good. These, says Hooker, are the "two sorts of feet" which God has placed in the soul.[10] So, while God's promise of grace and mercy draws the soul towards Him, it comes on its own "feet." In this way "the faculties of the soule hunt and pursue this mercy, and lay hold thereupon, and satisfie themselves herein" (SEC, p. 62). Hooker could fully agree with his Essex neighbor William Fenner that "as the body goes with its feet to that which it loves, so the soule goes out with its affections to that which it loves."[11]

Until these positive affections are activated, Hooker sees the understanding as the main component of man's nature involved in the process. He continues to warn against intellectual obstacles such as the "veile of ignorance," which is over every man's heart, and those "Desperate discouragements," which render a man spiritually impotent. But now he also urges the activation of the affections to see the *goodness* of the Gospel's promise, without which perception the mere intellectual recognition of the *truth* of that promise will not be effectual. To this end, in three successive sermons he takes up the four affections which he claims are most active in bringing the individual to the final assurance of grace.

Hope

Since Hooker and Fenner both followed Scripture in describing the affections as the "feet of the soul," the metaphor of the journey remained naturally suited to further elaboration of the soul's progress. Thus, Hooker's allegorical bent proves especially useful when, after initially saying that "the soule must learne, that it may be able in some measure to see the way, and learne the path that leadeth to everlasting happinesse," he then envisions the soul as actually being on a highway, waiting with gradually changing frames of mind for the arrival of that ultimate "good," faith (or mercy or grace), which is also personified as a figure on the road, still out of sight but coming towards the soul. Of hope he says, "It is the maine office of this affection in the heart to looke and expect for a good to come" (SEC, pp. 43, 112). Then he makes the picture more graphic:

It is a similitude taken from a man that looketh after another, and lifteth up it selfe as high as he may to see if any man bee comming neare him, looking wishly about him, so here the soule standeth as it were a tiptoe, expecting when the soule will come: as the man that is to meet another in such a place, they do set the time appointed, and then goeth up to a high hill, and looketh very earnestly round about him, wondreth he commeth not, and yet he hopeth he will come: so an humbled sinner, when the Lord saith, mercy is comming towards thee, mercy is provided for thee; now this affection is set out to meet mercy a farre off, namely hope; this is the stretching out of the soule. (*SEC*, pp. 112–13)

Hooker here conveys in dramatic and fully visual terms his somewhat paradoxical sense of the soul's concurrent activity and dependence on God for the conclusive action. He pictures the soul as *going out*, down the road and up the high hill, there to *wait*—"wishly," hopefully—for the one he goes to meet, namely Mercy. Hooker is never content to have his hypothetical soul simply sit where he is and wait; when the affections are called into play, they energize the spirit, so that it must be aggressive, on the move. But his theology will not allow that the soul simply keep going down the road until it discover its prize resting in some secluded bower. God is not like that, and neither is grace; they come seeking the properly prepared soul—the man who has gotten far enough along the road on his own steam. The implication sometimes seems to be that God demands the soul's activity because He is Himself active and energetic.

At one point Hooker contrasts this active and then hopeful man with a prisoner; the association of darkness and light imagery with the two men in this analogy makes eminently clear and forceful the differing appropriateness of hope on the part of the man who is on the right highway and of him who is not: "If a man be in a deepe darke dungeon, he cannot tell when it is light; hee may aske, is it light? but else hee cannot tell: But an humbled sinner is like a man standing full upon the Sunne rising, this face of Gods mercy shines full upon him, the Lord lets in the inclination of his kindnesse, and makes knowne the surenesse of his favour in the Lord Jesus Christ; now the soule hath some apprehension that he hath to doe with mercy" (*SEC*, p. 81). It is this "apprehension" which verifies the appropriateness of hope because for Hooker in his Calvinist framework of thought just as much as for Henry David Thoreau some two centuries later, the man whose spirit is properly attuned lives "in infinite expectation of the dawn." This "Sunne rising" is not a brightness to put out the eyes but to make us expect the imminent coming of the Light of Lights. And Hooker would have felt that Thoreau's final frame of mind in *Walden* was—

psychologically, at least—the appropriate one for full redemption: "Only that day dawns to which we are awake. There is more day to dawn. The sun is but a morning star."[12]

There are, of course, both true and false hopes, and Hooker partly concerns himself in this sermon with differentiating between the two. He details a number of false bases for hope to which the hypocrites cling; they make their prosperity or their sufferings signs of God's intentions to show them mercy in heaven. But Hooker warns that earthly signs can be deceptive. A properly "grounded" hope, on the other hand, endures "when all the rest of a mans abilities fail" (SEC, p. 140). This true hope is patient, despite seemingly abundant raw materials for discouragement. To let one's hope grow into impatience is to "stand upon tearmes with God" (p. 149). The hopeful Christian, while he stands on tiptoe on the rim of the high hill, must remind himself, "It is not for me to know the time."

Desire

Rather than impatience, the appropriate affection to follow hope in this period of anxious expectation is desire. The word obviously conveys an intensification of the heart's yearning for assurance. The sixth sermon in The Soules Effectuall Calling is on this desire, which Hooker says is "quickened" in a humbled and enlightened sinner by the Lord's spirit. Given Hooker's tendency to harp on the need for labor in the spiritual enterprise, his caution to his listeners is quite necessary: "You must not thinke to bring desire with you to the promise, but receive desire from the promise: It is a vaine thing to thinke that if the oares be in the boat, the boat must needs goe; indeed the oare will move the boat, but the hand of the Ferri-man must first move the oare: The soule is like the oare, and unlesse the hand of the Spirit moves our desire, it cannot move towards the Lord" (SEC, p. 151).

Other analogies from the secular lives of his hearers make his point all the more certain. He compares the soul to an infant who cannot walk without the help of his father and to a bowling ball which can "run" no farther than the strength of the hand of the bowler allows. The idea of the affections as the "feet of the soul" is thus kept before the listener, but the analogies used, which depend on the principle of motion and impetus, reiterate the point that they must be set in motion by some force beyond themselves. God thus has the active role, and the incipient saint is compared to inanimate objects such as oars and bowling balls or to an infant still lacking the strength or ability to be self-sufficient. The potential for meaningful movement rests entirely outside the self at this point. Quoting Matthew 12:20 ("A bruised reed shall he not break, and smoking flax shall he not quench"), Hooker warns that "the Lord must first strike fire by the promise upon the soule, before it can ever flame in a desire towards the Lord," but then offers the consolation that "when it doth once smoake in a holy desire, the Lord will not let it faile before he brings it to a perfect flame, and before it bee possessed of Christ and mercy which it longs for" (*SEC*, p. 152).

Hooker uses this opportune time to remind his listeners that, despite the Lord's having the initiating power, man's will ultimately has a crucial role to play. Hope and desire, he says, are each in their different turns serving "the great commandress of the soule, the *will*, for these affections are as hand-maids to serve the *will*" (*SEC*, p. 152). He uses personification to dramatize the subordination of these "hand-maids," the anticipatory affections, to the will. We see here again that there is no such thing as an armchair Christian; these characters are actively stirring the dust on the highway to grace:

> The will saith, I will have this or that good, and therefore hope wait you for it, and desire, long you after it: Hope is the furthest and greatest reach of the soule; for when the soule is doubting and quarrelling, and saith, will the Lord doe good to such an unworthy wretch as I am: yes saith the mind inlightned, mercy is intended towards thee, then hope goeth out to wait and looke for this mercy. Now when the soule hath waited a long time, and yet this mercy comes not, and he marvels at it and saith, the Lord hath said the weary soule shall bee refreshed: Oh where are all those precious promises? then the *will* sends out desire to meet with that good which will not yet come, and so desire goeth wandring from one ordinance to another, till it bring Christ home to the soule. As a gentleman doth when he expects some noble personage, hee sends out a man to wait in such a place, and bring him word whether he seeth him or no: afterwards when he returnes and saith he seeth him not, the gentleman sends out another messenger to meet him afarre off, and so likewise to bring him and give him entertainment: So it is with the soule of a poore sinner in this case. (*SEC*, pp. 152–53)

The eclecticism of Hooker's rhetorical method is evident when, having thus activated the listener's visual imagination, he drops the allegorical dramatics for most of the rest of the sermon, reverting to an analytical method whereby he first describes three "Motives" which produce spiritual desire and then describes the negative qualities of three kinds of hypocrites who pretend to have desire for grace. Each of these points is amply reinforced with similes, metaphors, or analogies which make concrete the abstract states of mind being described, while the several types and subtypes of hypocrites are rendered recognizable in biting "character" sketches. Hooker exerts himself conscientiously to attract the sensuous imagination of his listeners to identify the signs of both true and false desire and reinforces this with imagined dialogue (or monologue) of the characters he creates, frequently adding exclamations, either of his own or of the characters whose speech he imitates.[13] If rendered with any animation at all—as these passages surely must have been when delivered by their author, who became widely known as a "son of thunder"—this sermon would have commanded very forcefully the attention of all present. In fact, it is a virtuoso performance, demonstrating Hooker's mastery of his key rhetorical tools and clearly indicating why his preaching attracted large audiences and built a wide reputation in his native England.

Two of the analogies which Hooker uses to dramatize desire are particularly interesting and helpful in understanding both the message and the man. The first likens spiritual desire to the longing of a woman for the sexual love of her beloved. One of the signs of a true desire for mercy and Christ, he says, is manifest in the sinner's personal, almost selfish desire of Christ "for himself," not merely for the good that he can bring. It is as it is with "a maid that desires a man in wedlocke, she doth not desire the portion, but the person of the man, if I beg and die with him, saith she, if I never see good day with him, yet let me have him, and I care not" (SEC, p. 158). The same comparison occurs a little later, with clearer implication that the woman's desire involves the desire for sexual relations with her beloved. He observes that "the Lord breeds a thorow and sound desire in the hearts of those he intends good unto (not a flashy desire, but) like the desire of a longing woman that must have her longing, or else she dyes, so an humble soule must have a Saviour or else he dyes, for what she said in regard of children, the humbled soule that hath a true desire after Christ saith the same, Give me a Saviour or else I die" (p. 160).[14] It is not surprising that sexual desire provides a useful analogy here, but it is interesting that Hooker's only examples of it show a woman's rather than a man's desire. Though the biblical origin for this sexual perspective was present in Canticles, it is nevertheless clear that Hooker was aware of women's capacity for passionate love, an element in the Puritan mind more often ignored than recognized, despite an occasional Hawthorne among us.[15]

Another basic human craving—hunger, and alternately, thirst—provided an analogy that Hooker used even more fully in this and related sermons. Answering the rhetorical objection that great sins demand a great amount of grace, Hooker quotes Isaiah 44:3: "I will pour clean water upon the thirsty, and floods upon the dry ground" (*SEC*, p. 156). Several more times in this sermon he characterizes the sinner's desire as a thirst which the sufferer persists relentlessly in seeking to satisfy. The same, of course, is true of the person who hungers: "If a soule were hunger-starved, would hee not receive bread if it were offered him, or would he not call the man to him that sold bread, and buy it of him to supply his wants with the soonest, and say, let me be served first [?]" (p. 165). Or, in another place: "A [starving] man hung up in chaines cries onely for bread: so it is with a poore famisht soule, he desires nothing but Christ, and nothing else will satisfie him" (p. 158).

The hunger-and-thirst metaphors used in this manner form the central figures in another sermon by Hooker, which was printed anonymously as *Spirituall Thirst: A Sermon Preached upon John 7.37* (1638).[16] This book is a concentrated discussion of the nature of spiritual desire, which Hooker there calls "spirituall thirst," and it doubtless dates from the same period—the late 1620s—as the series on vocation. In *Spirituall Thirst*, the "man hung up in chaines" appears again as part of a very effective condensed definition of what Hooker has been calling true desire: "As it is with one hanged alive in chains, whatsoever is offered him hee sets light by it, unlesse it be bread; a Crowne of Gold, garments of silke contents him not without bread; oh bread, bread is that which he chiefly desireth: So it is with the true humbled soule, it is not riches, pleasures, honours that quiets his conscience, it is not gifts of memory, or of utterance, gifts of prayer or preaching which satisfyeth his distressed soule, so long as he goeth Christlesse, but he cryeth out with *Sampson, Oh, what availeth all these things, seeing I must die for thirst?*"[17] In this work Hooker gives what is probably his clearest and most succinct definition of both the affection of true desire and its metaphoric equivalent, spiritual thirst, when he says, "A spirituall thirst is a special work of the Spirit in a humble and contrite heart, wherby the will and affections finding nothing at home to satisfie them, but misery, are carryed forth with a vehement longing desire after the Lord Jesus Christ and his Righteousnesse, the soule never resting quiet untill it hath obtained them" (*ST*, p. 10). *Spirituall Thirst*, then, assumes the whole preparationist structure involving the preceding stages of contrition and humiliation and is, in effect, a simpler and perhaps less intellectually demanding sermon on the same subject as the sixth sermon in *The Soules Effectuall Calling*. Both draw heavily and unapologetically on the audience's awareness of their human appetites as analogues for spiritual desire.

As the emotional anticipation heightens at each progression from one affection to the next in the work of vocation, the ultimate possession of saving faith becomes all the more certain. As Hooker said in his prefatory Epistle to John Rogers's *Doctrine of Faith*, "In the hungrings and thirstings of the soule there is as it were the spawne of Faith, not yet brought to full perfection, the soule is comming toward God, but not yet come to him to rest so fully and wholly on him as hereafter it will." "All this while [during the progression of the affections] faith is a sowing into the soule" (*SEC*, p. 197). But the process is still by no means irreversible. Though Hooker says there are relatively few—"scarce one of a thousand," in fact (*ST*, p. 28)—who make it this far on the road to grace, this desire "is not a matter of complement and indifferencie; No, no, I may call it the very wheeles of faith, upon which faith is carried. . . . ; Looke as it is with a waggon, knocke off the wheeles, and all lyes in the dust; so take away this desire, and faith is in the dust" (*SEC*, p. 197). Only the thirsty and the hungry "shall be *satisfied*." The discovery of this true desire in oneself through self-examination, an extremely personal matter known only to the individual and God, is a glorious discovery, since Hooker promises, "Get this, and you get heaven, it is worth the while, Oh that we had hearts to labour for it" (*SEC*, p. 192).

This subtle evolution through a series of emotional developments within the soul is an eminently orderly process.[18] Stage follows stage in practically every case in an immutable sequence, so that the missing of a stroke could indicate the beginning of one's destined plunge into the torments of hell. It is precisely on this point of the predictability of the stages in the *ordo*, in fact, that Hooker can be most clearly distinguished from his Connecticut Valley descendant of a century later, Jonathan Edwards, who also gave considerable attention to the subject of the emotions in the work of conversion. Edwards, in fact, might have been speaking in direct opposition to Hooker when, in *A Treatise concerning Religious Affections*, he objected strenuously to preachers who were certain that they knew the way the Spirit works and could thus predict the sequence of the inner experience of the elect. Finding support in the writings of Thomas Shepard, Edwards wrote:

> Experience plainly shows, that God's Spirit is unsearchable and untraceable, in some of the best Christians, in the method of his operations, in their conversion. Nor does the Spirit of God proceed discernibly in the steps of a particular established scheme, one half so often as is imagined. . . . Very often, at first, their experiences appear like a confused chaos, as Mr. Shepard expresses it: but then those passages of their experience are picked out, that have most

of the appearance of such particular steps that are insisted on; and these are dwelt upon in the thoughts, and these are told of from time to time, in the relation they give: these parts grow brighter and brighter in their view; and others, being neglected, grow more and more obscure: and what they have experienced is insensibly strained to bring all to an exact conformity to the scheme that is established. And it becomes natural for ministers, who have to deal with them and direct them that insist upon distinctness and clearness of method, to do so too.[19]

Edwards is arguing that one describes one's own conversion in the way that will best conform to the locally accepted norm—a good insight, which Edwards might as appropriately have applied to his own situation as to those who insisted on "particular steps" in redemption. Hooker's own parishioners, in attesting their possession of saving grace when applying for church membership, undoubtedly traced their personal experiences through the stages of grace which Hooker preached in such detail. But what sounds like a theological difference here between Edwards and Hooker is really more a function of Edwards's new awareness of how the human mind operates, resulting from his familiarity with the new sensationalism in the writings of Newton and Locke. It was with this new thinking of Edwards that that aspect of Hooker's theology of redemption which insisted on a seemingly rational, strictly progressive framework for spiritual experience became once and for all outmoded.[20]

Love and Joy

Love and joy finally climax the work of the affections, says Hooker, just before the will accepts Christ. He explains their function in the seventh sermon of *The Soules Effectuall Calling* and the last of four in *The Soules Implantation*.[21] He was not alone in this view of the sequence of the affections before faith. William Fenner, in his *Treatise of the Affections; or, The Soules Pulse,* after noting the disagreements among Boethius, Galen, Aristotle, and Cardan as to how many affections there are, adopts the opinion of Plato, who "says they are innumerable." Even so, Fenner discusses only four, which are precisely the same four that Hooker describes. Fenner says these affections follow a "checker-wise order." "They are platted and woven together," but the sequence which Fenner describes is the same as Hooker's: hope, desire, love, joy.[22] Hooker and Fenner's Essex County colleague, John Rogers, also listed desire, hope, and joy (but not love) among the stages between contrition and faith.[23] Both Ames and Perkins as well refer to hope and desire,[24] though Hooker's discussion is fuller than theirs and he clearly differs from his mentors in discussing love and joy as they occur *before* grace; Ames and Perkins saw love and joy as the affections logically resulting from the acquisition of faith. Hooker insists that these are "saving," not "sanctifying" works.

At the outset of his discussion of love and joy, Hooker tactically notes that "many judicious Divines of late yeares," including especially the "judicious *Perkins*," have by "right and reason" argued their belief "that there is a saving desire, by which God brings in and breeds faith in the soule" (*SEC*, p. 203).[25] It is just as logical, he insists, that this desire should be followed immediately by love and joy before faith is fully acquired. "For looke with what authority and right there is thirsting before comming, and a desire before faith (for faith is all this while a hatching and breeding) by the same right and authority there is a saving kinde of love and joy before faith" (pp. 203–4). By thus citing precedent for his discussion of desire but none for his description of love before faith, he implies his sense that he is departing somewhat from standard doctrine. He knew, in fact, that he was directly opposing some of his most valued friends, including John Rogers, whose *Treatise of Love* was quite clear on this point: "Whereas Faith and Love being joyned together, yet Faith is set in the first place, note, that though in regard of *time*, they be wrought together in the soule, yet in order of *nature*, Faith goes first, vniting vs to Christ, from whom are derived into vs, Loue, and all other graces."[26] Here, for once, Hooker and Rogers argue different sides of the question.

Hooker continues his vivid depiction of the operation of the affections in his sermon on love and joy, relying especially on a variety of analogies, some of which are capable of allegorical elaboration. The first and longest of these convincingly conveys a full sense of the rising intensity of the Christian's anticipation of faith. Hooker pictures a "malefactour or traitour" who is pursued by the authorities all the way to the seashore, where he is captured, and returned to the Tower to await execution. When he is about to die, "he heares an inckling from the messengers, there is yet hope that his man may be pardoned" (*SEC*, p. 211). At this point "his heart is stirred up to hope," and when another messenger brings word that the king wants to see him at court, desire impels him there. After much earnest inquiring and running about the court, he perceives that "at last the King lookes out of the window, and seeth the malefactour and saith, is this the traitour? they say yes. . . . The King tells him the truth is his pardon is drawing, and comming towards him: with that his heart leaps in his belly, and his heart is inlarged to his Majesty; and he saith God blesse your Majesty, never was there such a favourable Prince to a poore traitour. His heart leaps with joy because his pardon is comming towards him; haply it is not sealed yet: Now when it is sealed and all, the King calls him in and delivers it, and that is the last stroke of faith" (pp. 211–12). The sinner, as Hooker goes on to explain, is the malefactor, God is the king, and the minister is the messenger. These affections of love and joy, then, are the very last reactions of the person before he achieves faith, just when he realizes he will receive it. The Spirit of God, says Hooker, "lets in some intimation," "some inckling" of God's love for the individual, and his response is, in turn, an outpouring of love to God and joy in his anticipated good fortune. An awareness of the presence of God's love, in other words, begets love in the soul. Hooker's analysis goes so far as to break the aspects of God's love down into three qualities, each of which "sets the soule all in a burning flame" of love (p. 224). These are the "sweetness" of God's love, the freeness with which it is offered, and the greatness of it, all of which at this point are merely anticipated, not yet fully enjoyed. Finally, putting himself in the role of the sinner newly aware that God will bless him in spite of his long record of ingratitudes to God, Hooker soliloquizes rapturously:

> If I had lien in a dungeon, and had beene plagued with torments all my life time; yea though I had another world of misery to live in, it is infinite mercy, so the Lord would pass by these base dealings, and pardon these rebellions of mine. But that God should send his Sonne to love mee, so incomparably, so unconceivably, that I could not hate him so much as he loved me; I could not so exceed in unkindnesse towards him, as he hath exceeded in kindnesse towards mee. Oh the height of this mercy beyond my desire! Oh the breadth of this mercy without all bounds! Oh the length of this mercy beyond all times! Oh the depth of this mercy beneath all miseries! Were my eyes made of love, I could nothing but weepe love; were my tongue made of love, I could nothing but talke love; were my hands made of love, I could nothing but worke love, and all too little for that God that hath loved mee so admirably, so unmeasurably. What shall I love if I love not the Lord? (*SEC*, pp. 225–26)

Here is Thomas Hooker in all of his pulpit mastery. Having just described a distinct though fleeting moment in the spiritual life of the saint—a point which his theological teachers had not bothered to specify at all—Hooker brings it to symbolic life through a dramatic rendering, with the king-God gazing out of his castle window above the head of the malefactor-sinner who looks eagerly up to the being who has the power of life and death over him and hears the news of his impending release from doubt and fear into new life and liberty. This is dramatically effective scene painting. The listener sees it all before him in his mind's eye as clearly as if he were watching the balcony scene in *Romeo and Juliet*. But the identification of listener with protagonist is here complete. Then Hooker, by his effusive example, teaches his congregation the joy of love for Christ in sentences which are rhythmically modulated through the parallel construction of repeated exclamations, culminating in the pure poetry of the three subjunctive clauses ("Were my eyes made of love," etc.), and climaxing in the brief rhetorical question, perhaps spoken with subdued volume but intense pitch, "What shall I love if I love not the Lord?" Having used the human analogy of the malefactor and the king and developed it at unusual length—the complete passage is some four pages of octavo text—as a way of simplifying the subtle psychological moment that he wants to define, he appeals to the emotional dimension of his hearers' spiritual yearnings, implicitly asking them to join him and his hypothetical redeemed sinner in ecstatic enjoyment of the love of God. At such high moments in Hooker's preaching, the plain style becomes a finely honed tool, capable of intellectual precision and emotional arousal of any man or woman in the audience, however high or low his or her social station or educational background. And in it Hooker shows himself eminently capable of combining the diverse arts of narrative and exhortation.

This mastery is important at this point because of the difficulty of the spiritual dissection which Hooker has set for himself in distinguishing a point in the life of the saint where he does not have faith and assurance of grace but knows he is about to get it. There is, in fact, a difficulty in maintaining this space between the lover and the beloved even for the duration of one sermon. He comes quickly to his first Use, where he instructs the audience that man cannot of his own accord respond to God with love and joy. Though his response requires the enabling power of the Holy Spirit, most men think it is easy enough: "What, not love the Lord Jesus Christ? why, who cannot love Christ? Who cannot? I say, neither thou, nor I, nor any man under heaven can love Christ by any power in himself" (*SEC*, p. 229). In fact, even religious duties will not help without God's assistance at this stage: "Thou mayst pray till thy eyes sinke in thy head, and till thy heart failes; and yet thou canst not love Christ, unlesse the Spirit enable thee thereunto" (p. 230).[27] No more here than at any other stage in the *ordo salutis* can the sinner save himself. Hooker goes right to the issue of God's initiative in the love between Savior and saved in the first of five "trials" to test the validity of one's love for God. If you can say, "I love God because hee loved me," then "this is a love of the right coine, it came from the right mint" (p. 239).

In each of these five trials, Hooker makes effective use of metaphor and especially of extended analogy. The principles of debate hold that analogy is a weak logical tool, subject to easy refutation. But it is also a persuasive tool where a popular auditory is concerned, as all successful propagandists know. The more the audience can understand and identify with the analogue, the more they will be inclined to transfer their assent to the primary subject. Hooker finds analogues in two very common aspects of English life which he uses to give his argument on love and joy a grounding in the objective lives of each of his listeners. In the first place, he had an affection for gardens and occasionally uses the imagery of gardens with particular poignancy. Early in his sermon on love and joy, he introduces the garden imagery, saying that "we will have garden love and joy, of the Lords own setting and planting" (*SEC*, p. 205). Here God is the gardener, and our own hearts are the soil he works. He picks up the figure again in the first Use, saying that "to love the Lord Jesus Christ, and to have a heart inlarged with joy to him, this is a worke of grace, which groweth not in our gardens" unless God plant it there (pp. 226–27). But the image is most fully and memorably developed as Hooker reveals his English love for the hybrid rose, already made famous above all other flowers by the English Renaissance poets and dramatists.

> Looke as it is with flowers, those flowers which are sowen and planted, and by the skilfull hand of the gardiner inocculated, are choise ones both for s[c]ent and sight, are your *province roses* and the like, are of great account; but your common *hedge roses*, no man cares for them: So it is with the worke of Gods Spirit, and all other common graces, there is *province love*, and *province joy*, which is planted and wrought in the heart by the skilfull hand of God and his blessed Spirit, these make a sweet smelling savour in the nostrils of God: Aye that love, saith the Father, Aye that love, saith the Lord Jesus [;] wee cannot better please them, than by entertaining them after this matter; but these hedge roses, this carnall love and carnall joy, that growes upon the hedge of our owne naturall hearts, the Lord cares not for this love and joy. (*SEC*, pp. 238–39)

As any reader of Shakespeare or other poets of the day knows, weed/flower imagery was a commonplace in the literature of Hooker's era.[28] Hooker's passage is a variation, then, on a common motif as he makes a central distinction between the common wild "hedge rose" and the finer, though widely known *provins* rose. The latter, a choice hybrid,

is created and nurtured by the gardener's "skilfull hand." Many in his
audience no doubt had hedges of wild roses at home, whereas relatively few would have identified personally with the implied landowner
who is wealthy enough to have "province" roses and a gardener to
"inocculate" and care for them. But the analogy is apt, both theologically and psychologically. Just as there are many more hedge roses
than *provins* roses, and more yeomen, laborers, and indigents than
wealthy landowners, so are there more souls in a corrupt than in a
blessed state. Hooker plays on this knowledge and the built-in attraction of both wealth and the natural beauty of the hybrid rose to urge
his hearers to identify with privilege, to desire to possess the hybrid
provins rose (and, by implication, the gardener who cares for this prize
possession). In this compact passage Hooker is carefully attentive to his
audience's subconscious awareness of social as well as horticultural distinctions. They are invited to give expression in the spiritual realm to
their longing for betterment of their social positions. If they could only
truly possess a spiritual love for Christ, they could be admitted to the
blessed garden of faith—and this entirely regardless of their worldly
social rank. Just as it would be the greatest imaginable blessing to have
wealth and leisure in the worldly realm, so in the spiritual realm would
it be the supreme blessing to possess grace.

In a second major analogy, which appears in the third and fourth
Uses of this same sermon, Hooker turns to the familiar biblical comparison of human marriage with the individual saint's "marriage" to
Christ. Even though this analogy was sometimes extended to startling
extremes, becoming overtly erotic or at least directly sexual, it was a
common one in Puritan literature and has been noticed frequently before.[29] Hooker, like some of his contemporaries, seems to relish the
opportunity to relate the soul's spiritual love for Christ to the individual listener's personal experience with the sexual expression of loving desire. As we might expect, there are numerous references in this
part of the sermon to Canticles, where the Puritans read a symbolic
dramatization of the soul's love for Christ. But Hooker's first clear use
of the analogy with sexual desire draws on the Gospels, referring to
Mary Magdalene's urgent physical attraction to the risen Christ, whom
she first mistook for the gardener. Hooker reminds his listeners that
when Mary recognized Jesus in the garden on the day of his resurrection, "she flew upon him and with marvellous violence embraced our
Saviour" (*SEC*, p. 256). Hooker dwells on the physical nature of her
attachment, which he interprets as symbolic of her intense spiritual
love for him. He is citing John 20:17 but going well beyond the details
of the biblical text as he offers this description of the scene and explica-

tion of the passage: "Hee saith unto her, *Touch me not, for I am not yet ascended;* as if he had said, I shall live many dayes upon the earth and thou shalt be satisfied with my presence, therefore do not *cling* so fast unto me; for the word *touch* signifies as much; and the same word is used in the *Corinthians* [I Cor. 7:1], *It is good for a man not to touch a woman,* that is, to cleave and to *cling* unto her; and it is taken from those peeces of buildings, which are let one into another: her affection was such, that she would not part with her Saviour, when she had met him" (pp. 256–57).[30] The most striking aspect of this passage is Hooker's obvious intention to stress Mary's physical expression of love. He was surely aware of the marginal note in the Geneva Bible for John 20:17, saying that "she was to muche addicted to the corporal presence" of Christ. And Hooker's notice of the etymological connection with the interlocking stone structure must be read as his suggestion that Mary at this moment, overwhelmed by her love for Jesus, has an actual desire for physical union with her Lord—a desire to be "let into" Christ. Certainly Paul's use of "touch," which Hooker quotes and relates to Mary's desire to "touch" Christ, specifically indicates sexual intercourse.[31] Hooker himself, however, supplies all the other emphases on Mary's passion, which is suggested in the biblical passage *only* in the word "touch." This emphasis on Mary's passionate attachment to Christ is not at all original with Hooker but had been quite popular among sixteenth-century mystical and doctrinal writers.[32] It was not so commonly stressed by seventeenth-century Puritans, though they surely knew the literature.

Mary Magdalene is thus the type of the loving, faithful believer. What is true of her love ought to be true of the love of all the faithful. The auditors of this sermon would have no trouble, Hooker assumed, in making connection in their personal lives with this experience of desire's merging into full and true love. He reminds them how they first received with a certain giddiness the initial sense of the return of their love by a beloved. It is the same in one's spiritual life. When the soul gets "incklings" of the Lord's love, "many of Gods Saints begin to bee light headed, because they are so ravished therewith, they are alwayes cleaving thereunto, insomuch that many times they are almost beside themselves" (*SEC*, p. 257). This love grows with further contact between the lovers: "Looke as it is with parties that live in the same family, and their affections are drawing on one towards another in marriage; they will cast their occasions so, that if it be possible, they will be together, and have one anothers company, and they will talke together, and worke together, and the time goeth on marvellous suddenly, all the while their affections are drawing on: so it is with the soule that loves Jesus Christ, and hath this holy affection kindled, it thinkes every place happy, where it hath heard of Christ, and thinkes that houre sweet, wherein it put up its prayers to the Lord, and enjoyed love-chat with him"(p. 257). The upshot of such meetings and love-chat is betrothal and marriage. The state of engagement, when love is expressed and recognized on both parts but not yet consummated (however much the consummation is desired), is the relationship most analogous to the soul's love for Christ before full faith is assured:

> A spouse that is contracted, thinkes every day [a] yeare, and every yeare twenty, till that [marriage] day comes; shee blesseth the very place where the bridegroom is, and shee thinkes the parties happy that talke with him, and she takes every token that comes from him marvellous kindly, but yet shee thinkes, if that day would once come wherein shee might possesse him, and be possessed of him, that she, and she alone might enjoy her husband; Oh this would bee a happy day, her heart would bee cheared, and exceedingly refreshed therewith: so a loving soule that hath beene truly humbled and inlightened in the apprehension of Gods love and mercie, and is contracted, as I may so say, unto Christ, hath many thoughts; when will it once be, that I may be married to Christ, and possesse him, and be possessed of him? (*SEC*, pp. 258–59)

Because of the lover's consciousness of "the strong and gluing nature of true love," she longs for full union. "There is a holy restlessnesse and impatience in the soule till it can attaine this" (*SEC*, p. 261). And why should one not be impatient for such a match, since Christ is "the fairest of all," "the strongest of all," and "more rich (if it be possible) than hee is strong"?[33] He is the ultimately desirable suitor, not the least of whose attributes is the ability to love even those who know they are unworthy.[34]

No human could be fully worthy of this love, of course, but the elect would be true, after their fashion. By contrast, the pretenders to worthiness, the hypocrites, who are never long ignored by Hooker, will reveal their corruption through infidelity to their professed beloved. Given his use of the common marriage metaphor for alliance with Christ in grace, it was natural for Hooker to depict the hypocrites metaphorically as sexual offenders against the marriage contract: "She is not accounted a loving wife, but an adulteresse, that when she hath plaid the harlot, will come and whine to her husband, and yet go to it againe. . . . So it is with the soule, it is adulterous and base love, and not the love of the Spouse of Christ, to confesse and bewaile sinne, and yet to commit it."[35] The logic as well as the metaphor is reduced to its simplest terms as Hooker differentiates between between true and false lovers of Christ: "You must not thinke to have heaven and hell too, to have Christ and the world too; It is impossible in reason that a wife should have a true affection of love to her husband, and an adulterous affection to her filthy mates too: the mate must be abandoned before the husband can be loved as he ought to be."[36]

The minister's role in all of this is clarified by Hooker at the end of the sermon. He sees himself as what Fenner called a "paranymph," or one in the role of an ambassador, from a prince to a woman in a distant land. God is, of course, this prince, and the listener is the woman. As in the king-prisoner scenario at the beginning of the sermon, the minister is the go-between, a necessary figure but not one of the principals. Here, it is interesting to note Hooker's use of a perennially fascinating subject to the British people, since the analogy would surely remind his audience of a recent episode in the love life of the royal family. In February of 1624 the Prince of Wales, soon to be King Charles, sent his courtiers to France to win for him the hand of Henrietta Maria, the sister of the king of France. They were married by proxy in the spring of the next year, finally consummating the marriage when she came to live with the by then King Charles in the spring of 1625. The analogic point was clear enough for Hooker's audience: just as surely as France was married to England in Henrietta and Charles could the world be married to heaven in the saint's loving acceptance of Christ's passionate proposal. For, as Augustine had said, a man is finally known by that which he loves.

The Will

Since loving involves exercising a preference, a choice, it is clear that loving and willing are closely related. In the redemption process, as soon as one is confirmed in one's love of Christ, one is ready to accept Christ fully—to settle into faith and to receive the benefits which the *sola fides* Calvinist doctrine promises as the consequence of this choice. In thus arguing that love of Christ and grace must precede union with them, Hooker appears comfortable in the camp of Renaissance voluntarists, one of whose early members wrote that "we are united more closely with God through the joy of love . . . than through knowledge."[37] It is love, said Marsilio Ficino, following Augustine before him and anticipating Hooker, Ames, and others after him, that leads directly to union with Christ, a union which is affirmed by the decisive act of the will's acceptance.

In Hooker's terms, by the time these "saving" affections of love and joy reach their highest pitch, the soul has done much laboring and trudging; it "hath walked a great while" along the rocky highway to faith (*SEC*, p. 299). Finally, though, "all the affections come to the will[,] the great commander" (p. 296). There comes a time when the will itself is effectually persuaded. Man finally "hears," in full clarity and with full understanding and affectionate yearning, the voice of Christ speaking of the sufficiency of his mercy. "Now when the soule heares this voyce, it saith, even *Amen* Lord, let it be so Lord. This is the hold of the heart, hope and desire, love and joy have discerned a world of mercy; and the will saith, so be it, let us stay and hold here, and goe no further" (p. 299).

The will, it would seem, has the final word in bringing the sinner to the comforts of grace. And so it does if we think of the process in the consecutive, orderly stages in which Hooker deals. But we must never ignore his reiterations here as elsewhere that in the elect "there is a kinde of prevailing sweetnesse of the grace of God in Christ, that will be at the roots of the heart, that it may give allowance unto it" (*SEC*, p. 291). This "prevailing sweetnesse" is the preliminary will of God to save the sinner, then, working to enable man's will to choose the good of faith. Only when "God hath gotten his good will" can justification follow and man's sins "be blotted out" (p. 292). "Thousands goe to hell," he says, by trusting their own ability to get faith. So an act of will does climax the active calling which Hooker has been describing, but it is a will *enabled* to act by God. On this point Augustine's argument with the Pelagians is echoed in Hooker's observation that latter-day Pelagians "put a kinde of ability in the will, to take or refuse Christ and grace when it is offered; but here is a deepe mistake, because the will of man is as farre averse from God, as the minde is blinde . . . therefore there must be this effectuall perswading, as the understanding must have the truth cleered to see a Christ, so the will must be perswaded, that it may receive power from him" (pp. 288–89). He compares the relationship of man's and God's power to stir the will to the effect of the moon on the tides in the Thames. The river itself has no innate power to create the tidal rising and falling; the power resides in the movement of the moon in the heavens. Man is the earthbound, downward-pulling Thames in this analogy and God is the moon, wherein lies all the power to raise and lower. The analogy is particularly appropriate, since the avenue by which the power of the moon is conducted to the river is invisible and in part mysterious, just as is the relationship between man's exercising his will and God's transmitting the enabling "sweetnesse" of grace into the corrupt will.

In this matter of the dependence of man's will on God, Hooker is, of course, merely being consistent with most of his predecessors and contemporaries in the Augustinian reformed tradition, all of whom held that the grace of faith is a gift from a merciful God to the elect, who are, in their own nature, grossly undeserving. But Hooker is decidedly different from one school of thought in this same tradition. As we noted in Chapter 6, not everyone agreed that the will was, as Hooker claims, "the great commander" of the soul. Some insisted that the intellect determined man's actions and was thus able to dictate to the will what course to follow. It was during Hooker's rise to prominence that this disagreement became pronounced. The Augustinian voluntarists vigorously denied the preeminence of the intellect, thus opposing the position defended by orthodox Protestant scholastics. The voluntarists insisted that "the will is the supreme faculty of the soul because it is within the will that the decisive movement takes place which determines man's final relation to God."[38] Norman Fiering's comment, quoting Ames as a prime example of voluntarist thinking, is equally applicable to Hooker, who was firmly allied with this school of thought: "As Ames has said, 'The Will is the true subject of theology since it is the true beginning of life and of moral and spiritual action.' . . . The will is the apex of the soul; or better, the free act of willing is the climactic movement of the soul, since the dispute with the intellectualists here is not simply over the power of rival faculties so much as over which faculty best represents what is in the end the quintessential element in both faith and virtue."[39] As we have already noticed, Hooker again and again warns his congregation that mere knowledge, mere intellectual insight, is not enough to get a man to heaven. In his treatise on the will in *The Soules Effectuall Calling*, he describes as one of four sorts of people who lack faith the "meere civilized and seemingly judicious professors" who *understand* the way to salvation but will not take it. Merely knowing and assenting to the truth is not enough, says Hooker. "The devills in hell have this faith too" (*SEC*, p. 460). Without the will's consent, faith is out of reach. An unpersuaded will can thus cancel any good work which may previously have been wrought on the intellect. Hooker entirely agrees with Ames's statement that a surrender of the self "to God in Christ as a sufficient and faithful Savior" is absolutely necessary but that one "cannot make that surrender through any assent of the understanding—only through a consent of the will."[40] Hooker and Ames go beyond both Calvin and Perkins in their outspoken advocacy of the primacy of the will in the act of faith.[41]

The effect of this act of will in grasping faith is profound. The sinner has, of course, been working toward the assurance of full faith ever since entering at the strait gate of contrition, and Hooker treats the acquisition of faith as the climactic event in the life of the soul. It is the great watershed, with everything on the near side characterized by laborious struggle and doubt, and everything on the far side blessed by the newly gained "ease" and comfort which faith brings. After struggling with Satan and the world, which have violently opposed the soul's progress, the soul is suddenly "content." Life becomes "most easie" as the burden is shifted from one's own shoulders to Christ himself. The change is dramatic: "Let thy heart be contented, and know that thou hast a childs part, and thy lot is fallen into a marvellous faire ground" (*SEC*, p. 400). The last image in particular depicts the sense of relief from the dark spiritual surroundings and rough terrain of the "way" up to this point. Knowing that one finally possesses true faith gives one the feeling of coming out of a dark and threatening wilderness onto a fresh meadow or clear plain. The dominant feeling of the Christian at this point is relief.

The title of Richard Baxter's famous work, *The Saints Everlasting Rest*, implies that after long and arduous labor toward faith, the acquisition of it finally brings peaceful relief. This "resting" in Christ, says Hooker, is "the marrow of faith" (*SEC*, p. 295). He proceeds to analyze "resting" in considerable detail, saying that it consists of five acts: (1) the soul "goes out" and "layes hold on Christ"; (2) it takes a firmer grip—"layes fast hold"—and will not let Christ go; (3) it accepts the offer of "ease" and flings all its troubles on Christ's back; (4) it derives power from Christ; (5) it "leaves the heart with God." Hooker's listeners might well have been excused for complaining that his "rest" was all too restless.

The dynamics of Hooker's conversion message are underlined in his description of these five acts. His metaphors give these obscure inner motions of the soul almost sensuous tangibility. The basic reference of the figures of speech is to the distribution of the weight of a carried burden. He implicitly recalls his many previous allegorical descriptions of the soul's labor on its journey to grace, bearing its own burden, having continuously to rouse itself to activity and new strength. In describing the first act of resting, for instance, he talks of relief for the foot-weary pilgrim in such a way as to suggest near-total exhaustion: "The soule goes out and falls and flings itselfe upon the riches of Gods grace" (*SEC*, p. 297). But it is the third of these acts of faith which is particularly characteristic in its description of the way a sinner disposes of his burden through his faith. Since Christ "promised to give ease," the soul—now at the outer limits of its capacity to endure—"flings the weight of all its occasions and troubles upon Christ, as the porter that is weary of his waight, and hath no way to helpe himselfe, but to be eased of his burden" (pp. 301–2). Hooker's weary pilgrim finds his rest simply by getting the weight off his feet; he leans on Christ, who is "not a broken staffe that will faile us, but a strong staffe which a man may trust to, and lay all the waight of life and happinesse upon it" (p. 303). The constant appeals to sensory experience in the imagery of weight and weariness engage the listener's imaginative participation just as fully as do the more famous slipping, sliding, and falling images of Hooker's Connecticut Valley successor, Jonathan Edwards, in his famous *Sinners in the Hands of an Angry God.*

The reason why the relief is so great and so permanent is that the power of Christ now operates *within* the individual. The pilgrim is literally given a new source of power; he is grafted to a good stock so that "there is sap and virtue communicated to the beleeving heart" which it never had before. Other liquid metaphors reinforce this idea. Since Hooker had previously warned his listeners that they could not get well water unless they went to the well and lowered the bucket, he now urges them to reap the benefit of that initial exertion: "It is not enough to let downe the bucket into the well, but it must bee drawen out also" (*SEC*, p. 306). An equally homely metaphor follows, as Hooker paraphrases Isaiah 66:11 and then elaborates the imagery somewhat: "*They shall sucke and be satisfied with the brests of the consolation, that they may milke out, and be delighted with the abundance of her glorie;* the Church is compared to a childe, and the brests are the promises of the Gospell; now the elect must suck out and be satisfied with it, and milke it out" (p. 306). In thus "leaning" on Christ, one taps the very source of the sap/water/milk of Life.

Faith, then, is the great and necessary ingredient in the life of the sinner. Once he meets the terms of the covenant of grace, the benefits follow. Faith, in effect, repairs the wagon that had its wheels knocked off. Those who lack faith, he says, are like "the cart that is from his wheeles; they draw heavily, and they are in great extremitie, and they tug and toile, but it will not be drawne with any ease or good successe: so unfaithfull soules sinck in their sorrowes upon every occasion, and their lives are tedious and wearisome; but faith sets the cart upon the wheeles, and carries all away easily and comfortably" (*SEC*, p. 391). Needless to say, this new ease in one's tasks brings with it great joy, a joy which can be differentiated from the affection which Hooker had described at length as just preceding faith. This new joy is a joy in the soul's satisfaction in Christ, the perfect spouse, rather than in anticipation of that satisfaction.[42] All affections, including joy, are transformed and made significantly different once grace is indwelling in the soul. In fact, it was apparently a Hooker sermon on this very topic which led

Thomas Shepard, who had just been grappling with doubts about his own faith but had settled them by leaving them "in the Lords bowels," to respond so favorably to Hooker's sermon the following day: "Now such was the goodness of Christ that when I came to hear my father preach at Boston the day after, my soul was settled on the same way again when he preached about contentedness. And so I was confirmed in the faith."[43]

Since Hooker's whole emphasis on preparation for and acquisition of grace stresses the rebirth of one's spiritual life as a process rather than an event, a continuum rather than a single moment, it is understandable that in the midst of his discussion of the winning over of the will to faith, he gives some consideration to the several hindrances, or "lets," to faith.[44] He is as optimistic and encouraging on this subject as he would ever be. There are, he assures his hearers, "cures" to all the hindrances. In fact, what is most striking about the last 280 pages of *The Soules Effectual Calling* is the general optimism and comforting frame of mind which they reveal. Except for the sixth Use in his final 400-page "sermon"—which is a Use of reproof identifying four types of people who are without grace—the final section of this work represents Hooker's nearest approach to a Puritan version of the power of positive thinking.[45] He always had tried to close on a positive note, but the length to which he goes here is unusual. For instance, in listing four rules for improving our approach to the gospel and grace, Hooker begins by saying, "Be sure to take thy soule at the best, doe not alwayes consider what is worst in thee, and goe no farther, doe not only see thy failings and infirmities on one side that accuse thee, but see if there bee any soundnesse and uprightnesse, any goodnesse and truth of heart, that may speake for thee: heare both sides, it is injustice to heare one side, and determine a cause thereby; as the Lord deals with his servants, so thou shouldst deale with thy self" (*SEC*, p. 577). The difficult task of getting faith never sounds easier in Hooker's preaching than when he tells his audience that "the promise requires no more of a man, but that he should come and lay hold on mercie, therefore doe thou require no more, than God in the promise requires; there is enough in the promise to doe thee good, therefore expect all good from it" (p. 608). With Richard Sibbes, Hooker obviously believes that "grief, sorrow, and humility are good; but discouragement is evil."[46]

After his circular digression back into the condition of men before faith, Hooker at the end of the book returns to consider the place and the condition of the man who is now assured that he has faith. He ends, logically enough, with instructions on how to "live by faith."[47] Here, an optimistic attitude seems much more appropriate than earlier, since Hooker is careful to specify that he is now talking to those who have faith. It was an accepted article of Calvinist doctrine that once true faith was acquired, it could not be lost. It might be surprising, therefore, to find here any very elaborate rules for how to hold onto it. But Hooker's interest in the meshing of theological doctrine and psychological experience is fully active here. He does not believe that true faith can be lost, but he does believe it can and must be "improved." It is important, he says, for us "to get matter for our faith to worke on," to store up extra promises against the day when they may be needed, and to "supple and oile the sinewes of faith" in order to keep it "limber and quick" (*SEC*, pp. 622–30). Further, one must be positive-minded and not spend his time doubting the faith which he has worked so hard to get. Too much self-examination now, Hooker acutely observes, can lead to inappropriate doubt and melancholy which would deprive the Christian of the ease and comfort which is finally available to him. Rather, he urges, one can now presume to make the promise "present and substantiall to thy soule" (pp. 630–36).

But the promise has two parts: "The present good and peace, and the eternall and everlasting good and comfort of it" (*SEC*, p. 648). We must never forget the latter part of it, nor should we expect too much from the former. The possession of faith brings no promise of exemption from the afflictions of either sin or worldly problems and cares. "I know not any one promise, from the beginning of Genesis, to the end of the Revelation, that ever sheweth any such thing as this, That the man which hath grace, should never finde the plague of a naughtie heart, and never be pestered with corruptions within, and sorrowes without; there is not one place which promiseth thus much" (p. 652). What you can expect is that God will make you (relatively) good, that he will give you some temporal and spiritual blessings in his own time and measure, and that his gifts will be suited to your needs.

Hooker holds back for his final point in the book an interesting admonition. The faithful must try, he says, to "overcome the Lord" (*SEC*, p. 666). In accepting the challenge of the covenant of grace to "believe and live," the redeemed saint has received a promise from the Lord which he should not be too hesitant to claim. Be somewhat bold, Hooker is saying, in approaching God with the confident expectation of his mercy: "The Lord loves to be overcome thus." "God is ready to give what he hath promised, but he will have us trie masterie with him." "God would have us wrastle with his Majestie" (pp. 666, 667). This is an admonition to confidence in one's condition and to an active Christian life. When the believer is assured of his possession of true faith, he should carry himself confidently in the world as a Christian.

This was impossible before faith, when uncertainty was expressed through relentless self-examination; but now the confidence even to "wrastle" with Majesty is not entirely out of order—so long as we never forget our subservient place. This confidence which the faithful have earned the right to assume provokes a lyrical conclusion to this long saga of the upward struggles: the Christian has come out of the dark wilderness and can now with full confidence "know and see your way, and use the meanes, and labour to get good thereby, that you may have sap and sweet of the promises, and goe singing, and rejoycing, & triumphing to heaven" (p. 667). The saint on the "way" is now possessed of full clarity of vision, together with both strength and emotional exuberance enough to get him easily, even joyously to his destination. A new frame of mind is clearly in command; the weary pilgrim is assured that his spiritual adventures will culminate in a happy ending. The individual saint could surely be excused if at this point he whispered to himself that it is all downhill from here.

11

Baconian and Platonic Aspects of the Approach to Spiritual Truth

Several of the details of Hooker's characterization of the life of the saint thus far considered suggest relationships to major intellectual currents of his day extending beyond the specific issues of theology, politics, polity, and psychology already noticed. It is all too easy to think of Hooker and his fellow Puritans only in relation to each other and earlier Reformers while ignoring the larger framework of intellectual ferment at the beginning of the seventeenth century. Yet Hooker spent some fourteen years as scholar, tutor, catechist, and fellow at Emmanuel College at a time when Cambridge was the main English center for those revolutionary thinkers who, throughout Europe, were beginning to reject the old habits of thought and methods of pursuing knowledge in favor of newer, more modern methods. Thus it is especially important to notice whatever signs of Hooker's position in this larger ferment of new ideas may work their way into his redemption sermons. The present chapter, therefore, departs from the ongoing consideration of Hooker's treatment of the *ordo salutis* in order to consider two important characteristics of his thinking which have become evident in the previous discussions. This temporary shift of focus ought to shed fuller light on the discussion of Hooker's writings which has preceded as well as that which follows.

Hooker does not refer directly in his writings to either Francis Bacon or Plato, and my concern is not to argue primary influence by either of them on his work. But each of these important and vastly different figures has come to represent a mode of thinking, a way of approaching both the known and the unknown, which has persisted in human history down to the present day under such labels as "empiricism" or "the inductive method" in the case of Bacon and "idealism" in the case of Plato. The habits of thought which each of these writers represents were receiving new attention in the Western world and particularly at Cambridge in the years of Hooker's mature life, both during and after his tenure at Emmanuel. By isolating tendencies in Hooker's writings which reflect affinities or partial sympathy with one or the other of these modes of thinking, we can perhaps better appreciate his intellectual qualities as well as the considerable range of methods which he felt were appropriate tools in his own central task, the preaching of the word in such a way as to be an effective "messenger" or "paranymph" between God and his listeners.

For centuries the university curriculum and the channels of thinking of its graduates had been dominated by scholasticism. In studying the curriculum at Cambridge in the seventeenth century, William T. Costello reduced the characteristics of scholasticism to "three distinguishing marks: it was dialectical, Aristotelian, and highly systematized." These characteristics all put a primary stress on man's rational faculty, a tendency which found direct expression in each of the three chief forms of the scholastic methodology at Cambridge—the lecture, the disputation, and the declamation. Commenting on the "vital influence" of this methodology on the students' minds and intellectual habits during and after their days at the university, Costello observes that "lectures, declamations, and, particularly, disputations had been serious occupations of the university student, and it is impossible to understand such a phenomenon as, for example, the mid-seventeenth-century pamphlet war without understanding the mechanical workings of the mind which had been trained to insist on an answer to an answer of an answer."[1] In using the term "mechanical" here, Costello puts his finger on the trait of the traditional scholastic mind which, with the advent of the seventeenth century, more and more bright young thinkers would find objectionable. As another scholar has observed, "The reason why scholasticism was [ultimately] held to be an obstacle to the truth was because it seemed to discourage further enquiry along experimental lines."[2] The Aristotelians, in other words, typically constructed their arguments on an a priori basis and came to have what Costello calls "an *a prioristic* regard for the system over the observable fact."[3] They were not enough inclined, according to their critics, to test their hypotheses.[4] It was on the basis of this objection that the intellectually revolutionary new generation at the beginning of the seventeenth century so profoundly changed the methodology of the search for truth.

After Thomas Aquinas "Christianized" Aristotle for the Schoolmen, the typical habit of mind on both scientific and theological matters had been to *accept* truth rather than to seek to *discover* it. In the age of Galileo, Bacon, and Descartes, when it was necessary to have, above all, a willingness to listen to possible new truths, a system which preferred to proceed syllogistically in its logic from its own known truths was increasingly exposed as inappropriate. So it was that Bacon propounded and popularized so successfully and lastingly his case for inductive reasoning, which allowed for extending, often by analogy, the conclusions drawn about a particular detail to conclusions which are much larger and more inclusive. Bacon's method demanded that one be attuned to the world around one for evidence which might suggest new conclusions about how the world operates. In speaking of Galileo in this regard, Basil Willey observed that "the argument upon which he, like all the anti-scholastics of the seventeenth century, really relies, is the appeal to observation."[5] Bacon implicitly opposed the Aristotelian aprioristic method with his own, which, he argued, made more allowance for the advancement of knowledge. "Our method," he said, "is continually to dwell among things soberly . . . to establish for ever a true and legitimate union between the experimental and rational faculty."[6] Personal experience, "the appeal to observation," thus acquired new authority.

Moreover, the chief motivation for Peter Ramus's "bombshell of a thesis"[7] claiming that "all that has been said from Aristotle is forged" was the lack of *utility* of contemporary scholastic Aristotelian logic. It proliferated terms and definitions, Ramus complained, without offering the student, who was asked to memorize them, any justification or explanation of the terms and definitions. The objection was essentially that if a man could not fully understand the tools he must use, he could not get very far in the use of them. And indeed, others were also shortly to object that the Aristotelian system of logic was a self-supporting, self-contained structure that could not effectively serve an age of transition from old knowledge and traditions to new ones. Even though Henry VIII had strengthened the centrality of Aristotle in the university curriculum with his 1535 royal order, which insisted on "the Philosopher's" primacy in the Cambridge curriculum, the long-standing reverential allegiance to Aristotle had been increasingly subverted in the latter half of the sixteenth century; the trend continued in the early decades of the seventeenth. If Aristotle was not expunged from the curriculum, as he was not, he was at least taught alongside others, most notably Ramus. When Hooker went up to Queen's College, Cambridge, in 1604 (he would emigrate to Emmanuel in the same year), the logic of Ramus had become more popular in the Puritan colleges than that of Aristotle, having been taught there by Laurence Chaderton, then of Christ's College, as early as the period 1568–77.[8] Ramus's central work, the *Dialecticae Libri Duo*, was in England in translation as early as 1574 and was defended at Cambridge from at least 1584, when Ramus's first major English exponent, William Temple of King's College, whose scholarly career was dedicated to defending Ramism from its Aristotelian attackers, saw his Latin edition through the Cambridge University Press.[9] After Temple, George Downame and William Ames solidified the fundamental tenets of Ramist logic in the Cambridge educational network; and, as Perry Miller has shown, from Ames the thinking extended to New England and eventually into the seventeenth-century curriculum at the young Harvard College.[10]

Ramus, of course, had never intended simply to discard Aristotle. Part of his defense against the modern Aristotelians was that he was interested in eliminating the obfuscations of scholastic Aristotelian logic, thus making Aristotle's logic more usable and its theory more accessible. Ramus was literally the first to say that Aristotelianism and Ramism could live comfortably together. In somewhat the same spirit, it might be argued, Francis Bacon was to separate science and theology so that, while scientific knowledge advanced through the new awareness of details in the universe all around men, the traditional theology, based on suprahuman revelation, could remain intact. In regard to religion Bacon was a conservative thinker. He served as spokesman for those of his day who felt that to subject theology to the same experimental revisionism as science was to pave the way for the downfall of traditional Christian belief. The metaphysical and the physical realms of truth were thus separate and governed by entirely different ground rules in Bacon's system, the one requiring acceptance, the other demanding constant investigation and revision. Change never comes easily, and even its most ardent prophets often go only part way, paving the way for those who follow. Ramus's disciples were more ardently anti-Aristotelian than their master had been, just as those who followed Bacon in the seventeenth century were much more willing than he to confront what they saw as necessary implications for religion in the new Baconian scientific approach to knowledge and truth.

It was into this time of intellectual turmoil that Thomas Hooker and his generation of Puritans were born. Peter Ramus's premature death had occurred in 1572, some fourteen years before Hooker's birth. But Francis Bacon's career was in full flower during Hooker's tenure at the University of Cambridge, and Hooker left England just five years after Bacon's death in 1626. Descartes, another antitraditionalist molder of thought in the Western world, was born ten years after Hooker, and their careers were contemporaneous. Thomas Hobbes was just two years younger than Hooker, though most of his important publication occurred after mid-century, by which time Hooker had gone to his New England grave. Thus Hooker lived in the midst of an extremely exciting time. He spent some fourteen years at the university, which was at that time the more liberal of England's major schools. During the early decades of the seventeenth century whatever new ideas were in the Anglo-European air would surely be fully discussed—either in formal sessions or informally—by students and faculty at Cambridge. There can be little doubt that Hooker, who became known as a master of disputation, was familiar with the new ideas of his day, whether theological or scientific. It is safe to assume that when Hooker reluctantly took his leave of England for his brief sojourn in Holland, he carried with him not only his chief resources of Calvinist theology and a perfected preaching style, but also a solid understanding of Ramus's logic and rhetoric and an ample exposure to the published thoughts of Francis Bacon. Though we have no precise evidence for claiming that he had read Bacon—apart from his being a willing participant in the intellectual activity of his day—there seems considerable reason to believe that he had, and that he applied his reading more directly in his preaching than did some of his equally well-known contemporaries.

Bacon's desire to separate the realms of science and theology recalls the approach of the scholastics—especially Thomas Aquinas—who thought in terms of two main branches of wisdom: on the one hand the metaphysical, which dealt with the "natural" world of sense experience, and on the other the theological. The scholastics were primarily interested in the latter, which was a higher realm than the former; but Bacon and the men who followed his lead in the new century were chiefly concerned with advancing knowledge of the natural world. For Bacon, as for Descartes, the stress was on original observation of the universe rather than on aprioristic thinking. To some extent Puritans were prevented from enjoying this liberation. In the first place, their primary interest was in that area of knowledge which Bacon set off-limits for revisionist thinking—the realm of theology. And though they saw their particular form of theology as a liberation from the latter-day corruptions of Roman Christianity, they inherited in the seventeenth century the Calvinist dogmatics, which very quickly became as self-enclosed a system of truth as any other. So for many, Calvinism—so fully explained in Calvin's *Institutes* and later in the writings of Theodore Beza, William Perkins, and William Ames—rapidly became a body of dogma to be mastered and believed rather than a prescription for personal discovery.

But with Hooker, at least, it was not so. While he did accept entirely such fundamental tenets of Calvinist thinking as the depravity of man, predestination, and irresistible grace to the few, he also determinedly believed that the religious life is deeply personal and based upon the individual's discovery for himself of the truth of the Calvinistic interpretation of the Scriptures. As we have seen, in Hooker's narration of the saga of redemption the central hero, the sinner-saint, is on a journey by himself in which experience is comprised of one discovery after another. The minister and one's Christian brothers and sisters are sympathetic as well as helpful, and the stages of progression are eminently predictable, but for the individual himself the experience is internal and thus highly personal. For him, in his slow progression from one level of the experience to the next, what might seem to an outsider to be a priori dictates from theological authorities became, one by one, verified truths of personal experience. As Hooker said repeatedly, intellectual acceptance of beliefs was simply not enough: "Thousands goe to hell that way." Only hard-earned experience could verify and validate the intellectual truths presented in the writings of the Fathers. "There is great ods," he wrote, "betwixt the knowledg of a Traveller, that in his own person hath taken a view of many Coasts, . . . and by Experience hath been an Eye-witness . . . and another that sits by his fire side, and happily reads the story of these in a Book, or views the proportion of these in a Map, the ods is great, and the difference of their knowledg more than a little."[11] Thus, while Hooker had no interest in throwing aside the *donńees* of Calvinism, any tendency of the reformed dogmatics to operate in an apriorist fashion is often overbalanced and obscured in the Hookerian insistence on first-hand knowledge coming from personal experience. By his preaching example he was leading in an anti-authoritarian, experimentalist direction which was to become standard for most Puritans.[12] They came to believe, as William Haller has said, that the minister must "teach nothing which he had not first tested in his own experience, and he must teach his people to subject all doctrine to the test of experience. Thus the preachers made experiment a familiar word on the plane of religion and morals long before it became supreme on that of natural science."[13]

There is yet another sense in which Hooker is in agreement with the spirit of his age. As Basil Willey has said, "The fundamental impulse of the [seventeenth] century was toward the 'explanation' of what had hitherto been mysterious, towards the statement in conceptual language of what had hitherto been expressed, or imagined, in pictures and symbols."[14] Certainly Hooker's elaborate stage-by-stage mapping-out of the mysteries of the soul's progress from degradation to regeneration to glorification, the progression which we have been following, is a characteristic expression of an age intending to banish mystery from the earth. It concretizes, through its utilitarian "conceptual language," the mysterious workings of the Spirit so that they finally seem not so mysterious after all. It is all the more impressive in that the achievement occurred in that realm of knowledge which Bacon had said had better be left well enough alone. Based upon a standard nucleus of Calvinist theology and Aristotelian physics, Hooker's description of the psychology of the soul was nevertheless an extension of traditional understanding on how the Holy Spirit and the human soul operate (or fail to operate) in religious experience. Thus, it is not inappropriate to speak of a Baconian-Cartesian dimension of Hooker's thought insofar as his redemption message assumed the primary importance of the individual's verifying spiritual truth experimentally for himself, thus making one's comprehension of religious truth a personally tested and truly felt grasping of otherwise elusive "truth."

Hooker's tendency to concretize the seemingly mysterious is expressed in still another dimension of his work. Here we need only recall the relentless consistency with which Hooker employs rhetorical tools such as metaphors, similes, analogies, tropes, and figures of all kinds to bring his spiritual message into the realm of sensual reality. Not only does he insist on a personal experience of redemption in all of its extended process, but he also—in an exceptional degree and consistency—provides the comparative bases in mundane experience through which a perception and comprehension of the spiritual is greatly enlivened and enhanced. Though he accepts intellectually the notion of Christian warfare between worldly and spiritual concerns, he is constantly fighting to reconcile that opposition in the way he employs his rhetorical tools. He and Richard Sibbes agreed that "there is no other principle to prove the word, but experience from the working of it."[15] He well knew that every man and woman in his congregation, no matter what their spiritual condition, could visualize a house in need of sweeping, a well with a rope and bucket, an oozing sore, a knotty piece of firewood, or a hedge rose. And it is only through his constant manipulation of such common natural elements as these that Hooker was able to make the meaning of his description of the otherwise elusive actions of the soul stick in the minds and hearts of his hearers. Likewise, it was only through his skill in appealing to the world they did know that he was able to make his admonitions to spiritual action take on that physical sense of stress and strain which so characterizes his message on the nature of redemption.

There is thus a sense in which Hooker's method is inductive rather than aprioristic and in which he extends the implications of Baconian thought on science into his practical exploration of theology. Bacon said that his desire was "to establish for ever a true and legitimate union between the experimental and rational faculty." Hooker, in explaining the often mysterious operations of the soul, wanted to connect the "experimental" not only with the rational faculty but with the affectional and volitional faculties as well. The unsubstantial soul, in other words, could be *observed* through the use of analogy with physical experience. Nor is there any theoretical inconsistency in this attitude with Puritan thought at large. As Perry Miller has shown, Alexander Richardson, the influential Ramist teacher at Queen's College, Cambridge, was a key formulator of the Puritan theory of technológia, which extended the confidence in God's purposeful creation of the universe to the idea that the smallest details of experience and of physical nature as well as of human art all had a divine *raison d'être* and a perfect order. Therefore, men should be attentive to the evidence of their own experience, ready to grasp new fragments of knowledge, whatever their shape or form. In his construction of his sermons and his selection of enlivening figures of speech, Hooker, who knew Richardson at Cambridge, was teaching by example and putting to use the basic truth observed in the following passage by Richardson:

> The *Genesis* of every thing is Gods, and man must see the rules of Art, therefore man must see them from singulars, by *analysis:* now then if man must learn these, and know them by his senses observation, induction and experience, then he must seek, and find out these, for they are not written in him: again, whereas every thing is in disposition, it is requisite that man find them out, and see them severally, therefore in this respect is this Art of reason called Invention, namely as he is sent by God to find out these things in his creatures; now if man must find them out with this act of his eye of reason, then is it fitly called invention. . . . And this teacheth man thus much, that he is to seek out, and find this wisdom of God in the world, and not to be idle; for the world, and the creatures therein are like a book wherein Gods wisdom is written, and there must we seek it out.[16]

Nowhere can we find a more explicit explanation for why Cotton Mather referred to the subject of his biography as that "most Richard-

sonian Hooker" or a clearer indication that the Puritans found the
theological application of Baconian induction eminently appropriate for
reading the truth of God's universe.

In the same regard, we need to recall the centrality of self-trial to
Hooker's directions on approaching grace. The touchstone, he urged,
should constantly be employed to verify the progress one was making toward one's goal. As we noticed in Chapter 9, when Hooker
outlines a Use of trial, he characteristically lists several attributes
which are or are not positive signs of progress. What he is doing,
quite simply, is suggesting an inductive approach to spiritual self-
knowledge. If you observe in yourself these four regular tendencies
of mind or these three habitual forms of action, you are (or are not)
safely on your way to redemption. This taking stock through small
details in order to enable larger conclusions about one's real spiritual
condition is patently an inductive approach. While the Puritan tendency to urge self-examination clearly predates Bacon's formulation
of the inductive method for arriving at scientific truth, the increased
popularity of the method among Puritans of Hooker's generation and
in Hooker in particular may be one way in which the age's desire
for personal verification of truth was spilling over into religion, despite Bacon's own warnings against applying his theories in this
realm. The same spirit of reaching large conclusions about oneself
through collecting numerous small details is reflected in other aspects of Hooker's preaching, including the use of character sketches
to enable typical hypocrites in the congregation and community to
identify themselves as such.

Bacon's interest in applying the tools of investigation to the acquisition of scientific, as opposed to theological, knowledge is undoubtedly a
latter-day extension of the Renaissance tendency to secularize wisdom
which Eugene Rice has traced.[17] Hooker says that it is often much
more difficult for the wise man to get true faith than it is for the humble "simplician," and to this degree he seems to accept the notion of
thinkers such as Bacon and Pierre Charron that religion is essentially
nonrational and paradoxical. Yet he does not follow them in separating
reason and faith.[18] The one is an essential tool—though not of itself
enough—in acquiring the other. Hooker, like any good Puritan, denies
that wisdom belongs merely to the secular realm. He incorporates intellectual exercise into the practical problem of getting faith, and he
describes intellectual enlightenment as the first stepping-stone in the
soul's journey. In fact, it is tempting to claim that in some sense he
uses Bacon in order to refute him. He has room in his system, at any
rate, for sympathy with Bacon's claim in *The Advancement of Learning*

that "the furthest end of knowledge" is for "the benefit and use of men." Bacon wrote, in similes that Hooker could appreciate, that knowledge ought "not be as a curtesan, for pleasure and vanity only, or as a bondwoman, to acquire and gain to her master's use, but as a spouse, for generation, fruit, and comfort."[19] Thus, utility is uppermost for Bacon as it was for Ramus. And so it was for the Puritans in their own sense of the teaching function of the ministry. It is to this point that William Haller speaks—all too briefly—in observing that Puritan "religion was made to justify devotion to practical and useful objects" and that the Puritans were "as deeply devoted as Bacon to the advancement of the kind of learning which, . . . [they] believed, would most directly express the glory of God and contribute to the relief of man."[20] In fact, it is worth noting that at the very time that Hooker was giving full popular expression to his doctrine of redemption at Chelmsford, the young John Milton was a student at Cambridge, where he, too, was attacking scholasticism's inutility and espousing something very like a Baconian approach to experience, while already being a devout and justified Puritan.[21]

The Puritan sermon, we have already observed, was organized in such a way as to lay out and explain a truth or doctrine and then to end with an explanation of how to *use* what the minister had just explained. The last section of the sermon—the Use, or Application— was just that, an attempt to give this new knowledge utility in the life of the hearer. And in the light of the other points of sympathy with the intellectual movements of his day, it ought not to be surprising that Hooker worked so hard at making his sermons *useful* rather than highly doctrinal or merely curious, delightful, or witty that he obtained a lasting reputation as an "experimental" preacher. So much was this the case that Cotton Mather could recall some fifty years after Hooker's death that Hooker "had a most excellent Faculty at the *Applications* of his Doctrine; and he would therein so Touch the Consciences of his Auditors, that a Judicious Person would say of him, *He was the Best at an Use that ever he heard.*"[22] It might be argued that in this Hooker was simply employing the opportunities which the plain style and the typical Puritan sermon structure handed down to him. And so he was. But he was doing so in a measure that exceeded that of most of his contemporaries. He was, at any rate, committed to the Baconian notion of the utility of knowledge and was meticulous in translating that commitment into his pulpit practice. In becoming widely known for his "practical divinity," Hooker was expressing another of his basic sympathies with the intellectual currents of the times. He was showing what some important non-Puritan thinkers had denied was possible:

that wisdom and faith were not incongruent and that spiritual knowledge had an essential utility if properly presented.

If, however, Hooker was in tune with such major intellectual currents of his world as the emphasis on observation of the natural world as a way to truth, the use of inductive reasoning to distill such observations, and the primary concern for utility, he was also attuned to a somewhat different—and on the whole, conflicting—strand of thought which had long roots in the past but would sprout anew at Cambridge after his departure for New England. In fact, it is curious and insufficiently explained that the rise of the Cambridge Platonists occurred in the seat of Puritanism itself, Emmanuel College, such a short while after the full flowering of Calvinism there. Hooker's tenure at Cambridge predates the heyday of the Cambridge Platonists, and his influence at Emmanuel during one and a half decades probably had little to do with their rise. Certainly the strong anti-Calvinist and anti-Augustinian bent of their thought, especially evident in their opposition to such fundamental doctrines as predestination and natural depravity, makes their theology radically different from that of the strongly Augustinian-Calvinist Hooker. In their return to the primary authority of the Greek philosophers Plato and Plotinus, the seventeenth-century Platonists were rejecting "the entire Western theological tradition from St. Augustine through the medieval schoolmen to the classic Protestantism of Luther, Calvin, and their variegated followers in the seventeenth century."[23] In addition, they were inclined to oppose organized religion and to sanction the view that Scripture is not necessarily consistent with itself. Such ideas necessarily place the Platonists at extreme odds with Hooker on very fundamental matters, so that it is possible to argue that any similarity of thought between Hooker's writings and those of the Cambridge Platonists is purely coincidental.

Yet there are factors which make it likely that Hooker, at the same time that he was developing his highly experimentalist approach to religious experience, was also more open to the appeal of certain central elements of Platonism than were some of his fellow Puritans.[24] One of the most important points of similarity between Platonic thought and Augustinian-Puritan thought was the anti-authoritarian thrust that both contained. In the growing antischolastic atmosphere of the early seventeenth century, this was no small matter. The stress on the individual experience of spirituality discussed above is common to Plato, Augustine, and preparationist Puritans alike. In addition, Hooker could share with the Platonists a sense of the central importance of love in the scheme of the individual's ascent to full communion with God. In

Hooker, this concept did not grow to the extent that it did in Plato and his Cambridge disciples, but Hooker's unique insistence on love as a pregrace affection which aids in pulling man and Christ together suggests his special responsiveness to this detail in Platonic thought. And finally, Hooker's preparationist idea of an upward aspiration to God as the central preoccupation of the Christian's energies in his worldly life is, in its general outlines and in its subjective potential for imaginative rendering, essentially similar to Platonic thought on aspiration toward and achievement of the Ideal.

Hooker's sympathy with these aspects of Platonic thought is implicit in many of his works but is nowhere so centrally present as in his narrative exegesis of the long ascent of the soul to eternal communion with God. His description of the stages of redemption—which extend from the darkness of ignorance in one's own sinfulness, through stages of gradual improvement, to the point of acquiring faith and with it the light of new insight into divine wisdom and mercy, and even beyond this stage to others of fuller, higher communion with divine light, wisdom, and beauty—takes a form very like that outlined in Plato. Near the end of the *Symposium* Plato captured the essence of this upward aspiration from earth to heaven. Plato is quoting a speech of Socrates on the aspiration through love to a perception of absolute beauty: "And the true order of going, or being led by another, to the things of love is to begin from the beauties of earth and mount upward for the sake of that other beauty, using these as steps only, and from one going on to two, and from two to all fair forms, and from fair forms to fair practices, and from fair practices to fair notions, until from fair notions he arrives at the notion of absolute beauty, and at last knows what the essence of beauty is."[25] It is not hard to see how the framework of this conception of a life of continuing aspiration to an ideal goal—one which is worth the total preoccupation of the individual, as Plato goes on to say—was adopted by Hooker in his attempt to give dramatic, imagination-capturing life to his own version of Calvinistic truth. His infusion of Christian belief into the Platonic outlines of the journey to the ideal is of course all-important.

We do not know whether Hooker ever read the above passage or others like it in Plato or the chief neo-Platonist, Plotinus, who became a primary source for the Cambridge Platonists. The opportunity for exposure to Plato and other Greek authors was increasingly present at Cambridge in the early seventeenth century, as the antischolastic movement had ever more recourse to Greek writers other than Aristotle.[26] But enough other opportunities for contact with Platonic ideas existed so that Hooker could well have developed his thoughts on the pathway to heaven from a variety of other sources. There is of course no doubt of his early and lasting affection for Augustine's writings, so that we can be sure he knew of Augustine's approving recognition of the Platonists in both his *Confessions* and *The City of God*, where Augustine acknowledged that of all non-Christian philosophers the Platonists represent "the closest approximation to our Christian position."[27] The upward yearning toward God's peace was also, of course, a Pauline notion, and Augustine found Paul's message more affecting, finally, than that of the Platonists.[28]

For centuries after Augustine's day, scholastic thinking paid homage to Aristotle, while Platonic writers were cast into the shade. Much nearer to Hooker's day, however, interest in Plato was revived in fifteenth-century Italy, where ideas were being generated on both Christian philosophy and art which were to become influential in England during the next century and a half. It was in Italy that Plato and Plotinus first became fully available to modern scholarship. Nicholas of Cusa, an influential Christian philosopher, first had access to them entirely.[29] They were rendered in new translation and interpreted in commentaries and in original works of philosophy by Marsilio Ficino and Coluccio Salutati. The influence of such men on the Puritan mind, relative to the Calvins, the Bezas, and the Perkinses, was of course minor. But it was probably greater than we have yet appreciated. Ernst Cassirer has outlined the transportation of Ficino's version of Platonic philosophy to England by John Colet, who returned from Italy to lecture at Oxford on the Pauline epistles in 1496, quoting profusely from Ficino's *Theologia Platonica*.[30] Colet was a friend of Erasmus, who was lecturing at Cambridge in the early sixteenth century.[31] Colet's influence on Erasmus's thought regarding the Christian life was considerable,[32] so that some of Colet's enthusiasm for the ideas of the Florentine humanists doubtless entered Cambridge at this time, but there is no doubt that Ficino's Platonic philosophy "seemed authentic and exemplary" to the Cambridge Platonists over a century later.[33] Thus the Platonist Academy in Florence, in which Ficino was a guiding light, ultimately reached as far in its influence as seventeenth-century Cambridge.[34] Despite this fact, Ficino, unlike his later Platonist readers at Cambridge, was a close follower and admirer of Augustine. He was, in fact, more in debt to Augustine than any other predecessor, including Aquinas, an affinity which suggests the likelihood of his appeal to orthodox seventeenth-century Puritans. This very mixture of a thorough knowledge of Platonism with a Christian belief and sympathy for the thought of Augustine is what makes the writings of the Italian Catholic Ficino often sound so much like those of the English Puritan Hooker.

Ficino and other Italian neo-Platonists, like Augustine before them, adopted and Christianized Plato's assumption of the upward aspiration to higher and higher degrees of beauty, love, and truth, replacing Plato's absolute Truth or Beauty with contemplation of and communion with Christ as the highest goal. In the following passage, Eugene Rice is speaking of the Italian Platonists' approach simply to wisdom, but his remarks on Petrarch and Ficino and his quotations from them represent the appeal of the Platonic thought process generally—a process which could be readily adapted to spiritual as well as intellectual experience:

> The effort to reach [true wisdom] . . . must always consist, as Plato said, in turning from terrestrial to celestial things, from the mobile to the immobile, from sensible to intelligible. Already Petrarch had seen this as the kernel of Plato's message: "For what does the doctrine of the heavenly Plato show," he asks, "but that the soul must separate itself from the passions of the flesh and tread down its imaginings before it can rise pure and free to the contemplation of the mystery of the Divine; for otherwise the thought of its morality will make it cling to those seducing charms." More accurately Platonic, Ficino says the same thing: in order to rise up to wisdom the intellect must purge itself of false opinions and the perturbations of the passions. It must turn from the forms of sensible things to the intellectual forms innate in it; and rise to them through intelligible forms, that is, to the Ideas.[35]

The turning from the low to the high, from the carnal to the divine, and doing so in a gradual process which enables one to shed in stages the weights of sin and self, is exactly the process which the preparationist preachers—Hooker especially—adapted and came to relish, though they of course had to add the complicating qualification of natural depravity.

As we have seen, for Hooker this process of ascent was by no means purely intellectual nor was it conceived in purely ethereal terms. But neither was it for Ficino, despite the terms which Rice uses at the end of the passage above. The affections, the will, and God all assist the intellect in the process of raising the soul from earthly to heavenly things. It is worth special notice, because of Hooker's particular attention to the subject, that the Platonists placed particular emphasis on the role of *love* in this heavenly aspiration. For instance, in his work on this subject, *De Amore,* Ficino writes that desire and love are immediately related to the soul's aspiration to the highest beauty (God). Ficino expresses this idea in terms which clearly have their origin in the same scriptural basis as Hooker's characterization of desire: "Thou oh God, Thou alone wilt extinguish this ardent thirst."[36] Ficino says elsewhere that "union with God, which is the goal of the soul, seems to be accomplished primarily through love,"[37] a notion which owes much to Plato's ideas, expressed near the end of the *Symposium*, that in attaining communion with divine beauty "human nature will not easily find a better helper than love."[38] Ficino extends his thinking on love to claim that it is a function of will, thus indicating his final opinion that the will is ultimately a higher power in the soul than the understanding.[39] In this he of course agrees with Augustine's anti-Aristotelian voluntarism, a position which we know was quite congenial to the voluntarist Hooker.

Rice observes that this voluntaristic association of love and the will is also characteristic of Coluccio Salutati, "the greatest of Petrarch's early humanist successors." "This emphasis on the will and love," says Rice, "is a traditional characteristic of those mediaeval thinkers who kept their Augustinian fervor undampened by Aristotle's intellectualism."[40] Since "the Platonic doctrine of Eros and the Platonic doctrine of beauty stand as the nucleus of the philosophy of the Florentine circle," it is not surprising that Ficino's most influential work in his own day was his commentary on Plato's *Symposium*.[41] This Platonic stress on the intimate association between love and will had a broad appeal that went well beyond the limits of the Florentine Academy and included most of those inclined to mysticism throughout the Renaissance. The tradition, for instance, includes not only the Spanish scholastic Francis de Sales, whose *Treatise on the Love of God* observes that "love urges on the mind to the ever more attentive contemplation of the beloved beauty, and the sight impels the heart to love it ever more ardently,"[42] but also the great English poet Edmund Spenser, who deals directly with the theme not only in *The Faerie Queene* but also in *An Hymne to Heavenly Love* and *An Hymne to Heavenly Beauty*. This aspect of the Platonic tradition finds agreement even in Hooker's dramatization of the will's sending out love as his ambassador to greet and embrace faith. Though the ultimate goal was expressed differently by Ficino, Salutati, Petrarch, Spenser, Hooker, and still others, they were all in essential agreement with Plato's claims for the importance of love to its attainment.[43]

What is at least equally important as the similarity of the Platonists' notion of how the soul moves in its ascent to union with God is the subjective sense of what this ascent consists of. Ficino and other Catholic Platonists are able to be much more openly Platonic than the later Calvinists because of their freedom from the doctrine of innate depravity. The result is that in their writings this ascent seems a much easier, more natural process than it does when described by a Thomas Hooker or a Thomas Shepard. In Ficino's thought, man had two tendencies, one upward to the eternal and one downward to the temporal. Those destined to move upward could do so without the intense sense of friction or drag that is captured in Hooker's figure of the wheel-less cart; they move, in fact, with a natural "lightness" in this ascent which is quite opposite to the burdensome weight of sin and unworthiness that Hooker's elect pilgrim must carry with him on the same journey.[44] Yet despite this important difference, both writers hark back to Augustine in the same metaphoric way when describing the sense of relief that comes when the soul reaches the end of the journey and discovers the availability of rest. Summarizing Ficino's thought in this regard, Kristeller says that "the love of the Soul for God is only a conceptual expression for that basic unrest which moves the consciousness inwardly and drives it upward from grade to grade, until at last it reaches its goal and finds rest in the highest act, the contemplation of God." Except for the final phrase, this sentence could well be a description of Hooker's account of the upward ascent through the stages of redemption. If the theology of the two men is not always the same, then, the two writers' conceptualization of the spiritual life is often strikingly close, whether it is due to Hooker's actual knowledge of Ficino's work, as it might be, or to their obvious mutual indebtedness to Augustine's Christianization of the Platonic stress on an upward ascent to the Ideal.[45]

On this acceptance of the centrality of the spiritual life and on the assumption that such a life was, ideally, a continuing upward-spiral of the individual soul aided by the informing power of the Holy Spirit Hooker could agree with just about any Platonist. But times were changing rapidly, especially at Cambridge, and it was not long after Hooker left Emmanuel College for his first clerical position in Esher that Platonism became more firmly ensconced at his alma mater.[46] Willey has said that "the Cambridge Platonists were mainly Puritan in affinity,"[47] but this claim rather quickly ceases to have much technical usefulness, at least in regard to theology, since the Puritan Hooker, despite his sympathy for Platonic ways of thinking about the spiritual life, would never have turned so far from Calvinism as did such Cambridge Platonists as Henry More and Ralph Cudworth. Hooker simply could not trust the power of human reason as far as they could; to him it was always "carnal reason," a term carrying implicitly all necessary warning against resting in it. Nor could he cast off his Puritan-Calvinist attachment to Augustinian theology in favor of Platonist idealism. But perhaps a Hookerian sympathy with and absorption of some elements of Platonic thought—those most consonant with Augustinian thought, as it happens—was a necessary prelude to the more radically rational doctrines of the later more thoroughgoing Platonists, whose theology Hooker could not, on the whole, have approved.[48]

What we find in the elements of Hooker's thought so briefly examined in this chapter is a fascinating merging of the experientialist with the idealist. These two intellectual forces, which were so actively straining—often against each other—for preeminence in Hooker's day in England, are epitomized in, on one side, Bacon, and on the other, the Platonists. And Hooker, within his ample intellectual reach, contains strong elements of both. He insists that what has seemed mysterious to many generations of Christians is, after all, a concrete, tangible, documentable experience; to prove this he conducts what amount to elaborate courses in religious psychology for the layman, including even the uneducated in his audience. But at the same time that he is showing the relevance of sense experience to spiritual tasks, he insists upon the idealist assumption that the essence of life is spiritual. The material world, though much more vividly present in Hooker's sermons than in those of many of his fellow Puritans, was after all only a means to an end, a way of making the mysterious, the wonderful, less mysterious and more real to the individual believer.

PART THREE

THE INNER WORLD
Going Beyond Faith

12

Going Beyond Faith
UNION, JUSTIFICATION, ADOPTION, SANCTIFICATION

In the unfolding saga of the soul's pursuit of grace, the great watershed is vocation, where one acquires firm assurance of his or her possession of saving faith. With this knowledge a great change comes over the soul. Though one never loses one's share of human depravity, grace alters the perspective towards this element of one's nature; one can now understand, feel, act, and react from the point of view of one assured of eternal happiness. Assurance of grace reveals a route which bridges over the debilitating effects of innate depravity, though one never totally shakes off the depravity itself. The faithful soul's acts may now become sanctifying acts—deeds which tend to the increased perfection of grace in the individual—rather than saving acts, which had contributed to the halting progress of the doubting soul towards faith. The soul, in other words, having passed through effectual calling, has been fundamentally altered. It is now more suitably fitted to complete the spiritual ascent which comprises the total Christian adventure.

This being so, the process of describing the ongoing life of the soul also, perforce, undergoes some changes. Once the great strain and stress is eased, the burden lifted, a new spiritual dynamics takes over. The antagonism between man's known inability and his wished-for ability, a topic which provided the constant refrain in Hooker's works on the earlier stages of the *ordo,* is now partially alleviated; assurance of grace brings calm of mind, and as a result the friction which made the soul's great labor so necessary is largely eliminated. The "rest" which had been promised is now available. Hooker's sermonic aesthetic in the works on the early stages of grace, stressing the perspective of the poor doubting Christian and the paradoxical necessity for exertion in the

251

face of the knowledge that exertion would be ineffectual, is not nearly so appropriate to the experience he must describe the rest of the way. Now he is faced with the problem, as he frankly admits, of explaining to his congregation of pragmatic merchants and farmers the "mysterious" interactions of the Holy Spirit with the human soul. His problem was essentially literary—a problem also faced by later writers in their efforts to bring an intangible truth before the imaginative consciousness of their audiences. Hooker—like Bunyan, Hawthorne, and Melville after him—faced the problem of discovering how to stretch the ordinary medium of language so as to reach the imaginations not only of those who already knew what he was describing as truth but especially of those who did not.

The result of Hooker's confrontation of this challenge is a series of sermons in *The Soules Exaltation* (1637) and later in *A Comment upon Christs Last Prayer* (1656) which often present carefully sharpened explanations of fine theological points but which sometimes lack the convincing concreteness, the metaphorical richness, and often the dramatic scene painting and character sketching so abundantly present in the volumes on the earlier stages of grace. The chief reasons for these changes lie in two sources: the nature of the material itself and Hooker's personal termperament. As we have seen in his willing confrontation of the challenges of his embattled era and in the figurative language of his sermons on preparation and vocation, this man of "mighty vigour and fervour of spirit" had a temperament which drew him to challenges requiring an energetic response. When the difficulty of the challenge was even partially removed, as it was for any sinner who had acquired true faith, the nature of the challenge to Hooker in describing the life of the soul was fundamentally altered. The language of striving and struggle, which had been his stock-in-trade, was no longer so immediately serviceable once the protagonist of his story, the laboring soul, had crossed the spiritual Jordan that separates the doubting sinner from assurance. Ironically, though Hooker's description of the soul's journey had now brought him and his congregation to the part of the journey which had seemed the ultimately desirable end, he now reveals a seemingly diminished level of enthusiasm for the task that remains.

As Hooker became aware that he was talking to increasingly fewer people in his congregation—he liked to recall Scripture's warning that "scarce one in twelve shall be saved"—and as he struggled to keep the subject matter from becoming too purely theological and abstract while discussing such subjects as the nature of holiness and of righteousness, and the interrelationship of the various persons of the Trinity, he ran up against a concurrent danger in himself, probably stemming from his academic training. He had a rather surprising tendency at this stage of his treatment of the redemption process to be drawn into theological controversies. As we have seen, his stated and, for the most part, practiced principle had always been to avoid formal controversy when preaching to a popular auditory. But now he is much more inclined to mention particular authorities or opponents on doctrinal points. *The Soules Justification,* for instance, is full of explicit disagreement with "Papists" and particularly the Jesuits. In the short space of the eighteen octavo pages of *The Priviledge of Adoption,* also, he breaks drastically with his own announced principle of avoiding explicit reference to his reading when preaching to people who in some cases "know not their ABC" by citing the opinions of Augustine three times, those of Gregory Nazianzene twice, and of Piscator once. This is more notice of authorities than he makes in works fifteen times as long (such as *The Soules Preparation* or *The Soules Humiliation*). The new tendency indicates Hooker's sense of his deeper involvement in issues which somehow require, both for his own assistance and that of his audience, frequent reference to intellectual predecessors. Hooker feels he is treading ground here that is less easily presented to a popular congregation than was the material of his preparationist sermons.

Thus, as Hooker gets beyond his main topic—the prefaith stages of redemption—his works become more uneven. Some of this is due to the incomplete state of surviving texts, which range from the garbled abstractions of parts of *The Soules Exaltation* to the striking clarity of treatment of fine theological points in *A Comment upon Christs Last Prayer.* Both of these books, in fact, contain work that is comparable to Hooker's best writing as well as work that is surely his worst. The difficulty for the critic in knowing precisely what to make of the unsuccessful portions at this distance in time is largely owing to the obvious imperfection of the texts. While Hooker's treatment of union, communion, and justification in *The Soules Exaltation* is complete, it is clear that some parts of the section on justification are imperfectly reproduced, perhaps by the printer but more likely by the note-taker, who occasionally mixed the organization rather badly and on one occasion seems not to have understood the point that Hooker was making.[1] Yet since this sort of problem does not often occur in Hooker texts printed from the notes of auditors, it suggests that Hooker himself may have been less than lucid at these points. Knowing nothing of the identity of the note-taker or indeed whether the printer actually might have had a

Hooker manuscript in hand, we can hardly be very decisive in assigning the full blame.

The case is somewhat different with *A Comment upon Christs Last Prayer*, since this work was, we know, printed from manuscripts in Hooker's own hand. Still, even this book was not totally ready for printing when he died, with the result that parts of it—most notably the first thirty pages—are rather sketchy notes, while other parts are fully written out. It is equally clear that the sermon on adoption, which was tacked on seemingly as an afterthought to the book called *The Christians Two Chiefe Lessons*, is extremely foreshortened. In addition, Hooker's doubtless full treatment of sanctification has survived only in parts, though the parts are usually complete sermons. What we have on these subjects, at any rate, does not approach the comprehensive treatment or the definitive concern of his treatment of the earlier stages. Only the very last stage in the redemption process was as fully described, apparently, as Hooker wanted it to be. This is in the latter half of *A Comment upon Christs Last Prayer*, where glorification is the main topic. To complete our examination of the entire saga of the soul's journey to heaven it remains only to explore Hooker's treatment of these four steps.

Union and Communion

One of the several works by Hooker published in London in 1638 was *The Soules Exaltation*, which is a sequel to *The Soules Effectuall Calling*. The book has three sections, each of the first two comprising two "lectures" on the consecutive subjects, "The Soules Union with Christ" and "The Soules Benefit from Union with Christ." The final portion of the book—and by far the longest—deals with the spiritual mechanics of justification. For the most part, the first two subjects in the book are handled in a manner comparable to Hooker's strongest pulpit literature. But the minister's awareness that he is now confronting a somewhat different kind of problem is everywhere apparent in the two sermons dealing with union with Christ.

At these later stages in his narrative of the soul's journey, Hooker continues his explotiation of the associationist force of figurative language. But now he is more inclined to develop single central metaphors for each stage, a practice which usually increases the clarity of his explanation but reduces the richness of his narrative. He first addresses the condition to which one is admitted on acquiring faith: "union" with Christ.

Hooker opens his treatment of this union by starting to create analogies in his usual manner, but is very soon obliged to notice that the literary problem of selecting earthly figures of speech for spiritual experience of this kind is considerable:

> What ever by way of comparison can be alleaged, concerning the neere combination of one thing with another, they are all tyed to this knitting of the soule to Christ: looke what a friend is to a friend; looke what a father is to a childe; what a husband to a wife; looke what a graft is to a tree; and that is neerer than a husband to a wife: nay, goe yet farther, *Galat.* 2.20. what the soule is to the body; the soule is not only knit to the body, as one member to another, as the hand is knit to the arme, and the arme to the shoulder; but the soule doth communicate it selfe universally thorow the least part of the body: so the Apostle saith, *Christ is the very soule of a beleever, I live, yet not I, but the Lord Iesus liveth in mee;* so that looke as the body liveth by the soule, the soule closing, and communicating, and quickning of the same, so Christ is in a Christian, and speaks in a Christian, and enableth a Christian to the performance of that he doth; hence the body of the faithfull is called Christ, 1 *Corin.* 12.12.[2]

Thus, the familiar metaphor of marriage, seemingly so appropriate in describing vocation, Hooker now considers inadequate for capturing the full essence of union (though he will fall back on it nevertheless). Now he needs metaphors which imply complete mixing in order to indicate the degree to which the spirit of Christ fully infuses the soul of a believer. Hooker meets the challenge here by comparing the process of growing into full union with Christ to chewing and digesting meat, which results in the creation of "good bloud," and to a woman's kneading two lumps of dough into a single one. It is in just this latter way, say Hooker, that faith kneads all of the soul's faculties together "and knits them unto God" (*SE,* p. 5).

The difficulty with these analogies, technically accurate though they seem to be, is that the elements of blood and dough have no feelings or thoughts enabling them to appreciate what has happened to them in their full combination into a new mixture. So Hooker resorts to comparisons involving human emotional connections and especially to the marriage analogy, since in this relationship we find the fullest "joining" of one person with another. When, after the long anticipation of hope, desire, love, joy, and moving of the will, one is finally united with Christ through faith, he is naturally delighted, "satisfied" with the union. Christ is, after all, the perfect spouse. There is a fine line between the spiritual and the sensual in Hooker's description of this "satisfaction," this "union." Hooker intentionally exploits the analogy between conjugal familiarity and spiritual oneness at the outset of the first sermon on union, where he says the satisfaction of the believer with the love of Christ is analogous to a husband's satisfaction with his wife's breasts. This husband will then be ravished with her love and will ultimately remain faithful to her. Hooker points out that this entire idea comes from Proverbs 5:19 (". . . let her breasts satisfy thee at all times; and be thou ravished always with her love."). But, as we see repeatedly in Hooker's sermons, he knew the fundamental importance of sexual love to the folk in his congregation, and he is always prepared to join their awareness of sensual experience to their knowledge of Scripture and their apprenhensions of spiritual experience. When he says, in fact, in his sermon on communion with Christ, that he wants to speak about the "intercourse betweene the Lord and the soule" which occurs "when the soule is married unto him" (SE, p. 59), one is forced to question the Oxford English Dictionary's claim that the use of intercourse to mean sexual relations did not occur until the late eighteenth century. Certainly Hooker does not mind inviting his audience to imagine the analogy of sexual intercourse as one more way of getting at the intimate completeness of the believer's marital joining with Christ through faith and grace.

In this grounding of spiritual experience in familiar examples from common experience, Hooker is working directly toward a philosophical point which is crucial to any idealist. This union with Christ is spiritual, he says, but that is not to say it is merely intellectual. He urges his congregation to appreciate the fact that this spiritual union is real; it joins the whole soul, "not onely . . . the apprehension," with Christ; it is "more than imagination" (SE, p. 7); it is total unification of life with spirituality. What we are seeing in this very interesting early section of The Soules Exaltation is Hooker's overt attempt to teach a spiritual interpretation of life to his worldly-minded congregation. In insisting so explicitly on the reality of spiritual experience, he is revealing his own awareness that he is getting into a part of his message on redemption that must seem especially unreal and intangible to a large portion of his audience. For the known elect, their spiritual marriage with Christ is the all-in-all, but for most it may very well seem insubstantial, unreal, imaginary, and therefore unbelievable—perhaps even uninteresting. These are the people whose attention Hooker hopes especially to attract.

Together with the problem of convincing both the newly elect (who are inexperienced in the ways of grace) and also the still reprobate of the essential spirituality of the Christian life, Hooker acknowledges, perhaps unwittingly in this case, another difficulty of the preacher's relation to his congregation once he has gotten to the stage of grace's actual indwelling. He intends to be reassuring to people of newly acquired faith but is actually acknowledging an implicit difficulty in his own task when he says, "Yee are now in the very gate of Heaven, . . . and I see no reason why a man may not say that hee is in Heaven in truth, though not in that measure and largenesse of glory he shall be afterwards. *I Thess.* 1.17" (*SE*, p. 10). If he could say to his audience that those who had reached the point of gracious indwelling of the Holy Spirit were not only at "the very gate of Heaven" but essentially already *in* heaven, certainly it had to occur to him that there would be some who would take this news as an invitation to complacency. The struggle, to their way of thinking, would be over. As he was to explain in other contexts, the struggle was *never* over for the faithful Christian—but that was an argument which would need more than a little voicing and defending, especially to an audience who had been hearing Hooker's repeated promises that if one could but get contrition, get humility, get faith, he would "have all." This having all, he points out, does not mean that the temptations of the world or the pains of sin will no longer hound the believer. The persecution of the saints, he notices, has been a constant in the history of Christianity. Such persecution was a worse sin than incest, but it is sure to continue. The saints must therefore take comfort in their knowledge that, like the two pieces of dough, once they have been united with Christ, they can never be separated from him or from the "benefits" of that union. In this sense, they are as good as standing at the gate of heaven and in no danger of "flying off" from faith when challenged. Yet being at the gate of heaven does not in any way justify spiritual complacency. The Christian must always "walke worthy" of the honor of this union; he or she must live as if in heaven. To be assured of rest is thus paradoxically to be admonished to further labor.

Recalling his metaphor of the moon and tides in order to remind his listeners that "my soule moves [toward Christ], but it is because it is moved" (*SE*, p. 32), Hooker assigns God the initiative. The first "stroke" of union comes from the Holy Spirit, who is thus the first of the three "persons" of God with whom the soul has union. This, Hooker admits, is a "deepe mysterie" (p. 25), but insists on his desire to do what he can to make it all clear for the "weake ones" who are listening (p. 34). Yet the latter half of the sermon is a curious mixture of abstruse logic-chopping on the question of whether the soul joins first with the human or the divine side of Christ's nature[3] with more characteristic, down-to-earth Uses, such as the last one, where, recognizing that man is a "sociable creature," he urges his hearers to associate with those with whom Christ associates (p. 53)—an interesting way of reminding his Puritan hearers of the importance of a covenanted community of believers and church members.

Hooker's subsequent sermon on communion between the soul and Christ attempts to clarify the doctrinal point that when the sinner has acquired the grace of God, he truly has all he needs. Here Hooker develops the marriage metaphor at considerable length. Christ is an infinitely wealthy spouse who brings to his marriage a great "dowrie and feofment" which he "makes over" to the believer (SE, p. 59). The believer's situation on entering union with Christ is like that of the average bride, who is concerned about her future security. "Every woman that matcheth with a man, would see what she might hold her selfe to; what if the man dye? and what if his meanes decay, what will hee estate her in?" (p. 63). The answer is discovered in consulting the dowry, the legal binding of the bridegroom's property into his commitment to his new wife. It promises the spouse protection against want in the event of the husband's death. The "covenant" or "conveyance" which Christ bestows on all his faithful involves four things, constituting all that the believing soul can possibly want: wisdom, by which "secret things," "deepe things," are revealed to the understanding; righteousness, which acquits us of guilt; sanctification, through which one is effectually purified of sin; and redemption, which saves us from death (p. 60). Hooker stresses the sufficiency of this "conveyance" to meet all one's needs, both during life and after.

As he thus resorts to worldly analogies in order to explain a mysterious doctrine to the "weake," Hooker reveals certain of his own assumptions about the nature of his society which are worth noticing for what they tell us about the all-too-obscure nontheological side of the man. In getting our ideas about Hooker almost entirely from his sermons—as we must do for lack of diaries, letters on nonreligious and nonpolitical subjects, or other personal writings—it is useful to note his observation at the end of his second sermon on union that man is "a sociable creature" who needs the companionship of others. Apart from recommending the companionship of the saints, he does not explore the implications of this observation, though it suggests that he himself took pleasure in sociability. But he does comment—albeit somewhat obliquely, in the form of an analogy meant to explain the sufficiency of God's grace—on the differing responsibilities of men in different roles in the social fabric. His essential point here is that every man who gets grace gets enough to serve his needs. The man who has only a "little faith" is no less saved than the man of "strong faith" (*SE*, p. 61). A wise father considers the different needs of his children in determining their inheritances, says Hooker: "He will stock his childe according to the calling wherein he is; . . . the merchant that ventures farre, hath great employments, many thousands will scarce furnish him: but a poore man, as a weaver, or a shoomaker, or the like, many thousands are more than hee can use in his trade" (p. 69). In just this fashion, "God doth apply to every man, according to his estate and condition; he that God hath set as a commander in his Church, as a Minister to teach, and a Magistrate to rule, and a master of a family, God fits graces unto them, according to their estates, the Lord takes measure of a mans estate as it were, and suits him proportionably with all graces necessary for his condition: againe, they that are meaner and poorer, they shall have wisdome, and sanctification, and redemption, but answerable to their conditions" (p. 71). This is not a purely democratic matter, then, but as Hooker says elsewhere, the point to remember is that a little grace is as good as a lot. It is the fact of possession which matters rather than the amount possessed.

Still, before he is through with this sermon, Hooker is moved to counter any inclination on the part of new believers to ignore their Christian duties toward God. He allows his hearers a question at this point which he poses rhetorically for them: How can we get these benefits from Christ? He gives two answers, saying first: "Eye the promise dayly, and keepe it within view, within the ken of the soule" (*SE*, p. 104). That is, read your Bible daily. Thus, for Hooker the Spirit is clearly tied to Scripture; it acts in man through the effect of the knowledge of Scripture on the heart of the believer. This is a point of central importance to the Puritans, though there came to be differences among them on the question of whether the Spirit ever communicates with a man apart from Scripture.[4] Hooker is clearly with the orthodox majority on this point. As we saw in the first chapter, his whole ministry was based on the assumption of the close interrelationship between the ministry, the Word, and grace. Not only does the Spirit *enter* its communion with the soul through the minister's presentation of the Word, but it *continues* there through the active acquaintance of the believer with the promise, the Word. Cultivating the qualities of the "good hearer" thus remains a crucial process in the saint's life, as Hooker also points out in his second answer: yield yourself to the power of the Spirit so that "thou maist bee inabled to doe what God requires" (p. 109). The doing effectually follows the indwelling. First, however, justification must be experienced and understood.

Justification

No theological issue was any more central for the Reformers than the doctrine of *sola fides,* justification by faith alone. Calvin devoted eight chapters of Book III of the *Institutes* to a defense of the Protestant position on justification, thus reflecting his agreement with Luther's earlier stress on the crucial distinction between works and faith as the source of justification. Hooker—who noted that the difficulties surrounding the doctrines of justification and sanctification have driven many a devout divine "to a stand"—fully recognized the centrality of the subject to his concern with the redemption process. Yet only five Hooker sermons dealing primarily with justification survive, and in these there is a noticeable absence of the persistent enthusiasm for his task that was typically present in sermons on earlier stages in the application of redemption.

His consideration of justification begins abruptly in *The Soules Exaltation,* interrupting his discussion of the soul's communion with Christ.[5] Hooker's initial comments on justification involve a rather casual definition of the term as "a conveyance of the merits of Christ, by way of imputation" (*SE,* p. 114), a definition which indicates his sense of the central importance of the concept of imputation but which fails to explain it. In a subsequent sermon, however, he offers a more careful and satisfactory definition. Justification, he says, is "an act of God the Father upon the beleever, whereby the debt and sinnes of the beleever are charged upon the Lord Iesus Christ, and by the merits and satisfaction of Christ imputed to the beleever; hee is accounted just, and so is acquitted before God as righteous" (p. 132).

Calvin had said that Paul's use of the term *justification* in opposition to the term *accusation* shows "that the form of expression is borrowed from the practice of the courts,"[6] a borrowing which struck Hooker as the key to explaining the doctrine to his audience. The meaning and value of the sinner's justification become dramatically clear in the morality-play scene which he sketches:

> When the soule of a poore sinner, shall appeare before the Tribunall of the Lord, and justice comes to put in a plea against him, Christ shall step in and say, Lord, for this poore soule that beleeves in me I have died: for this poore soule I tooke the nature of man upon me; therefore let thy justice bee fully satisfied with what I have done for him: well then saith justice, goe thy way, I have nothing to say to thee: the Lord makes a proclamation, Be it knowne to all men and angels, I acquit this soule; there is no imputation of sin he hath committed, no failing in any dutie shall condemne him. (*SE,* p. 121)

"This," Hooker concludes simply, "is the way of justification." His allegorical character Justice is only a slightly less dramatic figure than Edward Taylor's Justice, who remarks at the close of a dialogue with Mercy in *Gods Determinations touching his Elect:*

> Unto the Humble Humble Soule I say,
>   Cheer up, poor Heart, for satisfi'de am I.
> For Justice nothing to thy Charge can lay,
>   Thou hast Acquittance in thy surety.
> The Court of Justice thee acquits: therefore
> Thou to the Court of Mercy are bound o're.[7]

Taylor agreed with his Connecticut River valley predecessor that when God Himself is the judge, as He is in the final Judgment, the saint is like an accused man who discovers that the Lord Chancellor is his friend and that he has nothing to fear. Moreover, God's merciful decision is absolutely final; "a man never appeals from a higher court to a lower, but from a lower court to a higher" (*SE*, p. 148). If you are acquitted in heaven, says Hooker, no man can reverse the decision. This is precisely the degree of safety which a justified Christian enjoys.

Justification, as Hooker explains, is the first of two main ways that Christ conveys his grace to the elect. The second is sanctification. He explains this dual operation as follows: "Christ conveyes his grace two wayes; partly by imputing, partly by imparting: they are the termes of Divines, and I know not how to expresse my selfe better; but thus if you will, partly by imputation, partly by communication. . . . they are both reall, but one is habituall; both of these, both imputation and communication expresse a reall worke of God upon the soule, but the last onely leaves a frame and a spirituall abilitie and qualitie in the soule; the conveyance by imputation doth not" (*SE*, p. 113).

Initially Hooker limits his comments to imputation. This occurs, he says, when something which another person has or does is accounted mine, as if I had it or had done it. This implies, first, that "I have no help in my selfe in what I have, or what I doe" (*SE*, p. 114), and second, that something which another has is made essentially mine. Hooker draws on Calvin's law-courts analogy, observing "an old comparison that Divines use" in likening the situation of a justified man to that of a man in debtor's prison whose debts are suddenly paid for him by someone else; he does nothing, yet is totally free from punishment by the law. "God doth justifie a beleeving soule, not for what he hath, not for what he doth, but onely for what Christ hath, and hath done for him" (pp. 115–16). At no point in Hooker's description of the redemption process is man's inactivity so insistently underlined as here. In the act of justification, man is necessarily helpless, for justification is "by imputation onely, not by any action" of the sinner (p. 118).

Through this imputation, God's justice and law are entirely satisfied; the soul owes nothing for all its trespasses. The wonder of the doctrine which Hooker is preaching, he says, is that the Lord can "accept of mee, when I condemne my selfe" (SE, p. 124). He compares justification to Noah's ark; when everyone else is being swept away in the world's floods of evil, the justified can get "into Christ" and be safe from all dangers (pp. 122–23). Moreover, the safety is more than temporal; it is eternal, extending into the next world. One may well rejoice in the sense of escape which comes with his awareness of being justified. Hooker tangibly conveys just this sense in a passage which was doubtless admired for its powerful appeal to sensory experience by another Connecticut Valley successor, Jonathan Edwards, a century later: "You whose eyes God hath opened, whose hearts God hath humbled, and whose soules God hath called home to himselfe, you are now in the hands of the Lord; goe your way, and when you see hell flaming, and the devils roaring, and the damned yelling and crying out, looke backe I say and see this ditch out of which you are escaped; looke upon the pit which you were going over: you may blesse God and say, wee are past that, those dayes are gone, wee are past from death to life" (p. 129). Since all this relief is due to Christ, Hooker ends on the rhapsodic exhortation to "labour for a Christ," "oh, a Christ, a Christ, a Christ in all, above all, more than all" (pp. 128–29).

The basic distinction in Hooker's mind between justification and sanctification is that in the former a man's situation vis-à-vis the demands of God's justice is drastically changed, whereas in the latter the man *himself* is changed. This is the essence of his crucial distinction between "imputation" and "communication." A man in justification, he says, is like a servant whose indenture papers have been torn up and thrown away. He is now free from his debt to the master, though he has not changed inwardly in the least. This change in external circumstances Hooker calls a "moral" change, as opposed to a "natural" change, which would involve alteration in one's inward nature. This distinction occasions an interesting example which could have been partly based on the actual experience of the adventurous Captain John Smith. Take the case, Hooker says, of a faithful British subject who is captured and imprisoned as a traitor by the Turks. The man is charged with this crime only because he is in Turkey, not because he is any more or less traitorous than ever. When he is freed and returns to England, he is advanced in station and respect. He is still the same man; his change has been external—"moral," rather than internal or "natural." If he was ignorant before, he is still ignorant; if sinful before, he is still sinful. But he is far better off as a free man in England than as a prisoner in Turkey (*SE*, pp. 141–42).[8] Such is the case, says Hooker, for the justified man, who is, through the *imputation* of righteousness—not by any actual acquisition of it—let out from under the heavy weight of God's justice. He is a free man, though he has in no sense earned his freedom. No one—not even the purest saint—can truly merit release from the justice of God.

Hooker is here stressing an essential point of difference between the Reformers, who insisted on justification by faith alone, and "those merit-mongers, the Papists," who, as Hooker angrily observes, tend to take the saving power from God and assign it to men by giving works equal consideration with faith in the process of salvation. John Preston made the distinction very clear: "They [the 'Papists'] say that faith and works both are required to justifie; wee say, that nothing is required but faith, and that workes follow faith."[9] For Hooker, Preston, and all orthodox Calvinists, any change in man's inner nature and abilities comes after justification and adoption and as a direct result of the prior alteration in his spiritual circumstances. At that point, as the Christian begins to grow in sanctification, his efforts to turn away from sin become all the more important. His "labour" involves, especially at first, a willed attempt to imitate Christ. This imitation will always be destined to relative failure, but the faithful, once justified, will make every effort to dissociate themselves from both their former sins and their former corrupt companions. In giving an example of this new exertion against sin, Hooker anticipates his later discussion of sanctification. The example comes naturally at this point, however, since it is a first exhortation to the justified to act on their new sense of freedom. Man's will operates in cooperation with God's will in cases like the following, where a man is shown acting as a renewed individual for the first time:

> I have read an old story of a man that was carried away much by a harlot; at last the Lord [met] him and opened his eyes, and humbled his soule, and brought him out of his sinfull condition: many a day after the harlot met him againe, and the man would not looke on her, and she began to seft [*sic*] kindnesse upon him, and said, I am she, you know wee have had much sweet dalliance together: Oh, but saith he, blessed be God, I am not I; that is, I am not the man that I was before: so should we, though wee are nothing but sinne by nature, and know nothing but corruption, yet if the old sluggishnesse and stubbornnes of heart, and haughtinesse that wee have too too much received; if they come and say, we are

> the darlings that have had much sweet fellowship and communion
> with you, make them answer and say, I am not the man, I will
> have no more to doe with you. (*SE*, p. 162)

Here all of the sinner's former nature is epitomized in the character of
the rejected harlot, while the miraculous power of Christ's mercy to
transform the soul is expressed in the startlingly compact pronounce-
ment of self-awareness, "I am not I."

The doctrine of justification may well have remained a mystery for
most people, but for Hooker's congregation it came alive. He gave
character, shape, and substance to separate traits of personality, separate inclinations of the will. By transforming the abstractions of
psychology and theology to the immediacy of narrative dialogue, by
creating recognizable characters to act out abstract theological truths,
Hooker guided his audience into complexities of human nature that
would otherwise have been out of reach for many. Here his dramatic
imagination triumphs over just those obstacles that he had feared
would defy reduction to terms graspable by minds less sophisticated
than his own.

But Hooker pushes his explanation farther in order to explain still
more precisely just how justification operates. Coming up against the
complex issue of the Trinity, he resorts to simple logic and analogy to
explain how the various persons of the Trinity cooperate to bring the
believer through this stage. Justification, he says, is an act of the Father,
not of the Son or the Holy Ghost, because it was specifically the Father
who was offended by Adam's sin. The Father, then, is the proper judge,
and it is only He who can acquit a man of his guilt. If the sinner is a
debtor unable to pay his obligation, then the Father is the creditor, the
Son is the surety, and the Holy Spirit is the messenger who brings word
of the creditor's forgiveness of the debt. In bestowing justification, then,
God's three persons act in an orderly, sequential manner. God sent
Christ into the world to take the responsibility for the sins of the elect,
which he did in his crucifixion. Then the Holy Spirit enters the heart of
each believer to let him know inwardly that Christ's act has served effectually as his payment, his justification.

As he explains these complexities of the roles performed by the various members of the Trinity, Hooker's enjoyment of such theological
distinctions becomes quite evident. In the final months of his life, in
fact, he returned to the subject of the roles of the persons of God to
elaborate them at greater length in *A Comment upon Christs Last
Prayer*. In that work and in *The Soules Exaltation* Hooker fully characterized both God's demanding justice and His redemptive mercy. Both
of these divine qualities are active, and both are satisfied in the work of

redemption. God's justice absolutely requires that if Christ is to be our "scapegoat," as he volunteered to be, then he must be charged as guilty on our behalf. Since he assumes guilt, it is entirely just that he be punished. This submission demonstrates the Son's mercy just as fully as the Father's justice.

But Hooker recognized that human guilt remains a major psychological dilemma at the stage of justification. Given the fact of Christ's acceptance of our guilt, how much should one "charge himselfe" with one's own sin? Hooker answers for the believer only, saying that the believer must always examine his sin, constantly reminding himself that every single sin is enough of itself to damn a person eternally. He must, therefore, hate sin if he is to love God. At the same time, however—and here is the great comfort for the person who has true faith—"a beleever should not in his judgement conceive, nor in his heart be perswaded that any sinne, nor all his sinnes shall ever be able to fasten the guilt of sinne upon him, so as to cause revenging justice to proceed against him to his condemnation, if he seriously repent, and amend, and forsake his old wayes" (*SE*, pp. 191–92). "It is one thing [for a person] to be worthie of condemnation," as all people are, "and it is another thing to fasten guilt and condemnation upon him" (p. 192). Those who are both truly repentant and truly faith-full, can "shake off the guilt of all [their] abominations, and goe on cheerfully and comfortably to Christ, and yet humbly too" (p. 193). But at the same time those who are not among the faithful get only pain and sorrow from such doctrines: "This truth is like a thunder-bolt, and is able to shake the hearts of all unbeleevers, and to dash them all in peeces: . . . that every obstinate unbeleever is destitute of all hope of succour and pardon of his sinne: consider of this all you that are unbeleevers; you must pay your owne debts, and beare your owne burthens" (p. 197). The mercy of God "is limited onely to the faithfull" (p. 202). To guard against the tendency to overstress the quality of mercy in God, Hooker says, "you who thinke that Christ is made all of mercy, it is a God of your owne imagination, and your owne devising." What is perhaps most striking in all of this is Hooker's desire to balance the opposing characteristics of God's nature, justice and mercy, to assure that neither is forgotten. He implies that if each believer can keep this duality of divine traits carefully poised in his own conception of the nature of God, he can avoid being dominated by either of the twin dangers within himself: discouragement and overconfidence.

After his sermon on the satisfaction of God's justice, Hooker logically turns to focus on Christ's passion. The entire last half of *The Soules Exaltation* is a discussion of the atonement which seeks to stress both the role of Christ in obtaining justification for the elect and the responsiblity of each of the faithful as a result of Christ's actions. At times the discussion becomes unusually abstract as Hooker wades into the swamp of doctrinal dispute on matters of small importance to his congregation; at other times it is dramatically effective as he tries to help his congregation imagine the actual feelings of Christ in his passion in the Garden of Gethsemane and on the cross.

As Hooker begins to explore the how and why of Christ's serving as "surety" in paying man's spiritual debts, he makes use again of the notion of imputation. This time, though, it is to argue that man's sin was imputed to Christ just as righteousness is imputed to man. This is what is meant in the biblical text for his series on justification, 2 Corinthians 5:21, "For he hath made him to be sin for us, which knew no sin, that we might be made the righteousness of God in him." Christ was not a sinner, but he bore "all the sinnes of all the faithfull," just as a believer is not truly righteous even though justified (SE, p. 166). All the nonelect are simply and forthrightly sent "packing" to hell under this selective interpretation of the doctrine of atonement. This is clearly hard-nosed predestinarian doctrine, and Hooker is not at all interested in disguising the fact. Having achieved this emphasis, however, he proceeds to put primary stress on God's mercy thereafter, though the balance is difficult to maintain when sin's fearful power and consequences retain such a central position in his psychological appeal to his congregation. Christ's triumph over sin and death on behalf of his faithful was so great simply because they are such potent forces in the souls of men. Hooker cannot preach the one fact without stressing the other.

Hooker proceeds to explain that Christ was assigned responsibility for all of the elect by the Father in heaven. It was his duty then to take care of them, ultimately to deliver them safely into God's hand (SE, pp. 170–72). Christ thus put himself under the burden of God's law and paid the debts of all the sinful elect. Hooker would later emphasize the importance of this "sending" of Christ in saying that it was his distinctive role to become a willing servant, submitting "to that Under-condition" of servanthood, despite his equal divinity with the Father.[10] And Hooker is willing to spend over one hundred pages here discussing Christ's sacrifice and suffering simply because it was through this process that Christ accomplished the purpose of his "sending."

A large measure of the uniqueness of The Soules Exaltation rests in its consideration of the actual nature of Christ's suffering during the last hours of his life. The primary leitmotif of the final hundred pages of this book is the lament of Christ on the cross cited in Matthew

27:46, "Eli, Eli, lama sabachthani? that is to say, My God, my God, why hast thou forsaken me?" While this passage is not the text of these sermons, it is quoted numerous times as Hooker attempts to explain the exact nature of Christ's suffering.[11]

This imaginative re-creation of Christ's agony on the cross and its meaning for the Christian is sometimes movingly rendered, but the sermons' effectiveness is too often compromised by the double burden, increasingly obvious after the book's first half, of both faulty transcription and Hooker's own frequent reference to Roman Catholic authorities on justification. Though Hooker often attacks Jesuits in general, he particularly singles out Bellarmine, the Italian Jesuit cardinal whose death in 1621 probably preceded Hooker's references by only some four to nine years.[12] It is not surprising that he should have allowed himself to enter partisan theological debate on the doctrine of justification, since it is at the center of the Reformers' differences with the Roman church. And sometimes the statement of his disagreement with a Jesuit position—as, for instance, on whether and how God the Father forsook Christ on the cross (*SE*, pp. 264–67)—enables Hooker more easily to clarify his own position. Usually, however, with the exception of his "confutation" of the "Popish Purgatory," the issues are not major ones. The result is to increase the impression of distracting wrangling and theological nit-picking at the expense of consistently forceful conversion preaching. It was perhaps an awareness of these faults that caused Hooker to revise and condense parts of the sermon in *The Soules Exaltation* into the sermon published posthumously as *The Gift of Gifts; or, The End Why Christ Gave Himself*, which represents a more summary but better organized treatment of many of the issues of the earlier book.[13] Despite much effective preaching in *The Soules Exaltation*, therefore, the book remains an only partially successful production.

Adoption

Hooker's description of the next stage in redemption has survived only in a truncated sermon called *The Priviledge of Adoption*, published at the back of *The Christians Two Chiefe Lessons*, and in some scattered remarks in *A Comment upon Christs Last Prayer*. It appears that *The Priviledge* was originally a fuller treatment, but the surviving text was printed from notes which were not as complete as those used in printing most of Hooker's sermons. Still, given the intangible nature of the subject of adoption, it is unlikely that Hooker preached on it often or at length.

William Ames carefully placed adoption in the conversion scheme in saying that "although adoption follows from faith, justification comes in between. Adoption of its own nature requires and presupposes the reconciliation found in justification."[14] This same sense of the precedence of faith and justification is present in Hooker's main Doctrine on the topic of adoption: "None are the children of God by Adoption, but such as are so by Regeneration."[15] What distinguishes the man in adoption from the man in justification is simply his acquisition of a new "dignity" which comes with the status of adopted son of God. John Davenport described it compactly, saying that after Christians are justified "they are adopted, that is, accepted for Christs sake to the dignity of Gods children."[16] Hooker cites Gregory Nazianzene's observation that there are three ways of becoming sons of God: the way Christ did, by "generation"; the way Adam and the angels did, by "creation"; and the way all of the faithful do, by "adoption." The first two ways are, of course, impossible for mortal man since the Fall. The "ground," or basis, of one's adoption, then, is his prior union with Christ. The "end" of it is our admission to "a right and interest unto our heavenly inheritance" (*CTCL*, p. 288).

Just as the marriage and debtor's court analogies tend to dominate Hooker's explication of union and justification, the sonship metaphor controls his comments on adoption. Whereas Ames in his doctrinal explanation of adoption spent much of his effort in distinguishing differences between human adoption and divine adoption,[17] Hooker capitalizes on the availability of such a direct comparison and addresses chiefly the similarities. In fact, the problem in reading Hooker's account is to discover whether the doctrine is anything but a metaphor. His willingness to play word games with this figure very nearly obscures the meaning which it is intended to clarify. He begins by saying that the purpose of Christ's incarnation was "to make us the sons of God. The Son of God became the sonne of man, that wee sons of men might become the sons of God" (*CTCL*, p. 288). Adoption involves putting one in a new setting, a fact which encourages comparison to the ingrafting metaphor so often used to describe union in faith. Both metaphors enable the stress on a new beginning that is fundamental to the rebirth of the soul in grace. "As a child taken out of one family and translated into another, even so we are taken out of the houshold of Sathan, and inserted into the family of God" (p. 288). But this adoption does, after all, differ from a human one in that the Father into whose "family" the believer is adopted is not your ordinary *pater familias.* He is quite out of the class of the adopted child altogether. "If some beggarly roague were taken up to attend upon some great man (much more if to be the adopted son to a Prince) he must be stript of all his ragges; and washed and purified, and even (if it could be) have a new heart put into him too" (p. 291).

By using the analogy of gross social difference, Hooker stresses the unlikelihood—indeed the miraculousness—of the soul's adoption by God. He liked the opportunities for elaboration in the metaphor, and he developed them with particular effectiveness in commenting on the phenomenon of becoming the "sonnes of God":

> It is a wonder, that we can thinke of it without wondering. When it was told *David* that he might be the Kings sonne in law, what (sayes *David*) thinke you it a small matter to be the sonne in law to a King? *1 Sam.* 18.23. How can we then thinke it a small thing to be not a sonne in law, but an heire, not to a mortall, but to an immortall King, the King of Kings? How can wee but deeme it a speciall and unconceivable favour for us vile, wretched, wicked, and miserable sinners, dust and ashes, silly wormes, vessels of wrath, and vassals of Sathan, to be preferred to so great a dignity, as to be sonnes and heyres apparent unto the kingdome of God! (*CTCL*, p. 292)

It is this drastic alteration in one's spiritual circumstances which is formally recognized by God himself in adoption. Dignity is thereby acquired which is "so great, as greater cannot be conceived" (p. 294).

But predictably, the status of newly adopted son of God does not entail the right to lackadaisical ease. Rather, one must be "more circumspect over our selves, and more carefull of our courses, then ever heretofore we have beene" (*CTCL*, p. 298). Nor should one look for greater worldly dignity in the eyes of others. Instead, one is apt to experience afflictions such as poverty and contemptuous treatment by "worldlings." Nevertheless, the Christian who has become God's adopted son will be like Prince Charles, who in 1623 went searching for a wife on the continent: "When our King went into Spaine disguised, was he troubled (thinke ye) because he was not respected according to his worth by those amongst whom he came? No surely, he knew that when he returned he should find royall entertainement with his father" (p. 300). As at the final stages of vocation and union, Hooker finds a source of amazement in this proof of God's love. Adoption is truly a "priviledge"; "it is a wonder that we can think of it without wondering" simply because no one deserves adoption by a heavenly father.

Sanctification

Though it is understandable that a minister mainly interested in instructing and guiding what he called a "simple" congregation in the ways of grace might have been reluctant to give lengthy treatment to the stage of adoption, which is surely the subtlest and most fleeting of the distinguishable periods in the life of the saint, it is natural to assume that he would have given a good deal more time and emphasis to the next stage. Sanctification is the long period in the believer's life between his assurance of grace and his death—a period in which he grows in holiness and becomes more noticeably like the image of God. Sanctification was especially important not only because it involved a large portion of the earthly life of the saint but also because in New England it became a factor in determining one's political power as well as his role in the Church. Church membership was a prerequisite to suffrage in Massachusetts Bay, but such membership was granted only on the tripartite grounds of one's subscription to a congregational church covenant, indication of an understanding of church doctrine, and a convincing declaration of possession of saving grace, in conjunction with a scandal-free life, the latter serving in part to validate the claim of regeneration.[18] The entire church membership voted on whether or not an applicant's statements about his spiritual condition were convincing. And their basis for judgment was necessarily the outward deeds and speech of the applicant.

But despite all of this, we do not find in Hooker's surviving works any discussion of sanctification on the same scale as his treatment of most of the earlier stages. Since this may be due more to historical accident than to his own intention, it would be wrong to make too much of the fact in evaluating his emphases. It is probable that he did not slight this stage in the *ordo salutis* as much as the published remnants of his career suggest. The main early text we have on this subject is the brief book *The Soules Possession of Christ* (1638), while four of the seven sermons in the posthumous book discussed above in Chapter 4, *The Saints Dignitie and Dutie*, are an orderly restatement of the central issues in sanctification. And again, parts of *A Comment upon Christs Last Prayer* apply. Occasional other sermons are concerned with practical questions related specifically to that part of sanctification which is too often confused with the whole of it, morality. Since there is a theoretical side of sanctification which is prior to and above morality in the life of the saint, I shall for the moment address only Hooker's discussion of the theory of sanctification, leaving its ethical consequences to separate consideration in the next chapter.

It is only after the sinner has acquired faith, understood his justification, and realized his adoption that actual changes begin to occur in the nature of the individual's soul. Righteousness and holiness, as Hooker liked to say, can now for the first time be "habituall." That is, these qualities now actually spring from within the soul. This is possible because *"sanctification* puts a new frame of heart into us." No new faculties are added to the soul, but those which we possess are put "into right order," enabling holiness to increase (and, sometimes, to decrease) "many times." For this reason, William Ames could insist that sanctification brings a "real change." John Preston insisted that grace does not merely "make a little light alteration on the superficies of the heart, but alters the very frame of it." It does not just "put upon us a washy color of profession," but "dyeth us in grain with grace and holiness." When the soul of the formerly depraved sinner actually possesses "holinesse," this is a change indeed. Sanctification is thus not merely another term for good works. It includes these but is not limited to them. The essence of sanctification is an *inner* change. It involves the acquisition, as John Cotton put it, of "in-dwelling spirituall gifts of grace."[19]

The processive nature of the entire work of redemption is made especially clear in Hooker's treatment of sanctification. His stress here is characteristically on what goes on inside the soul of the newly justified and adopted Christian. Two major points emerge: that sanctification is hardly automatic as soon as one has been justified (though, paradoxically, one does follow hard on the heels of the other), and that the new indwelling of the power of the Spirit does not, as the Antinomians believed, take the responsibility off the backs of the saints. So while Hooker is stressing a doctrine which means liberation, at least relatively, from the great burden of sin under the Old Law, he seems aware that his listeners in their honest moments know that their lives are hardly easy or their souls particularly pure, for all their conviction of their own election. He is guarding against overconfidence and irresponsibility by those under grace while reassuring those who might be inclined to doubt that they really are eligible for the benefits of Christian union with the Lord. Through it all, he still recognizes the great importance of the minister's continuing role as spiritual guide. He still has much to tell the elect as well as the unregenerate, even those who have gotten so far as to enjoy the indwelling of habitual graces.

Hooker conveys the continuing responsibility of the saint to be active and energetic in pursuit of the spiritual life in his description of the general as well as the particular nature of sanctification. Here, as in the several preceding stages of redemption, he settles at the outset on a dominant metaphor which will serve him well throughout the entire first half of *The Soules Possession of Christ*. And again it is a metaphor which urges the Christian to spiritual action. The figure comes from his chief text for *The Soules Possession*, Romans 13:14, which reads in the Geneva translation he was using, "Put ye on the Lord Jesus Christ, and take no thought, or make no provision for the flesh to fulfil the lusts of it."[20] He urges this "putting on" of Christ as the chief responsibility of the Christian in grace. Christ in this instance becomes a protective garment whose fit improves with continued application. In order to perfect this fit, one must always continue to "go to" Christ, as Hooker insists in his first Doctrine; even those assured of their redemption "have daily need to fetch succour from Christ, and grace for the performance of every spirituall service which God requires at their hands."[21] Every man's grace, he explains, is like a garment that only partially covers his nakedness. You need therefore to go to Christ so as to become like "a man that hath a long garment, [and] is covered over from head to foote" (*SPo*, p. 15). The preacher aptly explains the continuing need for this "fitting" in saying, "You must not put on Christ as your holy day cloathes, a man must put on Christ, not onely in the morning in prayer time, as he confesseth and bewaileth his sinnes, and then leave Christ in his house or closet; no, no, you have as much need of your garments abroad, as in the house, therefore wear Christ all the day long, and goe clad with him continually, and bee able to converse and trade in Christ" (p. 60). The Christian must be conscious of his possession of grace even in his most mundane acts: "Put on Christ in every thing; in buying and in selling, in eating and in drinking, and in all things" (p. 60). The "robe" of Christ is thus not just an external badge; in a real spiritual sense the clothes make the man.[22]

In his catechism explanation of sanctification Hooker follows the pattern of Perkins, which was also the model for Ames and Shepard. He says that sanctification has two parts, mortification and vivification. The obvious Latin etymologies of the two words suggest precisely what the doctrinal argument is on sanctification. There must be a death of sin before there can be a rebirth of life in Christ. Just as surely as sanctification follows justification vivification follows mortification.[23] In mortification, says Hooker (taking his metaphors from Isaiah), we "put off" all our "menstrous clothes," our "bosome abominations" (*SPo*, p. 24). We renounce sin, in other words, thus renouncing ourselves and "all sufficiency and ability that is in us" (p. 26). In mortification, we strip our souls bare, so that "when the soul is once made naked, then *Faith* [in vivification] takes the *Robe*, this glorious *Robe* of Gods *grace*, and brings it home to the heart" (p. 35). This all sounds very familiar from the stages of contrition and humiliation, where sin was denied and self was left behind. But the difference is that now there is an indwelling principle in the soul which enables the sinner to make real, lasting headway against the enemy, whereas before, man's best actions were still unaided by grace.[24] In a late sermon on the subject of sanctification—though the term itself does not appear there—Hooker explains the notions of mortification and vivification by preaching on the Doctrine, "In whomsoever Christ is, there is a death of sin, and a life of righteousness."[25] This is necessarily a partial rather than an absolute change, in that no one can be permanently cleansed of "menstrous" sins. As Perkins had said, "Even . . . the best workes that a man can doe, . . . are good onely in part. . . . Because grace is onely begun in this life, therefore all the workes of grace in this life are sinfull and imperfect."[26] But he can be—and in sanctification is made to be—freed from the total dominion of sin which reigns in natural, corrupt people before grace. Hooker puts it in clear expository fashion in saying, "Who ever have Christ in them, they have the whole body of sin in every part of it weakned and destroyed, and the whole frame of holinesse and righteousnesse in every part of it begun in them, though both but in part" (*SDD*, p. 57). One is now freed from total subservience to sin. Real change occurs, he explains, in men's wills, affections, thoughts, words, actions, general and particular callings, and duties to man and to God. Sin, if not obliterated, is at least permanently weaker than formerly.

Vivification, on the other hand, brings with it a new spirit of grace (*SPo*, p. 36). The modern reader cannot help remembering Jonathan Edwards's account of his own experience of grace in his "Personal Narrative" as Hooker explains that in the life of righteousness there is a new seeking after God and the things of God together with an awareness that God's law contains not only justice and truth but also goodness and loveliness (*SDD*, pp. 62–64). There is also an increase in one's ability to perform "particular graces." As one goes to Christ "for particular strength and assistance in every performance," one finds that one has new abilities of patience, love, wisdom, and humility (*SPo*, pp. 38–41). In short, the heart itself is changed. No Old Testament passage could be more to the point or more in the spirit of the Puritan awareness of the meaning of grace than the passage in Ezekiel 36:26, which Hooker quotes in his sermon in *The Soules Possession:* "A new heart also will I give you, and a new spirit will I put within you: and I will take away the stony heart out of your flesh, and I will give you an heart of flesh" (p. 42).

As it had in earlier stages of the application of redemption, meditation plays an especially important role in sanctification. Hooker urges his listeners to focus on the "promise," the Gospel, for doing so "rivets the soule to the promise, and even fastens the promise into the heart" (*SPo*, p. 54). Since "the Scriptures are the very inspirations of God, the very breath (as one may say) of the Holy Ghost" (*SDD*, p. 135), then through meditation at the stage of sanctification, the Spirit and the Word are truly internalized—made a part of the soul of the believer. At the same time, however, one must be careful that in his meditations he does not somehow still "make provision" for the flesh, for sin. Since "the best of GODS children . . . have flesh and corruptions in them" (*SPo*, p. 65), one must not allow oneself to think privately about the delights of sin, because in doing so one will "give much advantage to *sinne* and *Sathan*" (p. 93). This would make no more sense than for an attacking army to send provisions into the city it is besieging. It would not—must not—happen. Certainly a woman who wanders out of her house at nine or ten at night does not provide for modesty and holiness "but whoredom and drunkennesse, for a prophane light heart, and therefore these guests will come afterward" (*SPo*, p. 122). "As it is in house-keeping, just so it is in heart-keeping" (p. 115). The faithful Christian, unlike the wayward housewife, severs himself from sin as fully as possible. One cannot be too careful, as Hooker shows through an unkind stereotyping of the Irish: "The *Irish man* being malicious and fearfull, never thinkes his enemy killed, till he hath cut off his head, he will bee sure to leave him past all hope of recovery: So a gracious heart never thinkes sinne mastered, till it see the very life and blood of his corruptions removed" (p. 147).

This kind of effective combat against sin is a rare thing in the world. "The Lord will put up righteousness in a short sum" (*SDD*, p. 68), so that even the truly righteous person must still work at his righteousness. Thus, even at a stage in the life of the saint when it would seem the Spirit is ready to take over, it takes further work to "increase the ruine of the old man" (p. 76). For God's saints to accomplish what He wishes, they must continue to "indeavor" in the use of the means. The sedentary, "lazie" Christian is simply a contradiction in terms: "If people lie still and will not up and be doing, God will not be with them" (p. 83).

There is a double paradox in this. In the first place, we recall the minister's holding out the promise of "rest" to the footweary pilgrim at the conclusion of vocation. For Hooker, however, resting does not mean ceasing to labor. And in the second place, it is surely a mark of Hooker's thought that, even as he is teaching that it is not the man himself who does the acting, who causes the tree to bear its fruit, he is also arguing that the individual in faith is bound to be an active person. This is because the faith which is in the heart of a man and which "causeth fruitfulness" simply "cannot be idle, it will have *footsteps*, it sets the whole man on work, it moveth feet, and hands, and eies, and all parts of the bodie" (*SDD*, p. 164). So it is that the elect soul was characterized by insistent spiritual labor not only in the preparatory stages; even now that it is "in faith," it is still entirely active. Hooker implies that there is a potential heroism in this activity of faith. The saint must be ready to *do* immediately "what God will have done," however great the danger or sacrifice, just as those heroic Christians Paul and Luther did. Whoever imitates them, whoever thus "walketh in the steps of *Abraham*," "is as sure of salvation as the Angels are" (p. 175). This is not because the works are efficacious but because they are clear signs of the heart's possession of saving faith. Those who are sanctified will surely be glorified.

The spiritual life, as Hooker envisioned it, is thus not a self-enclosed structure which, once achieved, is automatically self-sustaining. It is, rather, a process of continuous forward movement and growth. In describing the stage of sanctification, when the soul has become able to improve the quality of one's belief and action—to make a person an active Christian in the world—we do not find Hooker placing primary stress on specific deeds which the saint must perform. Instead, he emphasizes on the one hand the need for continued attention to the basic ingredient of faith—the nurture of the Word—and on the other hand the need to keep up one's guard against sin. The basic tensions are still operating. The confirmed believer is between God and the natural world, and even though now "married" to Christ, remains surrounded by evil and must continue the struggle against it. Yet the outcome of the struggle is no longer in doubt; perhaps this is the reason why Hooker's description of the *ordo* at this point tends to lack the dramatic vigor and narrative momentum which so energized his admonitions to labor in the earlier stages.

13

A Puritan Ethic

Since holiness, not works, was the essence of sanctification, Thomas Hooker never concentrated primarily on teaching morality. Despite his experimentalist emphasis and his skill in preaching effective Applications for his Doctrines, he stands with nearly all his generation of Puritan ministers in never preaching a doctrine such as "Do good deeds," but always stressing instead the importance of getting a humble heart and possessing Christ. Even after people had "put on" Christ and grace and reached the stage of sanctification, he urged them to work at improving the quality of grace and building a fuller relation to God rather than at performing charitable deeds. He agreed entirely with Perkins that "good workes make not good men in whole or in part: but men first of all made good by the goodnes of Christ imputed, make good works by their goodnes."[1] It was simply a matter of theological common sense; and since most of the people were unregenerate anyway, it was all the more absurd to preach a doctrine of good works at them. Everyone, after all, was capable of common graces, but only the habitual graces really meant anything lasting in one's spiritual life. Missing this point could lead to heresy, as the Puritans were quick to observe in their frequent attacks on the emphasis of the Pelagians and Roman Catholics: "The Romane Church makes very idols of works," said Perkins.[2] But it was also a point on which the Puritans differed with many Anglicans, who tended to be more optimistic about human ability to do good. The Puritan approach to morality was simply to preach spiritual renewal; good works, they believed, would come in due course. For a long while, therefore, Puritans—especially the New England immigrants—were not much given to the writing of works on morality.

Since the *sola fides* doctrine was so fundamental a tenet, Protestants from the first days of the Reformation on through the sixteenth century had avoided the notably Roman Catholic tendency to write instructional books on casuistry. For this reason William Perkins's *Cases of Conscience*, which was published posthumously in 1606, was a major landmark for the Puritans in the arousal of interest in casuistical writing, though it is apt to strike the modern reader as being a good deal less concrete in its moral instruction than one might have expected. William Ames imitated his predecessor in this regard, but arrives at his discussion of practical moral questions in his famous *Conscience with the Power and Cases Thereof* (1630) only after two sections discussing the primary question of the soul's salvation. And, like Perkins, Ames was often rather general in his treatment of moral questions,[3] though his book did become widely used among the Puritans.

Until at least the late sixteenth century, then, Protestants had to rely on Roman Catholic works of casuistry and moral theology.[4] But after the turn of the century, they began to break into the field more themselves. Both Ames's and Perkins's *Cases* as well as some Catholic books of moral instruction went with the first generation of New Englanders on the ships from England and the Netherlands, as did such other popular casuistical books as Richard Rogers's *Seven Treatises* (1603), John Dod's *A Plaine and Familiar Exposition upon the Ten Commandments* (1603), and a collection of writings by several anonymous authors, *A Garden of Spiritual Flowers* (1632). Dod's may have been the most popular of all of these, having gone through eighteen British editions in the thirty years before Hooker's departure for New England.[5] One can no doubt account for this stirring of interest in specifically Puritan works on the Christian life partly by observing the increasing distinction made by Puritans and Anglicans alike between their respective positions. The Puritans in the seventeenth century were ever more aware of the threat on the one hand of the imposition of "idolotrous" forms of worship by the church establishment and on the other of the repression of the godly preaching which was their chief spiritual resource. Thus, the encouragement and practical instruction offered by casuistical handbooks of their own was no doubt welcome to many, though they agreed with Anglican casuists on some, if not all, fundamental matters.[6] Once the Puritans had arrived safely in the New World, the threat of an established, authoritarian ecclesiastical enemy was remote, releasing the ministers to focus, for the time being at least, on the central issue of helping the elect home to God. This called for spiritual regimen more than moral exhortation, and thus it happened that there were no books of casuistry written and published by New England ministers until mid-century.[7]

Eventually this pattern broke down. After 1650—coinciding more or less with the cluster of deaths of such famous leaders of the first generation as Hooker, Shepard, Winthrop, and Cotton—it began to seem obvious that declining spirituality was a fact of life in the colonies. The ministers in the years leading up to the accommodations symbolized by the Half-Way Covenant tried to meet the problem head-on by preaching increasingly in the jeremiad vein and, finally, by publishing moral tractates with rules for one's ethical guidance. One of the first such works was a book for children, aimed at educating the new generation in the ways of the old, John Cotton's posthumous *Spiritual Milk for Boston Babes in Either England, drawn out of the breasts of both Testaments for their nourishment* (1656). From this point on, though the redemption of the heart remained a central concern, New England ministers were less purely concerned than they had been with spiritual instruction and more inclined to give direct attention to deeds and service. This is reflected in a distinction noticed by Robert Middlekauff between Richard and Increase Mather, the latter putting more emphasis than the former on the power of the will in the conversion process.[8] It was the third-generation Cotton Mather whose *Bonifacius* (1710) may be seen to symbolize the increasing stress on what men should do rather than on what they should be. The link between the general tendency to preach morality which Mather's book so fully represents and the Enlightenment's stress on humanitarian benevolence is clearly indicated in Benjamin Franklin's acknowledgement of his debt to *Bonifacius* both in his creation of his own humorous *Dogood Essays* and in his conscious pursuit of a service-oriented career later in life.[9] Franklin spent his boyhood, after all, in Mather's Boston. It was finally left to Jonathan Edwards, that great throwback to a purer Calvinism than his contemporaries knew, to perceive his fellow Christians' mistaken emphasis. His *Nature of True Virtue*, written in 1755, was an eloquent argument for a reordering of priorities in the ethical life, urging that the truly benevolent man is not the one who consciously sets out to do good in the manner indicated in books of moral guidelines but the one who *is* good.[10] Edwards's avowed preference for the preaching and thought of Thomas Shepard over that of later Calvinists was surely owing in large part to Shepard's having been, like his father-in-law, a conversion preacher who emphasized mainly the individual's relationship with God rather than his relationship with other people.

In this regard, Hooker and Edwards were of a similar mind. Both gave considerable attention to explanations of how God's Spirit works on the soul of man—Hooker especially in his discussion of the role of the affections in *The Soules Effectuall Calling* and Edwards on the same subject in his *Treatise Concerning the Religious Affections*—but neither ever became a casuist. Yet Hooker, also like Edwards after him, punctuated a great many of his sermons with instructions that are clearly moral in their implications. In his Uses he would frequently advise his hearers to avoid the company of the ungodly, to keep out of taverns and brothels, to respect and obey those in authority over them, and to encourage wives, children, husbands, and servants in the use of the means of grace. Certainly, in applying his Doctrines, then, Hooker did give his congregation some practical moral instruction. But he never framed his Doctrines on moral principles. Hooker's main value as a moral preceptor to his congregation was probably expressed in private, one-to-one conferences. He saved back at least one day a week for consultations in his study with people in his congregation who were troubled with "cases of conscience." As a spiritual counselor in such situations he was apparently much in demand. Sometimes, as in the famous case of Mrs. Francis Drake of Esher in Surrey,[11] these sessions were extensions of his pulpit efforts to bring individuals to grace, but at other times they could be occasions for explicitly moral instruction. In these instances, Hooker no doubt practiced the form of oral Puritan casuistry which, as Keith Sprunger notes, "was similar to modern pastoral counseling," though undoubtedly "it had more authoritative answers."[12]

Hooker's *Properties of an honest Heart* (1638), which apparently circulated in manuscript during his English ministry and perhaps even after his departure, came as close to being a casuistical work as any Hooker book would ever come. Yet this little work clearly stops short of overt moral instruction. It is divided into three unequal parts. The first lists five "Motives" which lead one to seek "truth of heart" and the second lists five "meanes" to pursue this motivation. But the main part of the book schematizes eight identifying "marks" of this inner uprightness which the Christian, through careful self-examination, ought to seek out. These marks are represented by the attitude one has toward each of eight major aspects of Protestant spiritual life—namely God, Christ, the Holy Ghost, Scripture, the Sabbath, the Saints of God, good duties, and one's self. In each case the author lists four "marks" which the "honest," or redeemed, heart will have toward these things. In thus describing what qualities of heart to look for in one's self, Hooker is presenting in a somewhat backhanded way instructions for how to act. For instance, the third characteristic mark of the Christian in regard to the Sabbath is described as follows:

> The *whole day* will he keepe *holy.* A carnall man dares be bold
> to clip Gods day, and take an houre in the *morning* in his bed
> longer than other dayes, and make longest dinners; *now,* hee
> sleeps it away in the day time; he prates it away, and trifles it out,

here and there in doing nothing: and at night hastens to bed be-
times, as one that is weary of Gods service, not knowing how to
spend the long winter evenings: whereas *an honest heart* dares not
be so bold, thus to rob God, & steale holy things; hee dares not
steale a penny from a man, much lesse an houre from God.[13]

In thus describing what does or does not characterize an "honest heart"
on the Lord's Day, Hooker is doing the next thing to giving explicit
moral instructions. But his stress remains on the prior concern of the
condition of one's heart.

This little duodecimo volume is unusual in Hooker's canon not only
for its near approach to a kind of casuistry but also for its author's
stated acknowledgement that it was written as a book rather than as a
sermon to be delivered orally.[14] *The Properties of an honest Heart,*
together with his other book of self-help, the catechism published as
An Exposition of the Principles of Religion, is valuable evidence of
Hooker's continuing pastoral concern that his parishioners receive all
possible help from him in their spiritual lives. Both works are clear
evidence that he did his best as pastor to follow the people out of
church and into their homes, providing them with written as well as
oral pastoral counsel. Both, however, keep the focus on the heart
rather than on the deeds.

Old and New Law

For a long while one of the dominant errors in our thinking about
Puritan beliefs was to insist on their Old-Testament-God-of-Justice
orientation. Beginning with the insights of Samuel Eliot Morison and
Perry Miller, we have come to see them differently. Careful attention
to Hooker's writings shows the need for avoiding the easy assumption
that the earliest American Puritans had a simply legalistic, Hebraic
frame of mind on morality. One of numerous dualistic concepts repeatedly stressed by Hooker is the opposition of the "Old Law" to the
"New Law." The Old Law (i.e., the Old Testament Law epitomized in
the Ten Commandments) made demands on men which Hooker and all
Puritans realized were impossible to fulfill, desirable though the goal of
complete obedience might be. Hooker addressed himself directly to
the question of the relationship between Old Testament Law and New
Testament Gospel, saying that the Law is important in preparing men
to receive Christ—schooling them for faith—but finally, the most valuable of all things comes from Christ and the Gospel. The net effect of
Christ's coming was to free men from bondage to the Old Law.[15]

This dualistic view of the two laws is closely related to the Puritans' stress on two covenants. In *The Saints Dignitie and Dutie,* Hooker explains that under the old covenant, the covenant of works, God demands perfect obedience but does not give postlapsarian man the power to obey. Besides these two "direct properties," the Old Law also contains two "accidental properties": it condemns men to hell for disobedience, and it causes men's hearts to rebel against the Law itself, thus multiplying their transgressions.[16] To be "under the law," says Hooker, is to be liable to all four of these properties. Under the Old Law man is required to be obedient but is forced to realize his powerlessness to prevent his own disobedience. The old covenant gave modern man no room to hope.

But in opposition to the Law is grace. The covenant of grace is at the very heart of Puritan thinking on morality. Without it, aspiration to moral action is entirely futile. In *The Faithful Covenanter,* as in *The Saints Dignitie and Dutie,* Hooker points to the contrast of man's situation before and after entering the covenant of grace. Previously, a legal performance of man's half of his covenant with God was required, but after one is justified, the requirement becomes "evangelical obedience," which means that men must simply express the goodness in their hearts as best they can and God will accept this attempt despite its imperfection. Paul's comment in Romans 6:14, "For sin shall not have dominion over you: for ye are not under the law, but under grace,"[17] is behind all that Hooker says on this subject. Under grace, says Hooker, past sins are forgiven, the strength and ability to do what is commanded is given to us, we are delivered from condemnation, and our corruption is hindered from multiplying. Thus, grace is "directly contrary to the Law,"[18] an answer to the impossible dilemma posed by the Law. None of this denies predestination, which Hooker always held firmly to,[19] but it does mean that those who are under grace—the faithful—are awarded "unspeakable consolation" in their paradoxical struggle to be morally obedient when they simply do not have the ability.

The effect of this opposition of grace to Law on the Puritans' ethical theorizing was, of course, not to negate the Mosaic Law but rather to eliminate the negative psychological potential in the old commandments. Hooker's constant concern was to nourish the inner man—to encourage as well as to admonish. The new concept of obedience enabled by grace's supersession of Law was a heartening doctrinal point that he was careful to underline for his congregations. And it indicates Hooker's sympathy with the modern Protestant tendency to move away from the legalism that had dominated medieval and early Renaissance casuistical thinking.[20]

Though Hooker nowhere in his published works systematically discussed the Ten Commandments, he did on occasion use the common reference to the First Table and the Second Table, which divides the commandments into what Hooker calls "the Law of God" and "the Law of Nature."[21] As William Perkins had earlier explained it, "The first table hath foure commandements" and relates to our love of God, while the second table "containeth sixe commandements" and "concerneth the loue of our neighbour."[22] Hooker pointedly stipulates that "Sinnes against the first table, are sinnes of a deeper dye, of a sadder nature, then Sinnes against the second table."[23] In doing so he was taking a fundamentally Puritan position in opposition to the characteristic Anglican ranking of the second table above the first in importance.[24] The reason for the Puritan position is simple: man's main allegiance is to God, not to man, and to violate the first four commandments is to violate one's primary allegiance. This hierarchy of allegiances is useful to Hooker, as we shall see, when he outlines ethical guidelines for his congregation. But we should also note that the distinction has important temporal implications for the struggles in England over the forms of worship and the need for popular preaching. The "treasons" charged against Laud and his Royalist/Anglican followers were all the worse in the minds of their Puritan accusers because false worship involved the breaking of the first commandment. Richard Sibbes spoke for his colleagues on the matter: the "rise of all sin against man is our sinning against God first. . . . The breach of the First Commandment is the ground of the breach of all the rest."[25]

In using this common differentiation between commandments of the First and Second Tables, Hooker does not intend to deemphasize the Second Table. *All* commandments must be taken to heart. Elsewhere he warned against three "False Shadowes" of the state of grace, giving brief character sketches of three types of self-deceived people. The second of these is the man of "Formall Righteousnesse." Such a man practices "the outward duties of the first Table" while neglecting the duties of the Second Table. Hooker cites scriptural examples of whores who pray to God but break wedlock at the same time (Prov. 7:14, 15; Jer. 7:9, 10). Such a person's self-deceit in believing in her own righteousness because she overtly obeys the First Table will lead to her spiritual ruin, says Hooker.[26] You cannot take only *some* of the commandments to heart.

The commandments were still basic to the Puritan view of morality, but, as Hooker was implying in insisting that grace had freed men from the bondage of the Law, they were more negative (particularly the duties of the Second Table) than the Puritan prescription for godly behavior. William Haller has correctly said that "the Puritan code was much more than a table of prohibitions. It was the program of an active, not a monastic or contemplative, life."[27] Hooker, like most contemporary Puritans, was not so much inclined to make lists of "Thou shalt nots" for his congregation as he was to confront them with positive spiritual challenges which, if properly met, might well lead to more diligent performances of one's duties. I have already mentioned that books and treatises outlining proper moral behavior were not characteristic products of the pens of first-generation New England preachers. Undoubtedly, this is partly owing to the availability of popular English works such as Dod's *Plaine and Familiar Exposition of the Ten Commandments*. But it is also true that the early New Englanders were singularly unfailing in remembering the necessary impurity of men's actions, and they never lost sight of the belief that any good works a man might accomplish were due, not to his own virtue, but to the mercy of God which had filled his heart with enough cleansing grace to make such acts possible. As Thomas Shepard wrote, "Consider, thy best duties are tainted, poisoned, and mingled with some sin, and therefore are most odious in the eyes of a holy God, (nakedly and barely considered in themselves;)."[28] Hooker liked to say simply that "the stumps of Dagon" remain in even the most obviously sanctified souls. A good deed was always seen as an effect rather than a cause, a result of the enabling grace of God rather than an action having any merit of itself.

Moral Priorities

Once this preference for avoiding an overt preaching of moral action is understood, Hooker's rare invention of a few moral "rules" for his parishioners' guidance appears all the more remarkable and important. Two sermons are particularly memorable for the directness and fullness with which they address themselves to the subject of the moral duties of the faithful Christian in a world which Hooker recognizes as essentially hostile to the believer. These sermons, though heretofore largely ignored, are available in very full texts and are both remarkable for their considerable metaphoric vitality as well as for their practical and usable advice on moral matters. One of these sermons, the last of the three published in *The Saints Guide* (1645), provides what amounts to a system of priorities which the believer ought to follow in determining what his most pressing "duty" is at a given moment. The other sermon, the first in the volume entitled *Foure Learned and Godly Treatises* (1638), provides instructions on how one ought to behave toward fellow believers on the one hand and toward the reprobate on the other. While these discrete sermons do not represent an attempt by Hooker to make a full description of the moral life, they do nevertheless present the basic principles of his ethic.

In the sermon entitled *The Plantation of the Righteous* Hooker makes much of the basic metaphor in the text, Psalm 1:3, "But he shall be like a tree planted by the rivers of water, that bringeth forth his fruit in due season." The psalm emphasizes the differing estates of the godly and the ungodly, a contrast which Hooker reinforces by implying that the planted tree was transplanted from a "barren land," a detail not present in the scriptural passage. In concluding his summary of the first psalm, he translates the Old Testament poetry into the symbology of the New: "So it is with those who having bin rooted out of the drie wildernesse of sin, and are by the great Husbandman God the Father, transported into the true Vine Jesus Christ, and set by the Rivers of his word and Ordinances, they grow fruitfull in grace and goodnesse, bringing forth flourishing fruite, and that in due season, when it may make most for the Glorie of God, and the good of his people."[29] This use of the fruit-bearing tree as a metaphor for the saint who does good "duties" is very common in Hooker's and other Puritans' writings.[30] The metaphor itself frequently implies the entire concept of visible sainthood—the notion held by all Puritans that the spiritual condition of one's heart determines the nature and quality of one's speech and actions. "Faith causeth fruitfulness in the hearts and lives of those in whom it is."[31] The difference between the fruitful tree which is now growing beside the river and the formerly barren tree in a desolate location emphasizes the difference that grace can make in one's ability to "bear fruit."

After the discussion of Psalm 1:3, Hooker puts his main stress on the phrase "in due season," saying, in summarizing the Doctrine, *"The duties of Saints ought to be seasonable"* (PR, p. 147). That this is a point seldom stressed from the pulpit is a factor which Hooker feels is worth mentioning; while this notion of seasonableness "may seeme strange to some, it is little knowne and lesse practised amongst most" (pp. 147–48). Then, after citing seven biblical passages which refer to the need to do things "in season" or in "due season," he goes on to ask the crucial question of how a man can discern the fit and proper time for doing duties. After a "general" answer that the Christian must act whenever both occasions and opportunities are suitable (as he puts it, there will be *time* enough in hell for repentance but no *opportunity*), he goes on to give three "particular" answers which appeal to common sense fully as much as to scriptural authority. He says: (1) we should *daily* "discharge those dutyes that are suited to the present day," since we may be dead tomorrow; (2) we should act when our bodies and spirits are in the fittest condition for action and not wait to decide to serve the Lord until we are too tired at night to pray or until we are too old to serve the Devil any more; (3) we should arrange to discharge *all* our duties adequately rather than use up all our energies on a single duty: one's "outward calling" must not prevent the nourishment of his soul, for instance (pp. 153–57).

None of these particulars is very startling to us, and certainly they would not have been to Hooker's congregation, though the reminders they contain would undoubtedly have seemed particularly timely to many. The main interest in this sermon, however, is in what follows, for it is in the rest of the sermon that Hooker lays down the fundamental system of priorities which one must obey if he is to do his duties both faithfully and seasonably. These crucial points are made in the course of a discussion of what Hooker calls "Duties occasionall," which means duties not a part of one's daily routine but needing to be done when the opportunity arises. He offers two rules to cover these cases. The first is that if you can do good at a certain time but some regular "duty" prevents it, then put off your regular duty for the time being. For illustration, he posits a hypothetical situation in which a man discovers that a neighbor's house is on fire just when he is going to pray with his family. At such a time, "we must for the present passe by our duty, and helpe our neighbour" (*PR*, p. 158). The issue is clarified somewhat when Hooker asks which duty one should do if he must choose between two or more. His answer is consistent with his notion of the relative importance of the two Tables in the commandments. He says that the "duty [which] is most excellent and necessary" must be done first—in other words, a duty of the First Table must be done before one of the Second Table. In the hierarchy of values, that is, man's first duty is to God, not to man. This is made clearer as Hooker raises and answers still another question: how do we know the preeminent importance of any duty? "We must have an eye more to Gods Glory, then to the Salvation of our souls, in all the duties that we performe" (p. 159).

The essential aim of Hooker's sermon, however, is to outline a system of priorities which will always enable a man to know just where his chief "duty" lies. God's glory comes first—even before our own souls—but as Hooker proceeds to state his second rule, which deals with duties to men, we learn that selflessness is not necessarily a consistent guide. In many situations, says Hooker, you must put *yourself* first. When the choice is between doing a duty for another or for yourself, if the two duties are "of the same ranke and quality," then do the duty for yourself. The fundamental Puritan soul-concern dictates that "we ought to love our owne personall good, more then the good of another."[32] He spells it out: "I must preferre my own occasions before another mans, my goods before his, my body before his, my life before his, serve my self in the first place, and my neighbour in the second" (*PR*, p. 160). One scholar correctly observes that such statements are liable to "make the modern reader suspect Hooker of being a Pharisee."[33] To overcome this suspicion, we must realize that, while our modern ethical thought tends to be based on a dualism which distinguishes mainly between the self and one's "neighbors," the Puritan ethical system depended on the basic distinctions between the body and the soul, the temporal, material world and the eternal, spiritual realm. Hooker isolates the central issue when he adds to his other statements the idea that "I must not preferre my body before his soule, my temporalls before his spiritualls, nor my goods before his life" (p. 160). While "occasional" departures are permitted (as in the burning house example), the rule is that after one's allegiance to God, one's own soul should be the next most important thing in the world. And certainly spiritual charity is of a higher order of importance than material charity. Oliver Cromwell made this distinction: "Building of hospitals provided for men's bodies; to build material temples is judged a work of piety. But they that procure spiritual food, they that build up spiritual temples, they are the men truly charitable, truly pious."[34] To Hooker, then, the hierarchy of values which determines one's moral actions looked like this:

1. God's glory
2. my soul
3. my neighbor's soul
4. my life
5. my neighbor's life
6. my body
7. my neighbor's body
8. my goods
9. my neighbor's goods.

Hooker knew, as did Edwards after him, that there is a sense in which self-love can be an entirely constructive act. The problem for the modern reader is to avoid confusing this self-love with selfishness. The one derives from a primary love of God, the other from a primary love of self.[35] Doubtless both Hooker and Edwards knew the passage in Augustine, which lists in a carefully ordered sequence the objects of man's responsibility: "Now God, our master, teaches two chief precepts, love of God and love of neighbour; and in them man finds three objects for his love: God, himself, and his neighbour; and a man who loves God is not wrong in loving himself."[36] And, Augustine goes on to say, where love of neighbor is involved, one's own family—the nearest parallel to self—comes first. "To *begin* with," he says, "a man has a responsibility for his own household—obviously, both in the order of nature and in the framework of human society, he has easier and more immediate contact with them."[37]

The five Uses which conclude Hooker's sermon constitute an admonition to be up and doing. As he puts it, being a Christian "is not an idle, but a laborious life," involving "much paines and travell [i.e., travail]" (*PR*, p. 167). In the third Use, which summarizes the sermon's major ethical implications, Hooker strikes his familiar *carpe diem* refrain, urging that we take advantage of "seasonable" opportunities when they appear, never losing sight of our priorities:

> For incouragement, seeing God doth now vouchsafe unto us so many glorious seasons and opportunities, which if improved might be to the eternall welfare of our soules, now to step in that we may be cured, . . . for so long as the Gospell is preached unto us, and tenders of mercie offered, so long our season of grace doth last, we should therefore now take these opportunities by the forelocke, for we know not how soone they may be removed from us, or we from them, and when the dore is once shut, though with the foolish virgins we may knock, yet it shall not be opened unto us: and for our helpe herein we should . . . learne so to order, and overlooke all our businesses, that we may be able to allot to every imployment a proportionable time, and we must alwayes take especiall care that our dutie to our neighbour never justl[e] out that homage and service that we owe unto our God, we must therefore never over-charge our spirits with multiplicitie of worldly businesses, but keepe our souls in such a frame, that we may be able when ever we goe to converse with God, in [a]ny holy ordinance, to set aside all worldly occassions, that neither our hearts, nor our thoughts, may run out upon them. (*PR*, pp. 168–70)

Thus, not only "sinfull sports, and pleasures" (p. 171) but even the doing of good works can interfere with one's spiritual health.

Love for Neighbor

One needs only to notice the great difference between Hooker's comments on self at the stage of contrition and those at the stage of sanctification to understand that, with grace, the individual did indeed acquire a new sense of self. But if one can now respect himself more than formerly, what of his relationships with others? Hooker recognized the need which that minority in his congregation, the elect, had for explicit instruction in how they, as saints, ought to relate to their fellow men. The sermon published under the title *The Carnall Hypocrite* in *Foure Learned and Godly Treatises* is his direct answer to this need. At the heart of this sermon Hooker gives a number of "rules for acting in grace." The sermon does not, however, dive right in to the problem of the saint's need for moral guidelines. Hooker commences instead with the matter of moral action at large, expressing with admirable succinctness what amounts to the Puritan approach to social and national reform when he says that "to humble and to reform our sins is the best means to maintain the safety of a kingdom or nation."[38] He cites Machiavelli, "that cursed politician," who, says Hooker, preached the very kind of hypocrisy that the present sermon is criticizing, urging men "to take up the name of virtue because there is no trouble in it, no disquiet which comes by it, but he would not have [them] take up the practice of it" (*CH*, pp. 92–93).[39] This Machiavellian approach, says Hooker, characterizes the carnal hypocrite, a type who is to be carefully avoided by the godly, according to the sermon's text, 2 Timothy 3:5 "*Having a form of godliness, but denying the power thereof: from such turn away*" (p. 91).

Having thus argued that society can be reformed only by the reform of individual souls, Hooker assures his congregation that the reformed soul *will* produce good works. The sermon's second Doctrine, in fact, is a summary of the fundamental Puritan doctrine of Visible Sainthood: "Sound godliness always shows and discovers itself where it is in the life and conversation of him that hath it" (*CH*, p. 94). For some ten pages Hooker seems to enjoy exploring this idea, creating numerous similes to illustrate the certainty of his claim that "if a man have an humble heart, he will have a holy life" because "the actions be proportionable unto the disposition of the heart" (p. 94). Hooker anticipates a question in the minds of his parishioners by asking if a man might not "have a gracious good heart . . . and yet be a retired Christian, and not express it outwardly?" His reply is blunt: "I answer no. If there be holiness in the heart, it will show itself without" (p. 95).

"We judge the tree by the fruit," says Hooker (*CH*, p. 97); and this is just as true when the fruit is bad as when it is good. This being so, he exhorts his congregation to *show* their grace, quoting Matthew 5:16 ("Let your light so shine before men that they may see your good works"). In doing so, one should be "neither cowardly in hiding his grace, nor vainglorious in expressing" it (*CH*, p. 101), and to insure such a proper balance, Hooker lists four rules which ought to be observed: (1) do not show off your own excellencies, but Christ's; (2) make sure that credit for your works goes not to you but to grace and Christ; (3) labor to make others love you and, through you, Christ; (4) aim always at showing the power of godliness.

Hooker follows these general admonitions by urging the faithful in his congregation specifically to turn away from ungodly people. In the realm of public intercourse, those in authority should excommunicate the "openly profane" (*CH*, p. 110). Later in his career, of course, Hooker is known to have been quite moderate in his own ecclesiastical practice on this point.[40] During the eleven years of his Hartford ministry, only one person was excommunicated from his church. But *The Carnall Hypocrite* was written and first preached while he was still in England, where it is likely that the percentage of "openly profane" church members was higher than in the new churches of New England, where, from the beginning, it was no simple matter to become a member in the first place. Hooker's "rules" insist that a "faithful man" who "hath . . . liberty" to choose must not "enter into communion with the wicked" (p. 111), though a servant or wife who is bound to a wicked master or husband must remain subject to him.

In one's private relationships ("mutable" or "voluntary communion") with the ungodly, the rule is even more firmly enjoined: "It is the duty of all the saints of God not to close in communion and unnecessary company and inward familiarity with those that are the deniers of the power of godliness" (*CH*, p. 113). Hooker admits that there are exceptions to this rule, as in cases where one's vocation necessitates communion with *all* people (as it does, for instance, for doctors, ministers, and lawyers) and when neighborhood or physical proximity necessitates it. And he adds a third exception, though rather begrudgingly, it would seem: "The bonds of religion and natural mercy binds sometimes to keep company with such, for the souls of all men should labor to do good unto all so far as necessity requires and opportunity is offered thereunto; for we are bound to preserve the honor, life, goods, good name of any man" (p. 113). This latter situation is of course subject to the general priorities outlined in *The Saints Guide* and, in any case, does not urge an active concern for the wicked. As Edmund S. Morgan has more than once observed, the Puritans were not much concerned about building bridges to the corrupt segment of mankind.[41] In fact, this deceptively charitable "exception" is followed just two pages later by two "rules" indicating how far the heart of a good man ought to be removed from the wicked, the first of which observes: "Every wicked man is a vile man; . . . [Christians] should despise and contemn them.

It is a badge of a Christian, the note of a holy heart in whose eyes a wicked man is vile" (p. 114). Yet when Hooker addresses himself to the question of just how far men's "outward carriage" must be turned away from the wicked, he somewhat contradictorily admonishes his listeners to do what they can for them. "You must bear a great deal of love toward them, and you ought to maintain a great deal of affection to them and do a great many services for them" (p. 115). This affection and these services are to include mourning "inwardly" for them, praying for them in secret, and using "all means to reclaim them": "Reprove them sharply, counsel them compassionately, and strive with them mightily, that so you may bring them home to know 'the things belonging to their peace' [Luke 19:42] here and everlasting happiness hereafter" (p. 116).

All of this might seem thoroughly contradictory—first warning the saints to shun the wicked and then to love them—were it not for what we know of Hooker's view of moral priorities. First allegiance is to God, then to one's own soul. Before being concerned about worldly matters, however, one's concern must be for the souls of others. While for the Puritans this never results in anything like a missionary approach, nevertheless it can be seen that this concern for the good of another's soul might well be expressed in such disciplinary acts as ostracism and excommunication, acts which Hooker sees as manifestations of love. In dealing with the question of how to treat those who have been Christians but are now fallen, he says that those who are now "obstinately incorrigible" can be publicly excommunicated and shut out of the company of the saints (CH, p. 118). He defends this position by anticipating an objection from his audience and promptly answering it. The passage is fundamental to our understanding of the close relationship between the Puritan concepts of church discipline and Christian love. Public excommunication and separation from the society of the saints

> is the practise of much love, nay, of the greatest mercy that a man can show to a wicked, profane wretch. I presume you will hardly think it so. You will say: 'This is love indeed, when a man cannot look upon another but he must disdain him! Doth a man show mercy to another when he will not keep his company? If this be your love, God bless me from such a love.' Take heed what thou sayest. God bless thee from folly and not from this love. And you shall plainly see it so, because this course and behavior is that which God hath appointed as a special means. It is that which is marvelous helpful and useful and profitable to withdraw a wicked man from his wicked course and work sound repentence in his soul. (CH, p. 118)

Thus, the motivation for the discipline of church members is not unlike that for the discipline practiced by parents on their children. It is rooted in love and a concern that, if at all possible, the discipline may serve to bring the offending person to a better course of action.

But there was another reason for this public and private ostracism—a reason which Hooker seems somewhat more enthusiastic about preaching. The saints need to defend themselves from the corruptions which dominate the outside world. This argument—which is essentially a doctrine of insulation, a doctrine which Edmund Morgan has argued insured the ultimate decline of the Puritans' dominance in New England—surely strikes us today as one of the least attractive aspects of Puritan piety. The following passage is nothing less than a warning to the church members to preserve the separation of the unequal. Sinfulness is, after all, contagious, as the metaphors insist:

> This reason concerns ourselves, that we may not be defiled, that we may not be infected with their wicked courses and polluted with their society. It is in this case with sin as it is with the plague of the body. He that will be clear of it, the old rule is: fly far enough, fly soon enough; he that is with those that are infected, likely he shall be infected. So it is with sin, which is the plague of the soul. He that hath a plague sore blossoming, he that hath a tongue belching forth his venom against the Lord of host, he that hath a plague sore of drunkenness, a plague sore of adultery, if ever you would be preserved, then go far enough, fly soon enough. The alehouse is the pest-house where the plague is; the drunkards are the persons infected. If thou wouldst be clear, come not near them. . . . As they say, one rotten apple spoils all the rest, and one scabbed sheep infects the whole flock; with the froward we shall learne frowardness, etc. (*CH,* pp. 118–19)

As we might expect, knowing the Puritans' admirable desire to explain everything as rationally as possible, all of this warning against keeping company with the wicked is not based on irrational fear. The particular way in which the "plague sores" of the corrupt were most dangerous was that contact with them would hinder the faithful from keeping the Lord's commandments. This is true, said Hooker, in "three particulars": (1) "If there be any desire or disposition of doing good, wicked company blast it even in the bud" (*CH,* p. 120). (2) Vile company deprives one of the benefits of the means and Ordinances. If one does come to the preaching of the Word, the wicked argue against its power and importance. If the Word does prevail, the wicked "peck out the good seed of the Word which is sown in the heart!" (p. 121). (3) "Cursed companions" comprise an army which will overpower one.

"This I observe by my experience: wicked men will never leave till others be worse than themselves" (p. 122). The war between the Spirit and the Flesh was no imaginary contest; it was a matter of spiritual life and death.

The sermon's conclusion furnishes just one Use, addressed, not to the faithful, to whom all of the foregoing moral instruction has been directed but "to the wicked themselves." These listeners are not to be displeased with the saints of God if "they judge meanly of you and estrange themselves from you":

> Oh, take heed of this! If the saints of God say, 'Depart from me, ye wicked!,' what will then the God of all saints? If the gracious saints will not abide thee here, will the God of all grace abide thee in heaven hereafter? No, no, the fearful sentence will pass upon you at the great day of account! [Mt. 25:41]: "Depart from me, ye cursed!" Therefore labor to be sensible of this and so to be humbled and abased for this, and labor for to be better, and then the saints of God will love and delight in your society. (CH, p. 123)

When one looks at this entire sermon in perspective, it becomes evident that Hooker's emphasis on the saint's safeguarding his own soul is far stronger than his stress on expressing love for the reprobate. Speaking to the saints, he can say, put yourself first: your own soul demands attention before the soul of a reprobate. In presenting a philosophy that will guide church members and even the Church itself in its relations with the outside world, Hooker in *The Carnall Hypocrite* is entirely true to the system of priorities outlined in *The Plantation of the Righteous*. The glory of God is served by keeping the wicked out of the Church, while at the same time the soul of the church member is safeguarded. In addition, but secondarily, the ungodly man is helped, through discipline, to see the need for throwing off his ungodliness and coming home to Christ. He is given an external motivation to virtue.

Obedience and Self-Denial

There is, in Hooker's system, only one valid reason for doing good: it is required by God. An entire sermon, entitled *Wisdome's attendants; or, The Voice of Christ to be obeyed*, is devoted to developing this idea.[42] The basic guideline for determining whether an action is a worthy one or not is to "remember who is your Leader." "In all our actions, let this be the question, would *Christ* do so? then will I." Thus the basic moral rule is, "What *Christ* did performe, doe you."[43] The two sermons which we have examined in some detail may be seen as

Hooker's practical recommendations for accomplishing this difficult admonition.

Such a task, of course, necessitates a denial of men's baser impulses so that obedience to God can remain the uppermost goal in one's life. These baser impulses or values, which, if permitted, would supplant Christ, are what Hooker calls simply "Selfe." "Selfe-denial" is necessary, therefore, and it is not surprising that it is described as one of the Christian's two chief lessons in Hooker's work by that title.[44] Nor is it any more surprising that the work of the individual soul to gain redemption must start with a recognition of his inadequacy to the task of salvation, a renunciation of self-reliance, and a seeking for assistance from Christ.[45] Selfhood, says Hooker, is slavery of a particularly base kind: "Sathan is a slave to sinne, and thou art a slave to him. It is a base thing to be a scullion, but to be a slave to a scullion no man can beare."[46] Being a servant of Christ is far better, Hooker explains, than possessing the apparent liberty of selfhood, which is really slavery. Hooker here appropriately reminds his congregation of the scriptural paradox that "the losing of a mans life is the next way to save it."[47]

In the Puritan scheme, good is accomplished, not by setting out to do it, but by admitting that you are incapable of doing it and thus opening yourself to the possibility of receiving grace, which, as Hooker repeatedly emphasizes, gives ability. It creates a "new creature" and enables one to accomplish at least a partial victory over the world in this life—a victory which is certain to be consummated in the next life. Faith and action in the Puritan scheme, then, are not only paired; they constitute a cause-effect sequence. The transplanted tree is the only tree which can bear fruit: "Faith causeth fruitfulness in the hearts and lives of those in whom it is." Such faith and its attendant fruitfulness receives the immense reward of eternal happiness.[48]

In view of the widespread notice and influence of the theories of Max Weber, Ernst Troeltsch, R. H. Tawney, and their followers on "the Protestant ethic," perhaps it is worth stressing one thing which is *not* involved in Hooker's version of the Puritan ethic. Although he agrees with other Puritans that idleness is sinful and that one should follow a worthy calling, in all of his frequent statements that good works are contingent on true faith, there is no mention whatever of any connection between good works and wealth. Weber himself, in pointing to what he saw as an ultimate connection between Protestant moral teaching and the capitalistic profit motive, was careful to say that this connection developed much later than the early seventeenth century.[49] More recently, Perry Miller and, from different vantage points, James

W. Jones and Emory Elliott, have insisted on important differences between first-generation American Puritans and their successors— differences which run parallel to those between early- and late-seventeenth-century Puritans in England.[50] It is a distinction which bears reemphasizing. Regardless of whether one grants Weber's ingenious argument or not, it is undeniable that Hooker never claimed a causal link between godliness, ethical action, and worldly prosperity. In fact, he frequently says, as he does in *The Danger of Desertion* (1640), that "riches, honors, and ease . . . will never establish a man . . . but his soul shall be gravelled and troubled. It must be the God of peace that must speak peace to a troubled soul."[51]

Hooker even finds it necessary, while speaking of morality and the way in which it follows justification, to point out that the practicing Christian may find that affliction rather than ease is his reward. As a result, a frequent admonition is that one must be able to endure hardships: "Every follower of Christ hath affliction allotted to him as a childes part." Afflictions are the saint's regular diet but "are no argument of Gods displeasure, sore persecution is no argument of a mans bad condition, but an ensigne of grace and goodnesse." Thus it is necessary for the believer to take up his cross with meekness and with great inner strength, always remembering "that all the promises of God are entailed upon the grace of Perseverance."[52] Hooker and most twentieth-century Christian theologians are in agreement in concluding, then, that it is not easy to be a Christian and that the rewards are not monetary or even tangible. Just as several major shifts in thought were involved in moving from the first-generation American Puritans' lack of primary concern for morality to Cotton Mather's *Bonifacius* and Franklin's "Art of Virtue," so was it a long way from the Puritan spiritual ethics of a Thomas Hooker to a later day's "Way to Wealth."

14

The Limits of Reason
GLORY AND WONDER

It is perhaps more than mere coincidence that the sermons which Hooker is known to have been preaching shortly before his death in July of 1647 deal with the final stage in the life of the saint. It seems safe to assume that he felt himself to be in that stage in his own spiritual life. But even more than this, it is clear that the consideration of glorification and the saint's ultimate union with God posed a special challenge to Hooker, as it did to any who might undertake to explain it. It is the stage in the *ordo salutis* which, above all others, challenges the preacher's descriptive and analytical powers. In the case of Hooker, in fact, it demonstrates the important fact that, for all of his confidence in his ability to lay out a clear map of the saint's way to heaven, he knew there were limits to his ability and his knowledge. In his sermons on glory, Hooker faced these limits and forthrightly admitted that he had reached the point in his explication of redemption—and probably in his own spiritual life—beyond which the reasoning faculty simply cannot go. His manner of dealing with glorification serves as a useful reminder that for all of its rationality the Puritan mind was far from being simply a reasoning machine.

For the Calvinist saint the highest hope and reward was to see and share in the glory of Christ in heaven. This process actually begins for the elect on this side of the grave, but its full realization must wait for the soul's final entry to heaven. Richard Sibbes called glorification the last link in "the golden chayne of salvation." In the final stage of one's earthly life, one arrives at the end of this chain, experiencing "the beginning of glory here; for all is not kept for the life to come, for God distils some drops of glory before hand."[1] As Samuel Willard later explained, glorification is a necessary extension of the experiencing of grace: "A state of Grace, and of Glory, have but their gradual differences: Grace is Glory begun, Glory is Grace finished or perfected: Grace is the seed whereof glory is the genuine Fruit: Grace, if it dy not, will bring forth glory undoubtedly; but it cannot dy, being an immortal seed, and abiding. True grace is a spring that never ceaseth flowing till it reach eternal Life."[2] In glorification, then, there is a built-in sense of climax. It is the beginning of the much-sought glorious end.

Hooker pursued his story of the Christian's pilgrimage all the way to this final stage of glorification in the book of sermons which in 1647 he was apparently simultaneously preaching and writing out in the manuscript which would be published a decade later as the last volume in his *summa* on the application of redemption. This major work of more than four hundred pages of octavo text is modestly entitled *A Comment upon Christs Last Prayer in the Seventeenth of John*. It gives evidence throughout that its author was conscious of describing the outer limits of spiritual experience and of putting his own rational and descriptive powers to their fullest test. He talks of the final stage in the life of the elect as being "the highest peak of happiness," the "highest step and stair" of human aspiration. The experience described is a culmination of the spiritual life, just as the act of describing it through a series of sermons represented for Hooker the ultimate extension of the minister's prophetic and rational powers. Finally, in fact, it was just a shade beyond those powers. He could *begin* to describe the experience, but inevitably his subject would outdistance him. Again and again throughout this final book Hooker calls his subject matter "unconceivable," "amazing," "mysterious," "incomprehensible." He saw his material as demanding not intellectual arrogance on the part of the preacher whose job it is to explain such doctrines but modesty, which often becomes simple awe, "wonderment." Here at the end of the long journey of the soul Hooker at times is willing to make the unfamiliar admission that he has stretched his mind as far as it will go and that there is still more beyond which must simply remain undescribed. He guides his people to the "highest peak" of the Hill Difficulty while at the same time admitting the limits of his own human abilities as a spiritual pathfinder. It is not that Hooker has suddenly become halting and insecure in his task but rather that his account of the long, steady ascent into the increasingly rarefied atmosphere of heavenly hope has simply reached a point beyond which no man can see clearly. Thus, in *A Comment* Hooker reflects more moments of mystical wonder than in any other work, revealing a dimension of his and the Puritan mind which it is all too easy to ignore but which is an essential component of the whole.[3]

This element of his work's emphasis is present from the very beginning of the book, where, having announced that he is going to preach a series of sermons on the last prayer of Christ, the prayer spoken in the Garden of Gethsemane on the night of Jesus' betrayal and capture, Hooker is hard pressed to find adequate superlatives to describe the importance of the prayer to mankind. He offers, not syntactically complete and rationally analytical sentences, but a series of clauses in which he seems to be searching for the phrase which will satisfactorily capture the essence of the high and mysterious doctrines he is about to approach. He calls the last prayer of Christ "a Prayer of unconceiveable and incomparable worth, above al that ever was expressed or recorded in the word: Like a confection or compound of those soveraigne excellencies; beyond the highest strayn of the desires or conceivings of the souls of the Saints. That which containes the quintessence or the pith of al the cordialls of the Gospel; the very marrow of al that great redemption, he had wrought and purchased: the highest pitch of al that happiness, which Heaven can afford, or the very richest Diamond in the crown of Glory."[4] Here Hooker's power to reduce theological complexity and scriptural good news to a communicable metaphor clearly falters. Except for the last phrase in the passage, containing a metaphor which will recur several times in the course of the book, the suggestions of figurative characterization of glory are at best stuttering and partial. Words like "confection," "cordialls," and "marrow," though they have figurative quality, are not fully developed metaphors. The terms which carry the weight of meaning are the superlative adjectives and adverbs "incomparable," "unconceiveable," "highest," "very," and "richest." These terms do not provide the visual or experiential equivalent which is customary in Hooker's descriptions of the spiritual world.

Yet such terms do suggest his sense of the climactic importance of this work's subject matter. The degree to which the miracle of grace exceeds the powers of human imagination and discourse is, in fact, a constant refrain—explicit and implicit—of this entire volume, perhaps most summarily expressed as Hooker begins to consider the second verse in his scriptural text. Having just finished an explanation of how Christ in his last prayer was praying only for believers, Hooker reads John 17:21 and then observes that "from this 21. verse to the end [of the chapter], we have the matter of our Saviors prayer in a most high, heavenly, and mysterious manner laid forth and presented to our consideration; wherein the incomprehensible worth of his love and wisdom seems to contend for precedency; and in truth both incomparable in themselves, & unconceiveable by the shallow scantling of the weak and feeble capacity of the Sons of Men" (*CCLP*, p. 35). While we should not expect such a meticulous spiritual analyst as Hooker to be put off entirely by such difficulties, he makes no secret of his sense that in this work he is climbing in an increasingly rarefied atmosphere of metaphysical truth. He ends the entire book on this note when in his penultimate Use, a Use of admiration, he remarks that Christ's mercy to sinners "is the wonderment of Angels, and the astonishment of Devils. And we should be amazed at this mysterious mercy" (p. 531).

The four hundred pages between the two statements just quoted[5] are by no means entirely in this vein of mystical awe at God's transcendence of the powers of human reason. Hooker approaches a number of important theological topics in his usual manner, combining analytical, experimental, and narrative methods. Still, there is a difference in this book which is most evident in two ways. In the first place, these sermons do not put so large a stress on elaborately detailed Uses as was his usual habit in his earlier work. This does not always mean that there are fewer Uses per sermon; in fact, nowhere else in his canon do we find as many as the eight which conclude one of his efforts in A Comment.[6] But the practical Applications do tend to be brief, frequently lacking the detailed analogic extension of the Doctrines to the everyday lives of the hearers that had become Hooker's preaching trademark. Perhaps this is explained in part by a second distinctive feature of this work, which is the relatively theoretical nature of its subject matter. The key issues in A Comment upon Christs Last Prayer include the meaning of divine love, the exact nature of the relationship between the Father and the Son, the roles in redemption of the various members of the Trinity, the meaning of the crucial term glory, and even the nature of heavenly happiness. The empirical approach to religion in the face of such issues must often take a back seat to pure theology.

In this regard A Comment resembles The Application of Redemption, The first eight Books more than any other Hooker work. As in that contemporary work, A Comment addresses a number of fundamental tenets of Hooker's theology—tenets without which he could never have constructed his conversion morphology. The whole notion that an undeserving soul can hope to go from spiritual degradation to heavenly glory depends upon the doctrinal tenets explained in A Comment. One important example can be seen on pages 56 through 76, where Hooker takes up the subject of God the Father's sending His Son to mankind. Nothing is more fundamental to the whole structure of faith and redemption than the belief that God intentionally sent His Son to live on earth. "Hereby the great work of our Redemption comes to be discovered, comes also to be acknowledged; when once this sending our Savior is rightly understood. Its the very Hinge upon which the Gospel turns: The very foundation, upon which the work of our Salvation hangs" (*CCLP*, p. 75). It is typical of Puritanism's intricate theological rationale and of the seemingly random structure of this book as well that discussion of this "hinge" involves Hooker in a partial explanation of the different roles of each of the members of the Trinity. Christ and the Father are one and the same in the Godhead, but in the matter of Christ's being sent, Jesus is God-man, as the Father and the Holy Spirit never are, and thus Christ is the center of the sinner's hope. The discussion of the different roles of Father and Son ultimately leads Hooker to an examination of certain of the Father's special characteristics, including Fidelity, Righteousness, Sovereignty, and Mercy. One basic theological issue spills over very readily into another. This sermon on "sending" begins by saying that Christ's last prayer aims chiefly at the praise of God's sovereignty, but the same sermon ends by giving great emphasis to God's mercy. The sermon thus involves an examination of the nature of God, the importance of the doctrine of the Trinity, and the relationship between this doctrinal theory and the all-important "work of our Redemption." The tenets mesh of their own accord. What we have, essentially, is an examination of the fundamental issues of the Puritan's covenant theology, which was itself a theological "hinge" on which the Puritan's hope for salvation turned.

But not only does *A Comment upon Christs Last Prayer* backtrack to the theological foundations of the soul's hope for grace; it also describes the climax of this whole process for the elect saint who has found his way from sinful corruption to heavenly glory. This is why Thomas Goodwin and Philip Nye published it as the seventeenth and last book in Hooker's *summa;*[7] it belongs at the end. In seeing *A Comment* as the final installment of this multivolume work, we need to remember, as the original editors pointed out, that the sermons in this last volume were preached "at the *Administration of the Lords Supper.*" In fact, the work deals directly with the sacrament of Communion only very rarely, though this context is always implied by Hooker's basing the entire work on the last prayer of Christ, which was offered on the night of the Last Supper. Yet Hooker's lengthy and sometimes redundant discussions of the soul's ultimate union and communion with Christ are motivated by the participation of the minister and his congregation in the sacrament of Communion, where spiritual communion between the faithful and their Lord was especially experienced and celebrated. One notes that Hooker's concern for Communion, while implicitly recognizing the importance of this sacrament, does not result in a stress on the symbolic importance of the elements of bread and wine themselves, as is so often the case, for instance, in Edward Taylor's private *Medita-*

tions, where the bread and wine as representative of Christ's body and blood are crucial to Taylor's sacramental symbology.[8] Hooker, though careful at one point to disassociate himself from the transsubstantiationist "conceit of the Capernaites, and the Papists" (*CCLP,* p. 113), chooses to stress the *ultimate* communion of the soul with Christ rather than to emphasize the recognition of such a union through the ordinance of Communion in Hartford Church on a given Sunday morning. The Communion service is thus clearly a "means" for Hooker, and he prefers to concentrate on the end to which it leads rather than on the means itself.

There is no doubt that Hooker sees the union between Christ and the believer as the climactic event in the Christian experience. It is equally clear that his description of this union is the climax of his own life's work. He begins his discussion of the text of Christ's last prayer by expounding on the Doctrine that "the chief Priviledg of the Saints, for which our Savior especially prayes, is; That they all may be one" (*CCLP,* p. 38). Christ's "choicest legacy," he says, is this unity of believers. But here he says he will "step aside from the common Road" in his interpretation. Most are inclined to say that this unity involves a "unity of amity, of love, and mutual and spiritual accord," a unity "of the same mind and Heart" among all Christians (p. 39), a fellowship of believers.[9] This is true, says Hooker, but it is not exactly what Christ was praying for. Rather, he was asking that each individual believer would be united with *him* and—since Christ is united to the Father—with the Father as well. There is an individual relationship with God, in other words, that must precede any hope of a Christian community. "The unity of affection or charity" between believers in society is secondary and pursuant to the primary relationship of unity "to Christ, and in him to God the Father" (p. 40). It is in this close relationship with both the Son and the Father, a relationship experienced fully at last in heaven, that man's glory resides. Once again, as in so many other parts of Hooker's redemption message, the individual's relationship with God is the central concern. Whether we are looking at Thomas Hooker as congregationalist, as voluntarist, or as spiritual psychologist, social relationships and social covenants always remain subordinate to the individual's concerns and the covenant of faith.

The final section of *A Comment* dwells on this union between Christ and believer—a condition of the soul beyond which, he insists, it is impossible to go, conceptually or spiritually. He again finds the familiar staircase metaphor especially appropriate to his description of the saint's gaining the highest possible level of spiritual fulfillment. He explains that the "chief aim" of Christ's last prayer was to ensure that the saints might be admitted to heaven, not to enjoy it for their own sakes, but so that they might behold the glory of Jesus Christ because "the Sight of his Glory is the highest step and stair of ours" (*CCLP*, p. 368). This is a contemplation of God which, for Hooker as for the more purely neo-Platonist Renaissance Christians, is the highest experience in one's existence, the end toward which all else leads. Hooker rhapsodizes on this attainment of the top stair, saying that one's ultimate union and communion with Christ is "the top of our happiness in Heaven" (p. 521). To go any farther than this, as he points out, would be to go beyond Christ, "which is unreasonably and unconceivably absurd." He has thus shown the reader and listener how to climb to the very top of the long staircase leading from "the lower-most Hel of sin and wretchedness, . . . the greatest estrangement from God" to "the neerest union and communion with God" (pp. 530, 531).

This achievement of a sense of structural as well as theological climax was accomplished by Hooker's approaching the biblical text, John 17:20–26, rather methodically, discussing it verse by verse, phrase by phrase. The book's editors, Goodwin and Nye, did not entirely conceal their criticism of this loose structural method when, in their "Epistle to the Reader," they implied that "this miscellaneous Treatment" and "Precursory handling" of such important subjects is at least better than none, "especially from so good a Hand, or Heart rather, so deeply experienced, and acutely insighted, as was our Author." Goodwin and Nye did not notice, however, that Hooker had actually managed to build into his book an additional structural principle beyond mere sequence of the verses in John 17 by proceeding from the doctrine of election and the act of Christ's "sending" to the saint's glorification. For the work does progress chronologically from the divine antecedents to the birth of Christ to the final full realization of the purpose of that birth in the saint's glorification. In this triumphant climax to both this volume and Hooker's lifelong explication of the sinner's progress to heaven, Hooker has seemingly made the most of what in the hands of less resourceful Puritan preachers might have been a merely slavish adherence to the successive verses of a biblical text. His "miscellaneous treatment" of seven verses of Scripture becomes nothing less than a structured consideration of the alpha and the omega of Puritan spiritual existence. In this respect *A Comment* has more sweep, a more comprehensive view of God's purpose for his people, than Hooker's other books. But this book's main purpose is nonetheless to focus on the final stage of redemption, so he moves purposefully to the subject of glorification.

Hooker several times undertakes to define *glory*. He says first that glory "somtimes signifies that unconceiveable excellency of al that incomprehensible worth and infinite goodness, that is in the Lord" (*CCLP*, p. 78). This meaning he renders more successfully as he adds visual imagery: "The shine and lustre of al those glorious Attributes of the Lord meeting together in that infinite fulness, as they be in him, like the beauty of so many thousand Suns in the Firmament, that is called, the GLORY of GOD, with which the Eyes of blessed Angels are dazelled, as not able to behold it, and therefore cover their faces. *Isa.* 6." But this is not a glory which the earth-bound faithful can share and is not the primary meaning of *glory* as the term is used in Hooker's analysis. In fact, he goes on to say, glory *is* grace, simply because "there is the greatest worth in it, greatest beauty Issues from it, the greatest esteem and highest account is acknowledged to be due thereunto by those who can judg" (p. 78). Christ had this grace in fullest measure, and he in turn gives it to his believers.

But despite this initial wish to equate grace and glory, Hooker usually uses the term *glory* in a way which is not quite synonymous with *grace*. So he offers a three-part "general" definition of the concept about midway through the book and then in a later sermon identifies glory more specifically as the final stage in the life of the saint. In these discussions, two qualities of glory emerge as most important, including, first, the worth or "excellency" of a thing which serves to put it above all other things (*CCLP*, pp. 325–26). This, in the more specific application of the definition, is described as "the worth and excellency of such Graces and Perfections, which are in Christ" (p. 368). "Grace whereby wee resemble Christ is glory," said Richard Sibbes.[10] A second way of using the term is to mean "the expression, and putting forth of such perfections" (p. 368). Glory, then, involves a supreme worth and supreme ability to act out, to shadow forth (as Christ does) that worth or to receive it (as do the redeemed). These qualities and abilities are precisely what the saint acquires when he receives grace.

A corollary of this discussion of glory is Hooker's frequent mention of the resurrection and ascension of Christ. These events, which express God's glory through Christ, are also acts which are repeated in the spiritual experience of all the faithful. This doctrinal concern supports Hooker's conceptual structuring of the life of the saint as an ongoing process and an ascending progression. The neo-Platonic/Augustinian pattern of spiritual experience at this end of the saint's journey, going from low to high, earth to heaven, bondage to freedom, is climaxed by resurrection—new birth of the redeemed—and finally by ascension to Heaven.[11] He finds his reasons for this pattern of spiritual life in Christian typology. Christ was of course "the second *Adam*," but since he had the power to raise bodies from the grave and to make them become spiritual bodies with continued life in heaven, his power "was beyond the power of Adam." By consequence, the "posterity of the second *Adam*" is better off than the posterity of even the prelapsarian Adam could have been. "The Faithful shal be raised and Translated from Earth to Heaven: whereas, had *Adam* stood in Paradise, he and his posterity had injoyed an earthly paradise, that is, God there only" (*CCLP*, p. 217). It is obviously better to be with God in heaven than on earth. We are especially fortunate, then, says Hooker, that we, the faithful, partake of Christ's resurrection and ascension to heaven as a part of our glorification. Mankind, through Christ, has thus advanced beyond the state of Adam even before the fall. Christ, being part of God, has been given glory by the Father and in turn gives it to his faithful. Richard Sibbes, in quoting Christ's prayer, says simply, "His glory is our glory,"[12] which is precisely what Hooker wants understood by all gracious people.

It is important to understand Hooker's use of the Adam-Christ typology at this stage, since it distinguishes his position from the positions of both sides of a dualism which has been argued by recent scholarship. Having particular reference to the Antinomian controversy, Jesper Rosenmeier has argued that Cotton's claim that the saints acquire the image of Christ in their justification is the key point distinguishing his position from that of the other leaders of Massachusetts Bay in the controversy.[13] Cotton's opponents, Rosenmeier claims, citing Thomas Shepard as their representative, believed that the change in the gracious Christian consists of a return to Adam's nature. Thus, in Cotton's view history is progressive; the regenerate soul is spiritually beyond and above the position of Adam. Shepard's supposedly orthodox view, on the other hand, presents history as circular, with the regenerate man simply returning to a version of Adam's innocence and preferment in the eyes of God.

Knowing that Hooker firmly opposed Cotton's views in the Antinomian controversy, we would expect Hooker to share the views of Shepard in this issue as in the others central to the dispute. And indeed, his earlier *Paterne of Perfection* involves an almost purely typological exploration of the traits of Adam which are worthy of imitation by all people. Hooker's aim there, however, was to get at the varying natures of man and God. His use of the prelapsarian Adam as exemplary *figura* worthy of everyone's imitation is a characteristic Puritan approach. In his later *Comment upon Christs Last Prayer*, however, his views vary widely from those of Shepard which Rosenmeier lays out. In the later work, though Hooker is not chiefly intending to present a theory of history, he clarifies what many of his earlier works had implied: that history is progressive, at least insofar as the modern believer, by acquiring full faith and entering true communion with Christ, enjoys a richer blessing of preferment than had Adam. We have already noticed how Hooker, when describing the saint's acquistion of faith, takes pains to point out that Adam never had to struggle to acquire faith, so that in effect, faith as we know it was a concept unfamiliar to Adam. In this respect, the new man moves beyond Adam himself. And we have seen how in the same manner the covenant of grace represents an improvement upon the covenant of works. Now at the point of the fullest earthly fruition of man's faith, the new man again clearly surpasses Adam in status. Christ was greater in power than Adam, and it is Christ with whom the elect enjoy union and through whom they unite with the Father in full glorification. Hooker even goes so far as to argue that since there is a contrary force working within many to prevent the soul's redemption, God's creation of a gracious Christian involves more power and wonder than his original creation of the world, where there was no contrary force in operation.[14] Moreover, Hooker explicitly states that the modern saint's relationship with God is a fuller one than was Adam's. Man's soul in grace engages with the Father, the Son, and the Holy Ghost "in the most initmate Union that can be imagined. Not as the Branches to the Vine, *John*, 15.1. nor as the Members to the Head, *Eph.* 1.22. but yet *neerer*, they are *bone of his bone, and flesh of his flesh*, . . . and this is beyond the compass of al that sufficiency, and excellency God implanted in *Adam*." Usually, however, it is simply the relationship between the soul and Christ that Hooker stresses. "*Adam*," he says, "had *Supernatural* Grace," but the grace of the faithful is "*more than Supernatural;* for that was not able to incorporate the Soul into Christ" (*CCLP*, p. 160).

A somewhat paradoxical element is added to Hooker's distinction between Adam and the new saint when he says that Adam was able to do all that he did from innate principles which "he had received, and the Lord had implanted in his Nature, coming into the World, gifted and qualified," while man does all that he does through the immediate assistance and action of God (*CCLP*, p. 160). Several times in the course of the book Hooker reminds his readers and listeners of Paul's statement that he did not live from a principle within himself. The *absence* of this innate ability is repeatedly cited by Hooker as a sign of the faithful soul's higher elevation than Adam and a cause for rejoicing. "Christ . . . hath given al unto them [the faithful]; for *all things are yours, and you Christs;* yea, *he hath advanced them, and set them in*

Heavenly places with Christ, their Bodies made Spiritual, which *Adams* could not be" (pp. 163–64).

God's relationship to Adam was quite literally that of a father, says Hooker, in that he gave him all his attributes, just as an earthly father is responsible, through sexual "generation," for the attributes of his son. But the gracious have a better relationship with God because they "look not to the Love of a Father meerly, but to the Love of his Faithfulness, and that wil not fail, nor shall they ever fal from it" (*CCLP*, p. 389). The latter distinction from the situation of Adam is of course all-important. Man, who is in his own *nature* much inferior to Adam, is by the great love of God, made superior in his *situation* to Adam because through grace he is set beyond the danger of a ruinous fall. And it is the very fact that it is *not* man's work which brings this incomparable good to him which must be especially noticed: "Herein lies the Crown of this glory, the Diadem of this Crown, the excellency above the happiness of Heaven, that none of al this did come from a man, by the power of any [human] Grace, or performance of any work" (p. 169).

This superiority of the condition of the faithful saint to that of the prelapsarian Adam is summarized in the distinction, which Hooker notices here in some detail, between the covenant of works and the covenant of grace. In the covenant of grace, to which God has bound himself entirely willingly, he does everything for man, thus expressing the immensity of his love for his elect. This loving-kindness by God is epitomized in Christ's coming as a man to earth. He put himself under the Father and made himself subject to undeserved punishment for the sake of his faithful, whom he promised the Father he would protect and guide back to heaven. This kind of love was never expressed to Adam simply because he did not need it. So much the better for the faithful today, says Hooker, since it is in fulfilment of the covenant of grace that man is enabled to enter into union with Christ.

There is thus a noticeable difference between the way Hooker talks about Adam and Christ as types and the way they are used in Shepard's arguments. This of course does not make Hooker an Antinomian. Rather, it suggests that his subject, glorification, a stage after justification and sanctification, forces him to think about the life of the soul as progressive while also moving him to a direct confrontation with the aspect of experience which is most mystical and mysterious. The yearning soul, having struggled through all the lower levels of the progression, is now ready for the ultimate experience. In glorification, as Ames explained, all that had been *potential* in the earlier stages of redemption becomes "real."[15] One now also glimpses in those fleeting moments of mystical awareness the full value of having shifted the burden of Adam's postlapsarian nature off one's back in becoming "married" to Christ. It is now Christ the husband and guardian, not Adam the brother, who gives the believer his identity.

Though it is common to observe that preparationist preachers, because of the seeming "legalism" of their depiction of the sequential stages of grace, were less likely than others to reflect a mystical side, this distinction is not exclusive or totally reliable. Certainly no man was a more profoundly committed preparationist than Thomas Hooker, and yet many of his works reflect a willingness to respond to God's love and mercy with awe and wonder. The ultimate experience for mystics has always been communion with the Divine, the experience to which Hooker's logically elaborated series of phases in the spiritual life inexorably guides him and his listeners.[16] So we find him recognizing that the powers of comprehension of even the most learned scholars characteristically falter on the doctrine of Christ and the sinner's union. In referring to John 17:23, for instance, he says, as he almost never does in any of his other works, that "there be some depths in some passages of the verse which are fitter to be admired, than comprehended, and exceed the reach, and discovery of the most Judicious Interpreter, that I can look into, and indeed, seem to be reserved for another world" (CCLP, p. 110). In the same vein is his previously mentioned frequent recourse to such words as "unconceiveable," "incomprehensible," "mysterious," "miraculous," "infinite," and "Splendida peccata." The reiteration of such terms indicates a sense—doubtless somewhat frustrating—on Hooker's part that not only are the powers of reason and imagination inadequate to the task of describing the union which is involved in glorification and the love of God which it exemplifies, but that language itself stumbles and falls short of the effects demanded of it.

Hooker had occasionally resorted to Uses of admiration or Uses of wonderment in his earlier sermons, especially where God's love for grossly unworthy men was his topic. He would sometimes explicitly suggest a stance of wonderment to his listeners as the most appropriate reaction, as in saying, "Let us stand amazed, and wonder at the admirable goodnesse, the riches of the kindnesse of the Lord, together with the depth of the stubbornnesse, rebellion, and evill of the soule."[17] The great contrast between God and man is most evident in the moment of recognition of God's love by the fortunate soul.[18] In the same vein, the following scattered passages are representative:

> Goe home and stand agast and amazed at the admirable unconceiveable goodnesse of the Lord to a poore miserable, sinfull,

damned creature. . . . This is not mercy, but the depth of mercy; this is not compassion only, but the bowells of compassion.

I thinke I shall never be able to conceive of the truths of God aright, how can the Lord accept of mee, when I condemne my selfe? . . . You would wonder that God should save such as you, and truly so you may well enough; for it is a wonder, it is a miracle indeed.

Indeed, it is a wonder, that we can thinke of [becoming the "Sonnes of God"] without wondering.

[Use of wonderment over the] everlasting admiration of this un-conceivable, unmatchable kindness of the Lord.[19]

Implicit in such passages is a basic humility on the part of this speaker about his own powers of reason and his own ability to convey all the subtleties of the Word and the nature of God described therein. Finally, in *A Comment,* Hooker resorts to a rhetoric of superlatives. The inadequacy of this literary approach is sometimes all too evident, as for instance in the following passage, where the topic is the Father's love for the Son: "The love of the Father being of greatest excellency, even of unconceivable vertue & efficacy, & our Savior being of un-matchable likeness to draw out the love of the Father, and incompara-ble worth to deserve it, it could not be, but so great love should give the greatest good to one of greatest desert: and therefore must give him that incomprehensible glory, which might be the amazement of the hearts of men and Angels, through al eternity" (*CCLP,* p. 348). In such a passage we are treated to a flood of superlatives but to very little of the more familiar and more successful substantiation of con-cepts through the use of figurative language which is the strength of Hooker's best prose.

The mixture of awe with considered metaphorical equivalents is somewhat more successful, however, in one of the longest passages of sheer wonderment in the entire volume. It comes at the very begin-ning of a sermon on the final two verses of Christ's prayer, John 17:25–26.[20] Hooker stresses the climactic quality of the final sentences of this prayer, mainly by constructing metaphors suggesting extreme altitude and brilliance, and in the context of these metaphors he is better able to superimpose superlatives on superlatives. In the follow-ing two paragraphs he conveys his own spiritual wonderment with his imagery of mountain peaks and gems in rulers' crowns; but the success of the passage is insured by the imagistic and syntactical shift in the surprising and summary last sentence (here punctuated as a final four-word independent clause):

We are then come to the Pinnacle of the perfection of happiness it self, and there seems to be somthing more, & one step higher, than the glorious Grace of Heaven; look we only to the glory of that Grace, that shal be imprinted upon the Saints and perfected in them at that time.

Here we have the Diamond of the Crown of glory even the love of the Father whereby he hath loved Christ himself, and which is better than life it self, or sanctifying Grace it self, when it is come to the greatest perfection, as we shal indeavor to speak to it, when we come to that place. Its the last resolution of *Pauls* confidence, and the top of the rock, whereon the Soul rests, Its beyond al gunshot. (*CCLP*, p. 384)

A Comment contains numerous other examples of Hooker's practice and advocacy of wonderment over the doctrine of the "glorious excellency" of God's love for unworthy man, but the passages already cited indicate clearly enough why two of the pillars of Hooker's Hartford congregation summarized his pastoral character after his death by saying that his "spirit most delighted in the search of the mystery of Christ, in the unsearchable riches thereof, and the work and method of the spirit, in the communication of the same unto the soul for its everlasting welfare."[21] Hooker had indeed been stressing "the mystery of Christ" and the "unsearchable riches" of the love of God in his last weeks. There was probably no dramatic shift in his last years to a more mystical interpretation of the ways of grace than he had held to earlier in his career. The difference rests in the subject rather than in him. In the Pauline-Calvinist insistence on sanctification's following justification and on the consequent acquisition of "habitual" grace, the life of the saint becomes increasingly controlled by the mysterious power of God's spirit, so that, in following the history of the redeemed soul to its ultimate resting place in the happiness of heaven, Hooker's themes and his style necessarily reflected more of his sense of the "inexplicable" aspects of the truths that he had spent a lifetime in explaining. At the end of his impressive, tangible description of intangible, psychological-spiritual experience, Hooker gave his congregation more of that mystical element which all along had "stood . . . at the very heart of Puritan faith"[22] than he had at earlier points in his explication. At the end of it all—and, as it turned out, at the end of his own earthly days—he was not at all a legalist or a proud Puritan rationalist. He was the amazed and fallible believer. For all of his exceptional ability to *explain*, then, we miss an important element in the man if we do not give due notice to his willingness to come to rest finally in a recognition of the failure of reason in the face of a God whose full attributes are, in the last analysis, beyond man's finding out.

The student who seeks to discover early roots for the mystical elements of American thought which became dominant in Emerson and Thoreau need not go back just to Edwards or just to Edward Taylor, though both are surely part of the continuum. He can go all the way back to the first-generation Hooker, whose own congregation well knew his "rellish" of the mystical elements of the spiritual life, even though modern readers have often been inclined to stress his and his colleagues' rationality above all. Having gone back to him, of course, one can readily trace the direct influences back through Richard Sibbes in England,[23] the early Renaissance neo-Platonists, Augustine, Paul and John. That is material for other studies. It is enough here to affirm that Thomas Hooker's voluntarist, preparationist stance was supple and broad enough to incorporate within it the genuinely mystical wonderment and awe that would be still another major facet of the American literary imagination in the centuries ahead.

Conclusion

For all of his memorable achievements in the external world, Thomas Hooker comes down to us most clearly as a voice. He was indeed a founder and a defender of the New England Way, but his strength in this role derived from his capacity to use the word. It was in his overlapping roles as prophet and shepherd that he had his most immediate impact on his contemporaries. And in his masterful execution of these roles he has a lasting appeal and importance to later generations.

As this examination of Hooker's writings has shown perhaps above all, the primary distinguishing characteristic of his best work is its vital energy. This reveals not only a quality of temperament but a philosophical commitment. Indeed, as he wrote of the stages in the Christian life and of particular dilemmas in the seventeenth-century Puritan's confrontation of worldly events, he developed what can best be called an activist aesthetic. While constantly urging his audience to an active, dynamic spiritual life, he remained aware that such a life was not easy, did not come naturally to most people. His sense of the need for constant searching, struggling, and laboring added integrity and believability to his message and thus increased his appeal to his immediate audience. Indeed, long after the doctrines of the Puritans had dropped away, major American thinkers and writers echoed his respect for the sense of difficulty in any attempt to assert the primacy of things of the spirit in a fallen world. Emerson, though in many respects characterized by a post-Calvinist frame of mind, carried forward the Hookerian sense of the individual's need to "explore the Active powers," to practice "the higher discipline of the heroic" in exerting one's soul to fuller, more productive activity.[1] Indeed, the Puritans' most fundamental legacy to later days in American life may be simply their full awareness of this constant tension between the present condition—of one's soul or of the nation's character—and the desired goal. If the great necessity for heroic exertion of the soul against the forces which oppose the principles of ideal fulfillment is repeatedly a major motif in the work of such varied authors as John Woolman, Ralph Waldo Emerson, Henry David Thoreau, Nathaniel Hawthorne, Herman Melville, Emily Dickinson, Henry James, T. S. Eliot, and William Faulkner, it merely serves as clear corroborative evidence of the degree to which Thomas Hooker had exposed a basic element in the American grain in his own writings. For it is in describing and dramatizing in his sermons these same tensions in the life of spiritual activity that Thomas Hooker laid permanent claim to our respect as a writer and orator just as fully as he did to our admiration for his achievements as a dynamic leader.

To be sure, Hooker did have a more immediate and identifiable impact on numerous disciples who continued to take his brand of Puritanism to their congregations for much of the rest of the seventeenth century: men such as John Eliot, Thomas Shepard, Samuel Stone, John Higginson, James Fitch, Edward Taylor, Solomon Stoddard, and his own son Samuel Hooker. Jonathan Edwards himself, as we have noticed, was occasionally touched forcefully by the writings of these men, and he is certainly a part of what has lately been called the "Connecticut Valley intellectual tradition," an important legacy of which Thomas Hooker was the original progenitor.[2] So while the doctrines and central spiritual commitment of the early days of Calvinist New England faded with the advent of the Age of Enlightenment, significant vestiges of the Hookerian tradition of expression did survive well beyond that era. His special literary method introduced a manner of thinking and a mode of depicting intangible experience which would ultimately occupy a central position in expressions of the American sensibility. Hooker perhaps above all his contemporaries introduced the allegorical literary mode into America. He was the first to give a New England habitation to that questing spiritual pilgrim, the Christian Soul, and, even more, to dramatize his adventures. When Hooker's sermons were most fully imaginative, when they most dramatically rendered the tensions, desires, and achievements in the life of this fallen but heroic saint, he most fully strained the limits of his genre, came closest to the creation of a new literary form. Hooker's representative soul, the imagined equivalent of the simple believer in the preacher's congregation, not only preceded Bunyan's Christian and Milton's Adam but also, in America, such secular equivalents as Cooper's Leatherstocking, Melville's Ishmael, Whitman's "Self," and Twain's Huckleberry Finn. All of these figures, had they heard Hooker preach, would have understood and identified with Hooker's Soul going down the road and standing on tiptoe to see over the next high hill, hoping to catch a glimpse of the source of all hope. And all of their creators, had they been able to hear Hooker preach or had they merely read his sermons, could have sensed an affinity—distant as it might at first seem—between his literary methods and their own.

There are, of course, particular connections that one is tempted to make between Hooker's dramatization of the essentials of life and later Americans' versions of them. For instance, though no one has ever proved that Nathaniel Hawthorne read Hooker, despite his well-known familiarity with many unspecified Puritan writers, if the chapter in *The Scarlet Letter* called "The Interior of a Heart" is placed next to Hooker's analysis of contrition in *The Soules Preparation* or Book Ten of *The Application of Redemption*, it becomes obvious that the same dramatic sense of spiritual reality informs them both. By the same token, it might be asked whether there is not more than a faint suggestion of similarity between the officers on Melville's *Pequod*—Ahab, Starbuck, Stubb, and Flask—and a lineup of fully developed Hookerian "characters" representing souls gone wrong because of inherent spiritual or psychological flaws.

These could, of course, be mere coincidences, parallels which defy proof of direct influence. But there remain other, still more fundamental points of relevance between Hooker and the writers of the American Renaissance and later. Most importantly, those writers had an interest which went even deeper than their tendency to imagine heroes in quest of an elusive spiritual ideal. They adopted a symbolic mode of expression which—as Charles Feidelson, Ursula Brumm, Sacvan Bercovitch, and others have shown—had its roots in the expression of the very earliest of the Puritan settlers. American literature's striking tendency to Romance, to symbolic rendering of experiential truth is based on a tendency to read the world emblematically, to accept Emerson's insistence that natural experience is the "dial plate" by which the spiritual dimension of life may be understood. The world before us is full of concrete symbols, signs of the divine force behind all experience. A skillful Puritan preacher such as Hooker, aware as he was of the degree to which the concrete world poses resistance to spiritual truth, sought especially hard for ways to render tangibly and convincingly his vision of that underlying reality. In their typology the Puritans were able to do justice to both their sense of the need to live energetically in the mundane world and their trust in the higher significance of the heavenly kingdom.

It was, finally, Hooker's ability to combine allegory, typology, epic-scale narrative, and sensuously grounded variations of figurative language with a deep understanding of the infinite complexity of human personality that made him such an exceptional interpreter of life to his contemporaries. His message ultimately proved especially suitable for a generation of New World colonists. His story of the epic experience of the elect soul had its equivalent not just in his imagined figures but in the real lives that he and his congregation lived. Through his preaching as well as his example he taught them the identity of a people transplanted into a fruitful garden. His was a clear and powerful voice in the wilderness, a prophecy which embodied the myth of a chosen people devoted to truth. For Hooker as for later generations of American interpreters of their cultural experience, the importance of America's promise was that it was spiritual as well as material. He firmly believed that for a movement from an Old World to a New World to realize its full potential and significance, it must be accompanied by a parallel movement within each person from the carnal world to the spiritual world. In his ability to make this movement seem both necessary and possible lies the particular secret of Thomas Hooker's success as a messenger of God.

Reference Matter

Notes

INTRODUCTION

1 Here and later in this study, except where otherwise noted, details of Hooker's life are from George Huntston Williams, "The Life of Thomas Hooker in England and Holland, 1586–1633" in *Thomas Hooker: Writings in England and Holland, 1626–1633*, ed. George Williams, Norman Pettit, Winfried Herget, and Sargent Bush, Jr., Harvard Theological Studies, 28 (Cambridge: Harvard Univ. Press, 1975), pp. 1–35; Williams's earlier biographical sketch, "The Pilgrimage of Thomas Hooker (1586–1647) in England, the Netherlands, and New England," *Bulletin of the Congregational Library*, 19 (Oct. 1967, Jan. 1968), 5–15, 9–13; Frank Shuffelton, *Thomas Hooker, 1586–1647* (Princeton: Princeton Univ. Press, 1977); the earlier but still largely reliable George L. Walker, *Thomas Hooker: Preacher, Founder, Democrat* (New York, 1891); Edward W. Hooker, *The Life of Thomas Hooker* (Boston: Massachusetts Sabbath School Society, 1849); and the single most important source for all of these, Cotton Mather, "Piscator Evangelicus; or, The Life of Mr. Thomas Hooker," in *Johannes in Eremo* (Boston, 1695), which was reprinted with minor revisions as "The Light of the Western Churches; or, The Life of Mr. Thomas Hooker" in Mather's *Magnalia Christi Americana* (Boston, 1702).
2 George Huntston Williams, "Called by Thy Name, Leave Us Not: The Case of Mrs. Joan Drake, A Formative Episode in the Pastoral Career of Thomas Hooker in England," *Harvard Library Bulletin*, 16 (April, July 1968), 111–28, 278–300. Also discussed in Shuffelton, *Thomas Hooker, 1586–1647*, chap. 2.
3 Sacvan Bercovitch, *The American Jeremiad* (Madison: Univ. of Wisconsin Press, 1978), p. 38. This "double focus" is a recurrent interest in Bercovitch's Chapter 2, "The Blessings of Time and Eternity."

Chapter 1: PURITAN PREACHER, SERMON, AND AUDIENCE

1 Darrett B. Rutman, *American Puritanism: Faith and Practice* (Philadelphia: J. B. Lippincott, 1970).

2 Daniel Boorstin, *The Americans: The Colonial Experience* (New York: Random House, 1958), p. 12. The importance of preaching to the Puritan community is discussed by nearly all historians of Puritanism, but see especially Christopher Hill, *Society and Puritanism in Pre-Revolutionary England,* 2nd ed. (New York: Schocken Books, 1967), pp. 30–78; Gordon S. Wakefield, *Puritan Devotion: Its Place in the Development of Christian Piety* (London: Epworth Press, 1957), pp. 11–27; Paul S. Seaver, *The Puritan Lectureships: The Politics of Religious Dissent, 1560–1662* (Stanford: Stanford Univ. Press, 1970), pp. 15–54; David D. Hall, *The Faithful Shepherd: A History of the New England Ministry in the Seventeenth Century* (Chapel Hill: Univ. of North Carolina Press, 1972); Rutman, *American Puritanism,* pp. 1–28; and Emory Elliott, *Power and the Pulpit in Puritan New England* (Princeton: Princeton Univ. Press, 1975).

3 Irvonwy Morgan, *Puritan Spirituality* (London: Epworth Press, 1973), p. 7.

4 Hall, *The Faithful Shepherd,* p. 71.

5 Mather, "Piscator Evangelicus; or, The Life of Mr. Thomas Hooker," in *Johannes in Eremo* (Boston, 1695), pp. 23–24. The phrase "Mr. Hooker's Company" is the designation used by John Winthrop, then governor of Massachusetts Bay. See *Winthrop's Journal: "History of New England,"* *1630–1649,* ed. James Kendall Hosmer (New York: Charles Scribner's Sons, 1908), I, 90.

6 Edward Hopkins and William Goodwin, "To the Reader," in Thomas Hooker, *A Survey of the Summe of Church Discipline* (London, 1648), sig. cv.

7 Samuel Stone, "In Obitum Viri Doctissimi Thomae Hookeri . . .," in Hooker, *A Survey,* sig. c3.

8 John Cotton, "On my Reverend and dear Brother, Mr Thomas Hooker . . .," in Hooker, *A Survey,* sig. [c4].

9 John Fuller, "Epistle," in John Beadle, *The Journal or Diary of a thankful Christian* (London, 1656).

10 Babette M. Levy, *Preaching in the First Half-Century of New England History* (Hartford, Conn.: American Society of Church History, 1945), p. 141.

11 Thomas Hooker (hereafter TH), *The Soules Preparation* (London, 1632), p. 69.

12 TH, *The Application of Redemption, The first eight Books* (London, 1656), p. 3.

13 TH, *The Soules Exaltation* (London, 1638), p. 62.

14 Ibid., p. 86.

15 TH, *The Application of Redemption, The Ninth and Tenth Books* (London, 1656), pp. 98, 101.

16 TH, *A Comment upon Christs Last Prayer* (London, 1656), p. 443.

17 TH, *The Application of Redemption, The first eight Books,* pp. 206–8. A shorter and earlier version of the same comments appears in *The Soules Implantation* (London, 1637), p. 65.

18 TH, *A Survey of the Summe of Church Discipline,* sig. b[1].

19 TH, *The Application of Redemption, The first eight Books,* p. 211.

20 TH, *The Soules Implantation*, p. 66.

21 TH, "The Preface," *A Survey of the Summe of Church Discipline*, sig. a4v.

22 John Higginson (1616–1708), son of the first minister at Salem, was one minister who recorded his debt to Hooker's formal and informal teaching. In an autobiographical preface to a work published late in his long career, Higginson tells of the "special care" given to him in Massachusetts Bay by the magistrates Winthrop, Nowel, and Dummer "and the ministers Mr. Wilson, Mr. Cotton, and Mr. Hooker." Writing of his early ministerial training, he says that "when the forenamed Honoured Gentlemen and Ministers saw meet, I was in the Year 1636. sent and employed by them, in the work of the Ministry (in the time of the *Pequot War*) at *Say-Brook Fort*, where I continued above four Years: and after I had been sometime a *School-Master at Harford* [sic], where I enjoyed the pullick [sic] *Ministry*, and private helpfulness of the Learned and Godly *Mr. Hooker*, and *Mr. Stone*, which was an invaluable mercy to me." "To the Reader" in Higginson, *Our Dying Saviour's Legacy of Peace to his Disciples* (Boston, 1686).

23 TH, *The Christians Two Chiefe Lessons* (London, 1640), p. 203.

24 This observation—sometimes a vehement accusation—is a recurrent one in times of spiritual enthusiasm and dissatisfaction with the established church system and practice. In Elizabethan times one John Bate, apparently a Puritan, in a dialogue between a Christian and a carnal man, had his Christian object that men who are "constant in the faith, painfull to til the Lordes husbandrie, faithful, zealous, watchful, laborious, & of a tried conuersation" are rare in the pulpit, while "oftentimes we see the contrarie, that ignorant men of corrupt conuersation haue that calling [the ministry] granted vnto them." John Bate, *The Portraiture of Hypocrisie* (London, 1589), p. 26. In Hooker's England of the 1620s and 1630s conforming Anglicans as well as half-hearted Puritans were charged with unregeneracy by their opponents, while in New England it would be a common refrain in such contexts as the Antinomian controversy and the Great Awakening a century later. See, for instance, the discussions of this phenomenon in *The Antinomian Controversy, 1636–1638: A Documentary History*, ed. David D. Hall (Middletown, Conn.: Wesleyan Univ. Press, 1968); and chap. 4, "The Danger of an Unconverted Ministry," in Alan Heimert, *Religion and the American Mind* (Cambridge, Mass.: Harvard Univ. Press, 1966), pp. 159–236.

25 TH, *The Application of Redemption, The Ninth and Tenth Books*, pp. 193, 195, 196. This sermon also had earlier publication in a rather different form; see *The Soules Preparation*, pp. 64–80. Sometimes titled *A Plain and Powerful Ministry*, it appears to have been intended for an audience of ministers. It may have been an ordination sermon. And it is possible that it was used as a commencement sermon at Emmanuel and perhaps even at Harvard College, since in it Hooker presumes to teach the ministers in his audience how to preach with the particular application which alone can strike the heart of the sinful listener.

26 TH, *The Soules Implantation*, p. 73.

27 TH, *The Application of Redemption, The Ninth and Tenth Books*, p. 198.

28 Ibid., pp. 198–9.

29 Ibid., pp. 199–200.

30 See A. F. Scott Pearson, *Thomas Cartwright and Elizabethan Puritanism* (Cambridge: Cambridge Univ. Press, 1925), pp. 40–45.

31 TH, *The Application of Redemption, The Ninth and Tenth Books*, p. 200.

32 Ibid., pp. 202, 200, 206, 200.

33 "The Relation of Mr Collins," in *The Diary of Michael Wigglesworth, 1653–1657: The Conscience of a Puritan*, ed. Edmund S. Morgan (New York: Harper and Row, 1965), p. 108 (reprinted from The Colonial Society of Massachusetts, *Transactions, 1942–1946*, vol. 35). Collins's attendance at a Hooker sermon in Cambridge could have occurred during any one of Hooker's several visits to the town from 1638, when Collins and his father settled in Cambridge, until June of 1647, when Hooker last visited there shortly before his death. See John Langdon Sibley, *Biographical Sketches of Graduates of Harvard University* (Cambridge, Mass., 1873), I, 186.

34 See "The Relation of Mr Collins," in *The Diary of Michael Wigglesworth*, pp. 107–21.

35 TH, *The Saints Dignitie and Dutie* (London, 1651), p. 234. John Preston, in a sermon published posthumously, also insisted that "every sermon which is heard sets us nearer Heaven or Hell." *A Pattern of Wholesome Words* (London, 1658), p. 288.

36 TH, *The Saints Dignitie and Dutie*, p. 239.

37 TH, *The Application of Redemption, The Ninth and Tenth Books*, p. 118. In a sermon called *Wisdomes Attendants; or, The Voice of Christ to be Obeyed*, Hooker treats at some length his thoughts on the proper way to "hearken" to the Word. The sermon is on the text in Prov. 8:32: "Now therefore hearken unto me, O ye children, for blessed are they that keep my ways." See *The Saints Dignitie and Dutie*, pp. 121–51.

38 TH, *The Soules Humiliation* (London, 1637), p. 151. See also *Spirituall Thirst* (London, 1637), pp. 25–26, where Hooker says that "God will not deny his Christ to him that thirsteth, because such an one . . . will use the meanes; hee will consciounably heare *Gods* Word, dutifully attend at the posts of Wisedomes doores, and with *Cornelius*, will waite for a faithfull Peter to be taught."

39 TH, *The Soules Effectuall Calling* (London, 1637), p. 70.

40 TH, *The Application of Redemption, The Ninth and Tenth Books*, pp. 118, 109.

41 Ibid., p. 106; TH, *The Application of Redemption, The first eight Books*, p. 296.

42 TH, *The Application of Redemption, The Ninth and Tenth Books*, p. 107.

43 TH, *Foure Learned and Godly Treatises* (London, 1638), p. 178.

44 TH, *The Soules Effectuall Calling*, p. 62.

45 Quoted in William Haller, *The Rise of Puritanism* (New York: Columbia Univ. Press, 1938), pp. 134–35.

46 Mather, "Piscator Evangelicus," p. 9.

47 See *The Workes of . . . William Perkins* (London, 1616–18), II, 668–69; and William Ames, *The Marrow of Sacred Divinity* (London, 1630), pp. 158–59.

48 See Chapters 8 and 14 below.

49 Mather, "Piscator Evangelicus," pp. 14–15.

50 On the general infrequency of hell-fire preaching in New England in the period 1620–70, see, for instance, Perry Miller, *Jonathan Edwards* (New York: William Sloane, 1949), p. 155; and Levy, *Preaching in the First Half-Century of New England History*, p. 25; on Hooker see also Everett H. Emerson, "Thomas Hooker and the Reformed Theology: The Relationship of Hooker's Conversion Preaching to its Background," (Ph.D. diss., Louisiana State Univ., 1955), p. 205; and idem, "Introduction," *Redemption: Three Sermons (1637–1656) by Thomas Hooker* (Gainesville, Fla.: Scholars' Facsimiles and Reprints, 1956), p. xv.

51 TH, *The Soules Exaltation*, p. 197.

52 TH, *The Application of Redemption, The Ninth and Tenth Books*, pp. 330, 331.

53 TH, *The Soules Effectuall Calling*, pp. 350–51.

54 TH, *The Paterne of Perfection* (London, 1640), pp. 255–56.

55 TH, *The Application of Redemption, The first eight Books*, p. 85.

56 TH, *The Saints Guide* (London, 1645), pp. 153–55.

57 TH, *The Vnbeleevers Preparing for Christ* (London, 1638), pt. 1, p. 177.

58 Ibid., p. 178.

59 Hooker, in fact, acknowledges Augustine in saying, "Do you as [Austin] did, and say, why not to day, Lord, why not to day; you could be content on your death beds to be drunke no more, why cannot you as well to day resolve to be sober; the adulterer when he lies upon his death bed wil not endure so much as to look upon his Quene, why should hee not as well abstaine from this base sinne to day, wee know not whether the meanes may be taken from us, or wee from the meanes, and therefore when the Lord saith, *My face seeke you*, answer againe and say, *thy face Lord will we seeke*." Ibid., p. 181.

60 John R. Wilson identifies a millenarian and apocalyptic strain in Puritan preaching during the interregnum, including that of Thomas Goodwin, Jeremiah Burroughs, and others of the Independent group in England and that of John Cotton in New England. See *Pulpit in Parliament: Puritanism during the English Civil Wars, 1640–1648* (Princeton: Princeton Univ. Press, 1969), pp. 223–30.

61 Book Six of *The Application of Redemption, The first eight Books* is on the text in Rev. 3:17; see pp. 283–301. The first long sermon in *The Vnbeleevers Preparing for Christ* uses the text Rev. 22:17; see pt. 1, pp. 1–80.

62 TH, *The Application of Redemption, The first eight Books*, p. 142. David D. Hall speaks directly to the issue of the Puritan ministers' desire to find a "middle way" between the extremes to which Hooker here refers. See Hall, *The Faithful Shepherd*, chap. 1.

Chapter 2: TROUBLES IN THE ENGLISH CHURCH AND COMMONWEALTH

1 Cotton Mather, "Piscator Evangelicus; or, The Life of Mr. Thomas Hooker," in *Johannes in Eremo* (Boston, 1695), p. 30.
2 See the discussion of this experience in George Huntston Williams, "Called by Thy Name, Leave Us Not: The Case of Mrs. Joan Drake, A Formative Episode in the Pastoral Career of Thomas Hooker in England," *Harvard Library Bulletin*, 16 (April, July 1968), 111–28, 278–300.
3 Evidence for such an assertion is simply the striking similarity between versions of particular sermons recorded by different note-takers. See, for instance, the variant versions of Hooker's English 'farewell sermon,' printed as *The Danger of Desertion* (1641) and again as *The Signes of Gods forsaking a People*, in *XXIX Choice Sermons . . . by . . . William Fenner* (London, 1657), pp. 251–62.
4 The works first published from 1645 to 1656, on the other hand, were probably all written in New England. See my bibliography of Hooker's works in *Thomas Hooker: Writings in England and Holland, 1626–1633*, ed. George H. Williams et al., Harvard Theological Studies, 28 (Cambridge: Harvard Univ. Press, 1975), pp. 390–425.
5 See the suggested dating for several early works in the headnotes in Williams et al., *Thomas Hooker: Writings in England and Holland*. Winfried Herget also comments on these problems in "Preaching and Publication: Chronology and the Style of Thomas Hooker's Sermons," *Harvard Theological Review*, 65 (April 1972), 231–39, and in "The Transcription and Transmission of the Hooker Corpus" in *Thomas Hooker: Writings in England and Holland*, pp. 253–70.
6 *Calendar of State Papers, Domestic Series, of the Reign of Charles I*, ed. John Bruce (London, 1859), III, 554. T. W. Davids prints substantial excerpts from the Collins and Browning letters in his *Annals of Evangelical Nonconformity in the County of Essex* (London, 1863), pp. 150–53.
7 Davids, *Annals of Evangelical Nonconformity*, pp. 150, 152.
8 *Calendar of State Papers*, III, 567; Davids, *Annals of Evangelical Nonconformity*, p. 152.
9 Davids, *Annals of Evangelical Nonconformity*, pp. 153, 158.
10 For comments on the methods of the Court of High Commission and on Hooker's response, see Allen French, *Charles I and the Puritan Upheaval: A Study of the Causes of the Great Migration* (Boston: Houghton Mifflin, 1955), pp. 282–84. Details of Hooker's career in this period are more fully treated in George H. Williams, "The Life of Thomas Hooker in England and Holland, 1586–1633" in Williams et al., *Thomas Hooker: Writings in England and Holland*, pp. 18–24; Keith L. Sprunger, "The Dutch Career of Thomas Hooker," *New England Quarterly*, 46 (March 1973), 17–19; and Frank Shuffelton, *Thomas Hooker, 1586–1647* Princeton: Princeton Univ. Press, 1977), pp. 130–33.
11 TH, *The Stay of the Faithfull* (London, 1638), pp. 19, 29.
12 Of the many books on British social history, the following works have been most helpful on the issues discussed in the following pages: Samuel R. Gar-

diner, *History of England from the Accession of James I to the Outbreak of the Civil War, 1603–1642,* vols VI–VII (London, 1884–86); Godrey Davies, *The Early Stuarts, 1603–1660* (Oxford: Clarendon, 1945); French, *Charles I and the Puritan Upheaval;* John Dykstra Eusden, *Puritans, Lawyers, and Politics in Early Seventeenth-Century England* (New Haven: Yale Univ. Press, 1958); and Paul S. Seaver, *The Puritan Lectureships: The Politics of Religious Dissent, 1560–1662* (Stanford: Stanford Univ. Press, 1970), esp. chap. 2, "Preaching and Politics."

13 G. M. Trevelyan, *English Social History: A Survey of Six Centuries, Chaucer to Queen Victoria* (London: Longmans, Green, 1942), p. 209.

14 Gardiner, *History of England,* VI, 198.

15 An unknown correspondent to Rev. Joseph Mead, London, Nov. 16, 1627, in *The Court and Times of Charles the First,* ed. Thomas Birch (London: Henry Colburn, 1848), I, 285; Gardiner, *History of England,* VI, 202.

16 French, *Charles I and the Puritan Upheaval,* p. 210. Gardiner, *History of England,* vols. VI and VII, makes frequent mention of Charles's "incapacity for recognising the real conditions of action" (VI, 22).

17 Quoted in Davies, *The Early Stuarts,* p. 44.

18 See the interesting first-hand account of the dissension surrounding this election in Rev. Joseph Mead to Sir Martin Stuteville, June 3, 1626, in Birch, *Charles the First,* I, 107–9.

19 Nathaniel Ward, writing from New England in the mid-1640s, charged the king with a number of gross evils, including "your own sinful mariage." *The Simple Cobler of Aggawam in America,* ed. P. M. Zall (Lincoln: Univ. of Nebraska Press, 1969), p. 55.

20 Birch, *Charles the First,* I, 363–64.

21 French, *Charles I and the Puritan Upheaval,* p. 101.

22 See Gardiner, *History of England,* VI, 375–76.

23 See Irvonwy Morgan, *Prince Charles's Puritan Chaplain* (London: Allen & Unwin, 1957), pp. 157–71.

24 It was from about this time, as Godfrey Davies has noted, that there was a noticeable increase in references in Puritan sermons to the differences between Calvinism and Arminianism, to the detriment of the Arminian position, a tendency which is amply represented in Hooker's sermons from the period. See Davies, "English Political Sermons, 1603–1640," *Huntington Library Quarterly,* 3 (Oct. 1939), 13.

25 See Seaver, *The Puritan Lectureships,* pp. 240–66.

26 In John Rushworth, ed., *Historical Collections* (London, 1682), I, 412.

27 French, *Charles I and the Puritan Upheaval,* p. 278.

28 TH, *The Stay of the Faithfull,* p. 46.

29 TH, *The Soules Exaltation* (London, 1638), p. 10. Subsequent quotations from this text will be indicated in parentheses with the abbreviation *SE.*

Always implied in these loaded nonconformist remarks is the point that a traitor of this sort is necessarily among the reprobate. J. Sears McGee comments on this belief in *The Godly Man in Stuart England: Anglicans, Puritans, and the Two Tables, 1620–1670* (New Haven: Yale Univ. Press, 1976), p. 172.

30 TH, *Spiritual Munition*, Document I in Williams et al., *Thomas Hooker: Writings in England and Holland*, p. 42. The work was originally published in London in 1638, twelve years after its delivery. Subsequent page citations to this sermon will be indicated parenthetically, with the abbreviation *SM*.

31 McGee discusses this tenet of Puritan belief in *The Godly Man in Stuart England*, pp. 119–42.

32 TH, *The Stay of the Faithfull*, p. 14. Subsequent page citations from this work will be indicated parenthetically, with the abbreviation *SF*.

33 Here the reference is left ambiguous so that the audience can decide for itself whether Hooker means specifically Anglican ministerial vestments or merely the lacy frills of foreign fashions to which Puritan ministers had been objecting since around the turn of the century, though in the context of references to the golden calf the preferred reading would seem to involve association with forms of worship.

34 "A Thomas Hooker Sermon of 1638," ed. Everett Emerson, *Resources for American Literary Study*, 2 (Spring 1972), 81, 82. He had ended his Chelmsford sermon in just the same way, saying, "And you that feare God, seeke his face, and seeke him still, and never give over seeking of him, in the simplicity of his pure ways." *SF*, p. 100.

35 Larzer Ziff, *Puritanism in America: New Culture in a New World* (New York: Viking, 1973), pp. 20–21.

36 John Rogers, *A Godly & Fruitful Exposition upon All the First Epistle of Peter* (London, 1650), p. 103. Quoted in Ziff, *Puritanism in America*, p. 21.

37 TH, *Foure Learned and Godly Treatises* (London, 1638), p. 26. See p. 6 for Hooker's comments on Machiavelli.

38 TH, *The Vnbeleevers Preparing for Christ* (London, 1638), pt. 1, p. 49.

39 TH, *The Faithful Covenanter*, in Williams et al., *Thomas Hooker: Writings in England and Holland*, p. 193. The sermon was first published in London in 1644, some fifteen years after its delivery.

40 Richard Sibbes, *A Rescue from Death*, in *The Riches of Mercie. In Two Treatises* (London, 1638), esp. pp. 71–72 and 124–27. Thomas Doolittle, referring to the plague of 1665, took the same view: "The word that signifies the 'plague' comes from a word that signifies to 'speak'. God in lesser judgments whispereth to a sin, but in a plague he speaketh out." Quoted in McGee, *The Godly Man in Stuart England*, p. 34.

41 See, for instance, TH, *The Churches Deliverances* (preached in 1626, the year after the worst of the plagues), in Williams et al., *Thomas Hooker: Writings in England and Holland*, pp. 61, 77–78, 80–81, 86.

42 Ibid., pp. 81–82. Hooker could employ an alarmist technique when raising the specter of a foreign invasion, as he did in *The Faithful Covenanter*, warning of the folly of overconfidence by instructing his hearers "not to depend upon privileges, not to boast of them and rest in them, and go away and say, 'What, the Spaniards come into England! What, the enemy overcome England! We have the gospel, the means of grace. No nation under heaven [has] so many in it that fear the Lord as our nation hath." The Jews took outward comfort from their temple, Hooker reminded his

Dedham audience. But "when the Babylonians came," "what good did their temple do them?" (ibid., p. 195). It is not at all impossible, he says, that England "should be overrun, and friends and means fail" (p. 219).

43 Ibid., p. 84.

44 Darrett Rutman, *American Puritanism: Faith and Practice* (Philadelphia: Lippincott, 1970), p. 23.

45 TH, *The Churches Deliverances*, in Williams et al., *Thomas Hooker: Writings in England and Holland*, p. 74. Subsequent quotations will be identified in parentheses with the abbreviation *CD*.

46 See discussion of the dating of this sermon in Williams et al., *Thomas Hooker: Writings in England and Holland*, pp. 53–59.

47 *The Works of George Herbert*, ed. F. E. Hutchinson (Oxford: Oxford Univ. Press, 1941), pp. 196–97. The lines quoted are ll. 235–40, 247. For Hutchinson's comments on the dating of this poem, see his note, p. 543.

48 Hutchinson, *The Works of George Herbert*, pp. 546–47.

49 William Fenner, *A Treatise of the Affections* (London, 1640), p. 189.

50 TH, *The Danger of Desertion*, in Williams et al., *Thomas Hooker: Writings in England and Holland*, pp. 245–46. Subsequent quotations from this sermon will be identified in parentheses with the abbreviation *DD*.

51 Thomas Shepard, *The Autobiography*, in *God's Plot: The Paradoxes of Puritan Piety, Being the Autobiography & Journal of Thomas Shepard*, ed. Michael McGiffert (Amherst: Univ. of Massachusetts Press, 1972), p. 55.

52 Rev. Joseph Mead to Sir Martin Stuteville, June 15, 1628, in Birch, *Charles the First*, I, 360.

53 See, for instance, John Winthrop's calmly rational "Generall Considerations for the plantation in New England . . ." in *Winthrop Papers*, II (Boston: Massachusetts Historical Society, 1931), 106–49. Similarly objective discussions of the reasons for migration appear in such works as Richard Mather's "Arguments tending to prove the Removing from *Old England* to *New* . . ." in [Increase Mather], *The Life and Death of that Reverend Man of God, Mr. Richard Mather* . . . (Cambridge, 1690), pp. 12–20, and John White's *The Planters Plea; or, The Grounds of Plantation Examined* . . . (London, 1630).

54 This point was so extreme that several years later on the other side of the ocean Anne Hutchinson's claim that Hooker had foretold the imminent destruction of England brought cries of disavowal from Hooker's closest associate during his last years at Chelmsford, John Eliot, who had helped Hooker run a school out of the Hooker home at Little Baddow. See *The Antinomian Controversy, 1636–1638: A Documentary History*, ed. David D. Hall (Middletown, Conn.: Wesleyan Univ. Press, 1968), p. 339.

55 Seaver, *The Puritan Lectureships*, p. 290.

56 See George H. Williams, "The Life of Thomas Hooker in England and Holland, 1586–1633" in Williams et al., *Thomas Hooker: Writings in England and Holland*, pp. 17–18.

57 Among those who appreciate the existence of the jeremiad as a common sermon form in England before the Great Migration are Sacvan Bercovitch in "Horologicals to Chronometricals: The Rhetoric of the Jeremiad,"

Literary Monographs, vol. III (Madison: Univ. of Wisconsin Press, 1970), and in *The American Jeremiad* (Madison: Univ. of Wisconsin Press, 1978); Christopher Hill in *The World Turned Upside Down: Radical Ideas during the English Revolution* (New York: Viking, 1972); and Darrett Rutman in *American Puritanism: Faith and Practice.* Several major studies of the New England cultural situation, however, have focused on the jeremiad only in an American historical context, thus, whether intentionally or not, encouraging the assumption that the form was a product of the New England experience alone. This tendency may stem from Perry Miller's groundbreaking chapter on the jeremiad in *The New England Mind: From Colony to Province* (Boston: Beacon, 1953), pp. 27–39, where 1652 is posited as the turning point in New England's self-view and the date of the beginning of the rise of the jeremiad in America. See also David Hall, *The Faithful Shepherd: A History of the New England Ministry in the Seventeenth Century* (Chapel Hill: Univ. of North Carolina Press, 1972); and David Minter, "The Origins of Interpretation: The Puritan Jeremiad as a Literary Form," in *The Interpreted Design as a Structural Principle in American Prose* (New Haven: Yale Univ. Press, 1969), pp. 50–66 (reprinted in *The American Puritan Imagination: Essays in Revaluation,* ed. Sacvan Bercovitch [Cambridge: Cambridge Univ. Press, 1974], pp. 45–55). Both Hall and Minter discuss the jeremiad only in the context of the latter half of the seventeenth century in New England. Joseph Haroutunian treats the same tradition as it existed in the eighteenth century in *Piety versus Moralism: The Passing of the New England Theology* (New York, 1932). The problem is accounted for, I believe, in my observation that the jeremiad was much less common in New England in the years 1620–50 than it was in England or than it would be later in the century in New England. Though Bercovitch claims in *The American Jeremiad* that the form was used in America from 1630 on, his examples tend to suggest its *relative* scarcity until after mid-century.

Chapter 3: BASIC QUESTIONS IN THE NETHERLANDS

1 These are the answers to John Paget's twenty questions, or as they are sometimes called, *The Twenty Propositions,* and the Preface to William Ames, *A Fresh Suit against Human Ceremonies in Gods Worship* (1633). Frank Shuffelton believes that Hooker probably "wrote out from his sermon notes the text of *The Soules Preparation*" (London, 1632) "during his first year in the Netherlands," though he offers no evidence for this hypothesis. It would seem equally possible that he left a manuscript in the hands of someone in England whom he trusted to have it printed. But it seems even more likely that he had nothing to do with its publication. *The Soules Preparation* is the first of the several works in Hooker's *ordo salutis* series of books published in England after his departure. Certainly some and probably all of these were published from auditors' notes rather than from authorial manuscripts. See Shuffelton's comments in *Thomas Hooker, 1586–1647* (Princeton: Princeton Univ. Press, 1977), p. 155.

2 TH to John Cotton, Rotterdam, c. April 1633, printed as Document IX in *Thomas Hooker: Writings in England and Holland, 1626–1633*, ed. George H. Williams et al., Harvard Theological Studies, 28 (Cambridge: Harvard Univ. Press, 1975), p. 297.

3 Consistory Register of the English Reformed Church of Amsterdam, quoted by Keith L. Sprunger in "The Dutch Career of Thomas Hooker," *New England Quarterly*, 46 (March 1973), 21. Sprunger's reconstruction of the sequence of events during Hooker's brief stay in Amsterdam and immediately thereafter is the fullest, and definitive, account of this part of Hooker's career and has been invaluable in the preparation of the present chapter. Other essential studies of the Dutch background are Raymond Phineas Stearns, *Congregationalism in the Dutch Netherlands: The Rise and Fall of the English Congregational Classis, 1621–1635* (Chicago: American Society of Church History, 1940); Alice Clare Carter, *The English Reformed Church in Amsterdam in the Seventeenth Century* (Amsterdam: Scheltema and Holkema, 1964); Keith L. Sprunger, *The Learned Doctor William Ames: Dutch Backgrounds of English and American Puritanism* (Urbana: Univ. of Illinois Press, 1972); and Shuffelton, *Thomas Hooker*, pp. 135–58.

4 Sprunger, "The Dutch Career of Thomas Hooker," p. 23.

5 Carter, *The English Reformed Church in Amsterdam*, p. 189. See also Stearns, *Congregationalism in the Dutch Netherlands*, pp. 29–30.

6 "John Paget's XX Questions (Propositions) and Thomas Hooker's Answers," Document VIII in Williams et al., *Thomas Hooker: Writings in England and Holland*, p. 278. Subsequent quotations from this text will be identified in parentheses with the abbreviation *XXQ*.

7 On relations in Amsterdam between Separatists and non-Separatists, including Paget's role in the opposition, see Carter, *The English Reformed church in Amsterdam*, pp. 22–24, 53–67.

8 Forbes, being minister of an English merchants' church not under the Dutch Classis, felt more or less free to offend the Classis if he chose. His ire on Hooker's behalf is understandable if based, as seems likely, on Paget's unnecessarily communicating his questions and Hooker's answers to the Amsterdam Classis, since Hooker, by volunteering to leave the city, had in effect silenced himself and gotten out of Paget's hair before the Classis even knew of the Twenty Propositions. John Davenport, who crossed Paget's path just two years after Hooker, complained of his treatment—and Hooker's—in three books. In one of them he addressed the issue of Paget's vindictive unfairness in making Hooker's answers public property. Davenport asked, "Why did the Answerer [Paget] make known Mr. H[ooker's] judgment to the Classis? seeing, in the conclusion of that wrighting, he [Hooker] expresseth himself thus[: ']Because I doe apprehend you conceive there cannot be a peaceable concurrence, in such distance of judgment, as I see my opportunity, to depart &c.['] Was not here a voluntary desistance? To what end was this wrighting carryed to the Classis, after he voluntarily desisted? Was it not to shelter and hide himselfe under the

Classis, that it might be thought, they deprived the Church of Mr. H. not he? was it not to expose Mr. H. to the more reproach and censure, when the Classis and Synod had judged against him?" John Davenport, *An Apologeticall Reply to a Booke Called: An Answer to the unjust complaint of W. B.* (Rotterdam, 1636). Other works in Davenport's controversy with Paget, which frequently make reference to Hooker's earlier case, are Davenport's *A Iust Complaint Against an Vnjvst Doer. . . .* ([Amsterdam,] 1634) and *A Protestation Made and Published by Iohn Davenporte upon occasion of a pamphlett Intitled a Ivst Complaint. . . .* (Rotterdam, 1635) and John Paget's *An Answer to the unjust complaints of William Best,. . . . Also an answer to Mr. John Davenport. . . .* (Amsterdam, 1635).

9 On the Delft experience, see Stearns, *Congregationalism in the Dutch Netherlands*, pp. 31–40, and Sprunger, "The Dutch Career of Thomas Hooker," pp. 37–42. Shuffelton, *Thomas Hooker*, pp. 150–55, gives a particularly good account of Hooker's experience in Delft.

10 Cotton Mather, *Magnalia Christi Americana* (Hartford, 1820), I, 308.

11 Sprunger, *The Learned Doctor William Ames*, pp. 71, 92. There is some disagreement on the date of Ames's arrival in Rotterdam. See the summary of opinions in George Williams's headnote to the preface in Williams et al., *Thomas Hooker: Writings in England and Holland*, pp. 305–6.

12 Sprunger, "The Dutch Career of Thomas Hooker," 43. Hooker's preface and Ames's text were even printed on different presses. See A. F. Johnson, "The Exiled English Church at Amsterdam and Its Press," *The Library*, 5th ser., 5 (March 1951), 241–42.

13 This "invitation" is itself merely a common surmise. It is possible that the preface and *A Fresh Suit* were written entirely independently and that a third party such as Hugh Peter saw the appropriateness of joint publication.

14 These were published anonymously, and it has been suggested that they were written by the Scottish divine David Calderwood, also an exile in Holland (see *DNB*, III, 697). Keith Sprunger, in his biography of Ames, does not question Ames's authorship.

15 Whether Burgess knew that he was responding to Ames or not is unclear, though there is a hint that he may have been aware of this in citing *The Marrow of Theology* and referring to its author as "*Doctor Ames* (a man which you and I loue better than any of the Schoolmen you name)." *An Answer Reioyned*, pp. 65–66. On the other hand, he cites Ames throughout as an authority on certain doctrinal points, something he would have avoided doing had he known he was arguing with Ames.

16 Ames married one of Burgess's ten children, but she died early, having borne no children. This may have been early in the second decade of the century, for it was Ames who replaced Burgess in 1611 as chaplain to Sir Horace Vere, commander of the English forces in Holland. Ames, according to his biographer, had remarried "sometime before the Synod of Dort in 1618." Sprunger, *The Learned Doctor William Ames*, p. 34. The family tie was thus not recent in 1633, but it may explain Hooker's accounting for

Ames's attack on his former father-in-law by saying in his preface that to correct the public errors of others is an expression of great *"love and mercy . . . to our fellow Brethren."* *A Fresh Suit,* sig. [c4].

17 The best modern account of Burgess's early nonconformity appears in Stuart Barton Babbage, *Puritanism and Richard Bancroft* (London: S.P.C.K., 1962), pp. 166–74. See also *DNB,* III, 310–12; *Alumni Cantabrigiensis,* pt. 1, I, 257; and George Williams's headnote in Williams et al., *Thomas Hooker: Writings in England and Holland,* pp. 303–6, 315–16. An interesting early account of Burgess's shift from nonconformist to conformist appears in Peter Heylyn, *Aërius Redivivus; or, The History of the Presbyterians. . . . From the Year 1536 to the Year 1647* (London, 1672).

18 Hooker's anonymous authorship of the preface is a long-standing tradition dating back to Cotton Mather's biography of him in 1695, wherein Increase Mather in a preface to the biographical sketch recalls his father, Richard Mather, a contemporary and friend of Hooker, attributing the preface to him. Stylistic details support the claim of Hooker's authorship. The enumeration of several "sorts" of "declyners" is a patently Hookerian use of the character tradition, as is the appearance in the list of the "Temporary Professor," or "Temporizer," whom Hooker also vilifies in other such lists. Also, such a phrase as "to justle Christ out of his prophetical & Kingly office" (sig. b) or "to jusle God out of the place of iustice" (sig. d3) is familiar Hooker terminology and even wordplay. Indeed, the style throughout bears the characteristic Hooker stamp. George Williams also discusses Hooker's authorship, in *Thomas Hooker: Writings in England and Holland,* pp. 307–15.

19 Preface to *A Fresh Suit against Human Ceremonies in God's Worship,* Document X in Williams et al., *Thomas Hooker: Writings in England and Holland,* p. 320. Subsequent quotations from this work will be identified in parentheses with the word "Preface."

Hooker was doubtless also remembering his own voyage from England to Holland, when his ship ran aground in a storm and was nearly wrecked. See Cotton Mather, *Magnalia,* I, 307.

20 Burgess, *An Answer Reioyned,* p. 27.

21 *Calendar of State Papers, Domestic Series, of the Reign of James I,* IX, 427; *DNB,* III, 311.

22 Burgess, *An Answer Reioyned,* p. 13.

23 Ibid., p. 16. He answers this objection simply by saying, "I haue, I thank God, learned something more then I knew 39 yeeres ago, & am now able to master those Objections which then mastered mee" (p. 16).

24 See George L. Walker, *Thomas Hooker: Preacher, Founder, Democrat* (New York: Dodd, Mead, 1891), p. 51; and George H. Williams, "The Pilgrimage of Thomas Hooker (1586–1647) in England, The Netherlands, and New England," Part I, *Bulletin of the Congregational Library,* 19 (Oct. 1967), 10. Shuffelton claims, without documentation, that Hooker's family accompanied him to Holland; see *Thomas Hooker,* p. 133.

25 Burgess, *An Answer Reioyned,* p. 8.

26 The court's spy network was fairly effective if we can judge from such evidence as the entry in the *Calendar of State Papers* for June 23, 1633, which summarizes the contents of a letter from Hugh Peter in Rotterdam to a Rev. Mr. Phillips in England: "Hugh Peters to Mr. Phillips, at Wrentham. . . . Dr. Burgess is answered, but how the books will come into men's hands was a question. Dr. Ames would be settled at Rotterdam the next month, and they shall desire to see the person addressed [*sic*]. Prays God to make them useful. . . . [*Endorsed by Bishop Laud*, 'Rece. Aug. 30, 1633,' *and* [*by Bishop Corbet*], '*This is a copy of a letter which I intercepted at Yarmouth. The prototype was sent to Phillips (after my reading) by a sailor's boy. I had hoped to receive his answer but the right reverend Phillips was too crafty*'. . . .]." *Calendar of State Papers, Domestic Series, of the Reign of Charles I*, VI, 113.

27 Williams notes the possibility that "the Printer rather than the Prefacist (Hooker) may well have prepared this last section after Hooker's departure" (p. 376n).

Chapter 4: "THE SAINTS DIGNITIE AND DUTIE": HOOKER AND THE ANTINOMIAN CONTROVERSY

1 Lawrence Shaw Mayo, *John Endecott: A Biography* (Cambridge: Harvard Univ. Press, 1936), pp. 84–90.

2 "Touchinge ye Crosse in ye Banners," *Proceedings of the Massachusetts Historical Society*, 3rd ser., 42 (April 1909), 274.

3 It seems likely that those individuals "without whoes invitation" Hooker would never have "sett penn to paper, on y^s point" included John Winthrop. The persuasion to make his mind known must have come from principals involved, and the court's subsequent agreement with Hooker that Endecott's act was unduly extreme at least suggests Winthrop as a possibility, as do Winthrop's solicitations of Hooker's counsel and assistance on other occasions both before and after this episode. (Hooker had recently been asked to debate Roger Williams on behalf of the authorities, and for the rest of his life his presence would be sought on important political and ecclesiastical occasions, beginning very soon after the Endecott debate with the Antinomian crisis.)

4 John Winthrop, *Winthrop's Journal: "History of New England," 1630–1649*, ed. James Kendall Hosmer (New York: Charles Scribner's Sons, 1908), I, 128. Norman Pettit treats the subject of Hooker's removal in "Lydia's Conversion: An Issue in Hooker's Departure," *Proceedings of the Cambridge Historical Society*, 40 (1964–66), 59–83, and briefly in *The Heart Prepared: Grace and Conversion in Puritan Spiritual Life* (New Haven: Yale Univ. Press, 1966), pp. 90–91.

5 *Winthrop's Journal*, I, 132. See Frank Shuffelton's discussion in *Thomas Hooker, 1586–1647* (Princeton: Princeton Univ. Press, 1977), pp. 199–210.

6 An inventory taken April 21, 1649, appraised Hooker's property at £1136. Two of the three main items are "Howsing and Lands . . . on both sides the Riuer," with a value of £450, and livestock (nineteen head of cattle,

five horses, and two oxen) valued at £143. This ample farmland and livestock apparently helped return enough cash to allow Hooker to accumulate
an impressive library, since the "Bookes in his studdy, &c." were valued at
£300, making it one of the most substantial collections in New England.
See the full inventory in George L. Walker, *Thomas Hooker: Preacher,
Founder, Democrat* (New York, 1891), pp. 181–83.

7 William Hubbard, *A General History of New England, from the Discovery
to 1680*, in *Collections of the Massachusetts Historical Society*, 2nd ser., 5
(1848), 173 (reprinted New York: Arno Press, 1972).

8 A letter from R. Stansby to John Wilson dated April 17, 1637, lists three
things which especially trouble him in the reports he has had regarding the
state of the Church in New England. Among these are "great diuision of
Iudgement in matter of religion amongst good ministers and people which
moued Mr. Hooker to remoue" and that "you are so strict in admission of
members to your church, that more than one halfe are out of your church
in all your congregations, & that Mr. Hooker before he went away
preached against yt (as one report who hard hym)." *Winthrop Papers* (Boston: Massachusetts Historical Society, 1943), III, 390.

9 William Hubbard, writing late in the seventeenth century, commented on
the comparative political influence of Hooker and Cotton, suggesting Cotton's greater clout: after "Mr. Cotton and Mr. Hooker came over," they
"did clear up the order and method of church government. . . . And such
was the authority they (especially Mr. Cotton) had in the hearts of the
people, that whatever he delivered in the pulpit was soon put into an
Order of Court, if of a civil, or set up as a practice in the church, if of an
ecclesiastical concernment." *A General History*, p. 182.

10 Introduction to *The Antinomian Controversy, 1636–1638: A Documentary
History*, ed. David D. Hall (Middletown, Conn.: Wesleyan Univ. Press,
1968), p. 4. This work supersedes Charles Francis Adams's books on the
same topic.

11 Thomas Hutchinson, *The History of the Colony and Province of
Massachusetts-Bay*, ed. Lawrence Shaw Mayo (Cambridge: Harvard Univ.
Press, 1936), I, 63.

12 Thomas Weld, Preface to John Winthrop, "A Short Story of the Rise . . . of
the Antinomians . . . ," in Hall, *The Antinomian Controversy*, p. 212.
Thomas Shepard recorded the same fact in his autobiography when he
wrote that "the elders . . . , having used all private brotherly means with
Mr. Cotton first . . . , they publicly preached both against opinions publicly
and privately maintained." *God's Plot: The Paradoxes of Puritan Piety,
Being the Autobiography & Journal of Thomas Shepard*, ed. Michael
McGiffert (Amherst: Univ. of Massachusetts Press, 1972), p. 65.

13 Frank Shuffelton is the only scholar to have suggested the connection of
The Saints Dignitie and Dutie with the issues of the Antinomian controversy. In his dissertation he argued that this book and *A Comment upon
Christs Last Prayer* were written more or less contemporaneously several
years after the controversy. In his published version of his Hooker biog-

raphy he is less inclined to date *The Saints Dignitie*. My analysis of the book places its seven sermons in the immediate temporal as well as intellectual context of the controversy. See Shuffelton, "The Light of the Western Churches: The Career of Thomas Hooker" (Ph.D. diss., Stanford, 1972), pp. 282–84, and idem, *Thomas Hooker*, pp. 258–62.

14 Among those who identify "T.S." as Thomas Shepard are J. Hammond Trumbull in "Thomas Hooker: Published Works," Appendix II in George L. Walker, *Thomas Hooker: Preacher, Founder, Democrat* (New York: Dodd, Mead, 1891), p. 193; and H. Clark Woolley, *Thomas Hooker: A Bibliography*, Center Church Monographs, no. 1 (Hartford, 1932), p. 30.

15 For instance, less than a year before his death, on September 17, 1646, in responding to a letter from Shepard, Hooker said, "My notes of Paedobaptisme are out of my hand, else you might have had them." Hutchinson Papers, vol. 240, Massachusetts State Archives, Boston. In the same letter Hooker enclosed a brief manuscript of his comments on the Sabbath, in response to Shepard's questions.

16 Hooker's will empowered his wife as executrix to see to the publication of "whateuer manuscripts shall bee judged meete to bee printed" and further appointed "my beloued frends Mr. Edward Hopkins and Mr. William Goodwyn" overseers of the will in order to assist Susanna in her duties. See the entire will in Appendix I in Walker, *Thomas Hooker*, pp. 178–81.

17 Shuffelton remarks that "the major ministerial disputants [in the Antinomian controversy] went on justifying themselves for years—nearly half of Shepard's collected works, for example, are detailed refutations of the grounds and practices of antinomianism, and Cotton went on defending moderate versions of his early opinions." Shuffelton, *Thomas Hooker*, p. 252.

In an undated letter to Shepard, when discussing a book by a "Mr. Buill" or "Mr. Ball"—probably John Ball's *Treatise of the Covenant of Grace* (London, 1645)—Hooker addressed a continuing point of disagreement with Cotton: "Only I confesse that all sett formes are unlawfull ether in publike or private, then to retyre to that defence of Mr Cottons: That its lawfull to use a forme in private, or occasionally in publike: but not ordinarily. For to my shallow conceit, he doth in such distinctions tradere causâ & y^t fully." Hutchinson Papers, vol. 240, Massachusetts State Archives, Boston; partially reprinted in John A. Albro, *Life of Thomas Shepard* (Boston: Doctrinal Tract and Book Society, 1853; rpt. New York: AMS Press, 1967), p. clx.

18 TH to Thomas Shepard, Sept. 17, 1646, Hutchinson Papers, vol. 240, Massachusetts State Archives, Boston. As Hooker was doubtless aware, Baillie had, in fact, quoted Cotton from *A Short Story* in his *Dissuasive against the Errours of the Time* (London, 1645). Cotton would in due course answer Baillie in *The Way of Congregational Churches Cleared* (London, 1648).

19 Hall so describes the spiritual climate in the colony in *The Antinomian Controversy*, p. 15.

20 *The Saints Dignitie, and Dutie. Together with the Danger of Ignorance and Hardnesse. Delivered in Severall Sermons By that Reverend Divine, Thomas Hooker, Late Preacher in New England* (London, 1651), pp. 71–72. Hereafter, quotations from this work will be indicated in parentheses with the abbreviation *SDD*.

21 David D. Hall sees the possibility of a collaboration against Cotton and the other "spiritists" by the "legalist" preparationists Shepard, Bulkeley, and Hooker. See *The Faithful Shepherd: A History of the New England Ministry in the Seventeenth Century* (Chapel Hill: Univ. of North Carolina Press, 1972), p. 166. And it is known that Winthrop, who had been mainly responsible for blocking a call to John Wheelwright from the Boston Church and was the key figure among the authorities in the calling of the synod, had sent out an urgent plea to Hartford that they spare a minister— probably Hooker, since Winthrop would have known he was prepared to meet Cotton head-on—to attend the synod. The entire Hartford congregation wrote to Winthrop in July 1637, lamenting "those heavy distractions" to which Winthrop had referred. They said quite clearly that times were very hard in their new settlement but that because the issue was great, their help had been sought, and they owed a great debt to Christ and his Church, they were "willing . . . not only to do what you desired, but may be more than you did expect, having resolved and purposed to send both our elders in the next fitt season, to be serviceable to you to the vtmost of ther ability." See the letter, signed by Hooker, Stone, and William Goodwin, the ruling elder, *"In the name and with the consent of the wholl church,"* in *Winthrop Papers*, III, 520–21.

22 Perry Miller writes of the Antinomian controversy as a head-to-head conflict of Hooker's and Cotton's views on church governance and theology in which Cotton "did not stand his ground, and his uneasy references to the affair in subsequent years are oblique admissions, that he and not Hooker made the concession." See Miller, "Preparation for Salvation in Seventeenth-Century New England," *Journal of the History of Ideas*, 4 (June 1943), 275.

23 "Mr. Cottons Rejoynder," in Hall, *The Antinomian Controversy*, pp. 97–98.

24 TH, *The Soules Exaltation* (London, 1638), pp. 226–27, 181–82.

25 "Mr. Cottons Rejoynder," in Hall, *The Antinomian Controversy*, p. 98.

26 Hugh Peter, "A Report of the Trial of Mrs. Ann Hutchinson . . . ," in Hall, *The Antinomian Controversy*, p. 379.

27 Wheelwright, "A Fast-Day Sermon," in Hall, *The Antinomian Controversy*, pp. 154, 157, 158, 163, 165–66.

28 It is hard to see why historians have until recently had such a difficult time in seeing this sermon as seditious, the charge on which the court found Wheelwright guilty. But even such an astute interpreter of colonial history as Charles M. Andrews wrote that the sermon "contains nothing that can possibly be construed as contemptuous or seditious." *The Colonial Period of American History: The Settlements* (New Haven: Yale Univ. Press, 1934), I, 482. The sermon, of course, contains a whole admission of the charge by

Wheelwright himself, though he would deny this in his trial—a denial singularly futile since the main evidence against him was a printed version of the fast-day sermon, which he admitted was indeed his work. See Hall, *The Antinomian Controversy*, pp. 152–53, 251–57.

29 Ibid., p. 8.

30 Cotton's letter replying to Shepard's questions ends with the request, "Remember my Deare affection to your selfe, Brother Hooker and others with you whom I deeply honor in the Lord." "Shepard-Cotton Letters," in Hall, *The Antinomian Controversy*, p. 33. Shepard's letter to the older Cotton was a rather bold expression of doubts about Cotton's doctrinal orthodoxy. His having written while Hooker was still in town invites the surmise that the latter knew of it and may well have had a silent role in its composition.

31 Winthrop, "A Short Story," in Hall, *The Antinomian Controversy*, p. 222.

32 "Mr. Cottons Rejoynder," in Hall, *The Antinomian Controversy*, p. 143. See also John Cotton, "A Conference . . . Held at Boston," in ibid., pp. 192–97.

33 See the exchange of letters between Bulkeley and Cotton in Hall, *The Antinomian Controversy*, pp. 34–42.

34 See ibid., pp. 34–35, where Hall quotes a relevant passage from Bulkeley's *The Gospel-Covenant; or, The Covenant of Grace Opened* (London, 1646).

35 Wheelwright, "Fast-Day Sermon," in Hall, *The Antinomian Controversy*, p. 161

36 Cotton, "A Conference . . . Held at Boston," in Hall, *The Antinomian Controversy*, p. 179.

37 On Hooker's differences with Cotton on this doctrine of the assurance of grace, see Norman Pettit, "Hooker's Doctrine of Assurance: A Critical Phase in New England Spiritual Thought," *New England Quarterly*, 48 (Dec. 1974), 518–34, esp. p. 528 on the use of "signs" in sanctification. John Coolidge describes John Cotton as epitomizing opposition to this use of "Marks and Signs"; see Coolidge, *The Pauline Renaissance in England* (Oxford: Clarendon Press, 1970), p. 131.

38 "The Examination of Mrs. Anne Hutchinson," in Hall, *The Antinomian Controversy*, pp. 331, 341–42, 342, 343.

39 Ibid., p. 316.

40 "A Report of the Trial of Mrs. Anne Hutchinson before the Church in Boston," in Hall, *The Antinomian Controversy*, pp. 380–81, 383.

41 Ibid., pp. 353, 370, 373.

42 Ibid., pp. 382–83.

43 His letter to Winthrop, probably written in October 1637 shortly after Hooker's return to Hartford from Cambridge, thanks the governor for "all your former kyndenesses and your last loving entertaynement." Then Hooker gives Winthrop some advice: "I have ever iudged it, in cases of difficulty which must come to scanning, most safe, to attend nothing for ground of determination, but that which will carry an undeniable evidence to an impartiall iudge. . . . For execution let it be so secret and suddayne that it cannot be prevented, so resolute and vncontrolable that it may tak

off hope from the adversary that it can be resisted: and this damps opposition and prevents hazard." See *Winthrop Papers*, III, 498–99.

Chapter 5: ADVOCATING THE NEW ENGLAND WAY

1 John Winthrop, *Winthrop's Journal: "History of New England," 1630–1649*, ed. James Kendall Hosmer (New York; Charles Scribner's Sons, 1908), II, 71. There were, in fact, five Independents at the outset (Philip Nye, Thomas Goodwin, Jeremiah Burroughs, William Bridge, and Sydrach Simpson) and more 'later.

2 These matters are more fully discussed in my "Thomas Hooker and the Westminster Assembly," *William and Mary Quarterly*, 29 (April 1972), 291–300.

3 The three exceptions are his guide to self-examination, *The Properties of an honest Heart* (London, 1638), and introductions to two works by friends: "To the Reader" in John Rogers, *The Doctrine of Faith*, 2nd ed. (London, 1627) and subsequent editions, and the Preface to William Ames, *A Fresh Suit against Human Ceremonies in Gods Worship* ([Rotterdam?], 1633). His most frequently reprinted book, *The Poor Doubting Christian Drawn unto Christ*, first published in 1629, was not a complete sermon but a sermon excerpt. See the explanation by Frank C. Shuffelton, "Thomas Prince and His Edition of Thomas Hooker's *Poor Doubting Christian*," *Early American Literature*, 5 (1970–71), 69–70.

4 At least six editions of both *The Poor Doubting Christian* and *The Soul's Preparation for Christ* had appeared by 1645, while *The Soul's Humiliation* had been printed at least four times. See my bibliography in *Thomas Hooker: Writings in England and Holland, 1626–1633*, ed. George Williams et al. (Cambridge: Harvard Univ Press, 1975), pp. 390–425.

5 John Fuller, an English Puritan minister who was examined and approved by the Westminster Assembly on January 31 and February 1, 1647, spoke of Hooker several years later as "that great Elijah, that renowned man of God in his generation." "Epistle" in John Beadle, *The Journal or Diary of a thankful Christian* (London, 1656).

6 Larzer Ziff, *The Career of John Cotton: Puritanism and the American Experience* (Princeton: Princeton Univ. Press, 1962), pp. 179–80.

7 See John Davenport's *Answer of the Elders of the Severall Chvrches in New-England unto Nine Positions, Sent Over to Them . . .* (London, 1643); Richard Mather's *Church-Government and Church-Covenant Discussed* (London, 1643); Mather's *Reply to Mr. Rutherfurd; or, A defence of the Answer to Reverend Mr. Herles Booke against the Independence of Churches* (London, 1647); and John Norton's *Responsio ad totam questionum syllogen a . . . Domino Guilielmo Apollonio . . . propositam* (London, 1648). B. R. Burg has recently discussed Mather's contributions to this literature and their historical context in *Richard Mather of Dorchester* (Lexington: Univ. Press of Kentucky, 1976), chap. 3.

8 The entry in the *Stationers Register* for January 31, 1645, reads: "*A briefe*

exposicõn of the Lords prayer by Mr John Hooker *in his familie.*" The stationer's clerk apparently omitted Thomas Hooker's name from the entry inadvertently, thus depriving the pronoun *his* of its referent. Thomas Hooker is clearly identified as author on the book's title page. It is also possible but less likely that John Hooker was Thomas's brother John, who was still living in Markfield, Leicestershire, about a hundred miles from London. For a fuller discussion of this and related evidence, see my "Thomas Hooker and the Westminster Assembly."

9 Herbert Palmer, *An Endeavor of Making the Principles of Christian religion . . . plain and easie* (Cambridge, 1640).

10 Alexander F. Mitchell, *The Westminster Assembly: Its History and Standards* (Philadelphia, 1884), p. 409. For detailed considerations of the main influences on the formulation of the Westminster Catechisms, see Mitchell, pp. 407–41; and Benjamin B. Warfield, *The Westminster Assembly and Its Work* (New York, 1931), pp. 379–400.

11 Mitchell, *Westminster Assembly*, p. 365.

12 Alexander F. Mitchell and John Struthers, eds., *Minutes of the Sessions of the Westminster Assembly of Divines* (London, 1874), p. 306. Nye was one of the "three men" mentioned by Hooker in his decision to stay at home and a major voice of Independency at the assembly.

13 Mitchell, *Westminster Assembly*, pp. 418–19.

14 These were the catechisms by Ezekiel Rogers, John Ball, William Gouge, M. N[ewcomen or Nicholl], Henry Wilkinson, Adoniram Byfield, and James Ussher. See ibid., p. 419.

15 See the informative discussions of the Scots' attitudes in H. R. Trevor-Roper, "Scotland and the Puritan Revolution," in *Historical Essays, 1600–1675, Presented to David Ogg*, ed. H. E. Bell and R. L. Ollard (London: Adam & Charles Black, 1963), pp. 78–130; and C. G. Bolam and Jeremy Goring, "English Presbyterian Beginnings," in Bolam et al., *The English Presbyterians: From Elizabethan Puritanism to Modern Unitarianism*, (London: Allen & Unwin, 1968), pp. 29–46.

16 Trevor-Roper, "Scotland and the Puritan Revolution," p. 91.

17 See ibid., pp. 86 ff.

18 Thomas Goodwin, Philip Nye, Sidrach Simpson, Jeremiah Burroughs, and William Bridge, *An Apologeticall Narration, Humbly Submitted to the Honourable Houses of Parliament* (London, 1643), p. 24. This edition has been reprinted with notes and a substantial essay by Robert S. Paul (Philadelphia: United Church Press, 1963).

19 The titles give some indication of Baillie's uncompromising tone and stance: *The Unlawfulnesse and Danger of Limited Episcopacie* (1641); *Ladensivm Αντοκάτακρισις. The Canterbvrians Self-Conviction* (1641); *The Life of William [Laud]* (1643); *Satan the Leader in Chief* (1643).

20 The Scots were not full-fledged members of the Assembly but were admitted by the two houses of Parliament "to debate upon occasion," an opportunity of which they made maximum effective use. See Mitchell and Struthers, *Minutes of the Sessions of the Westminster Assembly of Divines, p. lxxxiv.*

21 Goodwin et al., *An Apologeticall Narration,* p. 24.

22 See Henderson's *Reformation of the Church Government in Scotland Cleared from some Mistakes and Prejudices* (London, 1644).

23 Preface to John Norton, *The Answer to the Whole Set of Questions of the Celebrated Mr. William Apollonius, Pastor of the Church of Middelburg. . . . ,* trans. from the Latin by Douglas Horton (Cambridge: Harvard Univ. Press, 1958), p. xiii.

24 TH, Preface to *A Survey of the Summe of Church Discipline* (London, 1648), sig. [a2]v. Subsequent quotations from this volume will be indicated in parentheses with the short title *A Survey.*

25 John Spilsbery, *Gods Ordinance, The Saints Priviledge. Discovered and Proved in two Treatises. . . .* (London, 1646), sig. A2. Hooker attacked Spilsbery's views in *The Covenant of Grace Opened* (1646).

26 This reference indicates Hooker's knowledge of Rutherford's earlier book, *Exercitationes Apologeticae pro Divina Gratia* (1636), an anti-Arminian work for which Rutherford had been silenced.

27 Boniface III was pope for part of the year 607.

28 See Hooker's preface, *A Survey,* sigs. A2–A4v and sig. al for his sketch of the Church's history. Larzer Ziff comments on Cotton's eschatological interpretation of the historical moment in his *Career of John Cotton,* pp. 170–73.

29 See *Winthrop's Journal,* II, 98–105; and Edward Hooker's discussion of this in *The Life of Thomas Hooker* (Boston: Massachusetts Sabbath School Society, 1849), pp. 105–14.

30 The last of these works is the rare exception in that it is available in an excellent modern edition, translated and edited by Douglas Horton (see n. 23, above). Horton's "Translator's Preface" contains valuable comments on the work's historical context.

Like the responses of Hooker and Davenport to the challenges of the Dutch Classis two decades earlier, all of these works defending New England's church polity rely heavily on the thinking of the earlier antiseparatist Congregational leaders Henry Jacob, Paul Baynes, William Bradshaw, Robert Parker, and William Ames. Baynes's *Diocesans Trial* (1621), which attacked all ecclesiastical superstructures, was reissued in 1643 in London and thus had an immediate relevance to and impact on the debate. See Perry Miller, *Orthodoxy in Massachusetts, 1630–1650: A Genetic Study* (Cambridge: Harvard Univ. Press, 1933), pp. 75–77.

31 Hooker refers to Rutherford's *A Peaceable and Temperate Plea* as "lib. 1" (i.e., "book one") and *The Due Right of Presbyteries* as "lib. 2," never identifying either by title.

32 Preface to *A Survey,* sig. b2v. Winthrop provides the date and attests to the elders' unanimous approval of the manuscript. See *Winthrop's Journal,* II, 257. Hooker's preface was apparently written between July 1, 1645, and January 1646, when the manuscript was put aboard the ill-fated ship at New Haven.

33 Robert Gilmour, *Samuel Rutherford: A Study* (Edinburgh and London: Oliphant Anderson & Ferrier, 1904), p. 192.

34 Thomas Murray, *The Life of Samuel Rutherford* (Edinburgh, 1828), pp. 218–19.

35 Usually Hooker gives exact page references to the works he quotes, indicating immediate access to the books themselves.

36 Rutherford, *A Survey of the Survey of that Summe of Church-Discipline Penned by Mr. Thomas Hooker.* . . . (London, 1658), sig. A4.

37 W. M. Taylor, an early Rutherford analyst, said rather harshly that with Rutherford "there was only one side to every question, and that one his own and God's to oppose which was flat blasphemy and impiety. He could make no distinction between essentials and non-essentials; the form of church government was in his view of as much importance as the Deity of Christ; and what he judged to be right was so infallibly right, that all men were bound to conform thereto." Quoted in Gilmour, *Samuel Rutherford*, pp. 202–3.

38 Rutherford, *A Peaceable and Temperate Plea*, p. 16.

39 From Henry Wolcott's "Notes on Sermons," MS notebook, Hooker Family Memorial, MS. 73132, Connecticut Historical Society, Hartford, transcribed by Douglas H. Shepard.

40 This issue has been much discussed because early interpreters such as George Bancroft, John Fiske, James Truslow Adams, and Vernon Parrington were inclined to make Thomas Hooker into an early version of Thomas Jefferson when in fact his views were very much related to his own times. He must not be taken for a "democrat" in the modern sense. The best secondary comments on this matter are the following: Perry Miller, "Thomas Hooker and the Democracy of Connecticut," *New England Quarterly*, 4 (1931), 663–712, reprinted in *Errand into the Wilderness* (Cambridge: Harvard Univ. Press, 1956), pp. 16–47; Charles M. Andrews, *The Colonial Period of American History* (New Haven: Yale Univ. Press, 1936), II, 100–112; Clinton Rossiter, "Thomas Hooker," *New England Quarterly*, 25 (Dec. 1952), 459–88; Sydney E. Ahlstrom, "Thomas Hooker: Puritanism and Democratic Citizenship," *Church History*, 32 (Dec. 1963), 415–31; and Mary Jeanne Anderson Jones, *Congregational Commonwealth: Connecticut, 1636–1662* (Middletown, Conn.: Wesleyan Univ. Press, 1968), pp. 68–73.

41 Norman Pettit stresses this point more than others in *The Heart Prepared: Grace and Conversion in Puritan Spiritual Life* (New Haven: Yale Univ. Press, 1966), pp. 100–101, 161–62. Paul R. Lucas suggests that in the Connecticut Valley there was more difference in membership practices among the churches than has generally been noticed; see his analysis of these differences in *Valley of Discord: Church and Society along the Connecticut River, 1636–1725* (Hanover, N.H., Univ. Press of New England, 1976), pp. 25–35.

42 *A Survey*, pt. 1, pp. 250–88, esp. pp. 253, 274.

43 See Edmund S. Morgan, *Visible Saints: The History of a Puritan Idea* (New York: New York Univ. Press, 1963), pp. 104–10; and Pettit, *The Heart Prepared*, pp. 161–62.

44 Kenneth Lockridge, studying the church at Dedham, Massachusetts, cites just such a case: "When the wife of Robert Hinsdell became fearful and not able to speak in public, . . . fainting away there, . . . she was admitted on

the basis of a private conference." *A New England Town: The First Hundred Years* (New York: W. W. Norton, 1970), p. 31.

45 Lucius R. Paige, *History of Cambridge, Massachusetts, 1630–1877* (Boston, 1877), p. 251; *Winthrop's Journal*, I, 107.

46 Hudson, *A Vindication of the Essence and Unity of the Church Catholike Visible* (London, 1650), sig. A2v.

47 On December 31, 1655, Robert Baillie wrote to Simeon Ashe, a Presbyterian minister in London and former college friend of Hooker, that "Mr. Rutherfoord tells me you have his Answer to Hooker at last: let it be printed if yow think fitt." Ashe, in an undated letter soon after, responded, "Dr. [Thomas] Young is dead also; and his papers about Discipline are so voluminous, that no stationer will undertake to print them, because that controversie lyeth dead among us, and few inquire for any books of that subject: Hence it is that Mr. Crooke is so backward in putting to presse that Answere to Mr. Hooker, which Mr. Rutherfoord hath made and sent hither." *The Letters and Journals of Robert Baillie*, ed. David Lang (Edinburgh, 1841–42), III, 303–6.

48 John A. Lamb, "Samuel Rutherfurd, 1600–61," in *Fathers of the Kirk: Some Leaders of the Church in Scotland from the Reformation to the Reunion*, ed. Ronald Selby Wright (London: Oxford Univ. Press, 1960), p. 82.

49 Thomas Lechford, "To the Reader," *Plain Dealing; or, Nevves from New-England* (London, 1642). Lechford observed, speaking of New England membership and baptism practices, "When the major part are unbaptized, as in twenty years undoubtedly they will be, . . . what is like to become of it, but that either they may goe among their fellow-heathens the Indians, or rise up against the Church, and break forth into many grievous distempers among themselves?" The Half-Way Covenant, just twenty years later, was of course a more constructive solution to the problem than Lechford had forseen.

50 Robert G. Pope, *The Half-Way Covenant: Church Membership in Puritan New England* (Princeton: Princeton Univ. Press, 1969), pp. 22–25.

51 TH to Thomas Shepard, Sept. 17, 1646, Hutchinson Papers, vol. 240, Massachusetts State Archives, Boston. Shepard was apparently keeping his father-in-law supplied with books relevant to the controversy with the Anabaptists, for in the same letter Hooker acknowledges receipt of "Mr Geree his answer to Mr Tomes . . . together [with] Mr Blage agaynst Blackwood," commenting further that "they both seem iudicious" and that "it is a good hand yt many able have bestowed ther paynes this waye, that for myne owne part, I see no great need any more should be added." The books to which he refers are John Geree's *Vindiciae paedo-baptismi; or, A Vindication of Infant Baptism . . . .* (London, 1646), which answered John Tombes's *An Exercitation about Infant-baptisme* (London, 1646) and *An Examen of the Sermon of Mr Stephen Marshal, About Infant-Baptisme* (London, 1645) and Thomas Blake's *Infants Baptisme* (London, 1645), a response to Christopher Blackwood's *Storming of Antichrist* (London, 1644), which was itself an answer to Blake's earlier *Birth-Privilege* (London, 1644). Blackwood promptly answered Blake's *Infants Baptisme* with *Apostolicall Baptisme* (London, 1645).

52 Nathaniel Ward, *The Simple Cobler of Aggawam in America,* ed. P. M. Zall (Lincoln: Univ. of Nebraska Press, 1969), p. 6.

53 See *Winthrop's Journal*, II, 177.

54 TH to Thomas Shepard, Sept. 17, 1646, Hutchinson Papers, vol. 240, Massachusetts State Archives, Boston.

55 TH, *The Covenant of Grace Opened* (London, 1646), p. 16. Subsequent quotations from this work will be identified in parentheses with the abbreviation *CGO*.

56 Puritan views on the sacraments in both Old and New England are sensitively and clearly discussed in E. Brooks Holifield's important study, *The Covenant Sealed: The Development of Puritan Sacramental Theology in Old and New England, 1570–1720* (New Haven: Yale Univ. Press, 1974). His discussion of Hooker's views on baptism is particularly well-informed; see esp. pp. 150–56.

57 See also Thomas Shepard's use of the term in his posthumous *Church-Membership of Children and their Right to Baptisme* (Cambridge, Mass., 1668), p. 13, where he says, "It is a miserable mistake to think that inward reall holyness is the only ground of admission into Church-Membership, as some *Anabaptists* dispute, but it is a federal holyness, whether externally professed as in grown persons, or graciously promised unto their seed."

58 Pope, *The Half-Way Covenant*, pp. 123–24, documents the Farmington case, concluding that "Farmington could maintain the orthodoxy of the first generation because it softened the harshness of the practice which made the half-way covenant necessary."

Chapter 6: THE ANATOMY OF THE SOUL

1 Perry Miller, *The New England Mind: The Seventeenth Century* (New York: MacMillan, 1939), p. 105.

2 TH, *The Paterne of Perfection* (London, 1640), p. 61. Subsequent quotations from this work will be indicated in parentheses with the abbreviation *PP*.

3 William Perkins, *A Discourse of Conscience, Workes* (London, 1612–13), p. 517.

4 See Miller, *The New England Mind: The Seventeenth Century*, pp. 346–47. For additional comment on the functions of the parts of the sermon, see also Babette M. Levy, *Preaching in the First Half-Century of New England History* (Hartford, Conn.: American Society of Church History, 1945), pp. 94–97; and Millar Maclure, *The Paul's Cross Sermons, 1534–1642* (Toronto: Univ. of Toronto Press, 1958), p. 165.

5 William Ames, *The Marrow of Theology*, trans. and ed. John D. Eusden (Boston: Pilgrim Press, 1968), p. 193.

6 TH, *The Application of Redemption, The Ninth and Tenth Books* (London, 1656), p. 157.

7 I refer here to certain of the Italian Neoplatonists of the sixteenth century—Coluccio Salutati, Marsilio Ficino, and others—who were in many ways conscious followers of Augustinian thinking. See my discussion of these connections below in Chapter 11.

8 See, for example, John Downame, *The Christian Warfare Against the Devil, World and Flesh* (London, 1634). The title page of this book, which illustrates this conflict with emblematic art, can be conveniently consulted in William Haller's *Rise of Puritanism* (New York: Columbia Univ. Press, 1938), where it is the frontispiece.

9 *The Works of Anne Bradstreet*, ed. Jeannine Hensley (Cambridge: Harvard Univ. Press, 1967), p. 216.

10 On this dualistic world view, see, for instance, Larzer Ziff, *Puritanism in America: New Culture in a New World* (New York: Viking, 1973), pp. 8 ff.; Charles H. George and Katherine George, *The Protestant Mind of the English Reformation, 1570–1640* (Princeton: Princeton Univ. Press, 1961), pp. 105–6.

11 See the relevant discussion in Eugene F. Rice, Jr., *The Renaissance Idea of Wisdom* (Cambridge: Harvard Univ. Press, 1958), p. 92.

12 On Ramus, see Perry Miller, *The New England Mind: The Seventeenth Century*, chap. 5, esp. pp. 124—29; Wilbur Samuel Howell, *Logic and Rhetoric in England, 1500–1700* (Princeton: Princeton Univ. Press, 1956), pp. 146–281; and Walter J. Ong, *Ramus, Method, and the Decay of Dialogue* (Cambridge: Harvard Univ. Press, 1958), pp. 199–202. On Bacon, see Basil Willey, *The Seventeenth Century Background: Studies of the Thought of the Age in Relation to Poetry and Religion* (London: Chatto and Windus, 1934), pp. 24–30.

13 Sacvan Bercovitch, *The Puritan Origins of the American Self* (New Haven: Yale Univ. Press, 1975), p. 19.

14 TH, *The Application of Redemption, The first eight Books* (London, 1656), p. 302.

15 TH, *The Application of Redemption, The Ninth and Tenth Books*, p. 36.

16 Ibid., p. 53.

17 Ibid.

18 For Aristotle's distinction between practical and speculative wisdom, see *De Anima* III. 9. 432b26 and 10.433a 9–21. For a discussion of the physics curriculum at Cambridge, see William T. Costello, *The Scholastic Curriculum at Early Seventeenth-Century Cambridge* (Cambridge: Harvard Univ. Press, 1958), pp. 83–102. As Costello observes (p. 96), Aristotle divides the practical branch of knowledge—what Hooker calls "prudence"—into two habits: prudence and art.

Since Hooker occasionally cites Augustine, Aquinas, and others who knew Aristotle's thought, it is difficult to know how much ancient philosophy he actually read at first hand. His reluctance to cite nonbiblical authorities in his sermons—a policy based both on his awareness of his audience's limited familiarity with such sources and on his unwillingness to display what might seem pride in his own knowledge—serves to obscure the extent of his reading in the ancients. But Aristotle was still a very important part of the Cambridge University curriculum in Hooker's day, and he could not have avoided familiarity with Aristotle's definition of *soul*.

19 TH, *The Soules Effectuall Calling* (London, 1637), p. 287.

20 This precise use of the word *inlighten* occurs frequently in Hooker's writings and is an example of his attention to careful use of literal and figurative aspects of the language. It is the same word as our *enlighten* while also suggesting his essential meaning of illuminating within. Hooker delighted in and used with considerable skill this kind of double-edged term. An interesting study which bears upon Puritan usage generally is M. van Beek, *An Enquiry into Puritan Vocabulary* (Groningen: Wolters-Noordhoff, 1969).

21 TH, *The Soules Effectuall Calling*, p. 377.

22 TH, *The Application of Redemption, The Ninth and Tenth Books*, p. 98.

23 Ibid., p. 101.

24 TH, *The Soules Effectuall Calling*, p. 108.

25 TH, *The Saints Guide* (London, 1645), pp. 28, 29, 30.

26 TH, *The Application of Redemption, The first eight Books*, p. 36.

27 TH, *The Soules Preparation* (London, 1632), p. 31.

28 Ibid., p. 130.

29 TH, *The Vnbeleevers Preparing for Christ* (London, 1638), pt. 1, p. 127.

30 TH, *The Application of Redemption, The Ninth and Tenth Books*, p. 325.

31 Perry Miller mentions the important connection between heart and will (see *The New England Mind: The Seventeenth Century*, p. 248). Norman Pettit, whose book, *The Heart Prepared* (New Haven: Yale Univ. Press, 1966), is centrally concerned with the "heart" in Puritan thought, says simply that "the heart" is "the biblical metonym for the inner man." Hooker usually had a more precise meaning in mind.

32 William Perkins, *A Commentarie Upon the Epistle to the Galatians* in *Workes*. . . . (London, 1612–13), II, 277.

33 John Cotton, *Gods Mercie Mixed with His Justice* (London, 1641), pp. 3–4. This text is most readily accessible in a facsimile reprint (Gainesville, 1958), with an introduction by Everett H. Emerson.

34 TH, *The Vnbeleevers Preparing for Christ*, pt. 1, p. 57; *The Soules Effectuall Calling*, pp. 283, 58, 352–53.

35 See Perry Miller, *The New England Mind: The Seventeenth Century*, p. 249.

36 Vernon J. Bourke, *Will in Western Thought: An Historico-Critical Survey* (New York: Sheed and Ward, 1964), pp. 131–35; Norman S. Fiering, "Will and Intellect in the New England Mind," *William and Mary Quarterly*, 29 (Oct. 1972), 529.

37 Rice, *The Renaissance Idea of Wisdom*, p. 36.

38 Fiering, "Will and Intellect in the New England Mind," 537.

39 Miller, *The New England Mind: The Seventeenth Century*, p. 249.

40 Rice, *The Renaissance Idea of Wisdom*, p. 37. This connection of love with the will was also present in the thinking of both the ancient Hebrews and an important school of third-century Greek physicians. See Bourke, *Will in Western Thought*, pp. 129–31; and Claude Tresmontant, *A Study of Hebrew Thought*, trans. M. F. Gilson (New York: Deselee, 1960), pp. 119–21, quoted in Bourke.

41 TH, *The Application of Redemption, The first eight Books*, p. 322.
42 *St. Augustine's Confessions*, VIII. 12, Eng. trans. William Watts, The Loeb Classical Library (London and New York, 1912), I, 463.
43 TH, *The Soules Effectuall Calling*, p. 283.
44 TH, *The Soules Preparation*, pp. 77, 84, 104.
45 Ibid., pp. 116–17.
46 TH, *The Application of Redemption, The Ninth and Tenth Books*, pp. 273–74.
47 In *The Soules Preparation* (1632), Hooker calls conscience "a Sergeant" who approaches the sinner as if to arrest him, saying, "These are your sinnes; and as you will answer it at the day of Judgment, take heed of those sins upon paine of everlasting ruine. When conscience begins thus to arrest a man, then the heart comes and gives way to the truth revealed, and conscience thus settles it upon the heart." p. 124. See Chapter 9, below, for a fuller consideration of meditation as a tool in Hooker's ministry.
48 TH, *The Application of Redemption, The first eight Books*, p. 349, and pp. 351–451 passim.
49 See Miller, *The New England Mind: The Seventeenth Century*, pp. 241, 246–47, 257–59.
50 TH, *The Application of Redemption, The Ninth and Tenth Books*, p. 161.
51 Ibid., p. 165.
52 TH, *The Application of Redemption, The first eight Books*, pp. 322, 314, 374, 384. Hooker quoted the same passage from Augustine in an earlier version of the same sermon; see *The Vnbeleevers Preparing for Christ*, pt. 2, p. 68.
53 TH, *The Vnbeleevers Preparing for Christ*, pt. 1, p. 43.
54 TH, *The Application of Redemption, The Ninth and Tenth Books*, pp. 300, 301, 302–3.
55 Cotton, *Gods Mercie Mixed with His Justice* (London, 1641), p. 6.

Chapter 7: PREPARATION FOR GRACE: THE DOCTRINAL PREMISES

1 TH, *The Soules Humiliation* (London, 1637), p. 76.
2 Perry Miller and Thomas H. Johnson, eds., *The Puritans* (New York: American Book Co., 1938), p. 800.
3 See William Perkins, *A Golden Chaine; or, The Description of Theologie, contayning the order of the causes of Salvation and Damnation, according to Gods word* (London, 1597), pp. 139–72, and *A Treatise tending vnto a declaration whether a man be in the Estate of damnation or in the estate of grace* (London, [1589]); and William Ames, *The Marrow of Sacred Divinity* (London, 1638), pp. 109–33.
4 John Phillips, *The Way to Heaven* (London, 1625), p. 8.
5 Norman Pettit, *The Heart Prepared: Grace and Conversion in Puritan Spiritual Life* (New Haven: Yale Univ. Press, 1966), pp. 125–28.
6 John Cotton, *The New Covenant* (London, 1654), p. 54.
7 Quoted in Giles Firmin, *The Real Christian* (London, 1670), p. 19. Ward

arrived in New England in 1634, a year after Hooker, and returned to England in 1647, the year of Hooker's death.

8 See Pettit, *The Heart Prepared*, pp. 48–85.

9 Thomas Goodwin and Philip Nye, "To the Reader," in TH, *The Application of Redemption, The first eight Books* (London, 1656), sig. [C4]v.

10 Cotton Mather, "Piscator Evangelicus," *Johannes in Eremo* (Boston, 1695), pp. 32–33.

11 Perkins, *A Golden Chaine*, p. 140.

12 Ibid.

13 Ibid., pp. 142, 143.

14 TH, *The Application of Redemption, The first eight Books*, pp. 252–53.

15 Larzer Ziff, *The Career of John Cotton: Puritanism and the American Experience* (Princeton: Princeton Univ. Press, 1962), p. 16.

16 Ames wrote, for instance, that a part of predestination "is a purpose or intention of preparing and directing those means by which men elected are certainely lead [sic] through to salvation as to an end." *The Marrow of Sacred Divinity* (London, 1638), pp. 106–7.

17 TH, *The Soules Effectuall Calling* (London, 1637), p. 463.

18 TH, *The Christians Two Chiefe Lessons* (London, 1640), p. 64.

19 See Pettit's discussion of Hooker, Shepard, and Bulkeley, in *The Heart Prepared*, pp. 86–124.

20 William Goodwin, in particular, had a serious and long-lasting falling-out with Samuel Stone. See George L. Walker, *History of the First Church in Hartford, 1633–1883* (Hartford, 1884), pp. 146–81.

21 Goodwin and Nye, "To the Reader," in TH, *The Application of Redemption, The first eight Books*, sig. [C4], [C3]v. These editors were apparently more interested in making a good case for the necessity of this posthumous edition than in providing a disinterested comparison of the old and new editions. The newer versions are nearly always longer and more detailed, but there are relatively few passages in which it is clear that Hooker wanted to correct a doctrinal misrepresentation of the earlier and unauthorized books. Nearly always, the changes in the revised version are due to elaboration, expansion, and interpolation rather than to outright correction of doctrinal positions. A thoroughgoing comparison of the two texts, and new editions of each, would be highly desirable.

22 TH, *The Application of Redemption, The first eight Books*, title page. Subsequent quotations from this work will be identified in parentheses with the abbreviation *AR*, I, to distinguish it from the second volume of *The Application*.

23 TH, *The Vnbeleevers Preparing for Christ* (London, 1638), pt. 1, p. 109.

24 Ibid., pt. 1, pp. 6, 8.

25 Cotton Mather, "Piscator Evangelicus," pp. 41–42.

26 Samuel Eliot Morison, *The Intellectual Life of Colonial New England* (Ithaca: Cornell Univ. Press, 1960), p. 11. (This work was originally published as *The Puritan Pronaos*, in 1936.)

27 See Perry Miller, *The New England Mind: The Seventeenth Century* (New York: MacMillan, 1939), 404–5, for a discussion of the disagreement between Cotton and Twisse on predestination.

28 TH, *The Vnbeleevers Preparing for Christ*, pt. 1, p. 106.

29 See Miller, *The New England Mind: The Seventeenth Century*, pp. 36–40.

30 Perry Miller, " 'Preparation for Salvation' in seventeenth-Century New England," *Journal of the History of Ideas*, 4 (June 1943), 278–86. For a clear if very brief description of the century-long "steady drift toward Arminianism," see also Sydney E. Ahlstrom, *A Religious History of the American People* (New Haven: Yale Univ. Press, 1972), pp. 151–54. Gerald J. Goodwin addresses the issue in his article "The Myth of 'Arminian-Calvinism' in Eighteenth-Century New England," *New England Quarterly*, 41 (June 1968), 213–37. Though Goodwin's essay is an apparent attempt to refute Miller's thesis, it does not deal directly with Miller's claims of an increasing willingness among seventeenth-century Congregationalists to allow men more natural ability in their quest for salvation. Miller would not have disagreed with Goodwin's claim that the Calvinists never thought of themselves as Arminians.

31 Miller's discussion of the covenant theology in terms of a contractual relationship in which God is more or less *obliged* to keep his side of the bargain has been corrected by later scholars. See, for instance, Pettit, *The Heart Prepared*, pp. 219–20; Pettit, "The Order of Salvation in Thomas Hooker's Thought" in *Thomas Hooker: Writings in England and Holland, 1626–1633*, ed. George H. Williams et al. (Cambridge: Harvard Univ. Press, 1975), pp. 124–39; and Everett Emerson, "Thomas Hooker and the Reformed Theology: The Relationship of Hooker's Conversion Preaching to its Background" (Ph.D. diss., Louisiana State Univ., 1955), esp. chap. 4.

32 TH, *The Application of Redemption, The Ninth and Tenth Books* (London, 1656), p. 297.

33 Ibid., pp. 299–300.

34 Ibid., pp. 300–303.

35 Ibid., pp. 305, 305–6, 307.

36 TH, *The Soules Preparation* (London, 1632), p. 59.

37 Bernard's *Steps of Humility* implies the ladder metaphor in its title and contains occasional uses of it in the text, as in the first paragraph of chap. 9: "Ad quod tamen jam, ipso juvante, quo et vocante, mihi scalam erexi. Illic siquidem iter est, quo ostendat mihi salutare Dei." ("Yet I have already erected a ladder reaching up to this, with the aid of him who also calls me. For that is the path to where he shows me the salvation of God.") St. Bernard de Clairvaux, *The Steps of Humility*, trans. and ed. George Bosworth Burch (Cambridge: Harvard Univ. Press, 1950), pp. 172–73. Bishop Joseph Hall was one of many seventeenth-century writers who found the figure useful in describing the spiritual life: "This alone is the remedie of security and worldlines, the pastime of Saints, the ladder of heaven, and in short the best improvement of Christianitie." *The Arte of Divine Meditation* (London, 1606), p. 4.

Chapter 8: PREPARATION FOR GRACE: A TALE OF ADVENTURE

1 Though he did not write about his role in dealing with the Indians, except in scattered comments in correspondence with John Winthrop and Roger Williams, Hooker had an instrumental hand in the colonists' forceful attack on the Indians in the Pequot War in 1637. John Mason, the colony's military leader in that episode, wrote afterwards, "I still remember a Speech of Mr. HOOKER at our going aboard [the boat that took the soldiers downstream to the attack]; THAT THEY [the Indians] SHOULD BE BREAD FOR US." See Mason, *A Brief History of the Pequot War Especially of the memorable Taking of their Fort at Mistick in Connecticut in 1637* (Boston, 1736), with introduction and explanatory notes by Thomas Prince.

2 Cotton Mather, *Magnalia Christi Americana* (Hartford, 1820), I, 312–13.

3 Perry Miller and Thomas H. Johnson, eds., *The Puritans* (New York, 1938), p. 800. Miller mentions only six volumes specifically: *The Soules Exaltation, The Soules Humiliation, The Soules Implantation, The Soules Preparation,* and *The Application of Redemption*, presumably intending to indicate both volumes of the latter. He might also have included the other relevant volumes: *The Soules Ingrafting into Christ, The Soules Effectuall Calling, The Vnbeleevers Preparing for Christ, The Soules Implantation into the Natural Olive, The Soules Possession of Christ,* and *A Comment upon Christs Last Prayer*. Two other short books, which were as yet undiscovered when Miller wrote, can also be added to the list: *The Sinners Salvation* and *Spirituall Thirst*.

4 On the importance of Aristotle and Ramus to Puritan thought, see Perry Miller, *The New England Mind: The Seventeenth Century* (New York: Macmillan, 1939), esp. chap. 5; Wilbur S. Howell, *Logic and Rhetoric in England, 1500–1700* (New York, 1961); Walter J. Ong, *Ramus, Method, and the Decay of Dialogue* (Cambridge: Harvard Univ. Press, 1958); Keith L. Sprunger, "Ames, Ramus, and the Method of Puritan Theology," *Harvard Theological Review*, 59 (April 1966), 133–51; and David L. Parker, "Petrus Ramus and the Puritans: The 'Logic' of Preparationist Conversion Doctrine," *Early American Literature*, 8 (Fall 1973), 140–62. Eugene E. White suggests, with good reason, that this cumulative scholarship has resulted in a disproportionate emphasis on Ramus's influence on Puritan thought. The Puritans' use of such figures as Quintilian and Cicero doubtless needs further study. See Eugene E. White, *Puritan Rhetoric: The Issue of Emotion in Religion* (Carbondale: Southern Illinois Univ. Press, 1972), p. 202, and White, "Master Holdsworth and 'A Knowledge Very Useful and Necessary'," *Quarterly Journal of Speech*, 53 (February 1967), 1–16.

5 The subtitle of Hooker's *A Briefe Exposition of the Lords Prayer* (1645) was *Wherein the meaning of the words is laid open to the understanding of weake Christians, and what the carriage of their hearts ought to be in preferring each Petition*.

6 The odyssey which Hooker describes is, of course, highly personal, though repeated in the personal experience of all the elect. There are moments in some of his New England sermons, as I shall point out shortly, when his figurative language and his use of typology refer to the spiritual landscape in such a way as to invite a literal interpretation of the drama he describes. His questing hero in a spiritual wilderness turns out, in the New England setting, to be the same individual of whom heroic achievements are expected in the Connecticut wilderness. On such occasions, which would become more common in the sermons of later seventeenth-century New Englanders, there is a clear awareness by the preacher of both a spiritual and a "national" significance in his message of the kind discussed by Sacvan Bercovitch in *The American Jeremiad* (Madison: Univ. of Wisconsin Press, 1978), esp. chap. 2. See also Phyllis Jones, "Biblical Rhetoric and the Pulpit Literature of New England," *Early American Literature*, 11 (Winter 1976/77), 256. Hooker's "epic," however, does not consistently suggest a national application in the way that *The Iliad* and *The Aeneid* told of the glories that were Greece and Rome, or even in the way that Cotton Mather's *Magnalia Christi Americana* (1702) would tell the epic story of how Christianity was reaching its climax in the colonial history of America. The term *epic* must thus be somewhat more loosely applied in connection with Hooker's redemption sermons than, for instance, Bercovitch has applied it in discussing the *Magnalia* ("New England Epic: Cotton Mather's *Magnalia Christi Americana*," *ELH*, 33 [1965], 337–50). Hooker's story does, however, involve personal, agonizing struggle of the central character towards triumph over the ultimate antagonist through the collaboration of the divine power, a long and arduous time over which the action is enacted, and a cultural application of the myth to those who are hearing it orally related. Such important parallels of formal content with conventional epic, while not satisfying any purist definition of the genre, at least give ample warrant to the generic comparison which I am suggesting. Phyllis M. Jones and Nicholas R. Jones have recently noted this "heroic" dimension of Puritan sermons about the stages of redemption in their *Salvation in New England: Selections from the Sermons* (Austin: Univ. of Texas Press, 1977), p. 16.

7 U. Milo Kaufmann's discussion of *logos* and *mythos* as the terms apply to Bunyan's *Pilgrim's Progress* has been especially suggestive and helpful in my consideration of related aspects of Hooker's redemption sermons. See Kaufmann's *"Pilgrim's Progress" and Traditions in Puritan Meditation* (New Haven: Yale Univ. Press, 1966), pp. 8–15.

8 The growth of the pilgrim metaphor from a tool of didactic literature to its use in Defoe's work is briefly but suggestively sketched in J. Paul Hunter, *The Reluctant Pilgrim: Defoe's Emblematic Method and Quest for Form in "Robinson Crusoe"* (Baltimore: Johns Hopkins Press, 1966), pp. 93–124.

9 TH, *The Application of Redemption, The Ninth and Tenth Books* (London, 1656), p. 1. Subsequent quotations from this work and edition will be cited in parentheses with the abbreviation *AR*, II.

10 This has been a perennial problem in discussions of the federal theology. See, for instance, Perry Miller's restatement of his interpretation of the Puritans' covenant theology and its relationship to the doctrine of predestination in *Errand into the Wilderness* (Cambridge: Harvard Univ. Press, 1956), pp. 48–50. More recently Hooker has been mistakenly represented as reversing the Calvinistic priorities between election and faith. Quoting a passage from the opening sermon in the tenth book of *The Application of Redemption* as evidence, Parker claims that "for Calvin, election engenders faith; for Hooker, faith engenders election." Parker, "Petrus Ramus and the Puritans," p. 142. Such a claim, of course, misses the point of all that has gone before in Hooker's preparation for the opening section of his preparationist doctrine. His entire description of redemption, as he took pains to point out in Books One to Eight, is an account of how grace comes to the elect. The point is clearly established in the primary Doctrine to Book Eight: "God the Father by a Holy kind of violence as it were, plucks his out of their Corruptions, and Draws them to Beleeve in Christ" (*AR*, I, 349). The crucial word is "his"; belief comes only to "his," i.e. the elect. In Hooker's strictly Calvinist position on this point, faith cannot possibly be a condition for God's eternal decree of election.

11 Hooker was here practicing a relatively new form of typological interpretation, one which made the present-day Christian the antitype, whereas traditionally the Old Testament figures had been the types for which Christ presented the antitype. Murray Roston's comment is representative of others by recent explicators of typological methodology: "Here was an essentially new concept, with its roots in the soil of the temporal world, whereby mortal men, not elevated into sainthood, began to see their daily struggles, both spiritual and physical, in terms of a biblical archetype." *Biblical Drama in England from the Middle Ages to the Present Day* (London: Faber & Faber, 1968), p. 71. See also Sacvan Bercovitch, ed., *Typology and Early American Literature* (Amherst: Univ. of Massachusetts Press, 1972); Bercovitch, *The Puritan Origins of the American Self* (New Haven: Yale Univ. Press, 1975); and Barbara K. Lewalski, *Donne's "Anniversaries" and the Poetry of Praise: The Creation of a Symbolic Mode* (Princeton: Princeton Univ. Press, 1973), esp. chap. 5, pp. 142–73.

12 Lewalski, *Donne's "Anniversaries,"* p. 160; Bercovitch, *The Puritan Origins of the American Self*, p. 36.

13 The development and eventual phasing out in Luther's day of "allegorical" exegesis of scripture is described in Thomas M. Davis, "The Traditions of Puritan Typology," in Bercovitch, *Typology and Early American Literature*, pp. 18–38.

14 Alfred Habegger has discussed very briefly the principle of Ramist dichotomies as it relates to the organization of the *ordo salutis*, constructing a useful diagram after the manner of Ramist handbooks. See "Preparing the Soul for Christ: The Contrasting Sermon Forms of John Cotton and Thomas Hooker," *American Literature*, 41 (Nov. 1969), 347. Habegger does not extend the diagram into the structure of Hooker's discussion of contrition, which would look like this:

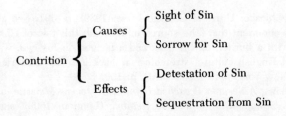

Parker also offers an informed discussion of Hooker's use of Ramist dichotomies, though he is mistaken in claiming that Thomas Shepard "apparently felt he had improved upon Hooker's doctrine" by "sub-dichotomizing Hooker's stage of contrition into . . . 'conviction of sin' . . . and 'compunction of sin.' " Parker, "Petrus Ramus and the Puritans," p. 152. Shepard was doubtless aware that this subdivision was the same as his father-in-law's "causes" and "effects" of contrition.

15 Owen C. Watkins, *The Puritan Experience* (London: Routledge and Kegan Paul, 1972), p. 6.

16 TH, *The Soules Preparation for Christ* (London, 1632), p. 202.

17 See M. van Beek, *An Enquiry into Puritan Vocabulary* (Groningen: Wolters-Noordhoff, 1969), pp. 52, 128.

18 This was a common usage of *way* in the sixteenth and seventeenth centuries. The *Oxford English Dictionary* offers examples from both secular and religious literature by William Tyndale, Thomas Gataker, and William Shakespeare, among others.

19 Louis Martz's observation, for example, that the following passage from Richard Baxter, written well before Bunyan's allegory, contains "metaphor and humor remarkably akin to Bunyan" is both true and predictable: "If lying down at the foot of the Hill, and looking toward the top, and wishing we were there, would serve the turn, then we should have daily travelers for Heaven. But *the kingdome of Heaven suffereth violence, and the violent take it by force:* There must be violence used to get at these first fruits, as well as to get the full possession. . . . But as the sluggard that stretched himself on his bed, and cried, O that this were working! So dost thou talk and trifle, and live at thy ease, and say, O that I could get my heart to Heaven!" Martz, *The Poetry of Meditation: A Study in English Religious Literature of the Seventeenth Century* (New Haven: Yale Univ. Press, 1954), p. 169. There is no denying the similarity to Bunyan here, but Baxter, like Hooker before and Bunyan after, is merely making his own effective use of a metaphor so common that by Bunyan's time it had become a cliché which provided a ready challenge to some devout Christian writer to convert into dramatic narrative, the achievement for which Bunyan is justly famous. M. M. Knappen made this point in saying: "When the propagandist had done his work, the prospective pilgrim needed accurate maps of the narrow path he was to follow, with all the gates and sloughs plainly marked. A century later Bunyan supplied the most famous and graphic answer to this demand." *Tudor Puritanism: A Chapter in the History of*

Idealism (Chicago: Univ. of Chicago Press, 1939), p. 391. See also Ola E. Winslow's comment that "the source underneath this tale of Christian, the pilgrim, with a burden on his back and a far goal in his eye, was a whole stratum of English culture, stretching far back into the centuries" in *John Bunyan* (New York: Macmillan, 1961), p. 150.

20 John Hopkins, *A Sermon Preached before the Qveens Maiestie at Hampton Court, on Sunday the 16 day of October* (London, 1609), sigs. B1–B2. Numerous titles of religious books from the early seventeenth century also indicate widespread popularity of the metaphor of the road to heaven as a central, organizing figure. One of the most popular of such works was Arthur Dent's *Plaine Mans Path-way to Heauen* (London, 1607), which went through a great many editions, spreading popularity of the "path-way" idea. But similar titles in circulation at the same time included Immanuel Bourne's *True Way of a Christian, to the New Ierusalem* (London, 1622), Robert Bolton's *Some Generall Directions for a Comfortable walking with God* (London, 1625), John Philips's *Perfect Path to Paradise* (London, 1626), Richard Byfield's *Light of Faith: and, Way of holinesse* (London, 1630), and Peter deMoulin's *Right Way to Heaven* (London, 1630). Many other writers, of course, employed the metaphor without using it in their titles. See, for instance, John Preston, *Grace to the Humble: As Preparations to Receive the Sacrament* (London, 1639), pp. 26–27; or John Bate, *The Portraiture of Hypocrisie* (London, 1589), pp. 59–60.

21 TH, *Spirituall Thirst* (London, 1638), p. 32.

22 TH, *The Application of Redemption, The first eight Books* (London, 1656), p. 58.

23 TH, *The Poor Doubting Christian* (Boston, 1743), p. 108.

24 The connections between Puritan literary methods and the later American symbolists of the nineteenth century were first discussed in detail in the seminal study by Charles Feidelson, *Symbolism and American Literature* (Chicago: Univ. of Chicago Press, 1953). See esp. pp. 77–101. Various aspects of these connections have since been developed by others, most notably Ursula Brumm, *American Thought and Religious Typology*, trans. J. Hoaglund (New Brunswick: Rutgers Univ. Press, 1970); and Sacvan Bercovitch, *Puritan Origins of the American Self*, chap. 5.

25 Rosemary Freeman, *English Emblem Books* (London: Chatto & Windus, 1948), p. 2.

26 *Calvin's Commentaries: The Acts of the Apostles, 1–13*, trans. John W. Fraser and W. J. G. McDonald, ed. David W. Torrance and Thomas F. Torrance (Grand Rapids: William B. Eerdmans, 1965), p. 77.

27 Hunter, *The Reluctant Pilgrim*, p. 95.

28 *Calvin's Commentaries: The Acts of the Apostles, 1–13*, p. 78.

29 An interesting, brief comment on the history of this technique appears in the preface to Joseph Hall's *Characters of Vertves and Vices* (London, 1608), where the author describes how "the Diuines of the olde Heathens" sometimes "bestowed their time in drawing out the true lineaments of euery vertue and vice, so liuely, that who saw the medals, might know the face: which Art they significantly termed *Charactery*. Their papers were so

many tables, their writings so many speaking pictures, or liuing images, whereby the ruder multitude might euen by their sense learne to know vertue, and discerne what to detest." Sig. [A5] and verso.

30 Hunter, *The Reluctant Pilgrim*, p. 94.

Chapter 9: PREPARATION, STAGE TWO: HUMILIATION

1 See TH, *The Application of Redemption, The Ninth and Tenth Books* (London, 1656), pp. 619–30.

2 TH, *The Soules Humiliation* (London, 1637), p. 6. Hereafter all quotations from this work will be identified in parentheses with the abbreviation *SH*.

3 TH, *The Christians Two Chiefe Lessons* (London, 1640), p. 58.

4 Henry Whitfield, *Some Helps to Stir Up to Christian Duties*, 1st ed. (London, 1634), p. 37.

5 TH, *The Properties of An honest Heart* (London, 1638), pp. 14–15.

6 TH, *The Christians Two Chiefe Lessons*, p. 211.

7 *Reliquiae Baxterianae; or, Mr. Richard Baxter's Narrative of The most Memorable Passages of his Life and Times*, ed. Matthew Sylvester (London, 1696), p. 6. While it is possible that Baxter heard Hooker preach, he was only about fifteen years old when Hooker left England; and since Baxter's home was in Shropshire, far from Chelmsford in Essex, it seems more likely that he read Hooker's early books, especially *The Soules Preparation* (1632), when he was engaged in private study for the ministry after Hooker had left the country.

8 TH, *The Properties of An honest Heart*, p. 48.

9 Adam Harsnett, *A Touchstone of Grace* (London, 1630), pp. 10–11. In this dual awareness of the need for self-trial and the mind's capacity for self-deception, Harsnett, Hooker, and other Puritans were following the eminently clear explanation of William Perkins in his *Treatise Tending vnto a Declaration, whether a man be in the Estate of damnation, or in the estate of grace. . . .* (London, 1589), a practical work intended for use by earnest self-examiners. This emphasis on the need to examine one's "marks and signs," however, is yet another point of difference between Hooker and John Cotton, who as John Coolidge has noticed, "again and again turns our attention away from signs and tokens of covenant conditions, whether outward or inward, and toward Christ." Coolidge, *The Pauline Renaissance in England: Puritanism and the Bible* (Oxford: Clarendon Press, 1970), p. 137.

10 The three parts are "The Prayer of Faith," "A Preparative to the Lords Supper," and "The Character of a Sound Christian, in 17 markes."

11 John Higginson, *Our Dying Saviour's Legacy of Peace To His Disciples in a troublesome World, from John 14.27. . . . Unto which is added, Some Helps to Self-Examination* (Boston, 1686), p. 187. See above, Chapter 1, n. 22, for Higginson's comments about Hooker's instruction.

12 This logical contradiction is noticed by Coolidge, who, after quoting Peter Bulkeley's *Gospel-Covenant*, observes, "This passage epitomizes the difficulty inherent in the strategy of urging men to search themselves for those very conditions of the Covenant of Grace which, as has been said, 'carry

man out of himself. It is like straining every nerve in an effort to relax—
'labor to get humiliation', Preston urges." *The Pauline Renaissance in England*, p. 132.

13 Everett Emerson, "Thomas Hooker and the Reformed Theology: The Relationship of Hooker's Conversion Preaching to Its Background" (Ph.D. diss., Louisiana State Univ., 1955), pp. 164–65.

14 Hooker's sermon *Culpable Ignorance*, published as the sixth sermon in *The Saints Dignitie and Dutie* (London, 1651), also stresses the point that the means in themselves are not efficacious. See pp. 189–215.

15 The word play on "all" as well as the consciousness of sound and use of parallel constructions here may well remind the reader of "The Preface" to Edward Taylor's *Gods Determinations touching his Elect*, where the poet exclaims:

> Oh! what a might is this Whose single frown
> Doth shake the world as it would shake it down?
> Which All from Nothing fet, from Nothing, All:
> Hath All on Nothing set, lets Nothing fall.
> Gave All to nothing Man indeed, whereby
> Through nothing man all might him Glorify.

The Poems of Edward Taylor, ed. Donald E. Stanford (New Haven: Yale Univ. Press, 1960), p. 387. In both the Taylor and Hooker passages there appears the same mental ability to absorb paradox into faith and express the acceptance in wordplay. In each, this attribute speaks simultaneously of intellectual command and stylistic finesse.

16 Richard Baxter, *The Saints Everlasting Rest* (London, 1650), p. 720.

17 Joseph Hall, *The Arte of Divine Meditation* (London, 1606), p. 85.

18 TH, *The Soules Preparation*, pp. 111, 85.

19 See Louis L. Martz, *The Poetry of Meditation: A Study in English Religious Literature of the Seventeenth Century* (New Haven: Yale Univ. Press, 1954); idem, "Foreword," *The Poems of Edward Taylor*, ed. Stanford; and idem, "Introduction," *The Meditative Poem: An Anthology of Seventeenth-Century Verse* (New York: Doubleday, 1963).

20 Martz, *The Poetry of Meditation*, p. 8.

21 See, for instance, John Preston's comments on the private use of "set forms of prayer" in his *Saints Daily Exercise: A Treatise Vnfolding the whole Duty of Prayer*, 9th ed. (London, 1635), pp. 80–87, a work edited by Preston's Puritan colleagues Richard Sibbes and John Davenport.

22 Martz, *The Poetry of Meditation*, pp. 25–39.

23 Ibid., p. 16.

24 Ibid., pp. 174–75.

25 Norman Grabo, "The Art of Puritan Devotion," *Seventeenth-Century News*, 26 (Spring 1968), 7–9. In this brief essay Grabo specifically answered Martz, pointing to several Anglicans and Puritans, including Hooker, who anticipated Baxter's reforms. Two years earlier, U. Milo Kaufmann had made a similar claim but offered less documentation, mentioning Hooker in

passing but concentrating on Richard Sibbes. See *"The Pilgrim's Progress" and Traditions in Puritan Meditation* (New Haven: Yale Univ. Press, 1966), pp. 133–50. The most comprehensive demonstration of the earlier interest in meditation by Puritans is by Barbara Kiefer Lewalski, *Donne's "Anniversaries" and the Poetry of Praise: The Creation of a Symbolic Mode* (Princeton: Princeton Univ. Press, 1973), chap. 3, "Protestant Meditation and the Protestant Sermon." Citing Grabo's work, Lewalski insists that "by the turn of the century Protestants were producing devotional and meditative tracts of their own in some numbers" (p. 80). All of these discussions mention Joseph Hall's *Arte of Divine Meditation* (1606), but Lewalski goes on to remind us that it was as early as Beza's *Chrestienne Meditationes sur huict Pseumes* (Geneva, 1582; Eng. trans. London, 1582) that Calvinist Protestants discovered the adaptability of their sermon form to private meditation.

26 See Edmund S. Morgan, *The Puritan Family: Essays on Religion and Domestic Relations in Seventeenth-Century New England* (Boston: Boston Public Library, 1956), pp. 80–82; Christopher Hill, *Society and Puritanism in Pre-Revolutionary England* (New York: Schocken Books, 1967), pp. 443–70.

27 See, for instance, William Haller's comments on the practice in *The Rise of Puritanism* (New York: Columbia Univ. Press, 1938), p. 136.

28 Lewalski observes: "The basis in Protestant theory for the near-fusion of the sermon and the meditation was the supposed identity of their purposes and their parts. . . . The sermon's purposes were twofold: instruction (carried on by means of an analysis of the text and doctrines), and stimulation of the affections and the heart (achieved through the searching application of text and doctrines to the particular audience)." *Donne's "Anniversaries" and the Poetry of Praise*, p. 85. Significantly, these aims were identical with those of meditation.

29 Martz, *The Poetry of Meditation*, p. 174.

30 Edmund Calamy, "To the Christian Reader," in William Fenner, *The Soules Looking-glasse* (Cambridge, 1640), sig. ¶ 4v.

31 Hooker's *Soules Exaltation* and *A Comment upon Christs Last Prayer* treat later stages of the Puritan's road to glory. As the individual comes closer to ultimate union with God, the immanence of the Spirit becomes more a concern of meditation than it could be in the earlier stages, so characterized by the great distance between man and God. At the later stages, the sinner/saint's topics for meditation as well as his inner experiences become at least potentially mystical. See below, Chapter 14.

32 Martz, *The Poetry of Meditation*, pp. 162–67.

Chapter 10: BECOMING FAITHFUL: THE AFFECTIONS AND THE WILL IN VOCATION

1 John Calvin, *Institutes of the Christian Religion* III. xxiv. 2, trans. Ford Lewis Battles, ed. John T. McNeill (Philadelphia: Westminster Press, 1960), II, 967.

2 Ibid. III. xxiv. 1 (II, 965).

3 John Rogers, "To the Reader," *The Doctrine of Faith*, 2nd ed. (London, 1627); Ezekiel Culverwell, *A Treatise of Faith* (London, 1633), p. 13; William Ames, *The Marrow of Theology*, ed. and trans. John D. Eusden (Boston: Pilgrim Press, 1968), pp. 80, 242; William Perkins, *A Treatise tending vnto a Declaration, whether a man be in the Estate of damnation, or in the estate of grace* (London, 1595), p. 34.

4 TH, "To the Reader," in Rogers, *The Doctrine of Faith;* Hooker's is the second of the two epistles "To the Reader." Quoted here from *Thomas Hooker: Writings in England and Holland, 1626–1633*, ed. George H. Williams et al., Harvard Theological Studies, 28 (Cambridge: Harvard Univ. Press, 1975), p. 144.

5 Pagination of *The Soules Effectuall Calling* begins with p. 33. This is because the printer intended to bind the book with the thirty-page work *The Soules Ingrafting into Christ;* this was done in some cases, but more often they were bound separately. Another publishing error resulted in the omission of some forty-seven pages of the text of the sermon on love and joy. These pages appeared, however, as pp. 220–66 in *The Soules Implantation. A Treatise* (London, 1637); see n. 21, below. Also, large parts of Hooker's earlier *Poor Doubting Christian* reappear in the text of *The Soules Effectuall Calling*. See my discussion of this in "The Growth of *The Poor Doubting Christian*," *Early American Literature*, 8 (Spring 1973), 3–20, an essay building on the partially correct findings in Frank C. Shuffleton, "Thomas Prince and his Edition of Thomas Hooker's *Poor Doubting Christian*," *EAL*, 4 (Winter 1971), 68–75.

6 TH, *The Soules Ingrafting into Christ* (London, 1637), pp. 5–7. Hereafter, quotations from this work will be identified in parentheses with the abbreviation *S Ing.*

7 Ames also discusses active and passive calling in *The Marrow of Theology*. See the Eusden ed., p. 159.

8 Robert Middlekauff discusses Mather's inclination to stress the activity of the affections in *The Mathers: Three Generations of Puritan Intellectuals, 1595–1728* (New York: Oxford Univ. Press, 1971), p. 64. Though B. R. Burg does not make the point directly, he quotes passages from Mather's manuscript sermons which bear it out: e.g., "the heart must needs go out in longing desyres after Christ." *Richard Mather of Dorchester* ([Lexington:] Univ. Press of Kentucky, 1976), p. 81. Hooker's response to the Antinomians' preference for passivity is discussed in Chapter 4, above.

9 Vernon J. Bourke, *Will in Western Thought: An Historico-Critical Survey* (New York: Sheed and Ward, 1941), p. 137. Bourke continues: "Willing becomes an activity motivated by a prior feeling." In contrast, "Continental European philosophy, from Descartes to Hegel, offers no parallel examples of the foregoing British trend toward a position in which feeling becomes a guide for will-activity." Pp. 137, 138.

10 TH, *The Soules Effectuall Calling* (London, 1637), pp. 58–60. This work is sometimes called *The Soules Vocation*, a title which it carried in its 1638 edition. Hereafter, quotations from this book will be identified in parentheses with the abbreviation *SEC*.

11 William Fenner, *A Treatise of the Affections; or, The Soules Pulse* (London, 1642), p. 3. Fenner died in 1640, and all of his published works were issued posthumously. In all likelihood, however, Hooker knew him personally. Both ministered in Essex County, both were befriended and protected by the earl of Warwick, and a manuscript version of Hooker's *Danger of Desertion* turned up in Fenner's papers and was published as Fenner's in his posthumous *Works* (1657) with the title *The Signes of Gods forsaking a People*. See my "Bibliography of the Published Writings of Thomas Hooker" in Williams et al., *Thomas Hooker: Writings in England and Holland*, pp. 411–12.

12 Thoreau, *Walden*, ed. J. Lyndon Shanley (Princeton: Princeton Univ. Press, 1971), p. 333.

13 For example: "Oh, . . . these old corruptions are ever dogging of me" (*SEC*, p. 154); "Oh that I had this free *grace* above all the rest" (p. 155); "Oh happy I that know it" (p. 155); "What, shall all my expectations be void?" (p. 156); "Oh the Gospell is a precious Jewell" (p. 167).

14 This is a rephrasing of Rachel's plea to her husband Jacob, "Give me children, or else I die" (Gen. 30:1). A similar passage occurs a little later in the book, where Hooker says, "Conceive two women, the one sicke, the other in love, both desire the Physitian; the sicke desires the Physitian, to bee healed by him, the other desires him not so much to be healed, but shee is desirous to be married to him. So it is with the soule that is carried in a kinde of love and affection to godlinesse, hee would not have Christ onely to heale him, but he would be married to Christ, that hee may enjoy the God of all pardoning, that he may enjoy the God of all purging and purifying" (*SEC*, p. 186).

15 The use of sexual love as a metaphoric equivalent for the love of God is discussed by Edmund S. Morgan in "The Puritan's Marriage with God," *South Atlantic Quarterly*, 48 (Jan. 1949), 107–12. Edward Taylor was much given to this type of imagery in his poetic "Preparatory Meditations," especially those on texts in Canticles. Karl Keller has discussed Taylor's erotic imagery, citing his particular debts to Calvin as well as to Canticles and the Gospel of John (Hooker's text for *The Soules Effectuall Calling* is, in fact, John 6:45). See Keller, *The Example of Edward Taylor* (Amherst: Univ. of Massachusetts Press, 1975), pp. 206–20. Stephen Fender suggests Hooker's imagery had a direct influence on Taylor's in "Edward Taylor and 'The Application of Redemption,' " *Modern Language Review*, 59 (July 1964), 331–34.

16 The text for the sermon, John 7:37 reads: "If any man thirst, let him come unto me and drink." The possibility of Hooker's authorship of *Spirituall*

Thirst was first suggested in print by Winfried Herget in "Preaching and Publication: Chronology and the Style of Thomas Hooker's Sermons," *Harvard Theological Review*, 65 (April 1972), 234. For detailed substantiation of this claim see my "Four New Works by Thomas Hooker: Identity and Significance," *Resources for American Literary Study*, 4 (Spring 1974), 3–26.

17 TH, *Spirituall Thirst* (London, 1638), pp. 13–14. Hereafter, quotations from this book will be identified in parentheses with the abbreviation *ST*.

18 Ames was in essential agreement with Hooker on the shape of this orderliness. See *The Marrow of Theology*, p. 241, points 12–16.

19 Jonathan Edwards, *Religious Affections*, ed. John E. Smith, in *The Works of Jonathan Edwards*, II (New Haven: Yale Univ. Press, 1959), p. 162.

20 For comment on this contrast between the proponents of a sequential morphology of conversion and Edwards, see Eugene White, *Puritan Rhetoric: The Issue of Emotion in Religion* (Carbondale: Southern Illinois Univ. Press, 1972), pp. 45–46, and Norman Pettit, "Hooker's Doctrine of Assurance: A Critical Phase in New England Spiritual Thought," *New England Quarterly*, 47 (Dec. 1974), 530.

21 The seventh sermon in *The Soules Effectuall Calling* begins on p. 202 and ends abruptly on p. 279, where a discussion of four kinds of hypocrites is only partially completed. The next sermon, which deals with the will, begins abruptly on the succeeding page. The fourth, and last, sermon in *The Soules Implantation* is nearly identical to the other text (after a difference in the opening section), except that it does not break off at the same point but considers all four types of hypocrites, adding a concluding Use of exhortation, and ending the whole sermon with the comment, "Thus you have heard the sermon read."

22 Fenner, *A Treatise of the Affections*, p. 128.

23 See Rogers, *The Doctrine of Faith*, pp. 157–75.

24 See Ames's description of hope in *The Marrow of Theology*, pp. 245–50, and his passing reference to desire, p. 252. Perkins explains that after humbling the sinner, "the Lord stirreth up in his heart a vehement desire and longing after Christ and his merites: this desire is compared to thirst [Rev. 21:6]: which is not onely the feeling of the drinesse of the stomack, but also a vehement appetite after drink, and David fitly expresseth it when he sayth; [Psalm 143:6] *I stretched foorth my hands vnto thee: my soule desireth after thee as the thirstie land* [Ps. 143:6]." Perkins, *A Treatise tending vnto a Declaration*, pp. 27–28. Thus, Hooker's innovation in treating desire comes, not in his perception of its existence, but in the degree of elaboration in his treatment of it.

25 In the version of this sermon printed in *The Soules Implantation*, Hooker identifies and quotes a particular passage in Perkins's *Cases of Conscience* as his reference here. See *The Soules Implantation*, p. 156.

26 John Rogers, *A Treatise of Love* (London, 1632), p. 11.

27 On this traditional connection between love and the third person in the Trinity, see William J. Scheick, *The Will and the Word: The Poetry of Edward Taylor* (Athens, Ga.: Univ. of Georgia Press, 1974), p. 76.

28 See, for instance, the discussion of John Donne's use of this imagery in Winfried Schleiner, *The Imagery of John Donne's Sermons* (Providence, R.I.: Brown Univ. Press, 1970).

29 Relevant discussions of this use of the marriage metaphor appear in Scheick, *The Will and the Word*, pp. 68–69 (previously published in "A Viper's Nest, the Feather bed of Faith: Edward Taylor on the Will," *Early American Literature*, 5 [Fall 1970], 47—48); and in the Morgan and Keller works cited in n. 15, above. A more broadly based but relevant discussion of the theological uses of sexual imagery in the Renaissance is Purvis E. Boyette, "Milton and the Sacred Fire: Sex Symbolism in *Paradise Lost*," *Literary Monographs*, v (Madison: Univ. of Wisconsin Press, 1973), 65–138.

30 The King James and Geneva versions say merely, "Jesus saith unto her, Mary. She turned herself, and saith unto him, Rabboni; which is to say, Master. Jesus saith unto her, Touch me not; for I am not yet ascended to my Father." The "marvellous violence" of a physical embrace is entirely Hooker's own embellishment.

31 The verse following the one that Hooker quotes reads, "Nevertheless, to avoid fornication, let every man have his own wife, and let every woman have her own husband" (1 Cor. 7:2).

32 See, for instance, Nicholas Breton's prose commentary on John 20:10–18, *Mary Magdalen's Loue* (1595), and Gervase Markham's *Marie Magdalene's Teares* (1601). Joseph Burns Collins, *Christian Mysticism in the Elizabethan Age* (Baltimore: Johns Hopkins Univ. Press, 1940), discusses some of this literature; see esp. pp. 147–49 and 183–85.

33 TH, *The Soules Implantation*, p. 256.

34 Karl Keller, in speaking of Edward Taylor's characterization of God as "the Great Lover," says that "Taylor is probing the nature of a God who should seek worthless man. God so loves mankind that he puts on the appearance of a young buck 'with the purest ruddy looks' (Christ as the young man of Canticles)." *The Example of Edward Taylor*, p. 214. Taylor's imagery in this respect is not different in kind from Hooker's.

35 TH, *The Soules Implantation*, p. 230.

36 Ibid., p. 247.

37 Marsilio Ficino, quoted by Paul Oskar Kristellar in *The Philosophy of Marsilio Ficino*, trans. Virginia Conant (New York: Columbia Univ. Press, 1943), p. 273.

38 Norman Fiering, "Will and Intellect in the New England Mind," *William and Mary Quarterly*, 29 (Oct. 1972), 537–41. See also Eusden, "Introduction" to Ames, *The Marrow of Theology*, p. 49.

39 Fiering, "Will and Intellect," p. 541.

40 Ames, *The Marrow of Theology*, p. 82.

41 See Eusden, "Introduction" to ibid., pp. 48–49. Scheick, *The Will and the Word*, demonstrates that Edward Taylor also belonged in this tradition; see his chap. 3, esp. pp. 49–51.

42 An essential point in Richard Sibbes's *Saints Priviledge; or, A Christians Constant Advocate* (London, 1639) is that the redeemed saint knows the sufficiency of grace in his soul by his inward feeling of joy.

43 Thomas Shepard, *Gods Plot: The Paradoxes of Puritan Piety, Being the Autobiography and Journal of Thomas Shepard*, ed. Michael McGiffert (Amherst: Univ. of Massachusetts Press, 1972), p. 122.

44 Though it is not quite accurate to say that "Hooker was the first of the Jacobean Puritan divines . . . to be concerned with the 'lets and impediments' that men set up" to block their assurance of grace (Pettit, "Hooker's Doctrine of Assurance," p. 521), his concern with these obstacles is nevertheless a distinguishing characteristic of his analysis. Similar examinations of "lets and hindrances" to faith appear in Ezekiel Culverwell, *The Way to a Blessed Estate in this Life* (London, 1633), p. 11, and John Rogers, *The Doctrine of Faith* (London, 1629), pp. 384–402.

45 In this section the volume incorporates parts of Hooker's first published book, *The Poor Doubting Christian*, a rapidly selling little work of encouragement to timid Christians. This helps to account for both the extraordinary length of the final sermon in *The Soules Effectuall Calling* and the comforting, positive encouragement which dominates the tone of the latter portion.

46 Richard Sibbes, "Discouragement's Recovery," quoted by Larzer Ziff in *The Career of John Cotton: Puritanism and the American Experience* (Princeton: Princeton Univ. Press, 1962), p. 31. Thomas Shepard comments personally to the same effect in *God's Plot*, p. 214. See also Pettit, "Hooker's Doctrine of Assurance," pp. 522–23.

47 This is just how John Rogers had ended his *Doctrine of Faith*; see pp. 454–501.

Chapter 11: BACONIAN AND PLATONIC ASPECTS OF THE APPROACH TO SPIRITUAL TRUTH

1 See William T. Costello, *The Scholastic Curriculum at Early Seventeenth-Century Cambridge* (Cambridge: Harvard Univ. Press, 1958), pp. 8–35. Quotations are from pp. 8 and 35.

2 Basil Willey, *The Seventeenth Century Background: Studies in the Thought of the Age in Relation to Poetry and Religion* (Garden City, N.Y.: Doubleday, 1953), p. 17.

3 Costello, *The Scholastic Curriculum*, p. 100.

4 Joseph Rickaby, *Scholasticism* (New York: Dodge, 1908), p. 50.

5 Willey, *The Seventeenth Century Background*, p. 27.

6 Quoted in ibid., p. 33.

7 Perry Miller, *The New England Mind: The Seventeenth Century* (New York: Macmillan, 1939), p. 123.

8 Wilbur Samuel Howell, *Logic and Rhetoric in England, 1500–1700* (Princeton: Princeton Univ. Press, 1956), p. 179. On Ramism at Cambridge see also James Bass Mullinger, *The University of Cambridge* (Cambridge: Cambridge Univ. Press, 1884), II, 404–19; Miller, *The New England Mind: The Seventeenth Century*, pp. 117–43 passim; Samuel Eliot Morison, *The Founding of Harvard College* (Cambridge: Harvard Univ. Press, 1935), pp. 60–78.

9 Miller, *The New England Mind: The Seventeenth Century,* p. 499; Walter J. Ong, *Ramus, Method, and the Decay of Dialogue* (Cambridge: Harvard Univ. Press, 1958), pp. 301–2.

10 Miller, *The New England Mind: The Seventeenth Century,* pp. 118–53.

11 TH, *The Application of Redemption, The Ninth and Tenth Books* (London, 1656), pp. 53–54. This passage is used to exemplify the spirit of experimental verification in the period by both Charles Feidelson, Jr., in *Symbolism and American Literature* (Chicago: Univ. of Chicago Press, 1953), p. 99, and Gabriel Josipovici in *The World and the Book* (Stanford, Calif.: Stanford Univ. Press, 1971), p. 145.

12 It is true, of course, that the Puritan preachers who emigrated to New England enjoyed an almost immediate acceptance as major voices in social and political matters. They ascended, in other words, to an authoritarian role in practically all dimensions of life—a position which they had certainly not so fully enjoyed in Anglican Caroline England.

13 William Haller, *The Rise of Puritanism* (New York: Columbia Univ. Press, 1938), p. 299.

14 Willey, *The Seventeenth Century Background,* p. 123. Bacon's comment in *The Advancement of Learning* speaks directly to this point: "Another error hath proceeded from too great a reverence and a kind of adoration of the mind and understanding of man, by means whereof men have withdrawn themselves too much from the contemplation of nature and the observations of experience, and have tumbled up and down in their own reason and conceits." Francis Bacon, *Essays, Advancement of Learning, New Atlantis, and Other Pieces,* ed. Richard Foster Jones (New York: Odyssey, 1937), pp. 211–12.

15 Quoted in Geoffrey Nuttall, *The Holy Spirit in Puritan Faith and Experience* (Oxford: Basil Blackwell, 1947), p. 39. Nuttall, in citing the inclination of the "radical Puritans" to make spiritual perception analogous to the physical perceptions of the senses, quotes this and other relevant remarks by Sibbes but nowhere in this connection mentions Hooker, whose writing is rife with working examples very much to Nuttall's point.

16 Quoted in Miller, *The New England Mind: The Seventeenth Century,* p. 162. Miller called this passage "an epitome of the Puritan Mind." Miller's whole discussion of technologia is relevant to my comments on the "inductive" aspects of Hooker's redemption message; see his chap. 6, pp. 154–80.

17 Eugene F. Rice, Jr., *The Renaissance Idea of Wisdom* (Cambridge: Harvard Univ. Press, 1958).

18 Rice discusses Charron's Baconian desire to separate entirely the realms of reason and faith; see p. 203.

19 Bacon, *The Advancement of Learning,* pp. 214, 215.

20 Haller, *The Rise of Puritanism,* p. 299.

21 See ibid., chap. 8, esp. pp. 293–308.

22 Cotton Mather, "Piscator Evangelicus; or, The Life of Mr. Thomas Hooker" in *Johannes in Eremo* (Boston, 1695), p. 9.

23 C. A. Patrides, *The Cambridge Platonists* (London: Edward Arnold, 1962), p. 4.

24 William Ames, for instance, was rather careful to avoid the taint of Platonism in his "Technometria." Miller, *The New England Mind: The Seventeenth Century*, p. 177, and Keith Sprunger, *The Learned Doctor William Ames: Dutch Backgrounds of English and American Puritanism* (Urbana: Univ. of Illinois Press, 1972), pp. 116–17, both comment on Ames's explicit denial of Platonic tendencies.

25 *Plato's Symposium*, trans. Benjamin Jowett (New York: Liberal Arts Press, 1956), p. 52.

26 A Latin translation of Plato's works was in the library of Emmanuel College early enough to have been included in the first surviving inventory of the library's contents. This inventory is undated but internal evidence indicates a date of ca. 1597. Emmanuel College MS, Lib. 1.3, fol. 185v. The only Latin *Opera* of Plato of appropriate date now in Emmanuel College's possession is the Basel, 1561, edition which includes Marsilio Ficino's commentary. There is no evidence in the volume to prove conclusively that this is the very copy that was present during Hooker's years at Emmanuel, though many such volumes do survive there. A Greek edition of Plato—probably the Basel, 1534, with Proclus's commentary—was added to the college's library sometime during the period 1622–26. Emmanuel College MS, Bur. 8.1, fol. 137. Carl Rasmussen and I are currently preparing for publication a complete catalogue of the Emmanuel College library's early holdings.

27 Augustine, *Concerning the City of God against the Pagans*, trans. Henry Bettenson (London: Penguin, 1972), p. 311.

28 This spirit is pervasive in Augustine's *Confessions* in passages such as the following: "For it is one thing, from the mountain's shaggy top to see the land of peace, and to find no way thither; and in vain to essay through ways unpassable, opposed and beset by fugitives and deserters, under their captain *the lion and the dragon*, and another to keep on the way that leads thither, guarded by the host of the heavenly General." Trans. E. B. Pusey (London: J. M. Dent, and Toronto: E. P. Dutton, 1907), p. 146.

29 Ernst Cassirer, *The Platonic Renaissance in England*, trans. James P. Pettegrove (Austin: Univ. of Texas Press, 1953), p. 93.

30 Ibid., pp. 11–16.

31 William Ralph Inge, *The Platonic Tradition in English Religious Thought* (New York and London: Longmans, Green, 1926), p. 39.

32 Geoffrey F. Nuttall, *The Puritan Spirit: Essays and Addresses* (London: Epworth Press, 1967), p. 51.

33 Cassirer, *The Platonic Renaissance in England*, p. 8.

34 For discussions of this influence, see Paul Oskar Kristeller, *The Philosophy of Marsilio Ficino*, trans. Virginia Conant (New York: Columbia Univ. Press, 1943), pp. 18–20; Frederick J. Powicke, *The Cambridge Platonists: A Study* (Cambridge: Harvard Univ. Press, 1926), pp. 12–13; James Deotis Roberts, Sr., *From Puritanism to Platonism in Seventeenth Century England* (The Hague: Martinus Nijhoff, 1968), pp. 26–30.

35 Rice, *The Renaissance Idea of Wisdom*, p. 64.

36 Quoted in Kristeller, *The Philosophy of Marsilio Ficino*, p. 268.

37 Ibid., p. 273.

38 *Plato's Symposium*, p. 53.

39 Ficino started out as an intellectualist but eventually swung to a firm voluntarist stance. See Kristeller, *The Philosophy of Marsilio Ficino*, pp. 271–76.

40 Rice, *The Renaissance Idea of Wisdom*, p. 37. The same emphasis is present in the psychological thinking of the medieval Franciscans, through whom it came down to later times in such works as the *Book on the Soul* by William of Varouillon. See Vernon J. Bourke, *Will in Western Thought: An Historico-Critical Survey* (New York: Sheed and Ward, 1964), pp. 132–37.

41 Cassirer, *The Platonic Renaissance in England*, p. 102.

42 Francis de Sales, *Treatise on the Love of God*, IV. 3, quoted in Joseph Burns Collins, *Christian Mysticism in the Elizabethan Age* (Baltimore: Johns Hopkins Press, 1940), pp. 208–9.

43 The Cambridge Platonists ultimately went further in their stress on love than their predecessors, managing to merge Reason and Will in their concept of Eros so that in Henry More's thought the once crucial distinction between voluntarism and intellectualism becomes meaningless. See Cassirer, *The Platonic Renaissance in England*, p. 126.

44 On the lightness of the ascent, see Kristeller, *The Philosophy of Marsilio Ficino*. English Renaissance writers sympathetic to Platonism did not necessarily see the spiritual life in the same way as the Cambridge Platonists, who, like Ficino, were inclined to minimize its difficulties. In fact, it is a more characteristic approach to stress the need for individual heroism. Spenser's Red Cross Knight, Bunyan's Christian, and Milton's Christ all appealed to Puritan readers partly because of their demonstration of heroic energy against very imposing opposition in their spiritual striving. And in the end they are rewarded, as is Hooker's "faithfull" soul. All followed the Platonic pattern of the quest for the ideal while also facing formidable opposition both in their own natures (Milton's Christ excepted) and in the world around them.

45 A manuscript in the Cambridge University Archives, CUR. 31. 1., lists the holdings of the Cambridge University Library in 1582–83. Though it does not mention Ficino, it does include two volumes of Pico della Mirandola and three of Nicholas de Cusa, both of whom influenced Ficino. The Emmanuel College Library acquired the two-volume Basel, 1601, edition of Pico's works in 1625 and two volumes of Cusa in the period 1622–26. Emm. Coll. MS, Bur. 8.1.

46 Benjamin Whichcote, the oldest of the Platonists and their long-time leader at Cambridge, arrived at Emmanuel College as a seventeen-year-old scholar in 1626, eight years after Hooker's departure.

47 Willey, *The Seventeenth Century Background*, p. 141.

48 Accounting for the rather sudden rise of Platonism at Emmanuel College after 1630 provides an interesting challenge which is beyond the scope of

this study. It is worth noting that in 1622 the influential John Preston became master there. One of Preston's biographers feels that his relatively intellectual version of Puritanism (a generalization which itself needs critical scrutiny) helped pave the way for the highly rational Platonists of Whichcote's generation. See Irvonwy Morgan, *Prince Charles's Puritan Chaplain* (London: Allen & Unwin, 1957), p. 205.

Chapter 12: GOING BEYOND FAITH: UNION, JUSTIFICATION, ADOPTION, SANCTIFICATION

1 See especially pp. 264–79 of *The Soules Exaltation* (London, 1638), where the organizational pattern of Hooker's points and subpoints becomes badly garbled.
2 TH, *The Soules Exaltation*, pp. 3–4. Hereafter, page references to this work will be indicated in parentheses with the abbreviation *SE*.
3 At this point Hooker successfully avoids dragging in comments on particular authorities, partly because he is at odds with them. He protests, "I am not greatly willing to meddle with this point in this popular congregation, because there are many wise and orthodox Divines, and godly too, which are of contrary opinion" (*SE*, p. 39).
4 For comment on this dispute see Geoffrey Nuttall, *The Holy Spirit in Puritan Faith and Experience* (Oxford: Basil Blackwell, 1947), pp. 22–25.
5 Adding to the deficiency in the note-taking, the printer, John Haviland, marked the apparent beginning of the section of the book called "The Soules Justification" with a decorative upper border and an enlarged type title on p. 131, some eighteen pages and one whole sermon after the actual beginning of Hooker's discussion of justification on p. 113.
6 John Calvin, *Institutes of the Christian Religion* III. xi, trans. and ed. John Allen (Philadelphia, 1932), I, 661.
7 *The Poems of Edward Taylor*, ed. Donald E. Stanford (New Haven: Yale Univ. Press, 1960), pp. 397–98.
8 In 1602, fighting in eastern Hungary (Transylvania), Smith was wounded and captured by the Turkish army, eventually being sold as a slave and transported to Constantinople. When he finally arrived back in England in 1603 he was wealthier by a thousand ducats and the proud possessor of a coat of arms showing three Turk's heads, representing his beheading of three Turkish heroes in single combat before his enslavement. Though Smith was not tried as a traitor, his story exemplifies the contrasting conditions mentioned by Hooker. Smith's own full account was not published until 1630 in his *True Travels, Adventures, and Observations of Captaine John Smith*, but a partial version appeared in *Purchas, His Pilgrimes* (London, 1625), where it became well-known.

Other published accounts of Englishmen's travels and captivities in Turkey in the first three decades of the century may, singly or cumulatively, have led to Hooker's interesting reference to a Turkish captive. See, for instance, George Sandys, *Relation of a Journey* . . . (London, 1615), and Anthony Munday, *The Admirable Deliverance of 266 Christians* (London, 1608).

Bradford Smith, *Captain John Smith: His Life and Legend* (Philadelphia: Lippincott, 1953), p. 357, mentions still more such accounts. Another Hooker reference to "a man that is led into captivitie, into Turkie, into Algeir, or the like" also occurs in *SE* on p. 75 and further suggests Hooker's recent exposure to some of this literature of Turkish wars and travel.

9 John Preston, *The Breast-Plate of Faith and Love*, 2nd ed. (London, 1630), p. 64.

10 TH, *A Comment upon Christs Last Prayer* (London, 1656), p. 59. He goes on to say that "this sending of our Savior" is "the very Hinge upon which the Gospel turns: The very foundation, upon which the work of our Salvation hangs" (p. 75).

11 See *SE*, pp. 203, 221–22, 235–36, 264–65, 267–71, 274–75, 281, 296.

12 The date of composition and/or delivery of the sermons in *The Soules Exaltation* is not and probably cannot be precisely known. Yet Hooker speaks of being "here" in England (p. 141) and describes his sermons on Union as "lectures." Such details encourage the dating of the work between 1625 and 1629, the years of his Chelmsford lectureship. This also appears to have been the period in which he preached most of those sermons that were finally published in London in 1637 and 1638.

The learned and skilled controversialist Bellarmine was of course the archetypal Roman Catholic antagonist for Protestant apologists, especially in England. A good example of Protestant defense of their doctrine of Justification, with frequent cuts at the Catholics, and especially at Bellarmine, is by the Bishop of Derry, George Downham: *A Treatise of Justification* (London, 1633).

13 TH, *The Saints Dignitie and Dutie* (London, 1651), pp. 1–43.

14 William Ames, *The Marrow of Theology*, trans. and ed. John D. Eusden (Boston: Pilgrim Press, 1968), p. 165.

15 TH, *The Christians Two Chiefe Lessons* (London, 1640), p. 289. Hereafter, quotations from *The Priviledge of Adoption* will be indicated in parentheses with the abbreviation *CTCL*.

16 John Davenport, *A Profession of Faith, made by the Reverend Divine, M[r] John Davenport at his admission into one of the Churches of God in New-England*, published in John Cotton, *The Covenant of Gods Free Grace* (London, 1645), p. 38. The view of Hooker, Ames, and Davenport is different from that of other Protestants such as George Downham, who said that adoption is simply a part of justification. See *A Treatise of Justification*, p. 77. Perkins seems to have been closer to this view than to that of his Puritan followers, claiming that adoption is "annexed unto" justification; see Perkins, *A Golden Chain* (London 1597), p. 148.

17 See Ames's *Marrow of Theology*, pp. 165–67, where he lists four such differences.

18 Hooker's particular opinions on the requirements and procedures for church membership are described in Chapter 5 above. See the basic study of the question for all of New England in Edmund S.

Morgan, *Visible Saints: The History of a Puritan Idea* (New York: New York Univ. Press, 1963), esp. pp. 87–93.

19 TH, *An Exposition of the Principles of Religion* (London, 1645), p. 24; Ames, *The Marrow of Theology*, p. 167; Preston, *Cuppe of Blessing* (London, 1633), quoted in J. Sears McGee, *The Godly Man in Stuart England: Anglicans, Puritans, and the Two Tables, 1620–1670* (New Haven: Yale Univ. Press, 1976), pp. 177–78; Cotton, *The Covenant of Gods Free Grace*, p. 27. William Perkins, in discussing predestination and sanctification, listed nine "effects" of sanctification. Good works are not among these, though in concluding his discussion of the subject he lists five things which "beeing the servants of Christ we are admonished," the fifth of which is "to doe good works." *A Golden Chaine; or, The Description of Theologie* in *Workes* (Cambridge, 1609), I, 115–16.

20 As is often the case, his quotation of this text actually merges the King James and Geneva translations. The wording is exactly that of the Geneva translation except for the phrase "or make no provision," which is slightly altered from the King James version. He may have been quoting from memory or, equally possible, his note-taking auditor may have mixed the passages.

21 TH, *The Soules Possession of Christ* (London, 1638), p. 6. Hereafter, quotations from this work will be indicated in parentheses with the abbreviation *SPo*.

22 An intriguing and as yet mysterious entry appears in the *Stationers Register* for May 6, 1639, which in all likelihood bears on Hooker's use of this clothing metaphor for sanctification. On that date the Stationer's clerk entered to the printers R. Young and Fulke Clifton, who had published other Hooker works, a work called "The Garments of Salvation first putt off by the Fall of our first Parents. Secondly, putt on again by the Grace of the Gospel. By T. H." To date, no copy of such a book has been found. It may not have been printed, but whether it was or not, it may well have been a fuller version of Hooker's treatment of sanctification.

23 TH, *An Exposition of the Principles of Religion*, p. 26. On the use of these terms by Puritans generally and by William Perkins in particular, see M. van Beek, *An Enquiry into Puritan Vocabulary* (Groningen: Wolters-Noordhoff, 1969), p. 63.

24 In *The Gift of Gifts*, the first sermon in *The Saints Dignitie and Dutie*, Hooker said, "Where ever there is faith, there is a victorie over the world, before there is faith, there the soul is a slave to the world, but if once there be faith, he is more then conquerour, he is not the worlds slave, but the world is his, the world is trampled under his feet, and is a dead flower to him, that hath neither beauty nor sweetness in it" (p. 7).

25 TH, *The Saints Dignitie and Dutie*, p. 54. Hereafter, quotations from this volume will be indicated in parentheses with the abbreviation *SDD*.

26 William Perkins, *An Exposition of the Creed* in *Workes* (London, 1609), I, 259–60.

Chapter 13: A PURITAN ETHIC

1 William Perkins, *The True Gaine: More in Worth then all the Goods in the World,* in *Workes* (Cambridge, 1609), I, 639.

2 Perkins, *A Warning against the Idolatrie of the Last Times,* in *Workes,* I, 665.

3 See Keith L. Sprunger, *The Learned Doctor William Ames: Dutch Backgrounds of English and American Puritanism* (Urbana: Univ. of Illinois Press, 1972), chap. 8, pp. 153–82. George L. Mosse, in *The Holy Pretence: A Study in Christianity and Reason of State from William Perkins to John Winthrop* (Oxford: Basil Blackwell, 1957), devotes a chapter each to Perkins and Ames on morality; see pp. 48–87. An important study of Anglican ethical thought in Hooker's era is H. R. McAdoo, *The Structure of Caroline Moral Theology* (London: Longmans, Green, 1949). J. Sears McGee has written an important comparative study on Anglican and Puritan approaches to morality, *The Godly Man in Stuart England: Anglicans, Puritans, and the Two Tables, 1620–1670* (New Haven: Yale Univ. Press, 1976). The Hookerian ethic which I describe in this chapter is closely consistent with the broadly Puritan position which McGee contrasts with Anglican moral teaching.

4 See Mosse, *The Holy Pretence,* pp. 34–47, and Sprunger, *The Learned Doctor William Ames,* pp. 153–60. My research currently in progress on the early library holdings of Emmanuel College, Cambridge, reveals that while the library had owned nearly from its beginning (1584) such standard works as Aristotle's *Ethics* (supplemented by several commentaries, including Melanchthon's) and Plutarch's *Moralia* (parts of which, at least, fall in the category of ethical teaching), an important cluster of more modern works on moral theology was added between 1622 and 1637. This includes the period of John Preston's Mastership at Emmanuel, but more importantly it was a period of growing interest in moral theology among Protestants. Most of the works on this subject added during the period are by continental Roman Catholic writers, such as the Spanish Jesuit Thomas Sanchez, the Austrian Jesuit Paul Laymann, and the Italian Jesuit moral theologian Vincenzo Fililucci.

5 See William Haller, *The Rise of Puritanism* (New York, 1957), pp. 117–20.

6 Both Anglicans and Puritans, though adopting medieval psychology, were postlegalist in moral theology. The similarity of the Anglican to the Puritan emphasis is underlined in McAdoo's statement that "the Anglican moralists endeavored to give emphasis in practice to that which moral theology had always stressed in principle, the liberty and authority of the individual conscience." *The Structure of Caroline Moral Theology,* p. 71. J. Sears McGee, however, has shown that in England, Anglicans and Puritans differed on the fundamental point of how much one could rely on the human will to produce good actions. McGee argues that "Anglicans were convinced that the things essential to salvation were easily comprehensible and few in number. All that was needed [to produce moral acts] was the effort of will to make use of them by applying them to conduct." "Unlike Puritans, Anglicans found it possible to think of themselves as achieving a significant measure of perfection in their 'conversation' among men. They could achieve

what He asked, because He had not asked for more than they could do."
The Godly Man in Stuart England, pp. 103–4. The drastic difference between this idea and the thinking of Hooker and other Puritans on human
nature and grace as well as morality is easily apparent.

7 This is not to say that they entirely avoided moral issues. But Thomas
Shepard's *Sound Believer* is a characteristic example in that in dealing with
life "according to the rule of the moral law," he actually concerns himself
chiefly with the condition of the heart. See *The Works of Thomas Shepard,*
ed. John A. Albro (Boston: Doctrinal Tract and Book Society, 1853; rpt.
New York: AMS Press, 1967), I, 275–84. The same is largely true of John
Cotton's *Way of Life* (1641).

8 Robert Middlekauff, *The Mathers: Three Generations of Puritan Intellectuals* (New York: Oxford Univ. Press, 1971), p. 173. A work which serves as a
good illustration of the kind of book not written by New Englanders in the
earliest generation of colonization but increasingly common in the later
decades of the century is Samuel Arnold's *David Serving His Generation*
(Cambridge, Mass., 1674). Arnold delivered this address to the Plymouth
General Court on June 3, 1674, arguing in it that "every Christian ought to
be . . . serviceable unto God and to the present generation," thus placing
primary emphasis on the idea that the *world* ought to be a primary ben-
eficiary of one's salvation. The inner-directed stress on cultivation of the
soul, so common a refrain in Hooker's day, had by 1674 already begun to
seem subordinate to moral action.

9 Franklin commented in his *Autobiography* that "there was also a Book . . .
of Dr. Mather's, called Essays to do Good which perhaps gave me a Turn
of Thinking that had an Influence on some of the principal Events of my
Life." *The Autobiography of Benjamin Franklin,* ed. Leonard Labaree et
al. (New Haven: Yale Univ. Press, 1964), p. 58.

10 The only book dealing primarily with Edwards's ideas on morality is Clyde
A. Holbrook, *The Ethics of Jonathan Edwards: Morality and Aesthetics*
(Ann Arbor: Univ. of Michigan Press, 1973). Norman Fiering, in "Will and
Intellect in the New England Mind," *William and Mary Quarterly,* 29
(Oct. 1972), concludes by indicating the close connection between the ideas
of seventeenth-century voluntarists and Jonathan Edwards, a connection
which leads one to the parallel patterns of thought in Hooker and Edwards
which I am here suggesting; see Fiering, esp. pp. 551–58.

11 See n. 2, Introduction, above.

12 Sprunger, *The Learned Doctor William Ames,* p. 163.

13 TH, *The Properties of an honest Heart* (London, 1638), pp. 35–36. John S.
Coolidge discusses the Puritan "doctrine of marks" and its implications in
the light of John Cotton's opposition to it. See *The Pauline Renaissance in
England: Puritanism and the Bible* (Oxford: Clarendon Press, 1970), pp.
126–32.

14 On p. 8 Hooker writes, "Now lay these Motives close to thy heart, and
apply them to thine owne conscience, who ever thou art that readest this
booke."

15 Hooker gives particular emphasis to the freedom-slavery metaphor throughout *The Saints Dignitie and Dutie* and *The Saints Guide*. See Norman Pettit's discussion of the concept of the two laws in *The Heart Prepared: Grace and Conversion in Puritan Spiritual Life* (New Haven: Yale Univ. Press, 1966), pp. 15–17.

16 This latter observation is typical of Hooker's psychological understanding of the problems people face in confronting scriptural admonitions to good action. He is never so simplistic as to assume that men can obey the Law just because they are told to do so. The easy (and often incorrect) use of the term "the Puritan ethic" in our day ascribes to the Puritans a mechanically legalistic and unfeeling way of thinking about morality which is simply not present in Hooker's thought.

17 See *The Faithful Covenanter* (London, 1644), p. 13.

18 TH, *The Saints Dignitie and Dutie* (London, 1651), p. 113.

19 In fact, his penultimate Use in the third sermon in *The Saints Dignitie and Dutie*, a sermon entitled *Grace Magnified; or, The Priviledges of Those that are under Grace*, instructs those still in a "natural state" that they are "under the Law" and will not go to heaven even though the saints of God may commit greater sins (see *The Saints Dignitie and Dutie*, p. 117). Coolidge comments very much to the point in his claim that the doctrine of grace, not predestination, was the central tenet for Calvin and his followers; see *The Pauline Renaissance in England*, pp. 115–16.

20 On this trend in England, see McAdoo, *The Structure of Caroline Moral Theology*, chaps. 1–2.

21 TH, *The Saints Guide* (London, 1645), p. 97.

22 Perkins, *A Golden Chaine*, in *Workes*, I, 32, 49.

23 TH, *The Saints Guide*, p. 92.

24 McGee, *The Godly Man in Stuart England*, chap. 3, "The Two Tables."

25 Richard Sibbes, *The Saints Cordialls* (London, 1637), p. 141, quoted in McGee, *The Godly Man in Stuart England*, p. 71.

26 TH, *The Christians Two Chiefe Lessons* (London, 1640), p. 224.

27 Haller, *The Rise of Puritanism*, p. 123.

28 Thomas Shepard, *The Sincere Convert*, in *The Works of Thomas Shepard*, I, 104. By contrast, the Anglicans, though they did not believe moral perfection to be attainable, did, as McGee points out, "generally regard the human will as more puissant than the Puritans did." *The Godly Man in Stuart England*, p. 108.

29 TH, *The Plantation of the Righteous*, in *The Saints Guide*, p. 146. Hereafter, quotations from this sermon will be indicated in parentheses with the abbreviation *PR*. This sermon was first published with the same title in a book called variously *Three Godly Sermons* and *Three Sermons* (1638). The later version in *The Saints Guide* (1645) is fuller and more polished.

30 Several scholars have discussed the sources and meaning of this metaphor. See, for instance, Ursula Brumm, "The 'Tree of Life' in Edward Taylor's Meditations," *Early American Literature*, 3 (Fall 1968), 72–87; Thomas Werge, "The Tree of Life in Edward Taylor's Poetry: The Sources of a

Puritan Image," ibid., 3 (Winter 1968–69), 199–204; Cecelia L. Halbert, "Tree of Life Imagery in the Poetry of Edward Taylor," *American Literature*, 38 (March 1966), 22–34.

"Duties" meant not only deeds done to or for other people but also included use of the "ordinances" of prayer, public worship, and Holy Communion.

31 TH, *The Saints Dignitie and Dutie*, p. 163.
32 TH, *The Paterne of Perfection* (London, 1640), p. 93. This work is especially concerned with the issues discussed in this chapter. See esp. pp. 86–113.
33 Everett Emerson, "Thomas Hooker: The Puritan as Theologian," *Anglican Theological Review*, 49 (April 1967), 201.
34 Quoted in McGee, *The Godly Man in Stuart England*, p. 189.
35 Holbrook distinguishes between "simple" and "compounded" self-love in Edwards, a distinction which also applies at this point in Hooker's thought. See Holbrook, *The Ethics of Jonathan Edwards*, pp. 58–64.
36 Augustine, *Concerning the City of God against the Pagans* XIX. 14, trans. David Knowles (London: Penguin Books, 1972), p. 873. This is the principle which validates a summary statement like that of James Deotis Roberts: "Reverence for self and God are so interrelated that Christian morals begin with the reformation of the inward man. . . . The actions of the good life proceed from the heart and only 'the pure in heart shall see God.' " *From Puritanism to Platonism in Seventeenth-Century England* (The Hague, 1968), p. 151. See also Richard Baxter's *Reasons of the Christian Religion* (London, 1667), pp. 90–92.
37 Augustine, *Concerning the City of God*, p. 873.
38 TH, *The Carnal Hypocrite*, Document III in *Thomas Hooker: Writings in England and Holland, 1626–1633*, ed. George H. Williams et al., Harvard Theological Studies, 28 (Cambridge: Harvard Univ. Press, 1975), p. 92. Hereafter, quotations from this work will be noted in parentheses with the abbreviation *CH*.
39 This direct opposition to the calculated "policy" of Machiavelli was a consistent position of the Puritans from Perkins through John Winthrop, though in the same period many English politicians were becoming more and more enamored of the practicality of the Florentine's theories on public morality. See Mosse, *The Holy Pretence*, pp. 26–33 and passim. See also Mosse, "The Assimilation of Machiavelli in English Thought: The Casuistry of William Perkins and William Ames," *Huntington Library Quarterly*, 17 (Aug. 1954), 315–26; Felix Raab, *The English Face of Machiavelli: A Changing Interpretation* (London, 1964); T. H. Breen, *The Character of the Good Ruler: A Study of Puritan Political Ideas in New England, 1630–1730* (New Haven: Yale Univ. Press, 1970), pp. 11–12; and F. J. Levy, *Tudor Historical Thought* (San Marino: Huntington Library, 1967), esp. chap. 7, "Politic History."
40 See Chapter 5, above.
41 Edmund S. Morgan, *Visible Saints: The History of a Puritan Idea* (New York: New York Univ. Press, 1963), p. 120, and *The Puritan Family: Reli-*

gion and Domestic Relations in Seventeenth-Century New England (New York: Harper & Row, 1966), pp. 168–86.

42 See TH, *The Saints Dignitie and Dutie*, pp. 121–51.

43 TH, *The Christians Two Chiefe Lessons*, pp. 27–28. McGee claims that the Puritans did not speak nearly so much of the *Imitatio Christi* as a goal capable of realization as did the Anglicans. It is not explicitly a major motif in Hooker's writing, certainly, but the typology which set up Christ as the second Adam enabling us to return, through grace, to *a measure of* our former glory, always suggests the *imitatio* as a high and worthy goal. See McGee, *The Godly Man in Stuart England*, pp. 107–13. On the Puritans' attitude towards the *imitatio*, see also Sacvan Bercovitch, *The Puritan Origins of the American Self* (New Haven: Yale Univ. Press, 1975), esp. pp. 8–15.

44 TH, *The Christians Two Chiefe Lessons*, pp. 1–101; see esp. pp. 35–37.

45 See Chapter 7, above, and Hooker's *Soules Preparation, The Soules Humiliation,* and *The Application of Redemption, The Ninth and Tenth Books.*

46 TH, *The Christians Two Chiefe Lessons*, p. 59.

47 Ibid., p. 62.

48 TH, *The Saints Dignitie and Dutie*, p. 163.

49 Max Weber, *The Protestant Ethic and the Spirit of Capitalism*, trans. Talcott Parsons (New York: Scribner's 1958), chap. 5, pp. 155–83. Weber uses Richard Baxter as the key exemplar of Puritanism and, in a characteristic Weberism, says, "In Baxter's view the care for external goods should only lie on the shoulders of the 'saint like a light cloak, which can be thrown aside at any moment.' But fate decreed that the cloak should become an iron cage" (p. 181).

50 See Perry Miller, *The New England Mind: From Colony to Province* (Cambridge: Harvard Univ. Press, 1953); James W. Jones, *The Shattered Synthesis: New England Puritanism before the Great Awakening* (New Haven: Yale Univ. Press, 1973); and Emory Elliott, *Power and the Pulpit in Puritan New England* (Princeton: Princeton Univ. Press, 1975). For relevant comment on changes in English Puritan thought in the seventeenth century, see Robert S. Michaelson, "Changes in the Puritan Concept of Calling or Vocation," *New England Quarterly*, 36 (Sept. 1953), 315–36.

51 TH, *The Danger of Desertion*, Document VII in Williams et al., *Thomas Hooker: Writings in England and Holland*, p. 238.

52 TH, *The Christians Two Chiefe Lessons*, pp. 65, 245.

Chapter 14: THE LIMITS OF REASON: GLORY AND WONDER

1 Richard Sibbes, *A Breathing after God; or, A Christians Desire of Gods Presence* (London, 1639), p. 152.

2 Samuel Willard, *The Childs Portion; or, the Unseen Glory of the Children of God Asserted and proved* (Boston, 1684), p. 84.

3 This "*mystical Union* with *God* and *Christ*" is, as Thomas Goodwin and Philip Nye pointed out in their "Epistle to the Reader," "a Subject but

rarely handled by *Divines*." The mystical element of the Puritan mind has been discussed in several helpful articles, including James Fulton Maclear, " 'The Heart of New England Rent': The Mystical Element in Early Puritan History," *Mississippi Valley Historical Review*, 42 (1955–56), 621–52 (reprinted in *The New England Puritans*, ed. Sydney V. James [New York, 1968]); Jerald C. Brauer, "Puritan Mysticism and the Development of Liberalism," *Church History*, 19 (Sept. 1950), 151–70; and Clarence Gohdes, "Aspects of Idealism in Early New England," *Philosophical Review*, 39 (Nov. 1930), 537–55. Geoffrey F. Nuttall considers mystical dimensions of Puritan thought in *The Holy Spirit in Puritan Faith and Experience* (Oxford: Basil Blackwell, 1946), esp. chap. 9.

4 TH, *A Comment upon Christs Last Prayer* (London, 1656), p. 2. Hereafter quotations from this work will be indicated parenthetically with the abbreviation *CCLP*.

5 Although the text ends on p. 532, there are actually only 432 pages in the work since the pagination skips from p. 222 to 323.

6 See *CCLP*, pp. 117–28.

7 On the leaf opposite the book's title page appears this description: "Mr. Hooker *On The Seventeenth of* John *Being his Seventeenth Book, made in* New-England."

8 As one would expect in Communion sermons, there are occasional references in *A Comment* to Christ as "liveing bread," and "the Food of thy Soul" (pp. 112, 142), but these traditional metaphors receive no special elaboration.

9 Hooker may have had in mind a work like Richard Sibbes's *Bowels Opened* (London, 1639), which, though dealing with the concept of union, stresses the role of the Church much more than does Hooker's *Comment*.

10 Richard Sibbes, *The Excellencie of the Gospell above the Law* (London, 1639), p. 452.

11 Richard Sibbes, writing at length on glory, insisted even more explicitly on this process as something continuing beyond death: "There be degrees of glory. . . . A Christian is glorious while he lives, and hee growes in glory while he lives, he is more glorious when he dyes, for then his soule hath perfectly the image of Christ stamped upon it; but he is most glorious at the day of resurrection, when body and soule shall be glorious, when he shall put downe the very Sunne it selfe, all glory shall be nothing to the glory of the Saints." *The Excellencie of the Gospell above the Law*, pp. 536–37.

12 Sibbes, *The Saints Cordialls* (London, 1637), p. 298. Sibbes also expressed views on the Christ-Adam typology which were in agreement with Hooker's in *The Excellencie of the Gospell above the Law*, where he said that the glory of Christ in the Gospel is greater than Adam's glory (p. 242). See also p. 148, where Sibbes argues that the "second Adam's" liberty is greater than that of the first Adam.

13 Jesper Rosenmeier, "New England's Perfection: The Image of Adam and the Image of Chist in the Antinomian Crisis, 1634 to 1638," *William and Mary Quarterly*, 27 (July 1970), 435–59.

14 "It's beyond the power of darkness to bring light. . . . It is the height of power, not only to work something out of nothing, but something out of that which is contrary to it; And therefore this work of the Application of Redemption to a lost sinner, is harder than the work of Creation it self, for as the Lord had nothing then to help him, so he had nothing to hinder him in Creating the World; but here the Lord must take away the heart of stone, he must turn the heart of flint into a heart of flesh, he must *cause light to shine out of darkness*, and work one contrary out of another." TH, *The Application of Redemption, The first eight Books* (London, 1656), pp. 131–32.

15 See William Ames, *The Marrow of Theology*, trans. and ed. John D. Eusden (Boston: Pilgrim Press, 1968), pp. 171–74, where he explains glorification.

16 For a useful historical survey of mystical Christian and pre-Christian thought, see Joseph Burns Collins, *Christian Mysticism in the Elizabethan Age, with Its Background in Mystical Theology* (Baltimore: The Johns Hopkins Press, 1940).

17 TH, *The Saints Guide* (London, 1645), pp. 57–58.

18 John Calvin, whom we hardly consider a mystic, argued in the same pattern as does Hooker for the *limits* of man's reason, citing as his precedents the attitudes of Augustine and Paul. In 1552 Calvin wrote that "Augustine's word should never be forgotten: Attend to who God is and who you are. He is God, you are man. Should you think you are talking of justice, is the fount of justice dried up? You as a man expect an answer from me. But I also am a man. Let us both therefore listen to one who speaks: O man, who art thou? Better is the ignorance of faith than the temerity of knowledge! Seek for merit, and you will find only punishment. O the height and the depth! Peter denies, the thief believes. O the height and the depth! You ask a reason. I stand in awe before the height and the depth. You ratiocinate, I admire; you dispute, I believe. I see the height, but I do not comprehend the depth. Paul rests quietly because he found wonder. He calls the judgments of God inscrutable—do you mean to scrutinise them? He says His ways are past finding out—do you propose to find them out? Similarly in another place he says: Will you dispute with me? Rather admire with me and exclaim: O the height and the depth! Let us agree to tremble together lest together we perish in error." John Calvin, *Concerning the Eternal Predestination of God*, trans. J.K.S. Reid (London: James Clarke, 1961), p. 118.

19 TH, *The Vnbeleevers Preparing for Christ* (London, 1638), pt. 2, pp. 70, 74; *The Soules Exaltation* (London, 1638), pp. 124–25; *The Christians Two Chiefe Lessons* (London, 1640), p. 292; *The Application of Redemption, The Ninth and Tenth Books* (London, 1656), p. 322.

20 The King James version reads: "O righteous Father, the world hath not known thee: but I have known thee, and these have known that thou hast sent me. And I have declared unto them thy name, and will declare it: that the love wherewith thou hast loved me may be in them, and I in them."

21 Edward Hopkins and William Goodwin, "Epistle to the Reader," in TH, *A Survey of the Summe of Church Discipline* (London, 1648), sig. C2.
22 Maclear, " 'The Heart of New England Rent,' " p. 621.
23 Maclear notices the connection between stress on the role of the Holy Spirit in the Christian life and an increase in mystical tendencies, noting especially the preaching of Richard Sibbes. Ibid., p. 626. Nuttall also has frequent recourse to the writings of Sibbes in this connection in *The Holy Spirit in Puritan Faith and Experience*, esp. chaps. 1 and 9.

CONCLUSION

1 *The Early Lectures of Ralph Waldo Emerson*, vol. II, *1836–1838*, ed. Stephen E. Whicher, Robert E. Spiller, and Wallace E. Williams (Cambridge: Harvard Univ. Press, 1964), p. 229.
2 The phrase is Karl Keller's in *The Example of Edward Taylor* (Amherst: Univ. of Massachusetts Press, 1975), pp. 223–36. See also John Seelye's discussion of the Connecticut Valley in *Prophetic Waters: The River in Early American Life* (Oxford: Oxford Univ. Press, 1977).

Thomas Hooker's Works

MANUSCRIPTS

Very few of Hooker's manuscripts have survived. There are, however, a few letters and a treatise on the Sabbath called "Theses Sabbaticae" in the Hutchinson Papers, Massachusetts State Archives, Boston. This collection also contains the manuscript of "Touching ye Crosse in ye Banners." The Connecticut Historical Society owns a manuscript book called the "Hooker Family Memorial" containing miscellaneous notes by several hands including primarily Thomas Hooker's.

PRINTED WORKS

For a full listing of all known editions of Hooker's writings, including published letters, consult my bibliography in *Thomas Hooker: Writings in England and Holland, 1626–1633*, ed. George H. Williams et al., Harvard Theological Studies, 28 (Cambridge: Harvard Univ. Press, 1975), pp. 390–425. The attribution of some titles to Hooker is discussed in my essays "Four New Works by Thomas Hooker: Identity and Significance," *Resources for American Literary Study*, 4 (Spring 1974), 3–26, and "Establishing the Hooker Canon," in Williams et al., *Thomas Hooker: Writings in England and Holland*, pp. 378–89. The variants in several editions of Hooker's most popular work is a primary subject in my "Growth of Thomas Hooker's *Poor Doubting Christian*," *Early American Literature*, 8 (Spring 1973), 3–20. Everett Emerson contributed useful observations about one correct and two false attributions by previous bibliographers in "Notes on the Thomas Hooker Canon," *American Literature*, 27 (Jan. 1956), 554–55. Other useful comments of this kind appear in Hubert R. Pellman, "Thomas Hooker: A Study in Puritan Ideals" (Ph.D. diss., Univ. of Pennsylvania, 1958), and Andrew T. Denholm, "Thomas Hooker, Puritan Preacher, 1586–1647" (Ph.D diss., Hartford Seminary Foundation, 1961).

The following is a chronological listing which indicates the date of first publication of each of Hooker's works. Unless otherwise indicated, the place of publication was London.

"To the Reader," in John Rogers, *The Doctrine of Faith* (1627).

The Poor Doubting Christian Drawne unto Christ, in [Richard Sibbes, ed.,] *The Saints Cordials* (1629).

The Soules Preparation for Christ; or, A Treatise of Contrition (1632).

"The Praeface" to [William Ames,] *A Fresh Suit against Human Ceremonies in Gods Worship* (1632).

The Soules Humiliation (1637).

The Soules Ingrafting into Christ (1637).

The Soules Effectuall Calling to Christ (1637). Also called *The Soules Vocation* (1638).

The Soules Implantation (1637). A revised and enlarged version published as *The Soules Implantation into the Naturall Olive* (1640).

Foure Learned and Godly Treatises (1638).

The Properties of an honest Heart: Laid out in a Sermon (1638).

The Sinners Salvation (1638).

The Soules Exaltation (1638).

The Soules Possession of Christ (1638).

Spirituall Munition: A Funerall Sermon (1638).

Spirituall Thirst: A Sermon Preached upon Iohn 7.37 (1638).

The Stay of the Faithfull (1638).

Three Godly Sermons (1638). Also published as *Three Sermons* (1638). A revised and enlarged version published as *The Saints Guide, in Three Treatises* (1645).

The Vnbeleevers Preparing for Christ (1638).

The Christians Two Chiefe Lessons (1640).

The Paterne of Perfection: Exhibited in Gods Image on Adam (1640). Reissued as *Gods Image on Man, and His Covenant made with him in his state of Innocency* (1653).

The Danger of Desertion; or, A Farewell Sermon of Mr. Thomas Hooker (1640). Also attributed to William Fenner and published in his posthumous *XXIX Choice Sermons* as *The Signes of Gods Forsaking a People* (1657).

The Faithful Covenanter (1644).

A brief Exposition of the Lords Prayer (1645). A revised version published as *Heavens Treasury Opened in a Fruitful Exposition of the Lords Prayer* (1645).

An Exposition of the Principles of Religion (1645).

A Survey of the Summe of Church Discipline (1648).

The Covenant of Grace Opened (1649).

The Saints Dignitie and Dutie (1651).

The Application of Redemption, . . . The first eight Books (1656).

The Application of Redemption, . . . The Ninth and Tenth Books (1656).

A Comment upon Christs Last Prayer in the Seventeenth of John (1656).

"Abstracts of Two Sermons by Rev. Thomas Hooker. From the Shorthand Notes of Mr. Henry Wolcott," *Collections of the Connecticut Historical Society,* 1 (Hartford, 1860), 19–21.

"Touchinge ye Crosse in ye Banners," *Proceedings of the Massachusetts Historical Society*, 3rd ser., 42 (April 1909), 272–80.

"Mr. Paget's 20 Propositions to Mr. Hooker with his Answers thereto," in Raymond Phineas Stearns, *Congregationalism in the Dutch Netherlands: The Rise and Fall of the English Congregational Classis, 1621–1635* (Chicago: American Society of Church History, 1940), pp. 105–13. Also available in slightly variant versions in Alice C. Carter, *The English Reformed Church in Amsterdam in the Seventeenth Century* (Amsterdam: Scheltema and Holkema, 1964), pp. 189–200, and in *Thomas Hooker: Writings in England and Holland, 1626–1633*, ed. George H. Williams et al. (Cambridge: Harvard Univ. Press, 1975), pp. 277–91.

"A Thomas Hooker Sermon of 1638," ed. Everett Emerson, *Resources for American Literary Study*, 2 (Spring 1972), 75–89.

Thomas Hooker: Writings in England and Holland, 1626–1633, ed. George H. Williams, Norman Pettit, Winfried Herget, and Sargent Bush, Jr., Harvard Theological Studies, 28 (Cambridge: Harvard Univ. Press, 1975). Contains ten newly edited, previously published works:

> *Spiritual Munition*
> *The Church's Deliverances*, from *Foure Learned and Godly Treatises*
> *The Carnal Hypocrite*, from *Foure Learned and Godly Treatises*
> "To the Reader," from John Rogers's *The Doctrine of Faith* (1627)
> *The Poor Doubting Christian Drawn unto Christ* (1629)
> *The Faithful Covenanter*
> *The Danger of Desertion*
> "John Paget's XX Questions (Propositions) and Thomas Hooker's Answers"
> Thomas Hooker to John Cotton, Rotterdam, c. April 1633
> "Preface" to William Ames's *A Fresh Suit against Human Ceremonies* (1633).

Index

377

DESIGNED BY ED FRANK
COMPOSED BY CREATIVE COMPOSITION
ALBUQUERQUE, NEW MEXICO
MANUFACTURED BY CUSHING MALLOY, INC., ANN ARBOR, MICHIGAN
TEXT IS SET IN CALEDONIA, DISPLAY LINES IN TIMES ROMAN

Library of Congress Cataloging in Publication Data
Bush, Sargent.
The writings of Thomas Hooker.
Bibliography: p. 373.
Includes index.
1. Hooker, Thomas, 1586–1647.   I. Title.
BX7260.H596B87   285.8′092′4   79–5404
ISBN 0-299-08070-6